*Nisekoi* is now an anime!

Seeing the characters I created move and talk is

both touching and slightly embarrassing...

Still, I'm looking forward to it.

Naoshi Komi

NAOSHI KOMI was born in Kochi Prefecture, Japan, on March 28, 1986. His first serialized work in *Weekly Shonen Jump* was the series *Double Arts*. His current series, *Nisekoi*, is serialized in *Weekly Shonen Jump*.

# NISEKOI: False Love
## VOLUME 8
**SHONEN JUMP Manga Edition**

Story and Art by
NAOSHI KOMI

Translation — Camellia Nieh
Touch-Up Art & Lettering — Stephen Dutro
Design — Fawn Lau
Shonen Jump Series Editor — John Bae
Graphic Novel Editor — Amy Yu


First published in Japan in 2011
by SHUEISHA Inc., Tokyo.
English translation rights arranged
by SHUEISHA Inc.



Printed in the U.S.A.

Published by VIZ Media, LLC
P.O. Box 77010
San Francisco, CA 94107

10 9 8 7 6 5 3 4 2 1
First printing, March 2015

# NISEKOI

## False Love

### vol. 8: Last Minute

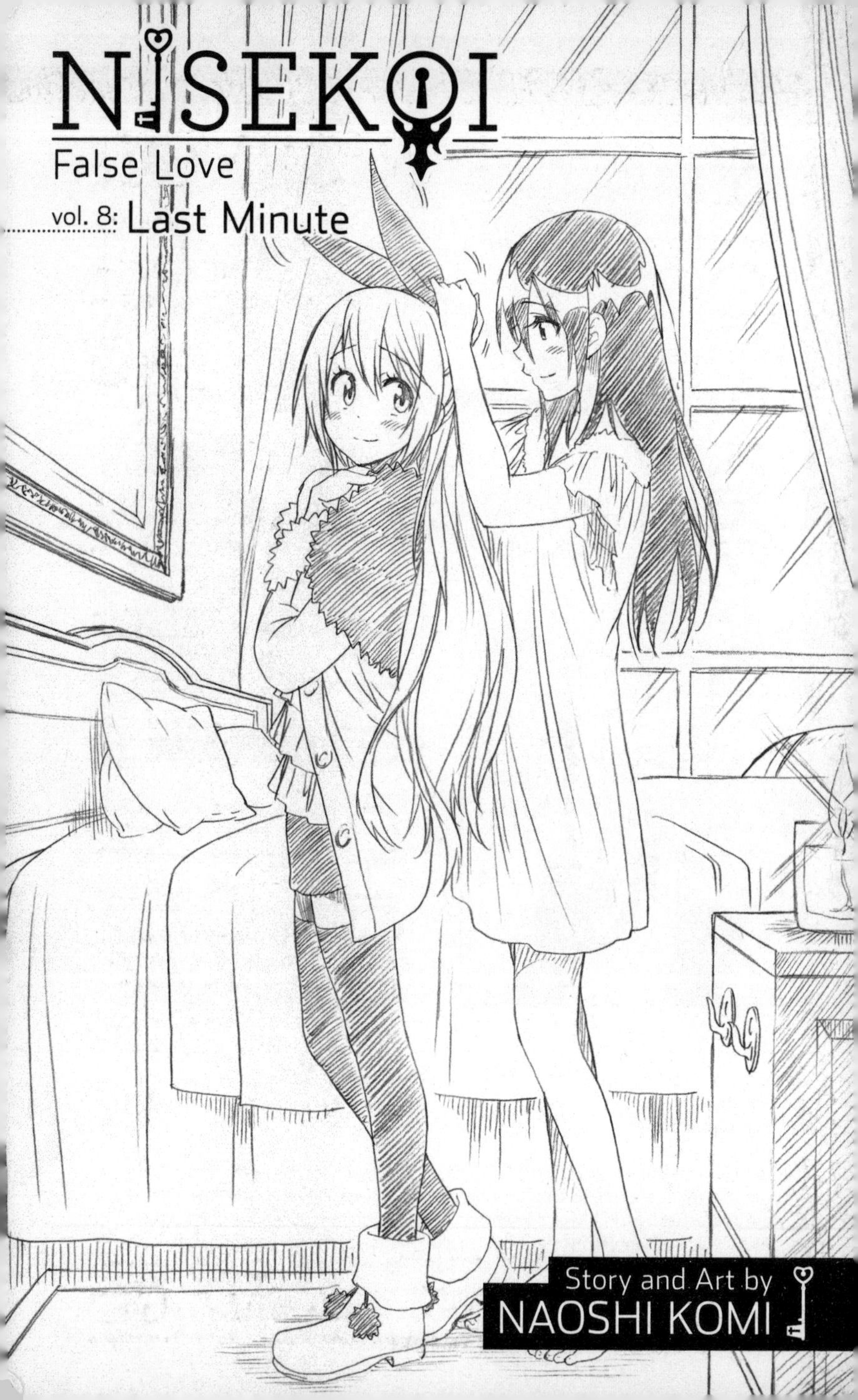

Story and Art by
NAOSHI KOMI

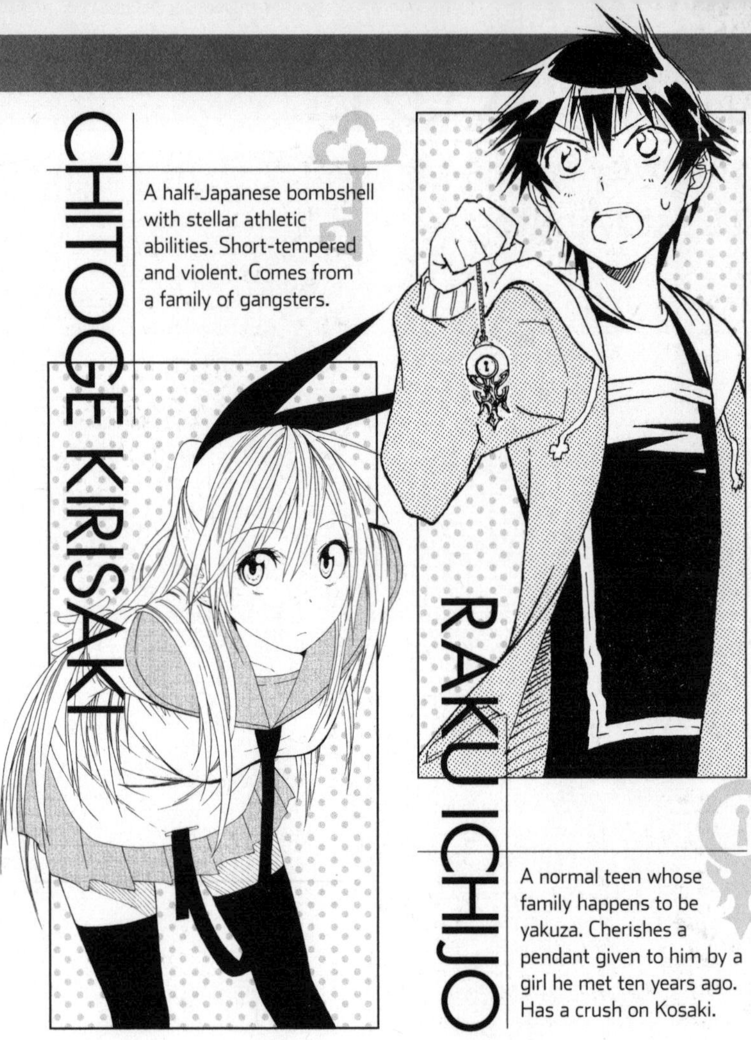

## CHITOGE KIRISAKI

A half-Japanese bombshell with stellar athletic abilities. Short-tempered and violent. Comes from a family of gangsters.

## RAKU ICHIJO

A normal teen whose family happens to be yakuza. Cherishes a pendant given to him by a girl he met ten years ago. Has a crush on Kosaki.

Raku Ichijo is an ordinary teen...who just happens to come from a family of yakuza! His most treasured item is a pendant he was given ten years ago by a girl whom he promised to meet again one day and marry.

Thanks to family circumstances, Raku is forced into a false relationship with Chitoge, the daughter of a rival gangster, to keep their families from shedding blood. Despite their constant spats, Raku and Chitoge somehow manage to fool everyone. One day, Chitoge discovers an old key, jogging memories of her own first love ten years earlier. Meanwhile, Raku's crush, Kosaki, confesses that she also has a key and made a promise with a boy ten years ago. To complicate matters, Marika Tachibana, a girl who claims to be Raku's fiancée, has a key as well and remembers a promise ten years ago. Meanwhile, Chitoge finally admits to herself that she has feelings for Raku. What will become of everyone's love lives?

# THE STORY THUS FAR

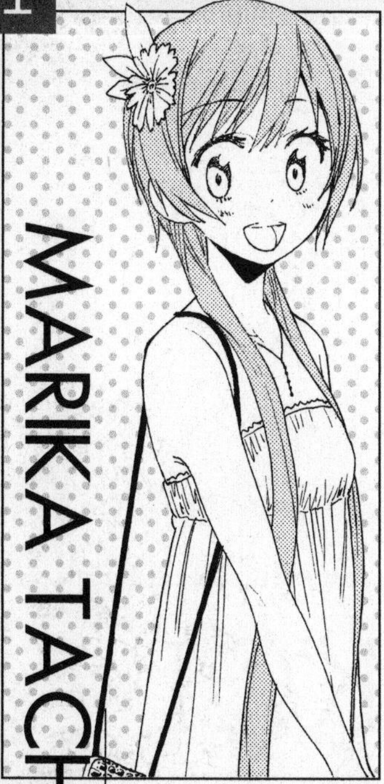

## MARIKA TACHIBANA

Daughter of the chief of police, Marika is Raku's fiancée, according to an agreement made by their fathers—an agreement Marika takes very seriously! Also has a key and remembers making a promise with Raku ten years ago.

## KOSAKI ONODERA

A girl Raku has a crush on. Beautiful and sweet, Kosaki has no shortage of admirers. She's a terrible cook but makes food that *looks* amazing.

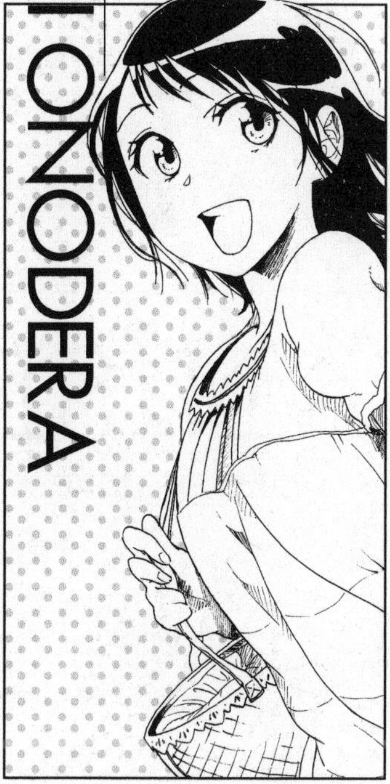

### SEISHIRO TSUGUMI

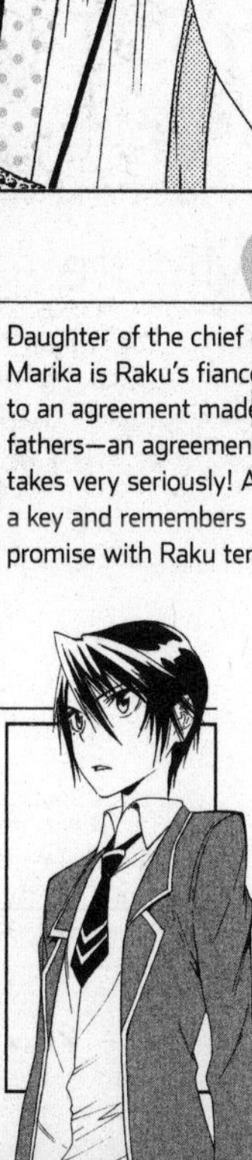

Adopted by Claude as a young child and raised as a top-notch assassin, Seishiro is 100% devoted to Chitoge. Often mistaken for a boy, Tsugumi's really a girl.

### SHU MAIKO

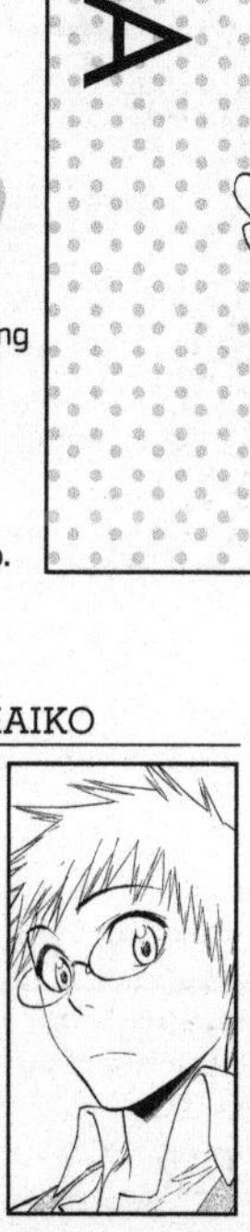

Raku's best friend. Outgoing and girl-crazy. Always tuned in to the latest gossip at school.

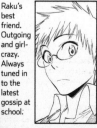

### RURI MIYAMOTO

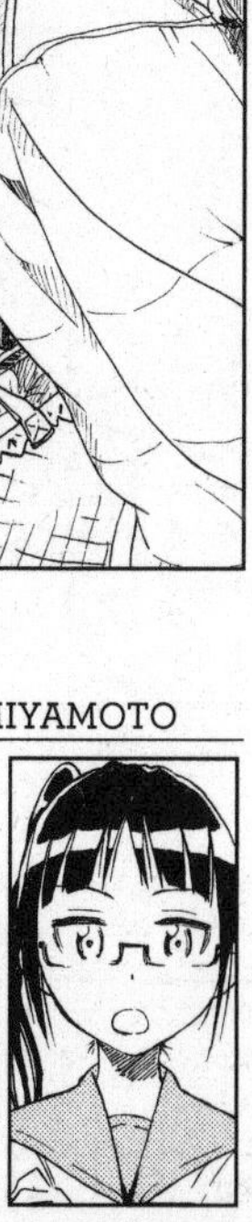

Kosaki's best gal pal. Comes off as aloof, but is actually a devoted and highly intuitive friend.

# NISEKOI
## False Love

### vol. 8: Last Minute

TABLE OF CONTENTS

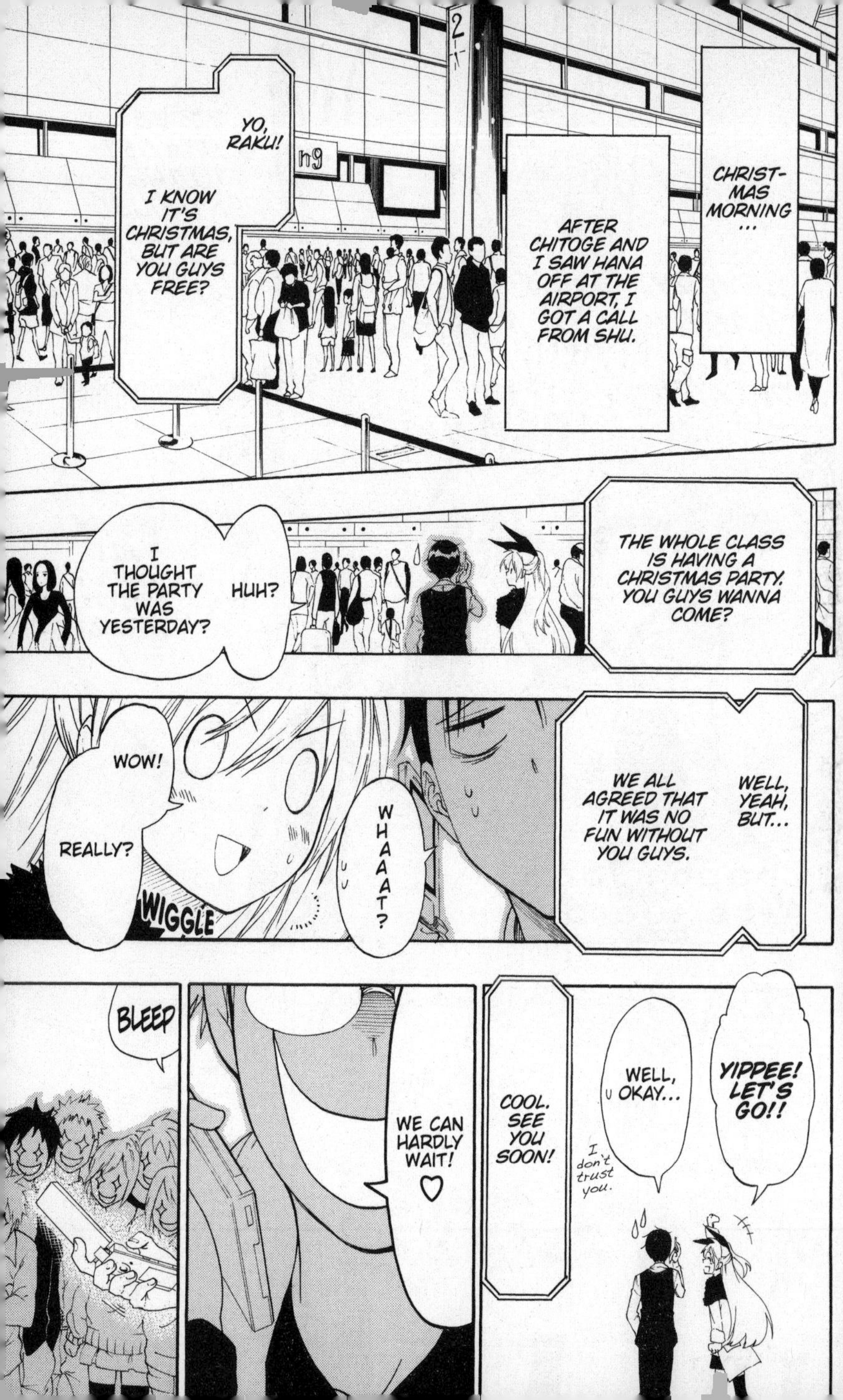
CHRISTMAS MORNING...
AFTER CHITOGE AND I SAW HANA OFF AT THE AIRPORT, I GOT A CALL FROM SHU.
YO, RAKU!
I KNOW IT'S CHRISTMAS, BUT ARE YOU GUYS FREE?
THE WHOLE CLASS IS HAVING A CHRISTMAS PARTY. YOU GUYS WANNA COME?
HUH?
I THOUGHT THE PARTY WAS YESTERDAY?
WELL, YEAH, BUT...
WE ALL AGREED THAT IT WAS NO FUN WITHOUT YOU GUYS.
WHAAAAT?
WOW!
REALLY?
WIGGLE
YIPPEE! LET'S GO!!
WELL, OKAY...
I don't trust you.
COOL. SEE YOU SOON!
WE CAN HARDLY WAIT! ♥
BLEEP

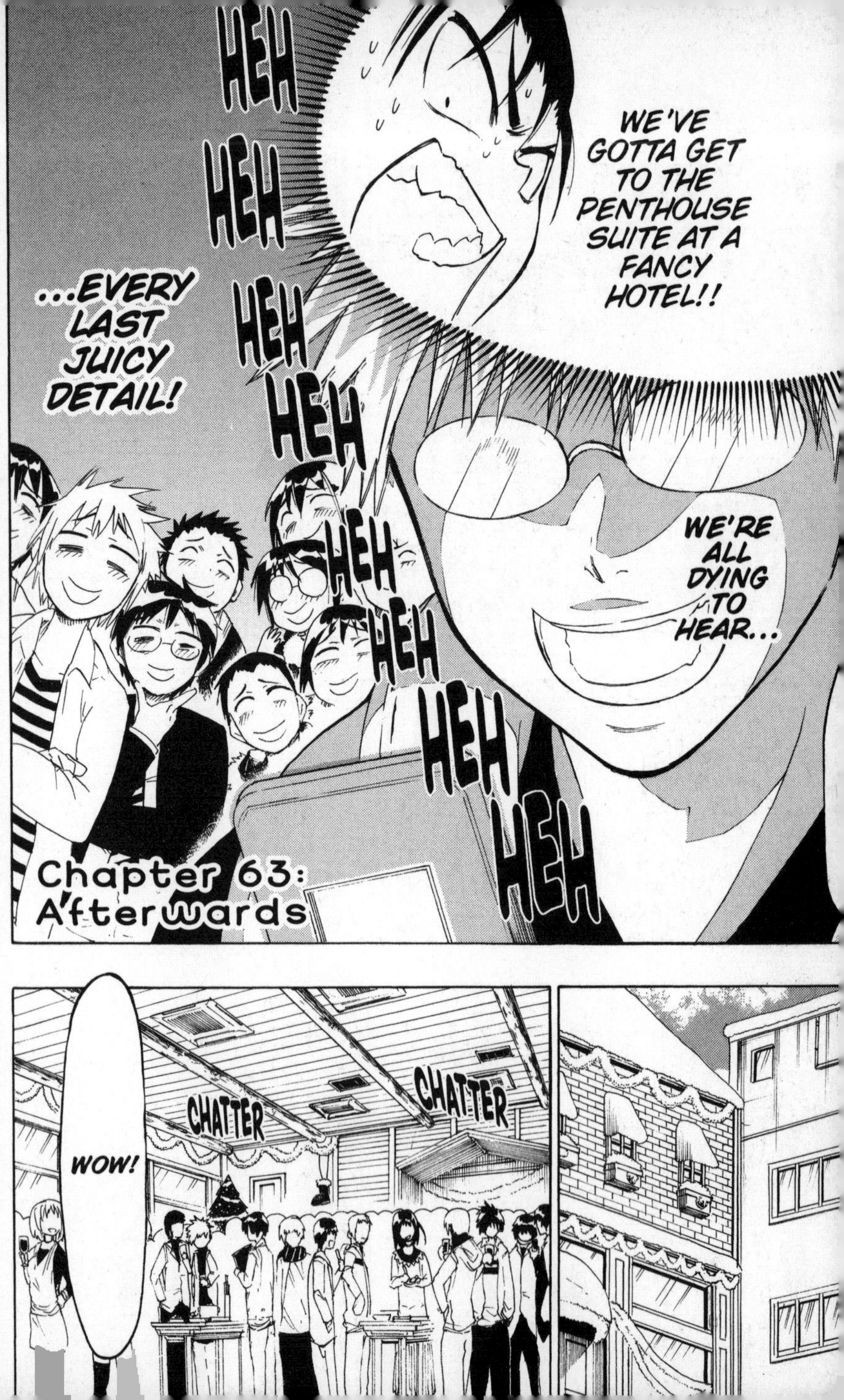
WE'VE GOTTA GET TO THE PENTHOUSE SUITE AT A FANCY HOTEL!!
HEH HEH HEH HEH HEH HEH HEH HEH
WE'RE ALL DYING TO HEAR...
...EVERY LAST JUICY DETAIL!
Chapter 63: Afterwards
CHATTER
CHATTER
WOW!

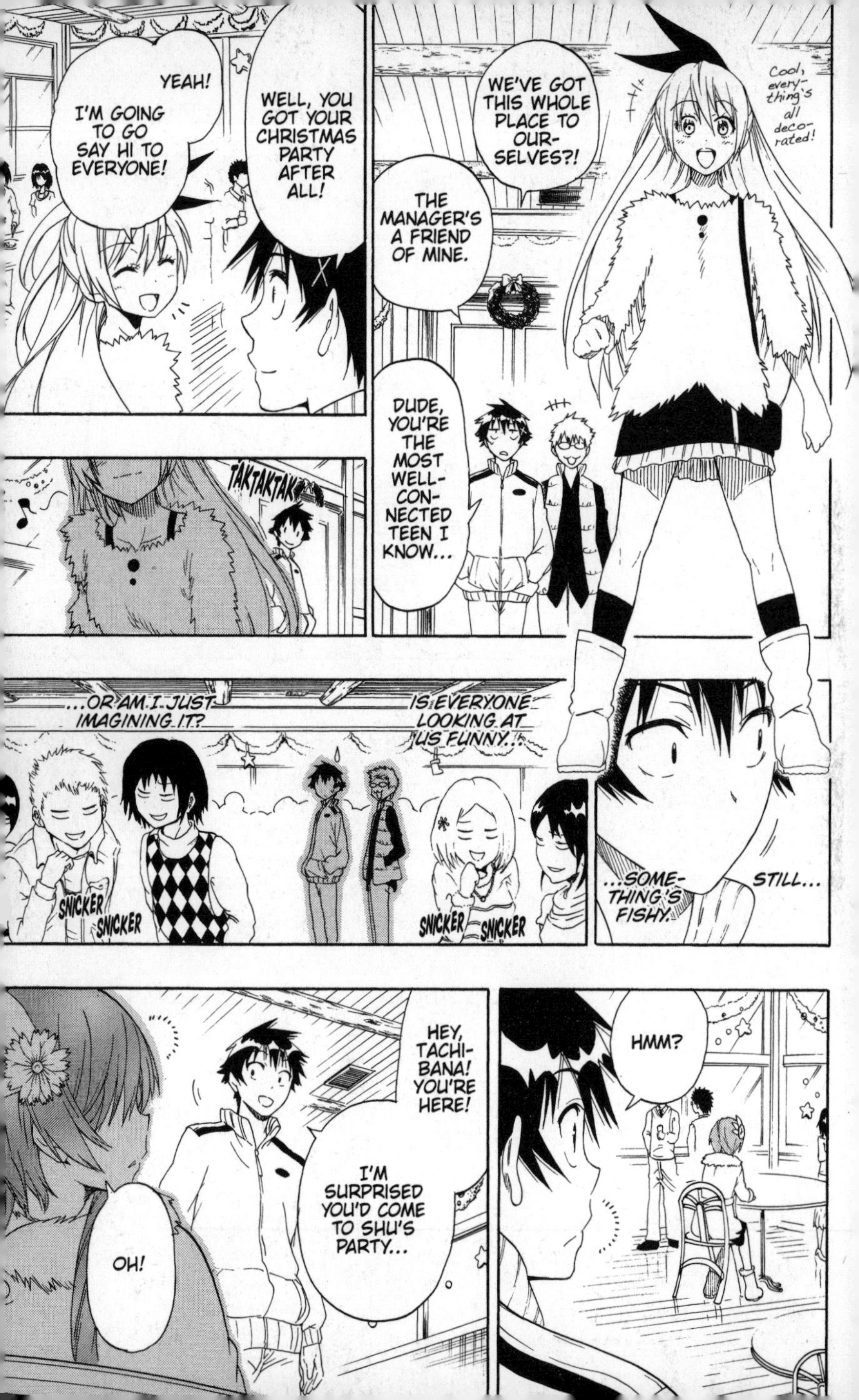
WE'VE GOT THIS WHOLE PLACE TO OURSELVES?!
Cool, everything's all decorated!
THE MANAGER'S A FRIEND OF MINE.
DUDE, YOU'RE THE MOST WELL-CONNECTED TEEN I KNOW...
WELL, YOU GOT YOUR CHRISTMAS PARTY AFTER ALL!
YEAH!
I'M GOING TO GO SAY HI TO EVERYONE!
TAKTAKTAK
STILL...
...SOMETHING'S FISHY.
IS EVERYONE LOOKING AT US FUNNY...
...OR AM I JUST IMAGINING IT?
SNICKER
SNICKER
SNICKER
SNICKER
HMM?
HEY, TACHIBANA! YOU'RE HERE!
I'M SURPRISED YOU'D COME TO SHU'S PARTY...
OH!

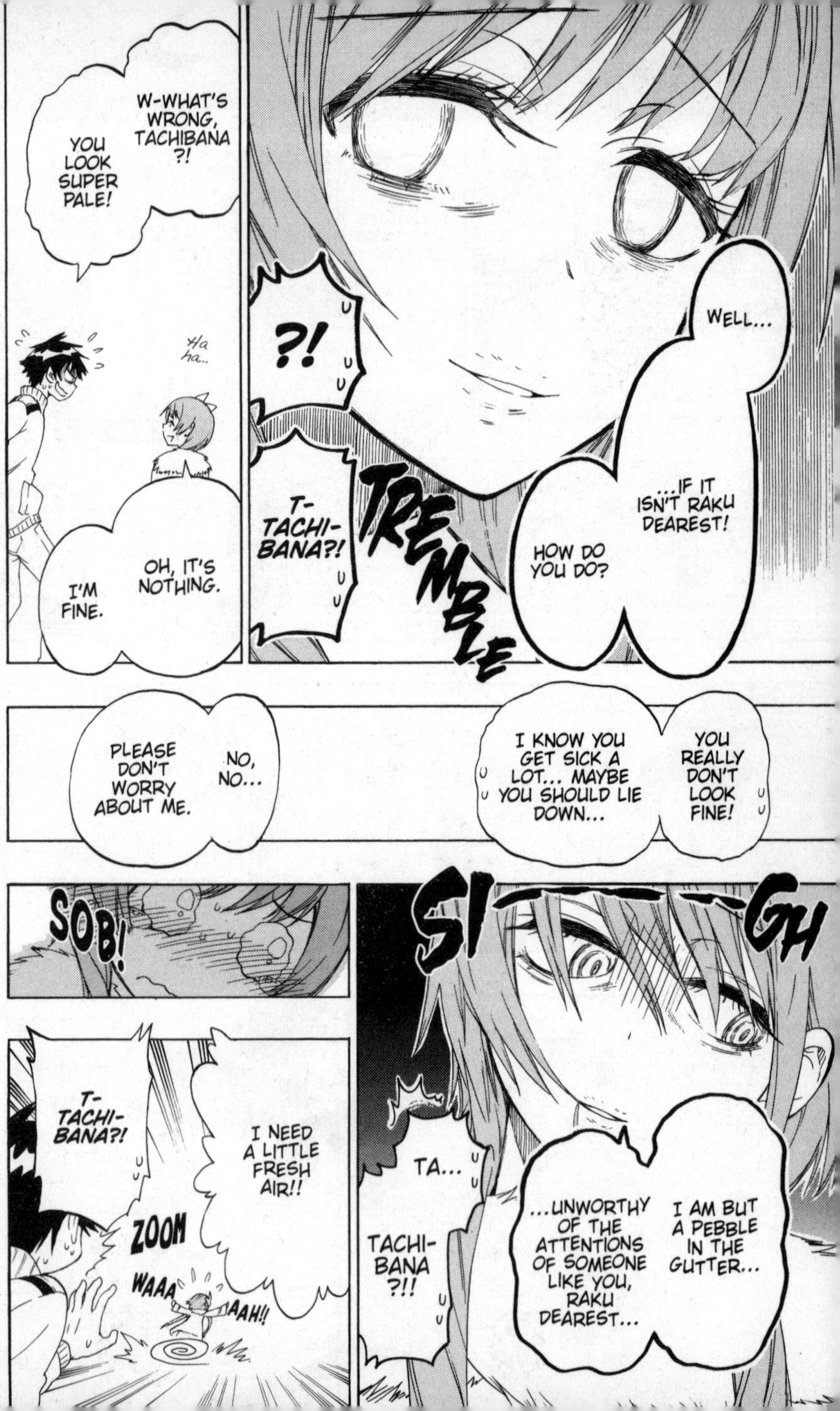
WELL...
...IF IT ISN'T RAKU DEAREST!
HOW DO YOU DO?
?!
T-TACHIBANA?!
TREMBLE
W-WHAT'S WRONG, TACHIBANA?!
YOU LOOK SUPER PALE!
Ha ha...
OH, IT'S NOTHING.
I'M FINE.
YOU REALLY DON'T LOOK FINE!
I KNOW YOU GET SICK A LOT... MAYBE YOU SHOULD LIE DOWN...
NO, NO...
PLEASE DON'T WORRY ABOUT ME.
SI———GH
I AM BUT A PEBBLE IN THE GUTTER...
...UNWORTHY OF THE ATTENTIONS OF SOMEONE LIKE YOU, RAKU DEAREST...
TA...
TACHIBANA?!!
SOB!
I NEED A LITTLE FRESH AIR!!
T-TACHIBANA?!
ZOOM
WAAAAAH!!

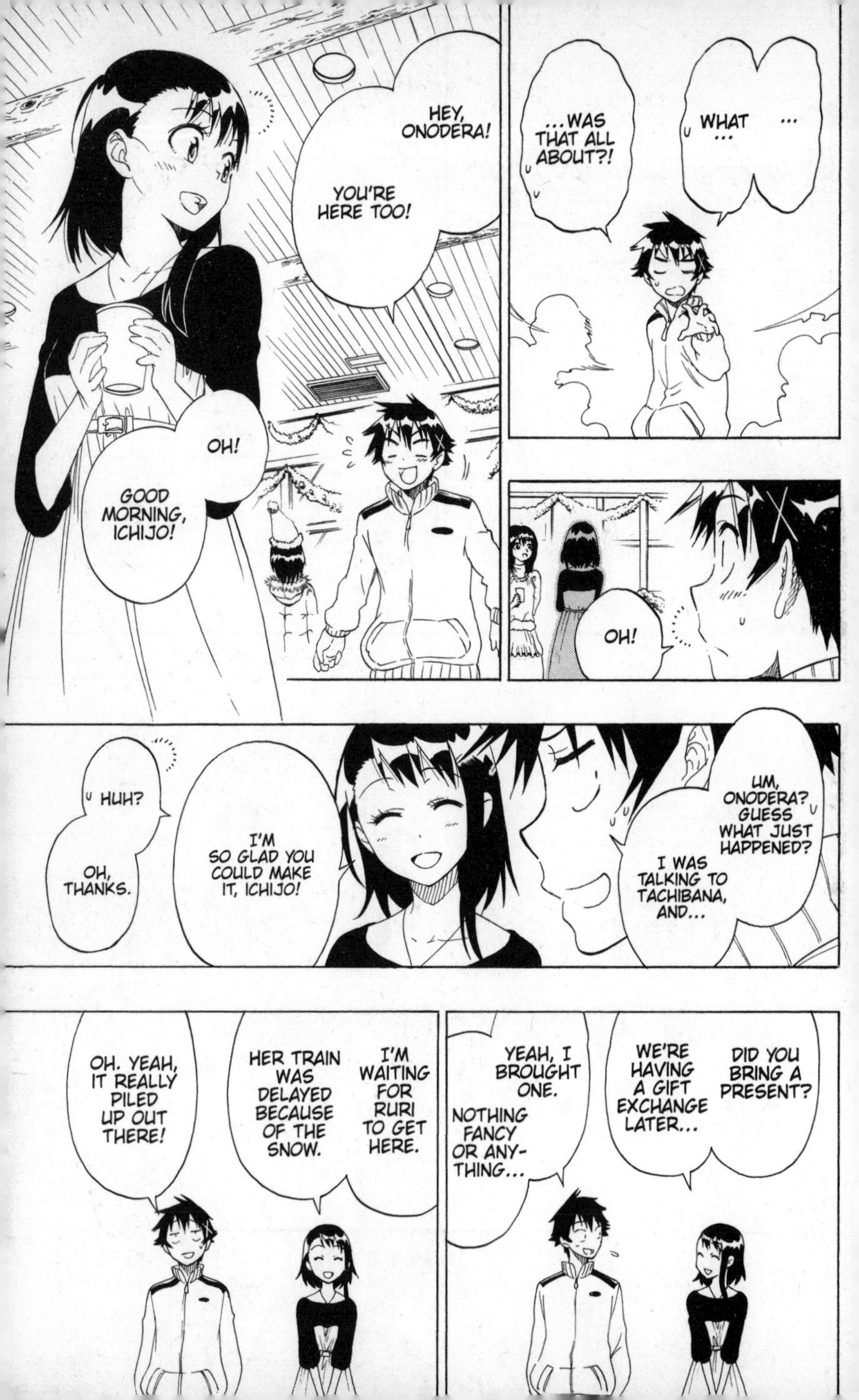
WHAT ... ...
...WAS THAT ALL ABOUT?!
OH!
HEY, ONODERA!
YOU'RE HERE TOO!
OH!
GOOD MORNING, ICHIJO!
UM, ONODERA? GUESS WHAT JUST HAPPENED?
I WAS TALKING TO TACHIBANA, AND...
I'M SO GLAD YOU COULD MAKE IT, ICHIJO!
HUH?
OH, THANKS.
DID YOU BRING A PRESENT?
WE'RE HAVING A GIFT EXCHANGE LATER...
YEAH, I BROUGHT ONE.
NOTHING FANCY OR ANY-THING...
I'M WAITING FOR RURI TO GET HERE.
HER TRAIN WAS DELAYED BECAUSE OF THE SNOW.
OH. YEAH, IT REALLY PILED UP OUT THERE!

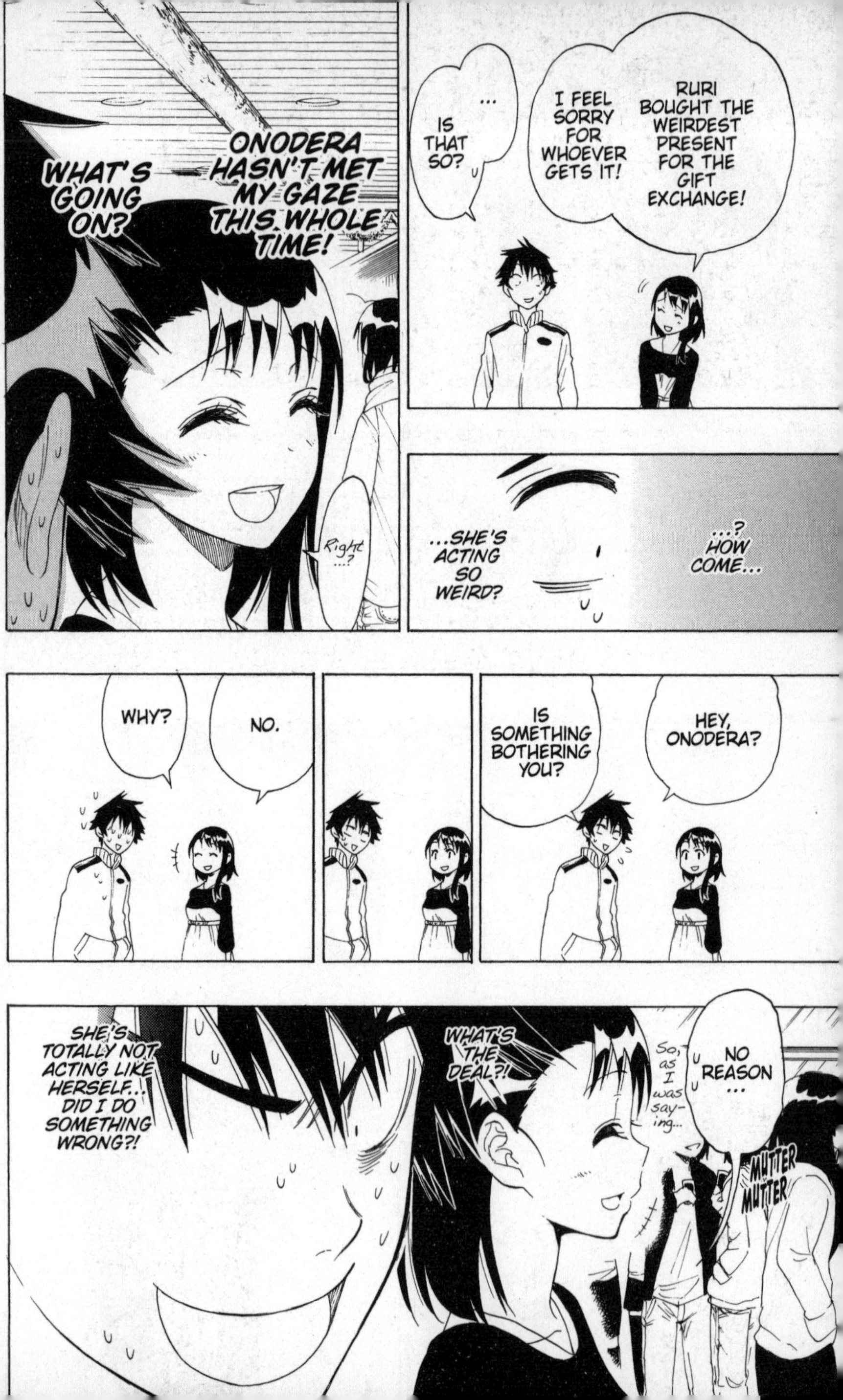
RURI BOUGHT THE WEIRDEST PRESENT FOR THE GIFT EXCHANGE!
I FEEL SORRY FOR WHOEVER GETS IT!
... IS THAT SO?
...? HOW COME...
...SHE'S ACTING SO WEIRD?
ONODERA HASN'T MET MY GAZE THIS WHOLE TIME!
WHAT'S GOING ON?
Right...?
HEY, ONODERA?
IS SOMETHING BOTHERING YOU?
NO.
WHY?
NO REASON...
So, as I was saying...
MUTTER MUTTER
WHAT'S THE DEAL?!
SHE'S TOTALLY NOT ACTING LIKE HERSELF... DID I DO SOMETHING WRONG?!

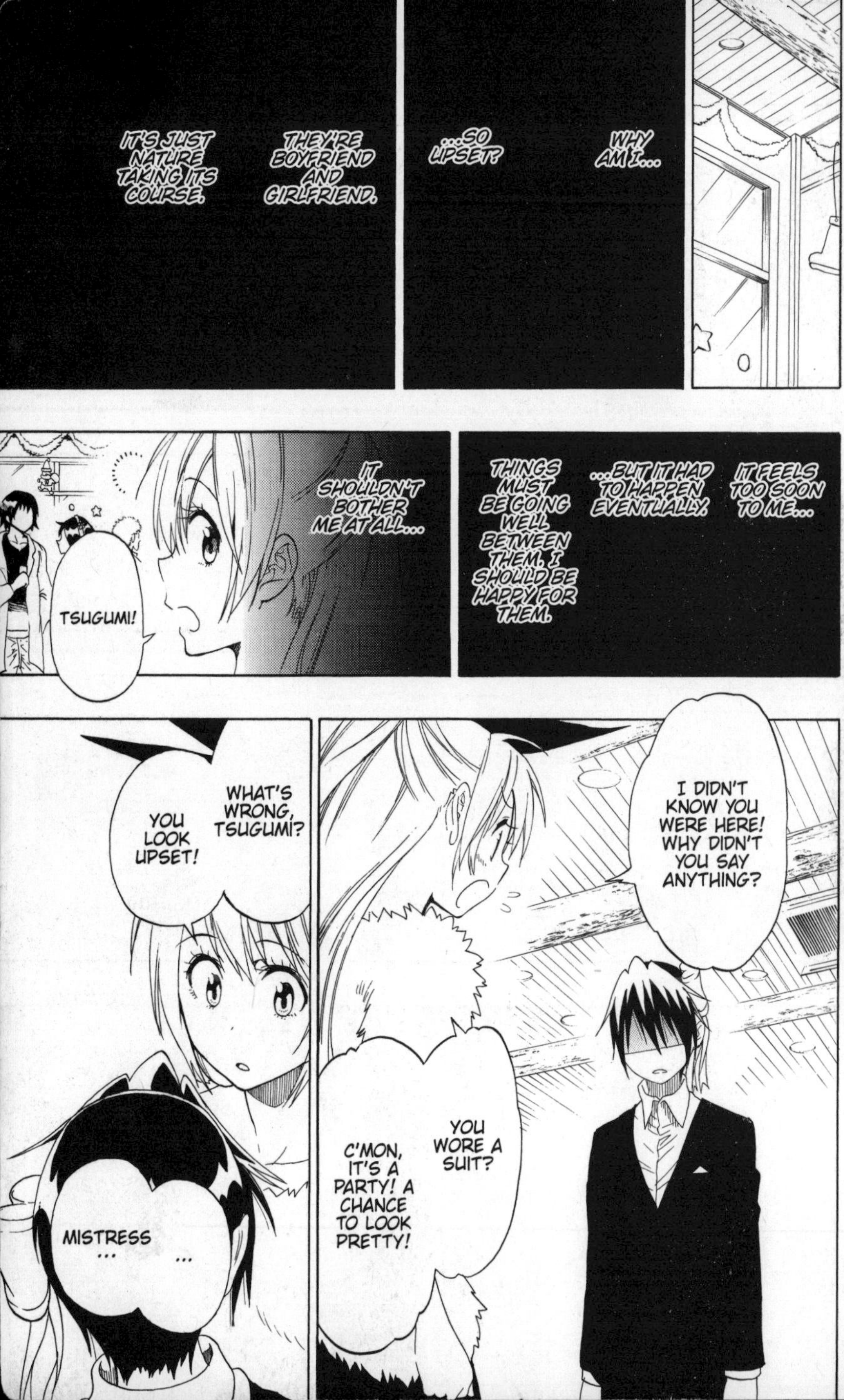
WHY AM I...
...SO UPSET?
THEY'RE BOYFRIEND AND GIRLFRIEND.
IT'S JUST NATURE TAKING ITS COURSE.
IT FEELS TOO SOON TO ME...
...BUT IT HAD TO HAPPEN EVENTUALLY.
THINGS MUST BE GOING WELL BETWEEN THEM. I SHOULD BE HAPPY FOR THEM.
IT SHOULDN'T BOTHER ME AT ALL...
TSUGUMI!
I DIDN'T KNOW YOU WERE HERE! WHY DIDN'T YOU SAY ANYTHING?
YOU WORE A SUIT?
C'MON, IT'S A PARTY! A CHANCE TO LOOK PRETTY!
WHAT'S WRONG, TSUGUMI?
YOU LOOK UPSET!
MISTRESS ... ...

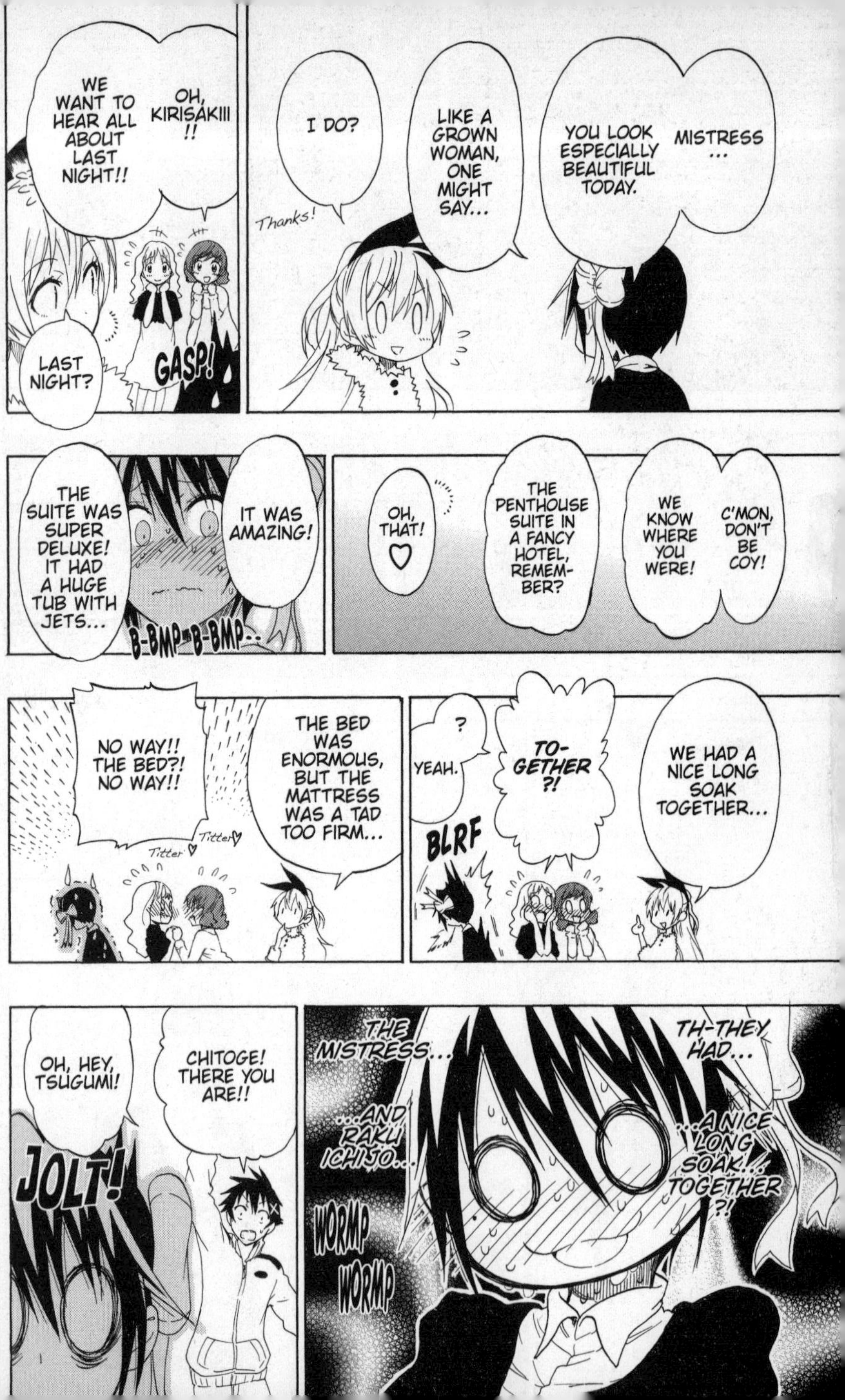
MISTRESS...
YOU LOOK ESPECIALLY BEAUTIFUL TODAY.
LIKE A GROWN WOMAN, ONE MIGHT SAY...
I DO?
Thanks!
OH, KIRISAKIII!!
WE WANT TO HEAR ALL ABOUT LAST NIGHT!!
GASP!
LAST NIGHT?
C'MON, DON'T BE COY!
WE KNOW WHERE YOU WERE!
THE PENTHOUSE SUITE IN A FANCY HOTEL, REMEMBER?
OH, THAT! ♡
IT WAS AMAZING!
THE SUITE WAS SUPER DELUXE! IT HAD A HUGE TUB WITH JETS...
B-BMP B-BMP...
WE HAD A NICE LONG SOAK TOGETHER...
TO-GETHER?!
?
YEAH.
BLRF
THE BED WAS ENORMOUS, BUT THE MATTRESS WAS A TAD TOO FIRM...
NO WAY!! THE BED?! NO WAY!!
Titter♡
Titter♡
TH-THEY HAD...
THE MISTRESS...
...A NICE LONG SOAK... TOGETHER?!
...AND RAKU ICHIJO...
WORMP
WORMP
CHITOGE! THERE YOU ARE!!
OH, HEY, TSUGUMI!
JOLT!

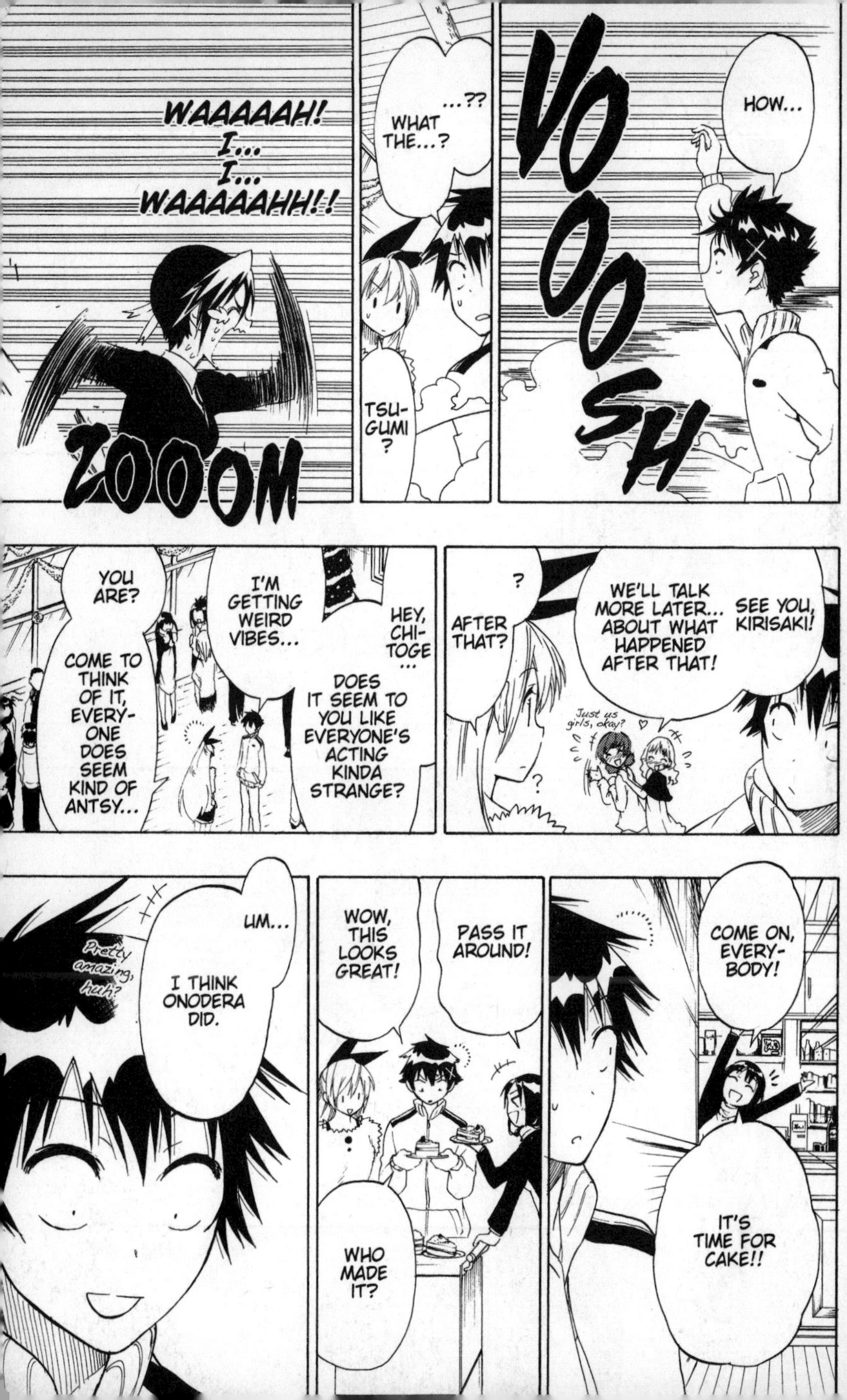
HOW...
VOOOSH
...??
WHAT THE...?
TSU-GUMI ?
WAAAAAH! I... I... WAAAAAHH!!
ZOOOM
SEE YOU, KIRISAKI!
WE'LL TALK MORE LATER... ABOUT WHAT HAPPENED AFTER THAT!
Just us girls, okay?
?
AFTER THAT?
HEY, CHI-TOGE...
I'M GETTING WEIRD VIBES...
DOES IT SEEM TO YOU LIKE EVERYONE'S ACTING KINDA STRANGE?
YOU ARE?
COME TO THINK OF IT, EVERY-ONE DOES SEEM KIND OF ANTSY...
COME ON, EVERY-BODY!
IT'S TIME FOR CAKE!!
PASS IT AROUND!
WOW, THIS LOOKS GREAT!
WHO MADE IT?
UM...
I THINK ONODERA DID.
Pretty amazing, huh?

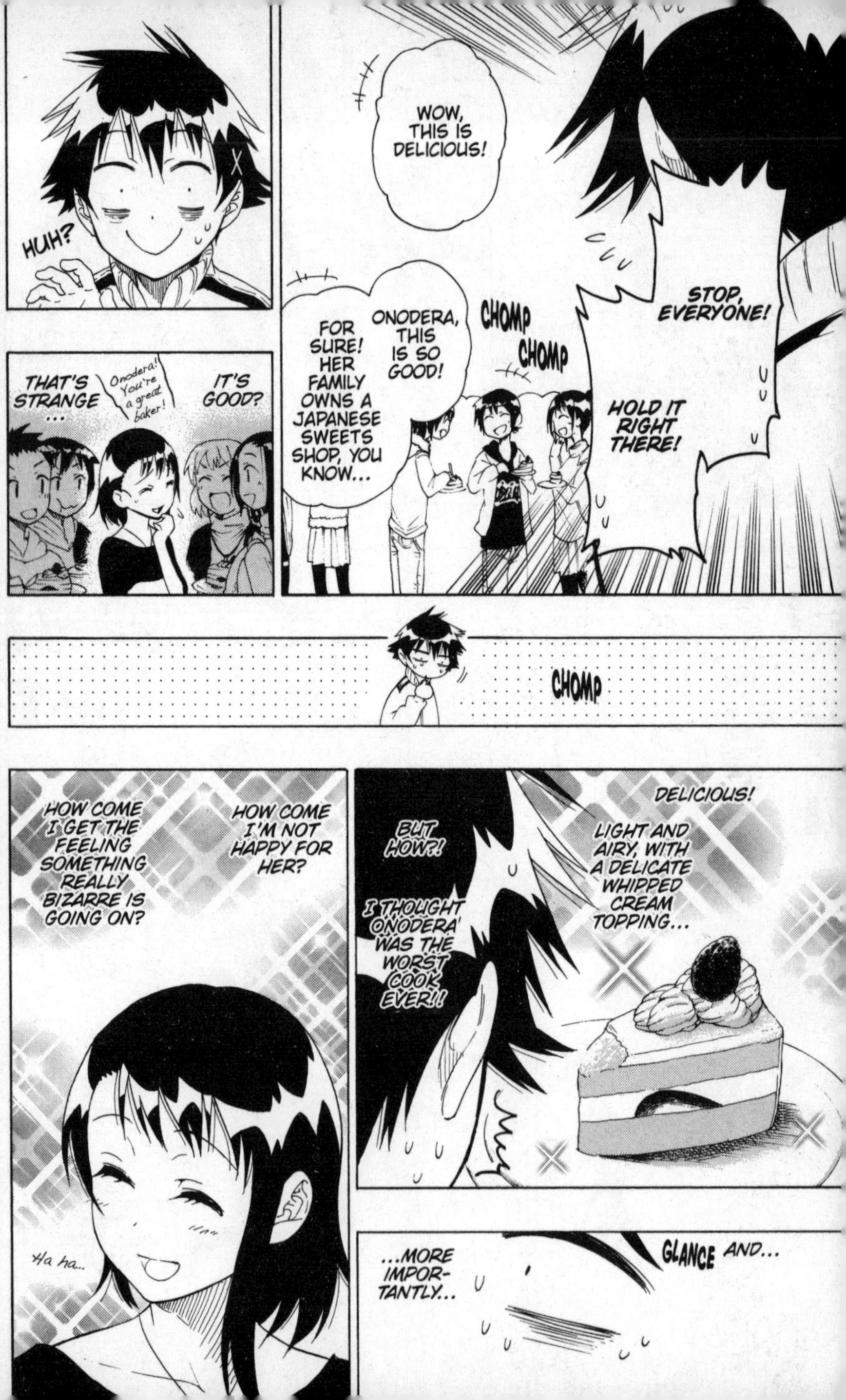
STOP, EVERYONE!
HOLD IT RIGHT THERE!
WOW, THIS IS DELICIOUS!
CHOMP
CHOMP
ONODERA, THIS IS SO GOOD!
FOR SURE! HER FAMILY OWNS A JAPANESE SWEETS SHOP, YOU KNOW...
HUH?
IT'S GOOD?
Onodera! You're a great baker!
THAT'S STRANGE...
CHOMP
DELICIOUS!
LIGHT AND AIRY, WITH A DELICATE WHIPPED CREAM TOPPING...
BUT HOW?!
I THOUGHT ONODERA WAS THE WORST COOK EVER!!
AND...
GLANCE
...MORE IMPORTANTLY...
HOW COME I'M NOT HAPPY FOR HER?
HOW COME I GET THE FEELING SOMETHING REALLY BIZARRE IS GOING ON?
Ha ha...

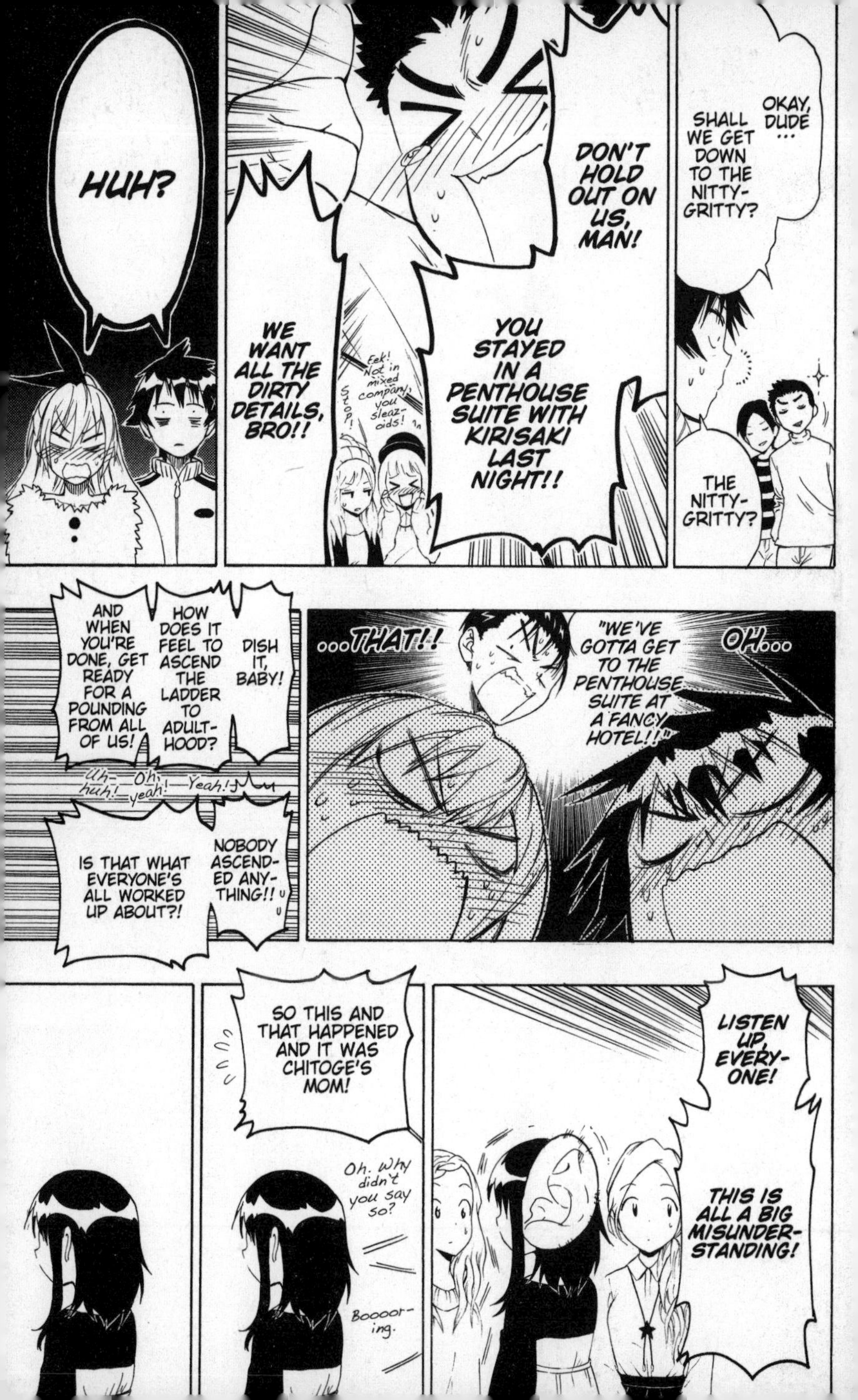
OKAY, DUDE...
SHALL WE GET DOWN TO THE NITTY-GRITTY?
THE NITTY-GRITTY?
DON'T HOLD OUT ON US, MAN!
YOU STAYED IN A PENTHOUSE SUITE WITH KIRISAKI LAST NIGHT!!
WE WANT ALL THE DIRTY DETAILS, BRO!!
Eek! Not in mixed company, you sleazoids!
Stop!
HUH?
OH...
"WE'VE GOTTA GET TO THE PENTHOUSE SUITE AT A FANCY HOTEL!!"
...THAT!!
DISH IT, BABY!
HOW DOES IT FEEL TO ASCEND THE LADDER TO ADULTHOOD?
AND WHEN YOU'RE DONE, GET READY FOR A POUNDING FROM ALL OF US!
Uh-huh! Oh, yeah! Yeah!
NOBODY ASCENDED ANYTHING!!
IS THAT WHAT EVERYONE'S ALL WORKED UP ABOUT?!
LISTEN UP, EVERYONE!
THIS IS ALL A BIG MISUNDERSTANDING!
SO THIS AND THAT HAPPENED AND IT WAS CHITOGE'S MOM!
Oh. Why didn't you say so?
Boooor-ing.

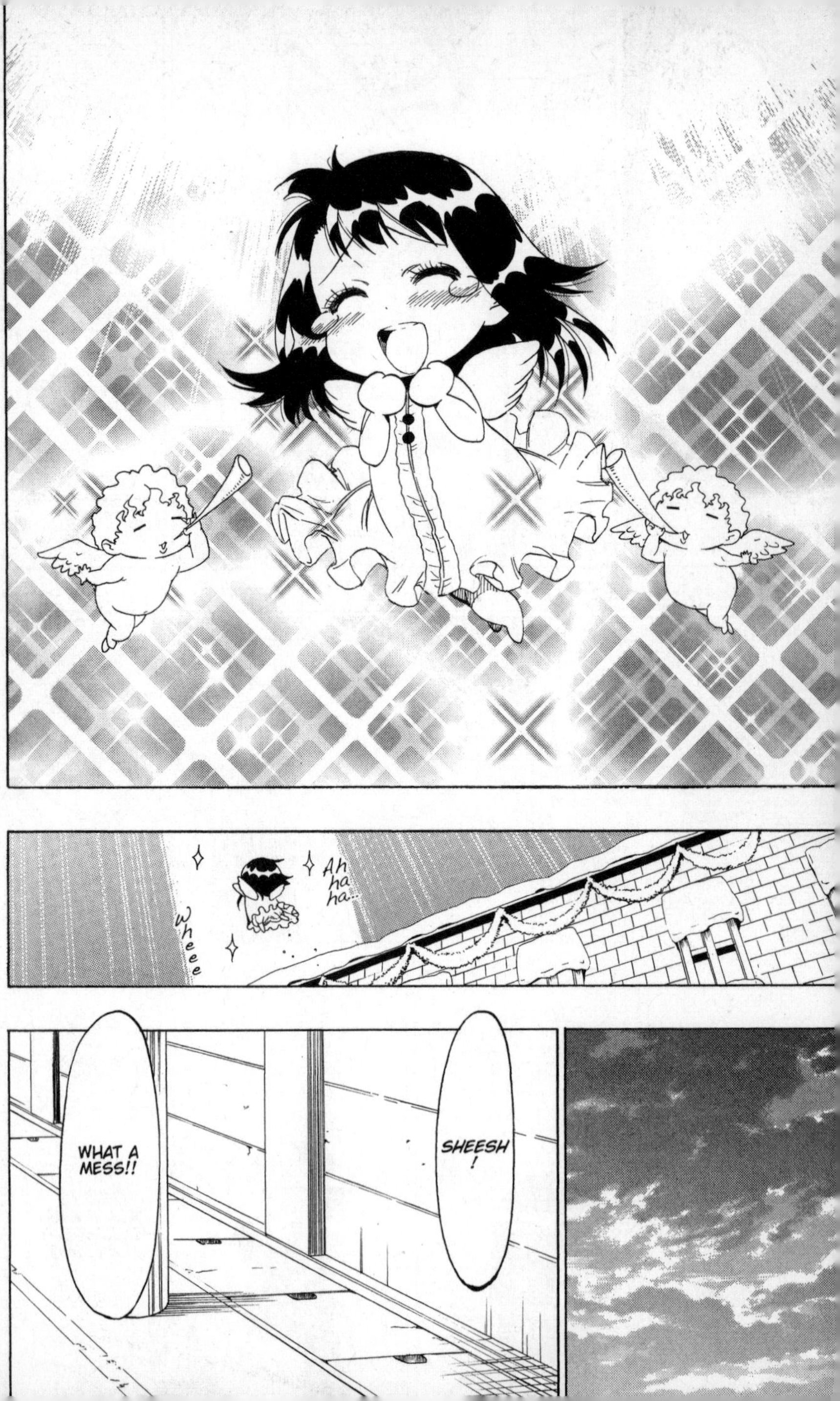
Ah ha ha...
Wheeee
SHEESH!
WHAT A MESS!!

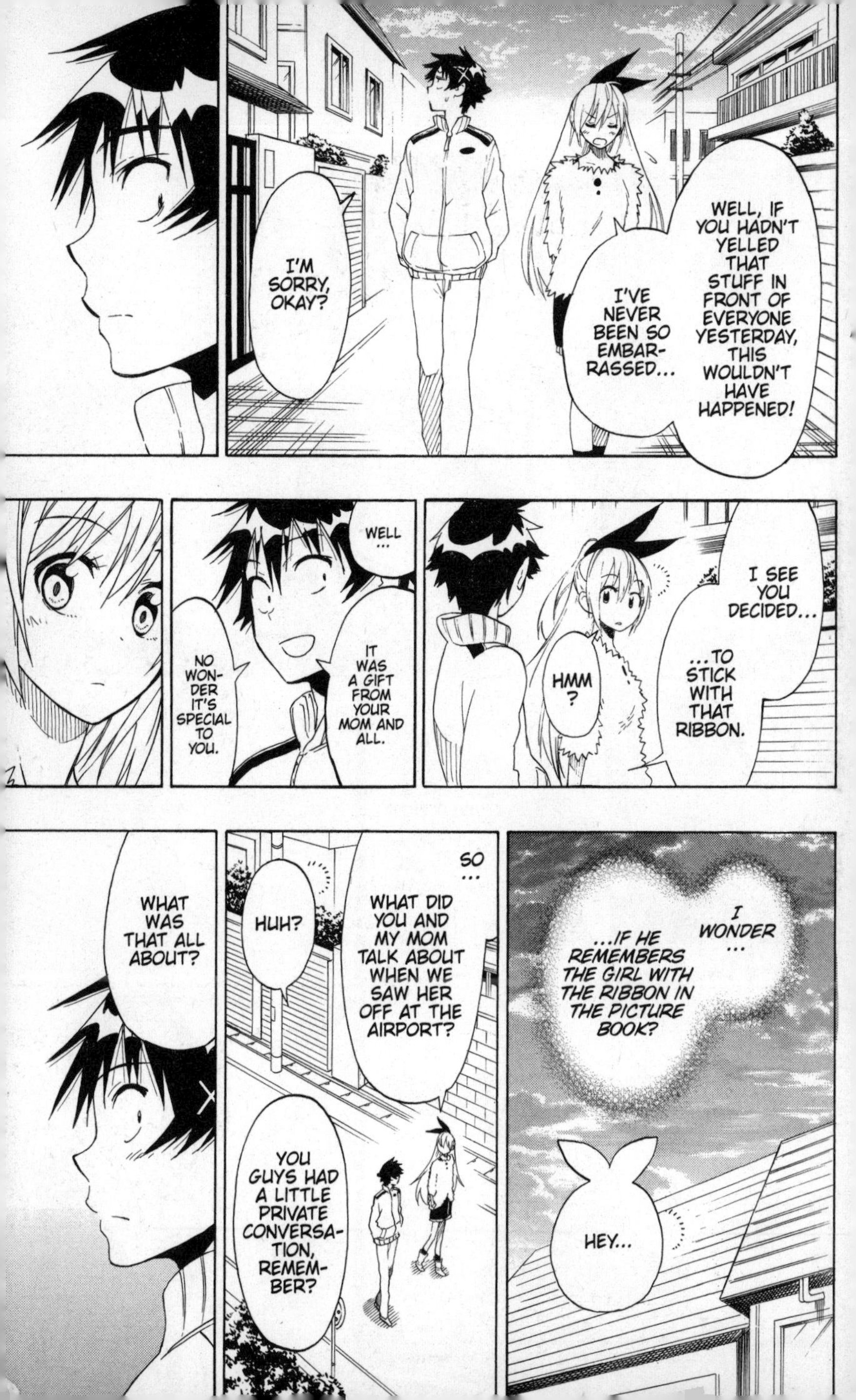
WELL, IF YOU HADN'T YELLED THAT STUFF IN FRONT OF EVERYONE YESTERDAY, THIS WOULDN'T HAVE HAPPENED!
I'VE NEVER BEEN SO EMBARRASSED...
I'M SORRY, OKAY?
I SEE YOU DECIDED...
...TO STICK WITH THAT RIBBON.
HMM?
WELL...
IT WAS A GIFT FROM YOUR MOM AND ALL.
NO WONDER IT'S SPECIAL TO YOU.
I WONDER...
...IF HE REMEMBERS THE GIRL WITH THE RIBBON IN THE PICTURE BOOK?
HEY...
SO...
WHAT DID YOU AND MY MOM TALK ABOUT WHEN WE SAW HER OFF AT THE AIRPORT?
HUH?
YOU GUYS HAD A LITTLE PRIVATE CONVERSATION, REMEMBER?
WHAT WAS THAT ALL ABOUT?

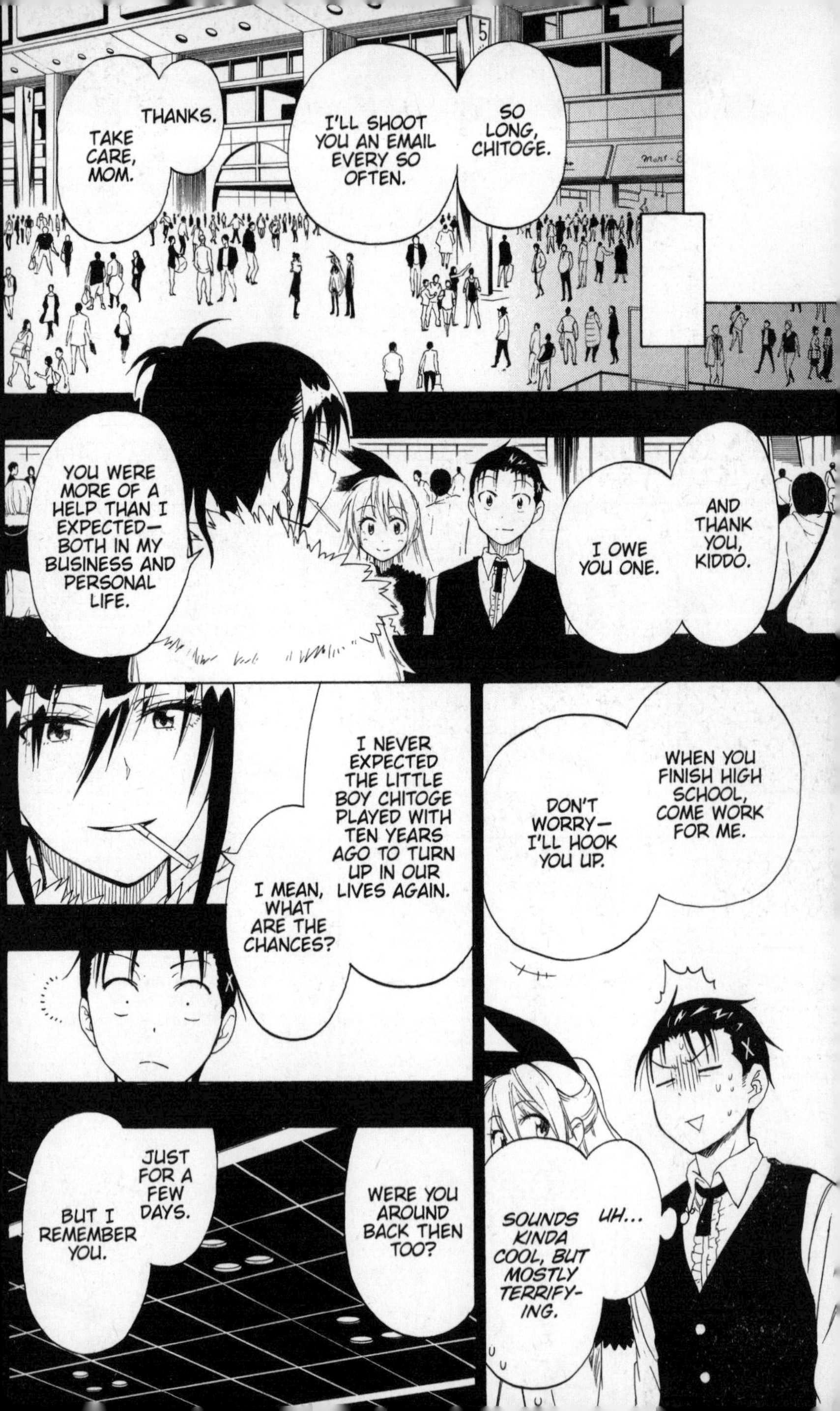
SO LONG, CHITOGE.
I'LL SHOOT YOU AN EMAIL EVERY SO OFTEN.
THANKS.
TAKE CARE, MOM.
AND THANK YOU, KIDDO.
I OWE YOU ONE.
YOU WERE MORE OF A HELP THAN I EXPECTED—BOTH IN MY BUSINESS AND PERSONAL LIFE.
WHEN YOU FINISH HIGH SCHOOL, COME WORK FOR ME.
DON'T WORRY—I'LL HOOK YOU UP.
UH...
SOUNDS KINDA COOL, BUT MOSTLY TERRIFYING.
I NEVER EXPECTED THE LITTLE BOY CHITOGE PLAYED WITH TEN YEARS AGO TO TURN UP IN OUR LIVES AGAIN.
I MEAN, WHAT ARE THE CHANCES?
WERE YOU AROUND BACK THEN TOO?
JUST FOR A FEW DAYS.
BUT I REMEMBER YOU.

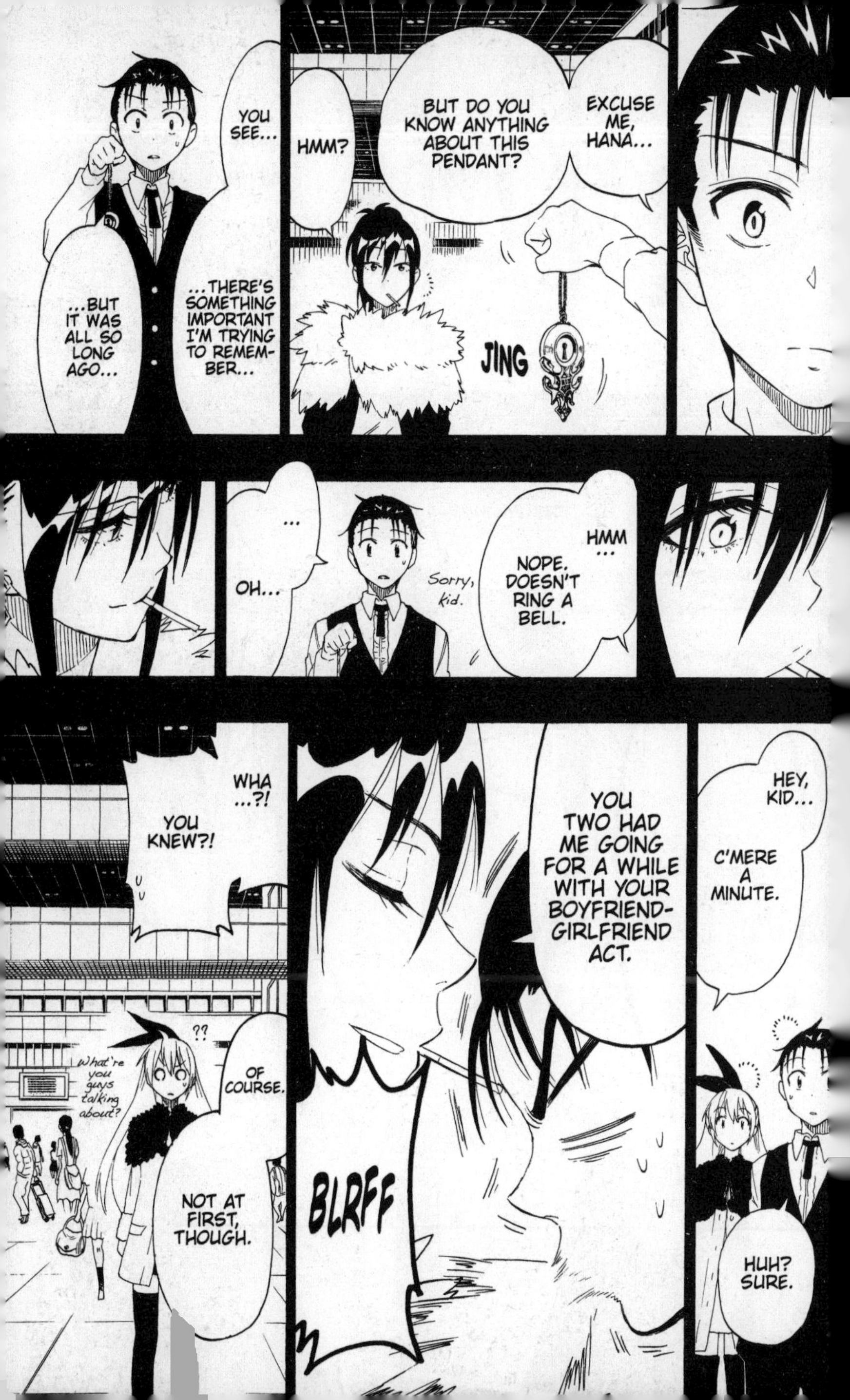
EXCUSE ME, HANA...
BUT DO YOU KNOW ANYTHING ABOUT THIS PENDANT?
HMM?
JING
YOU SEE...
...THERE'S SOMETHING IMPORTANT I'M TRYING TO REMEMBER...
...BUT IT WAS ALL SO LONG AGO...
HMM ...
NOPE. DOESN'T RING A BELL.
Sorry, kid.
...
OH...
HEY, KID...
C'MERE A MINUTE.
HUH? SURE.
YOU TWO HAD ME GOING FOR A WHILE WITH YOUR BOYFRIEND-GIRLFRIEND ACT.
BLRFF
WHA ...?!
YOU KNEW?!
OF COURSE.
NOT AT FIRST, THOUGH.
??
What're you guys talking about?

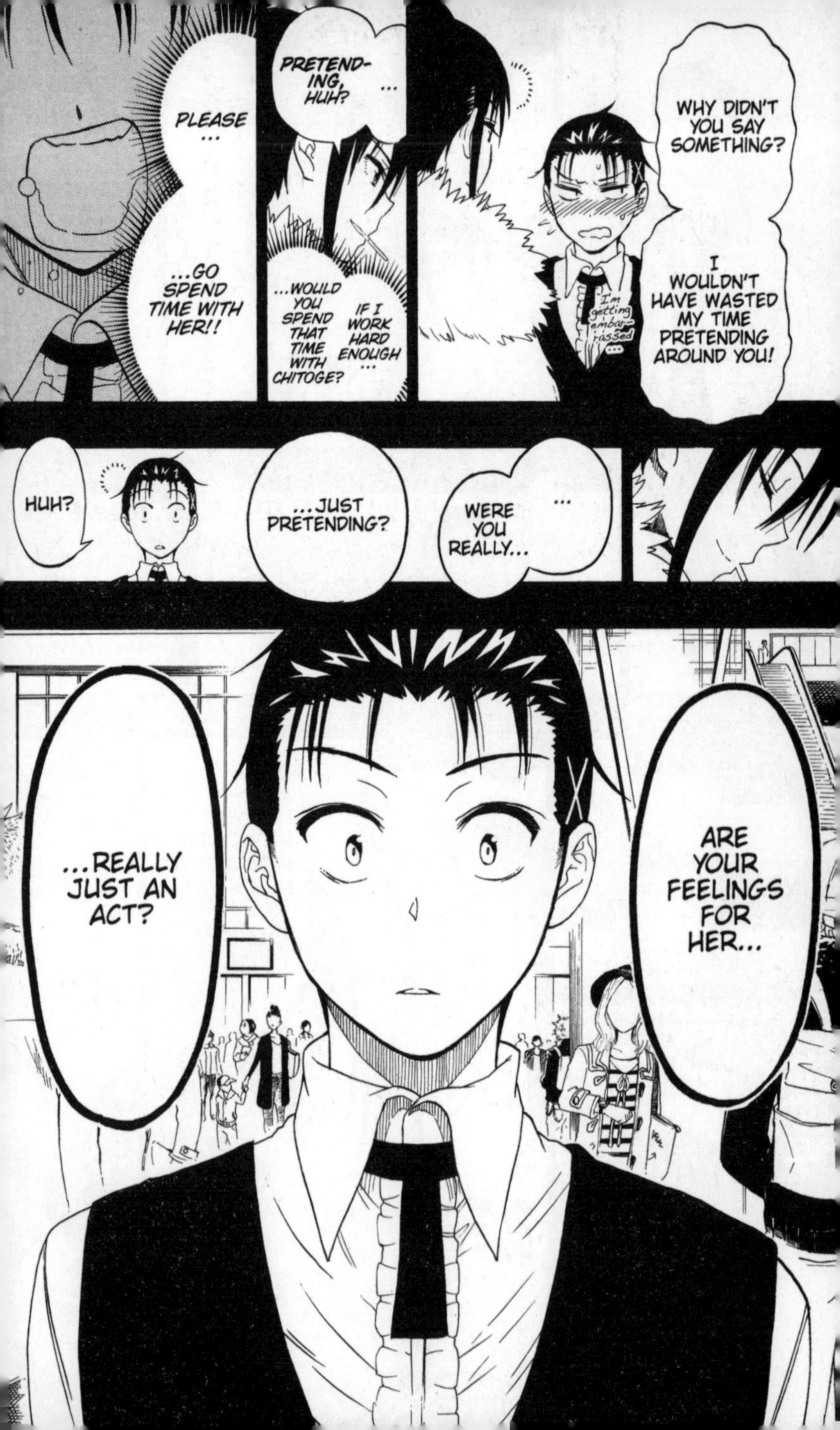
WHY DIDN'T YOU SAY SOMETHING?
I WOULDN'T HAVE WASTED MY TIME PRETENDING AROUND YOU!
I'm getting embarrassed ...
PRETENDING, HUH?
...
IF I WORK HARD ENOUGH ...
...WOULD YOU SPEND THAT TIME WITH CHITOGE?
PLEASE ...
...GO SPEND TIME WITH HER!!
...
WERE YOU REALLY...
...JUST PRETENDING?
HUH?
ARE YOUR FEELINGS FOR HER...
...REALLY JUST AN ACT?

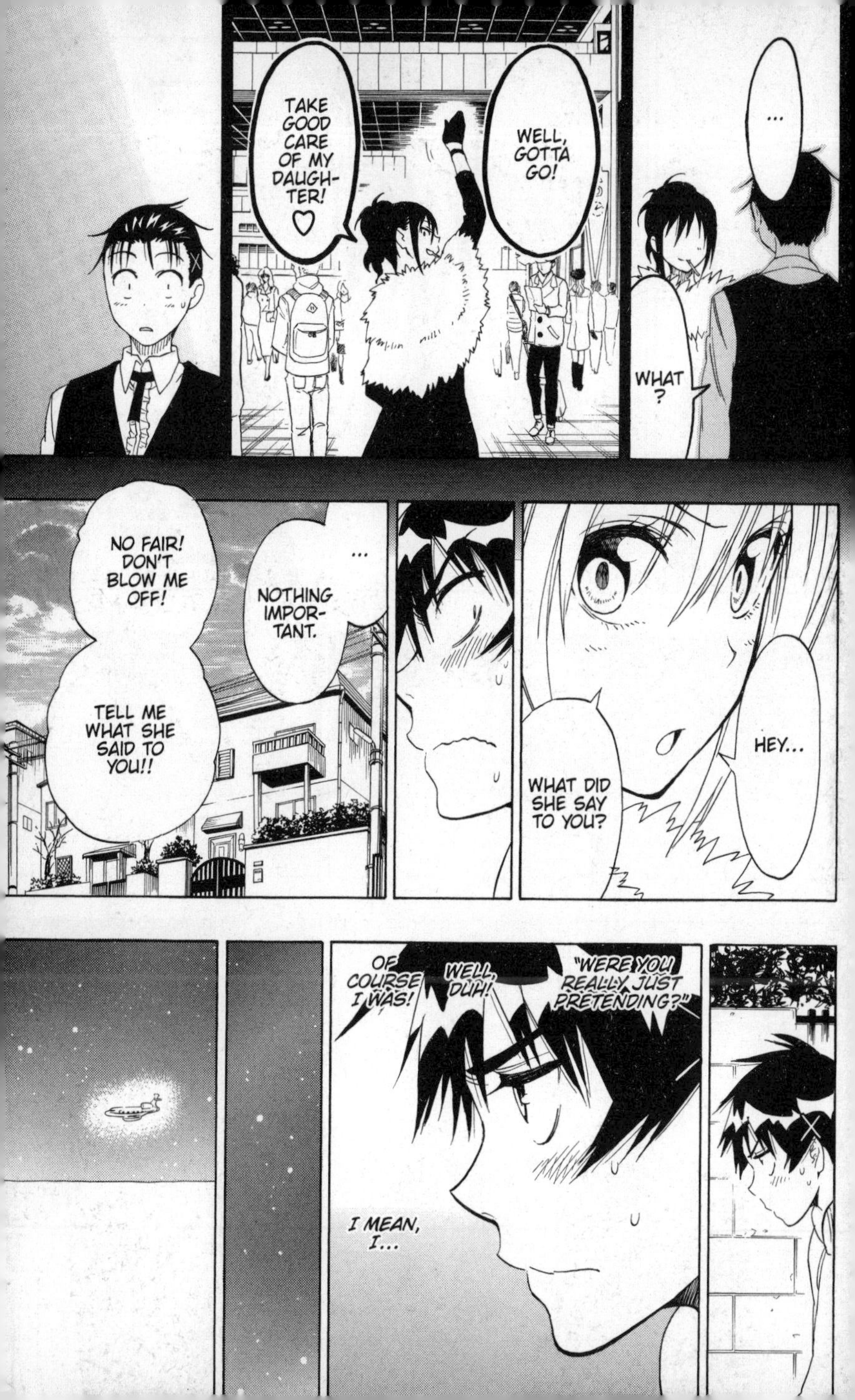
...
WHAT?
WELL, GOTTA GO!
TAKE GOOD CARE OF MY DAUGH-TER! ♡
HEY...
WHAT DID SHE SAY TO YOU?
...
NOTHING IMPOR-TANT.
NO FAIR! DON'T BLOW ME OFF!
TELL ME WHAT SHE SAID TO YOU!!
"WERE YOU REALLY JUST PRETENDING?"
WELL, DUH!
OF COURSE I WAS!
I MEAN, I...

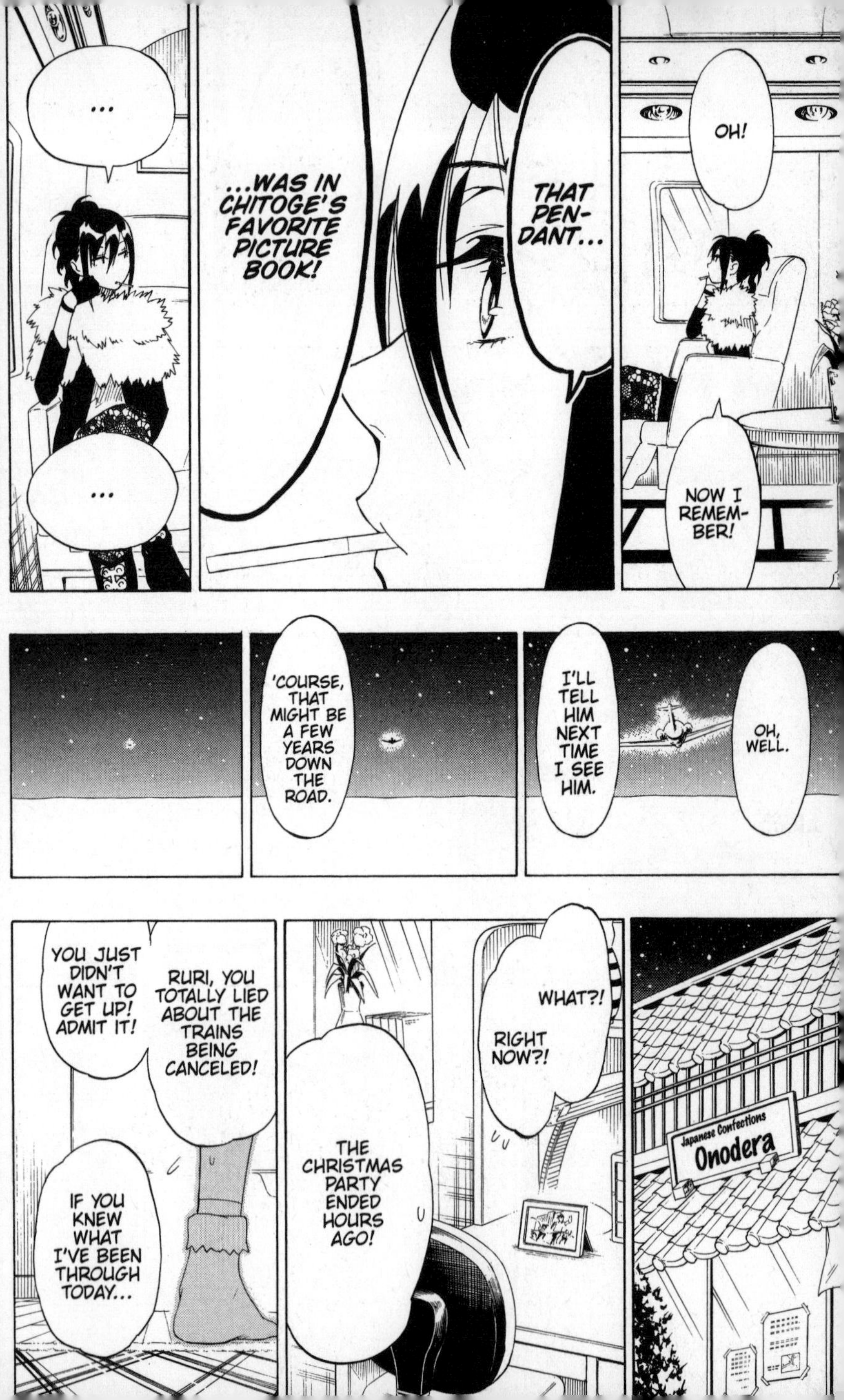
OH!
NOW I REMEMBER!
THAT PENDANT...
...WAS IN CHITOGE'S FAVORITE PICTURE BOOK!
...
...
OH, WELL.
I'LL TELL HIM NEXT TIME I SEE HIM.
'COURSE, THAT MIGHT BE A FEW YEARS DOWN THE ROAD.
Japanese Confections
Onodera
WHAT?!
RIGHT NOW?!
THE CHRISTMAS PARTY ENDED HOURS AGO!
RURI, YOU TOTALLY LIED ABOUT THE TRAINS BEING CANCELED!
YOU JUST DIDN'T WANT TO GET UP! ADMIT IT!
IF YOU KNEW WHAT I'VE BEEN THROUGH TODAY...

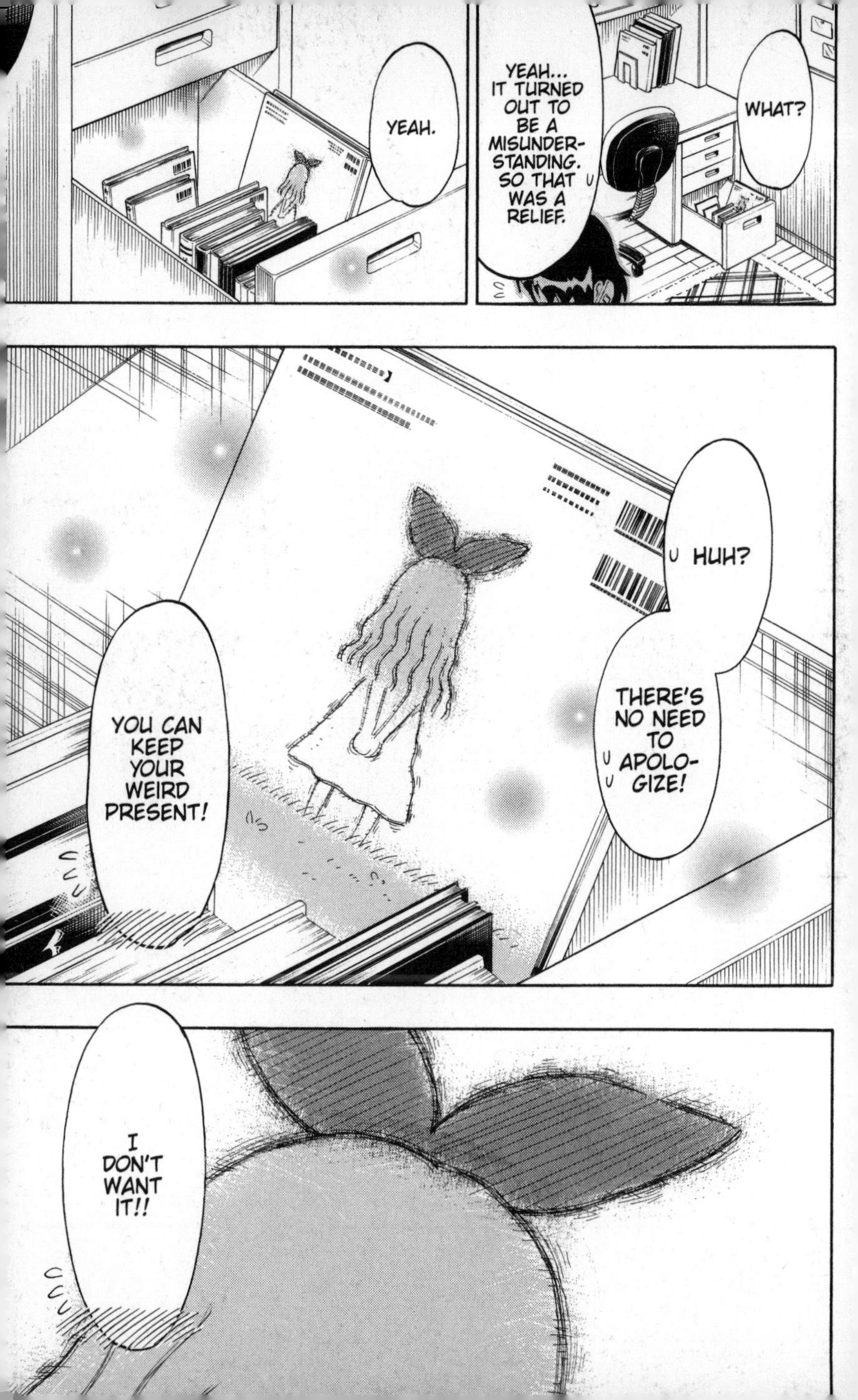
WHAT?
YEAH... IT TURNED OUT TO BE A MISUNDERSTANDING. SO THAT WAS A RELIEF.
YEAH.
HUH?
THERE'S NO NEED TO APOLOGIZE!
YOU CAN KEEP YOUR WEIRD PRESENT!
I DON'T WANT IT!!

A Gift from Ruri

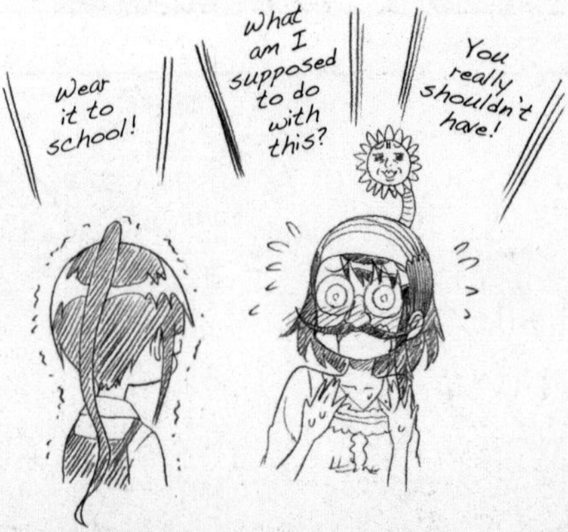
You really shouldn't have!
What am I supposed to do with this?
Wear it to school!

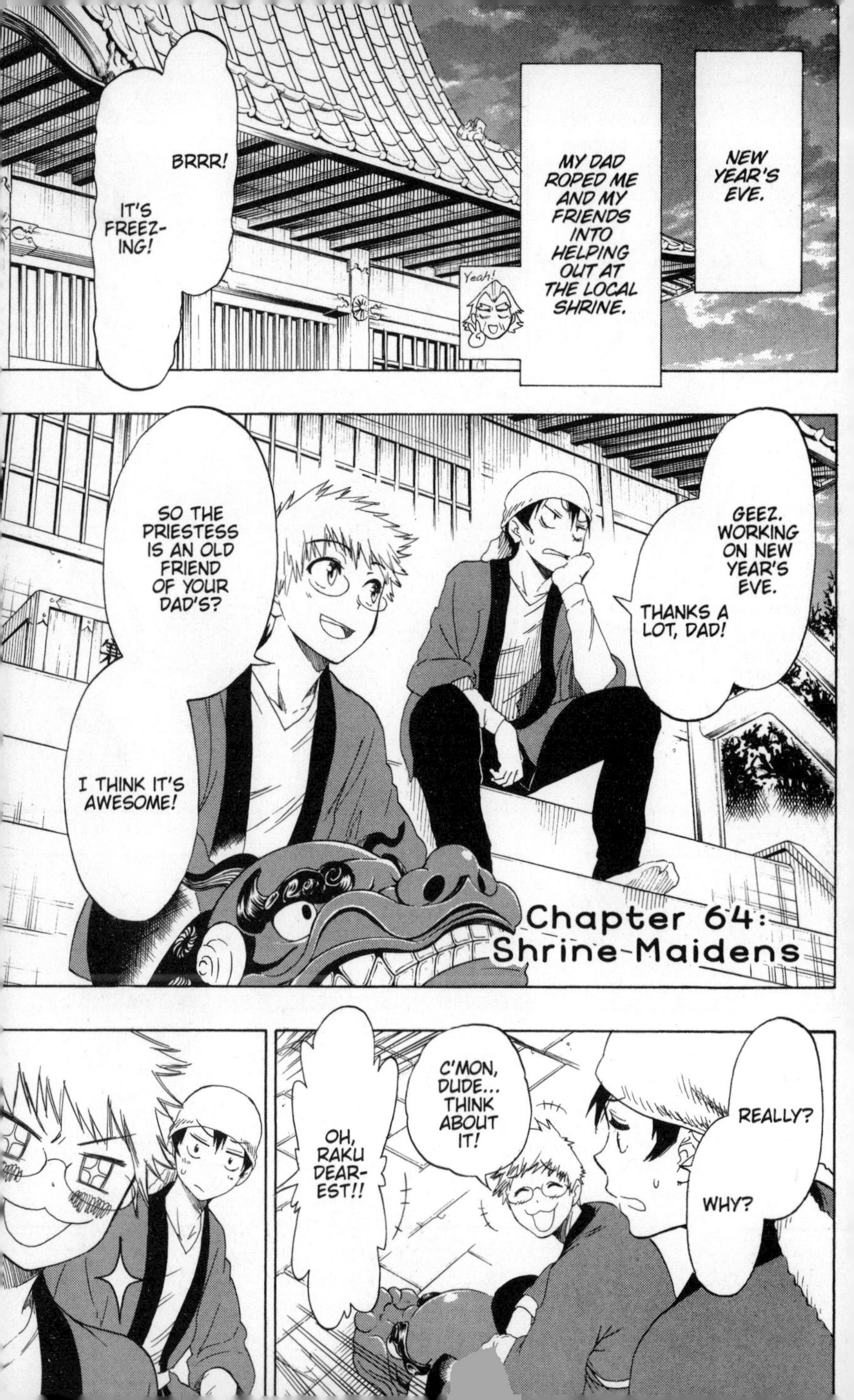
NEW YEAR'S EVE.
MY DAD ROPED ME AND MY FRIENDS INTO HELPING OUT AT THE LOCAL SHRINE.
Yeah!
BRRR!
IT'S FREEZ-ING!
GEEZ. WORKING ON NEW YEAR'S EVE.
THANKS A LOT, DAD!
SO THE PRIESTESS IS AN OLD FRIEND OF YOUR DAD'S?
I THINK IT'S AWESOME!
Chapter 64: Shrine Maidens
REALLY?
WHY?
C'MON, DUDE... THINK ABOUT IT!
OH, RAKU DEAR-EST!!

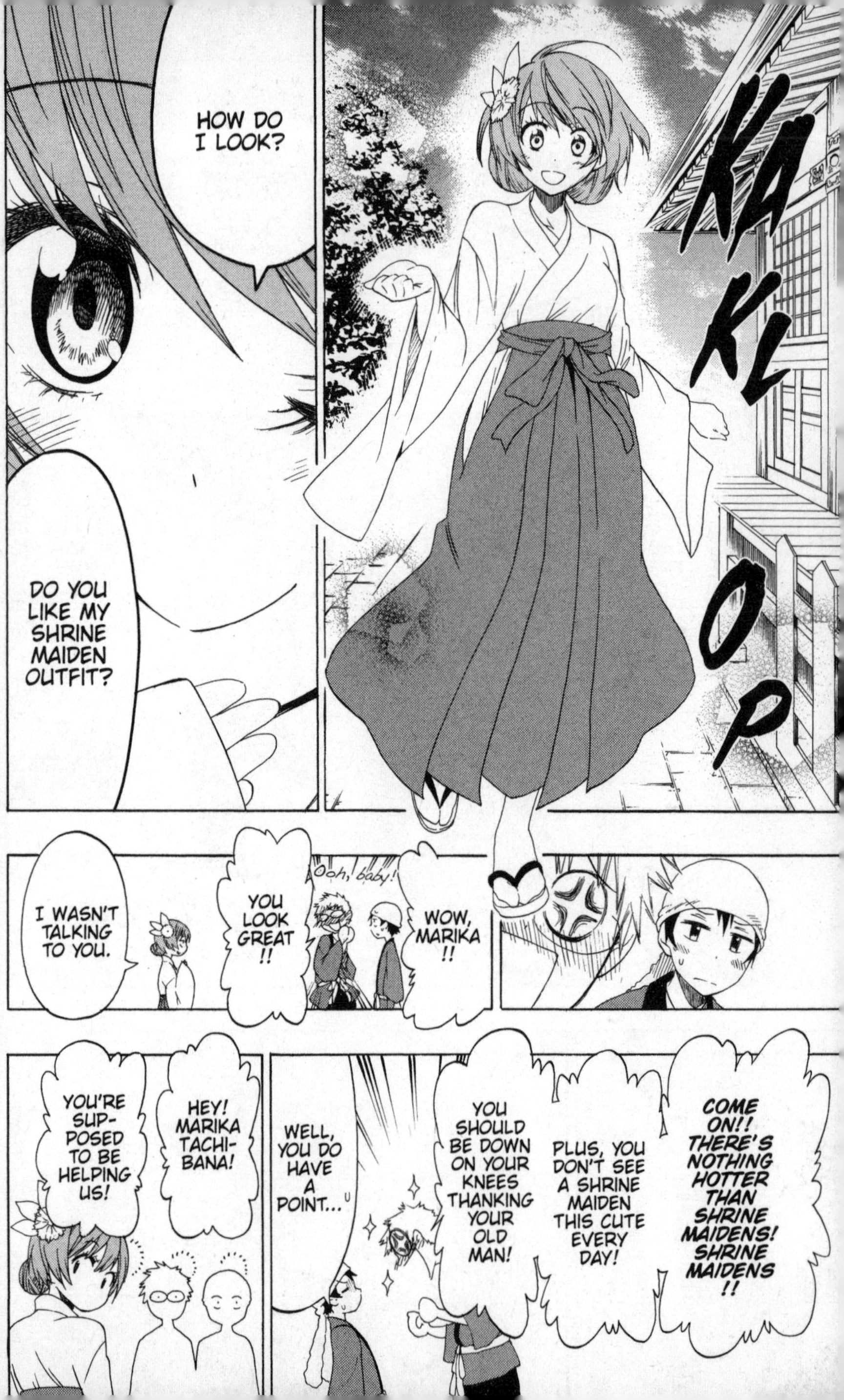
KA KLOOP
HOW DO I LOOK?
DO YOU LIKE MY SHRINE MAIDEN OUTFIT?
WOW, MARIKA!!
Ooh, baby!
YOU LOOK GREAT!!
I WASN'T TALKING TO YOU.
COME ON!! THERE'S NOTHING HOTTER THAN SHRINE MAIDENS! SHRINE MAIDENS!!
PLUS, YOU DON'T SEE A SHRINE MAIDEN THIS CUTE EVERY DAY!
YOU SHOULD BE DOWN ON YOUR KNEES THANKING YOUR OLD MAN!
WELL, YOU DO HAVE A POINT...
HEY! MARIKA TACHI-BANA!
YOU'RE SUP-POSED TO BE HELPING US!

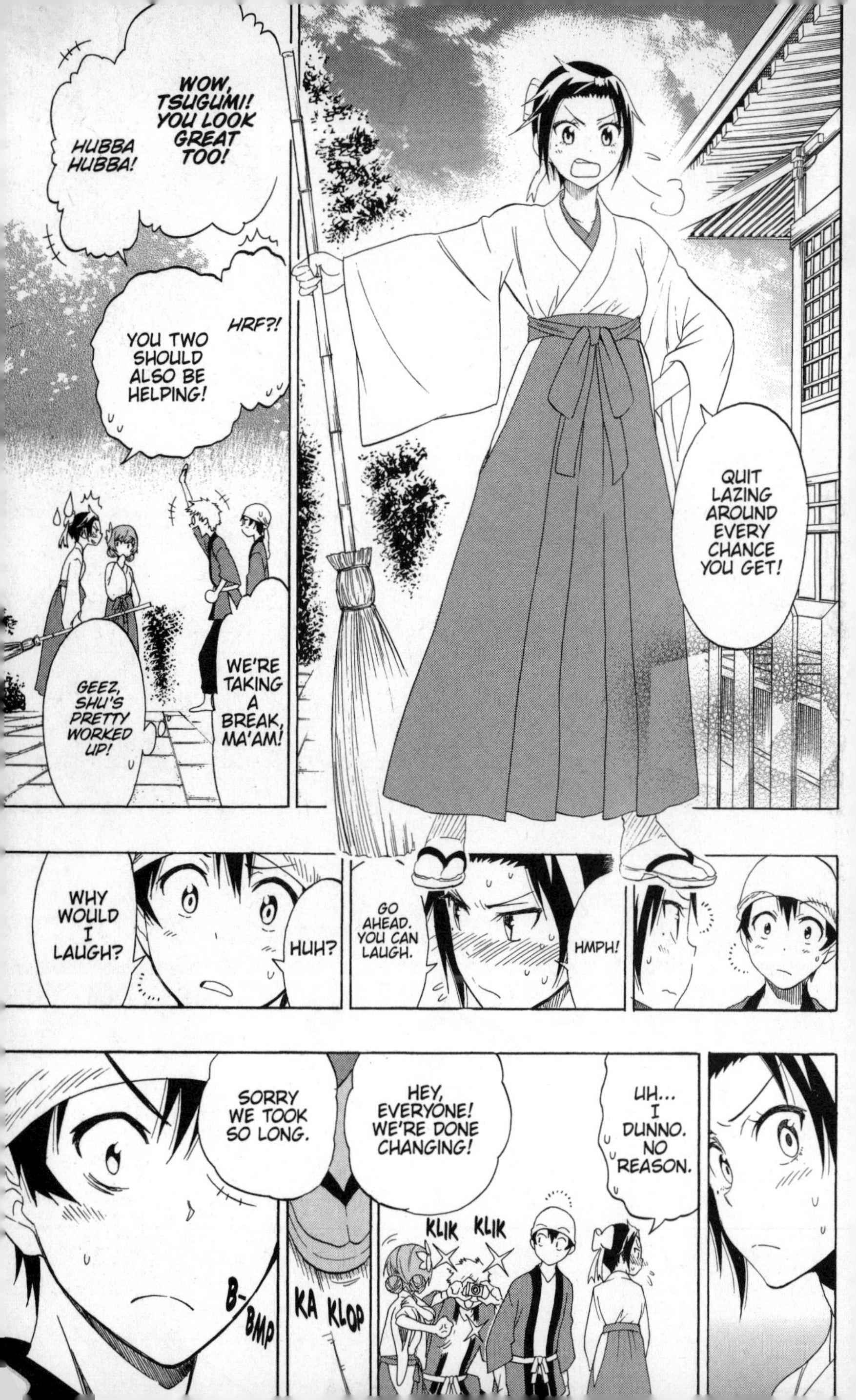
QUIT LAZING AROUND EVERY CHANCE YOU GET!
WOW, TSUGUMI! YOU LOOK GREAT TOO!
HUBBA HUBBA!
HRF?!
YOU TWO SHOULD ALSO BE HELPING!
WE'RE TAKING A BREAK, MA'AM!
GEEZ, SHU'S PRETTY WORKED UP!
HMPH!
GO AHEAD. YOU CAN LAUGH.
HUH?
WHY WOULD I LAUGH?
UH... I DUNNO. NO REASON.
HEY, EVERYONE! WE'RE DONE CHANGING!
KLIK KLIK
SORRY WE TOOK SO LONG.
KA KLOP
B-BMP

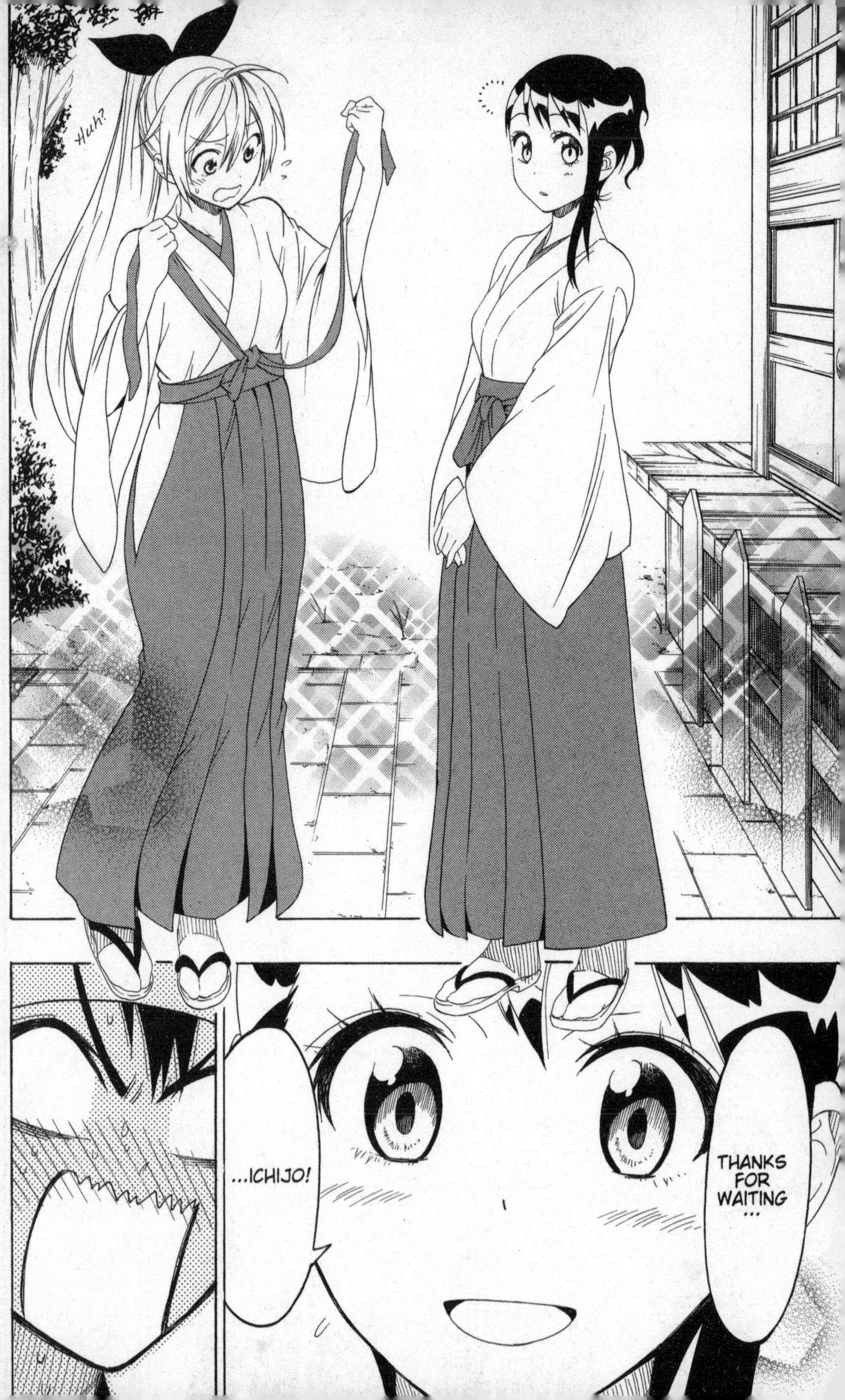
Huh?
THANKS FOR WAITING...
...ICHIJO!

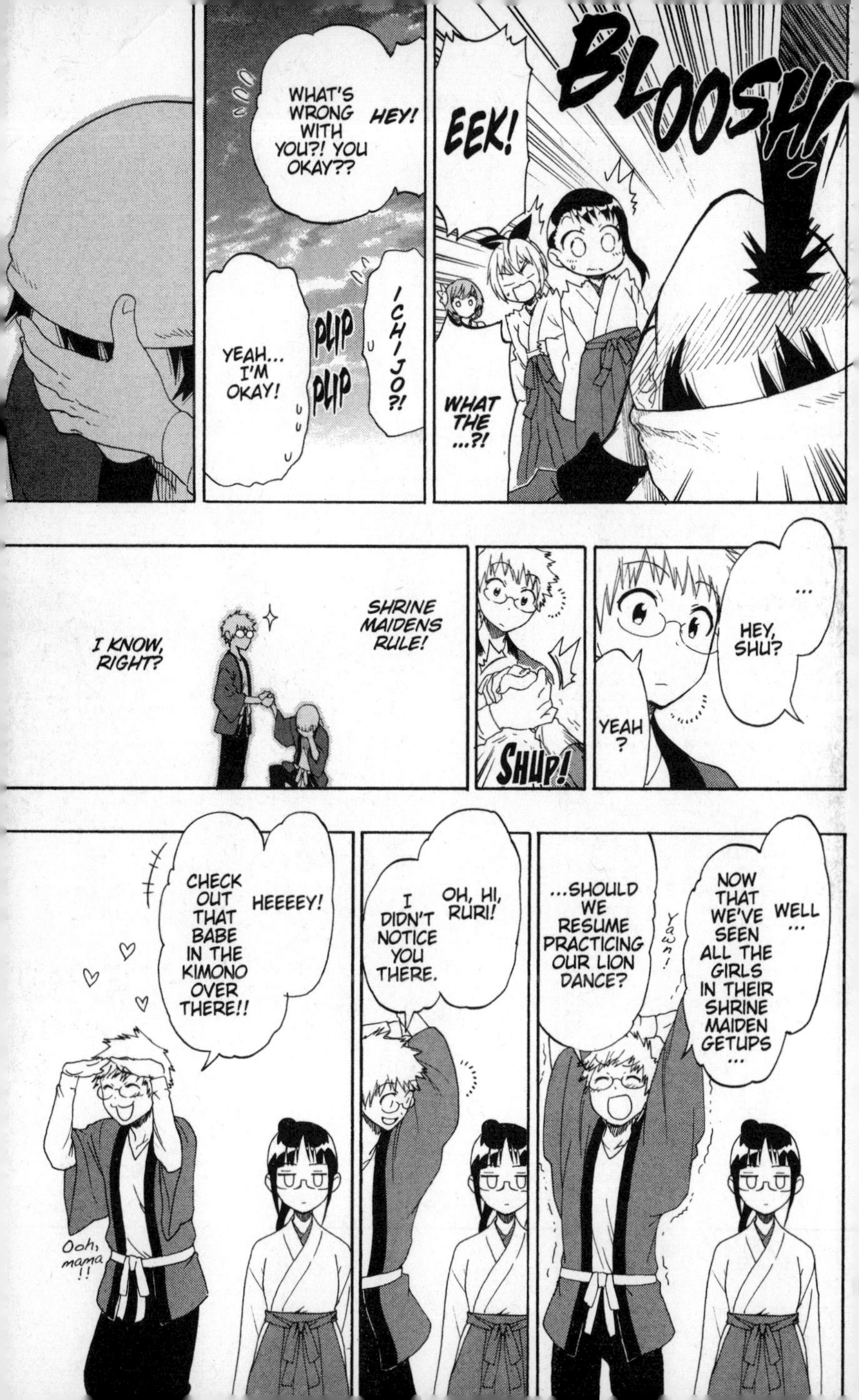
BLOOSH!
EEK!
WHAT THE ...?!
HEY!
WHAT'S WRONG WITH YOU?! YOU OKAY??
ICHIJO?!
PLIP
PLIP
YEAH... I'M OKAY!
...
HEY, SHU?
YEAH?
SHUP!
SHRINE MAIDENS RULE!
I KNOW, RIGHT?
WELL...
NOW THAT WE'VE SEEN ALL THE GIRLS IN THEIR SHRINE MAIDEN GETUPS...
Yawn!
...SHOULD WE RESUME PRACTICING OUR LION DANCE?
OH, HI, RURI!
I DIDN'T NOTICE YOU THERE.
HEEEEY!
CHECK OUT THAT BABE IN THE KIMONO OVER THERE!!
Ooh, mama!!

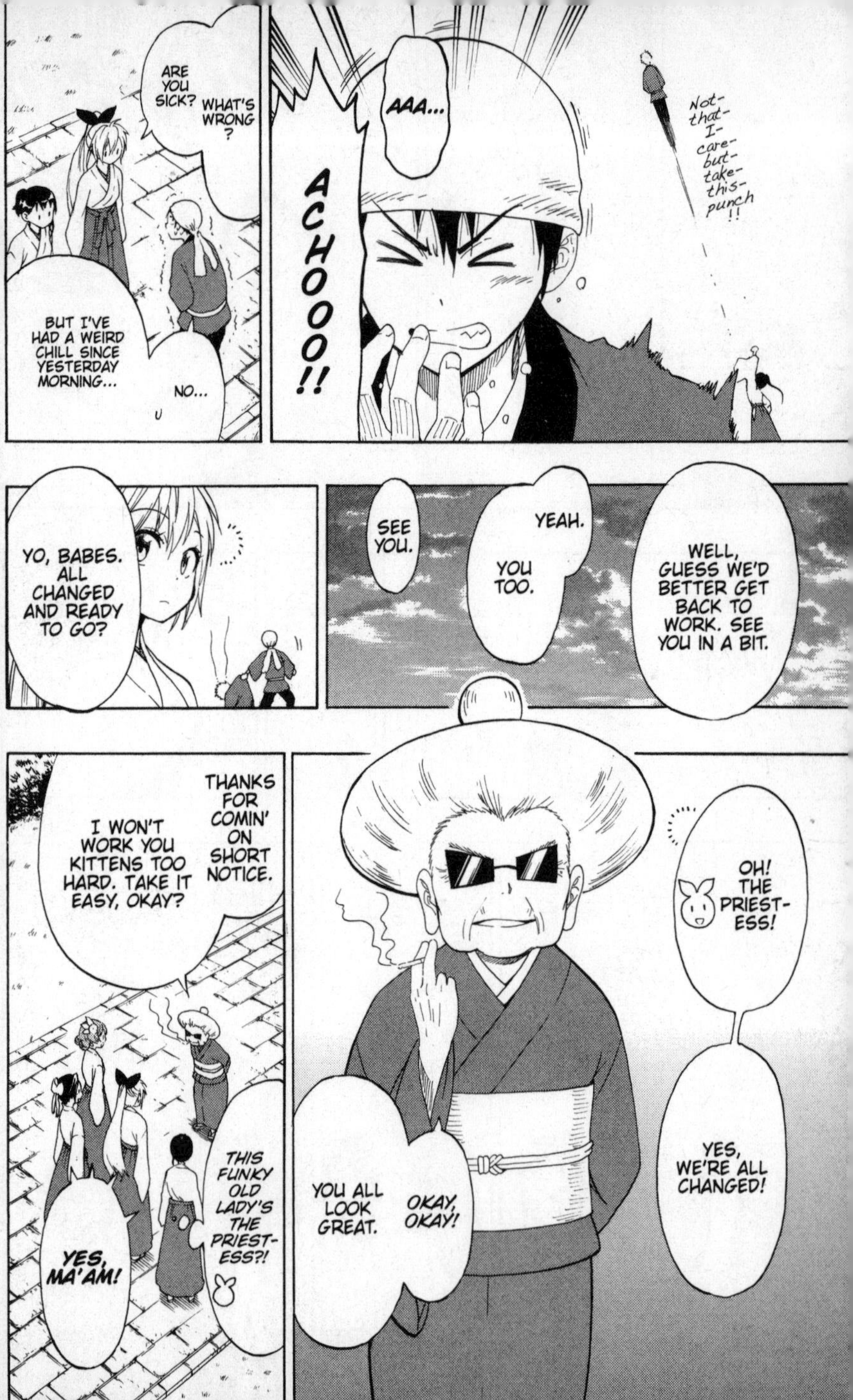
AAA...
ACHOOOO!!
Not-that-I-care-but-take-this-punch!!
WHAT'S WRONG?
ARE YOU SICK?
NO...
BUT I'VE HAD A WEIRD CHILL SINCE YESTERDAY MORNING...
WELL, GUESS WE'D BETTER GET BACK TO WORK. SEE YOU IN A BIT.
YEAH.
YOU TOO.
SEE YOU.
YO, BABES. ALL CHANGED AND READY TO GO?
OH! THE PRIEST-ESS!
YES, WE'RE ALL CHANGED!
OKAY, OKAY!
YOU ALL LOOK GREAT.
THANKS FOR COMIN' ON SHORT NOTICE.
I WON'T WORK YOU KITTENS TOO HARD. TAKE IT EASY, OKAY?
THIS FUNKY OLD LADY'S THE PRIEST-ESS?!
YES, MA'AM!

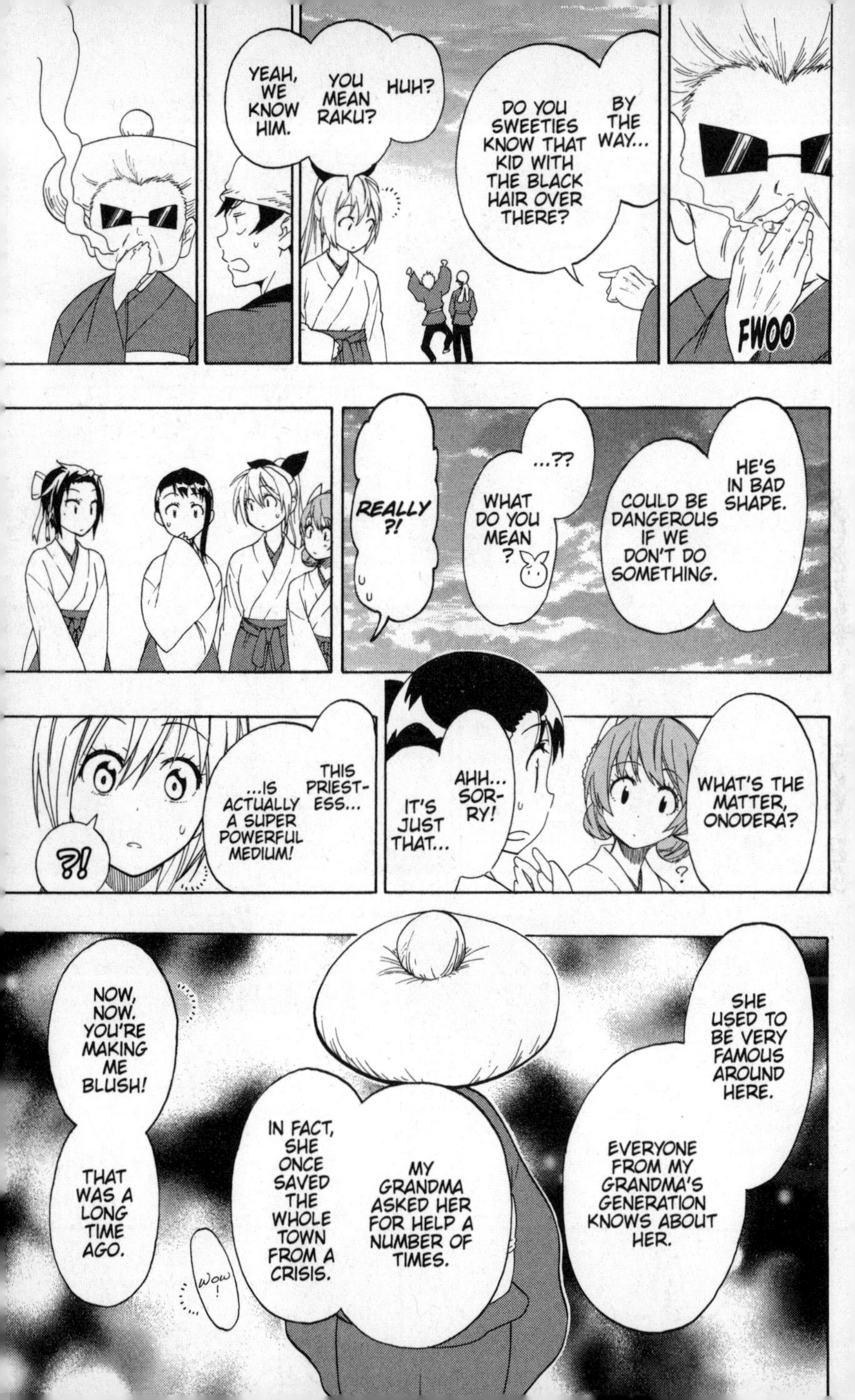
FWOO
BY THE WAY...
DO YOU SWEETIES KNOW THAT KID WITH THE BLACK HAIR OVER THERE?
HUH?
YOU MEAN RAKU?
YEAH, WE KNOW HIM.
HE'S IN BAD SHAPE.
COULD BE DANGEROUS IF WE DON'T DO SOMETHING.
...??
WHAT DO YOU MEAN?
REALLY?!
WHAT'S THE MATTER, ONODERA?
AHH... SORRY!
IT'S JUST THAT...
THIS PRIESTESS...
...IS ACTUALLY A SUPER POWERFUL MEDIUM!
?!
SHE USED TO BE VERY FAMOUS AROUND HERE.
EVERYONE FROM MY GRANDMA'S GENERATION KNOWS ABOUT HER.
MY GRANDMA ASKED HER FOR HELP A NUMBER OF TIMES.
IN FACT, SHE ONCE SAVED THE WHOLE TOWN FROM A CRISIS.
NOW, NOW. YOU'RE MAKING ME BLUSH!
THAT WAS A LONG TIME AGO.
WOW!

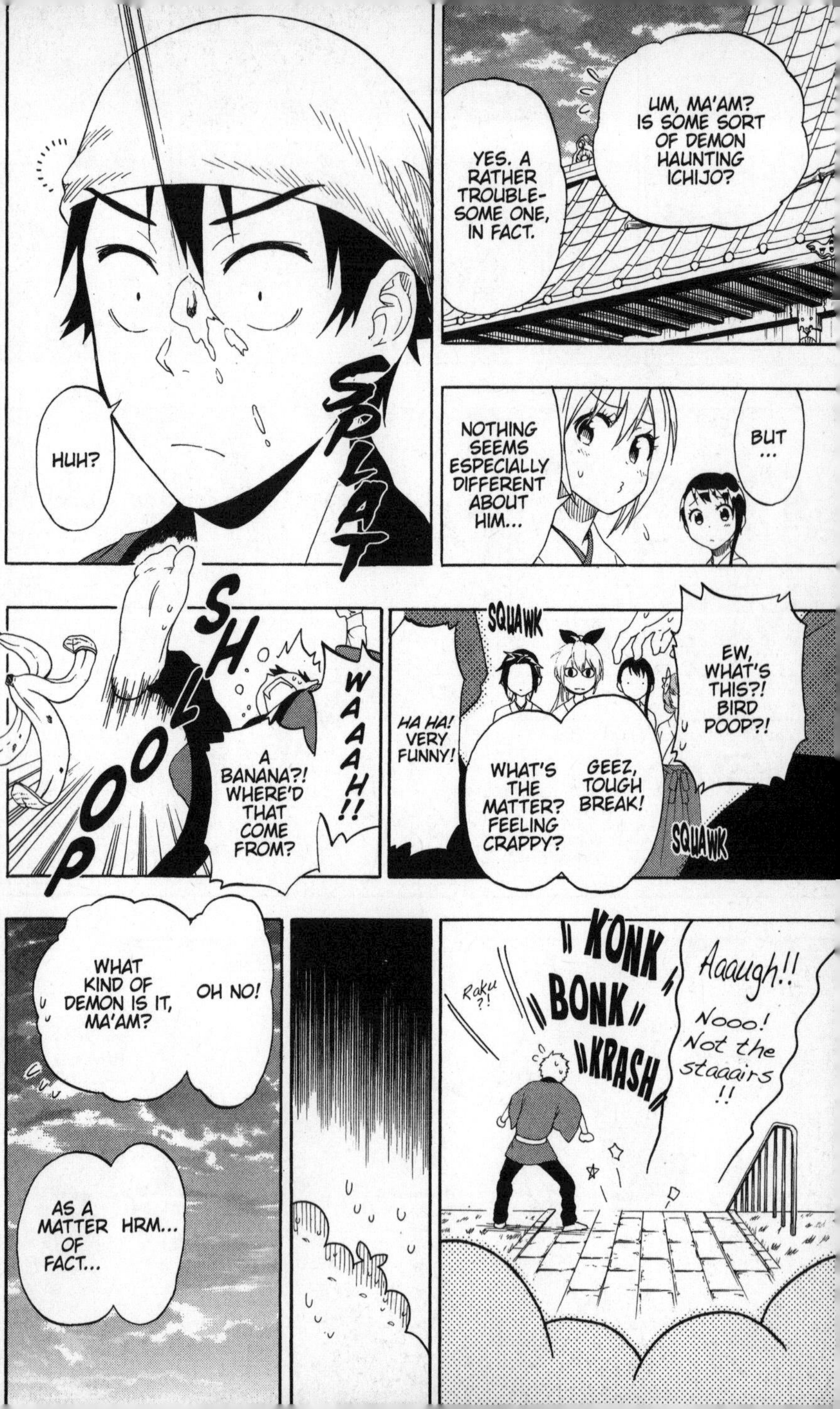
UM, MA'AM? IS SOME SORT OF DEMON HAUNTING ICHIJO?
YES. A RATHER TROUBLE-SOME ONE, IN FACT.
BUT ...
NOTHING SEEMS ESPECIALLY DIFFERENT ABOUT HIM...
HUH?
SPLAT
EW, WHAT'S THIS?! BIRD POOP?!
SQUAWK
GEEZ, TOUGH BREAK!
WHAT'S THE MATTER? FEELING CRAPPY?
HA HA! VERY FUNNY!
SQUAWK
WAAAAH!!
SHLOOOOP
A BANANA?! WHERE'D THAT COME FROM?
Aaaugh!!
Nooo! Not the staaairs !!
KONK
BONK
KRASH
Raku ?!
OH NO!
WHAT KIND OF DEMON IS IT, MA'AM?
HRM...
AS A MATTER OF FACT...

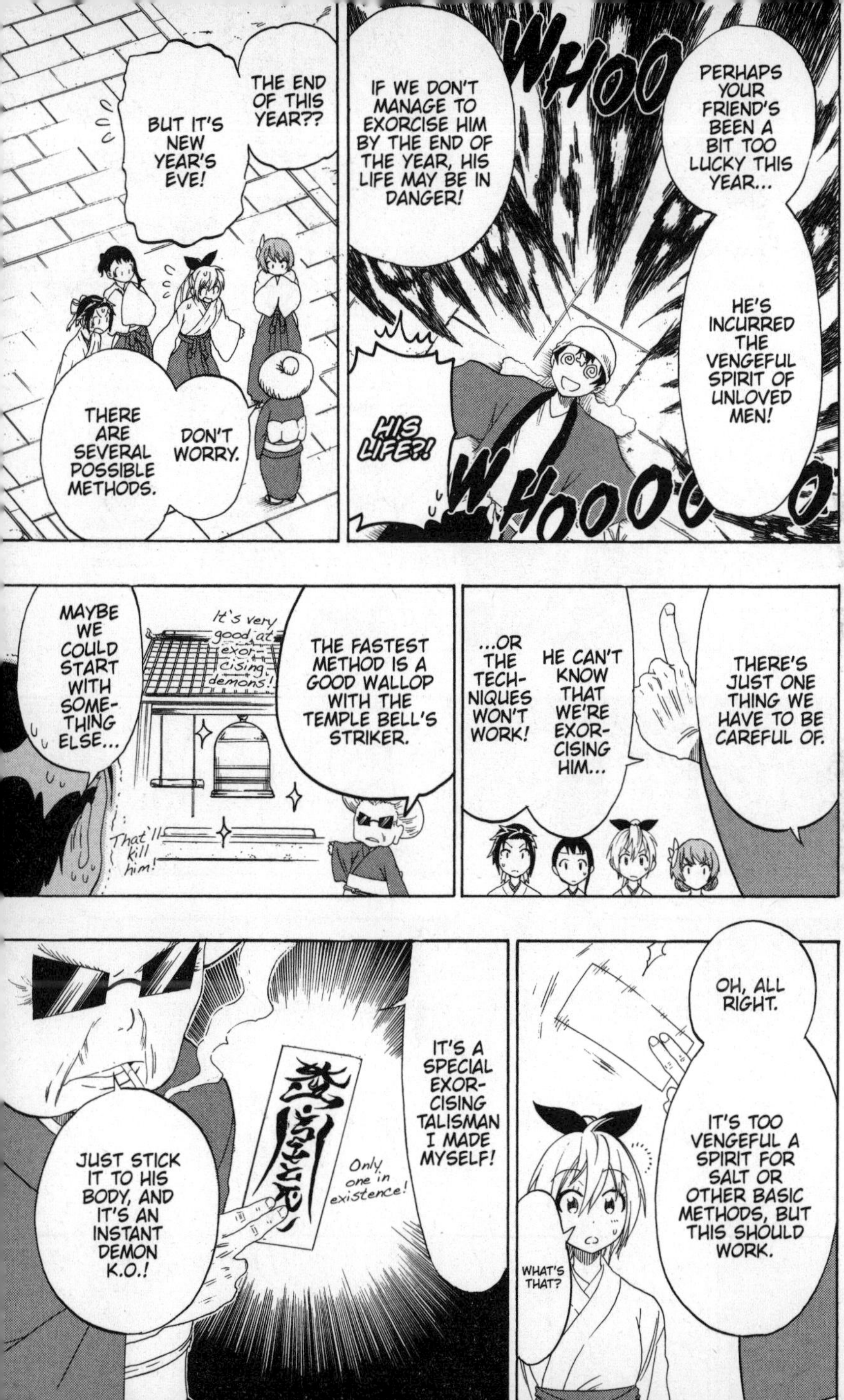
PERHAPS YOUR FRIEND'S BEEN A BIT TOO LUCKY THIS YEAR...
HE'S INCURRED THE VENGEFUL SPIRIT OF UNLOVED MEN!
WHOO
IF WE DON'T MANAGE TO EXORCISE HIM BY THE END OF THE YEAR, HIS LIFE MAY BE IN DANGER!
HIS LIFE?!
WHOOOOO
THE END OF THIS YEAR??
BUT IT'S NEW YEAR'S EVE!
DON'T WORRY.
THERE ARE SEVERAL POSSIBLE METHODS.
THERE'S JUST ONE THING WE HAVE TO BE CAREFUL OF.
HE CAN'T KNOW THAT WE'RE EXORCISING HIM...
...OR THE TECHNIQUES WON'T WORK!
THE FASTEST METHOD IS A GOOD WALLOP WITH THE TEMPLE BELL'S STRIKER.
It's very good at exorcising demons!
MAYBE WE COULD START WITH SOMETHING ELSE...
That'll kill him!
OH, ALL RIGHT.
IT'S TOO VENGEFUL A SPIRIT FOR SALT OR OTHER BASIC METHODS, BUT THIS SHOULD WORK.
WHAT'S THAT?
IT'S A SPECIAL EXORCISING TALISMAN I MADE MYSELF!
Only one in existence!
JUST STICK IT TO HIS BODY, AND IT'S AN INSTANT DEMON K.O.!

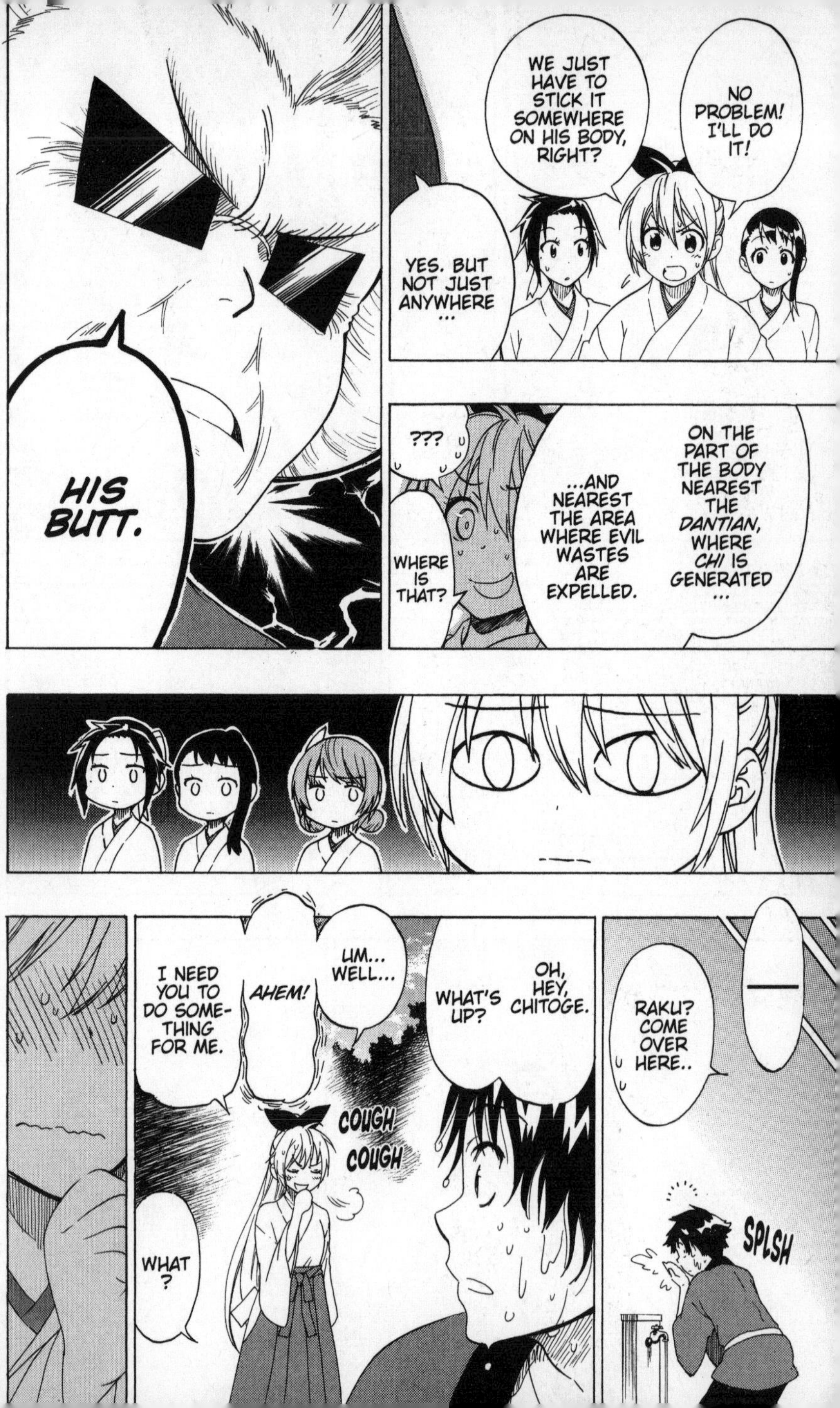
NO PROBLEM! I'LL DO IT!
WE JUST HAVE TO STICK IT SOMEWHERE ON HIS BODY, RIGHT?
YES. BUT NOT JUST ANYWHERE ...
ON THE PART OF THE BODY NEAREST THE *DANTIAN*, WHERE *CHI* IS GENERATED ...
...AND NEAREST THE AREA WHERE EVIL WASTES ARE EXPELLED.
???
WHERE IS THAT?
HIS BUTT.
——
——
RAKU? COME OVER HERE..
SPLSH
OH, HEY, CHITOGE.
WHAT'S UP?
UM... WELL...
AHEM!
I NEED YOU TO DO SOME-THING FOR ME.
COUGH COUGH
WHAT?

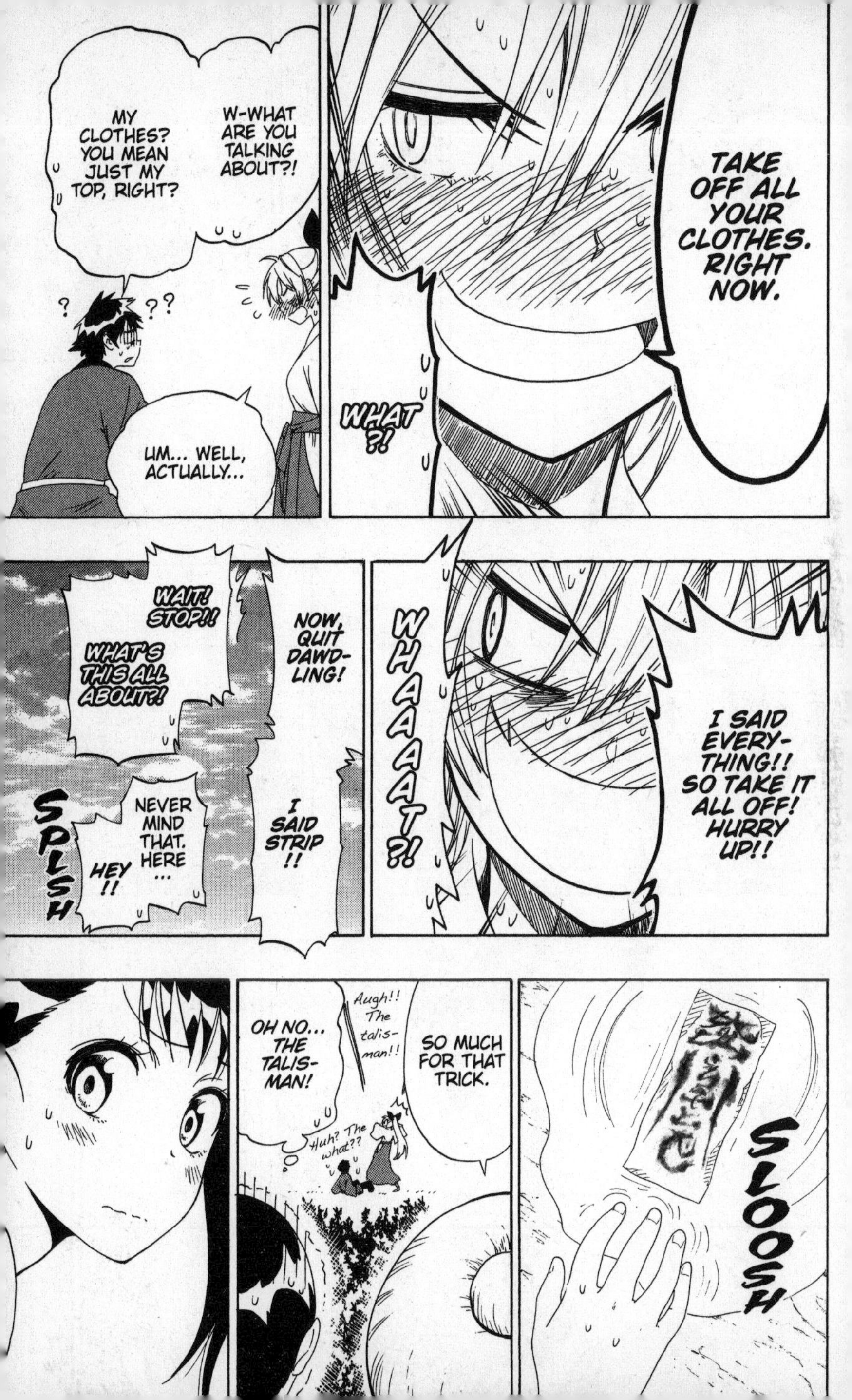
TAKE OFF ALL YOUR CLOTHES. RIGHT NOW.
WHAT ?!
W-WHAT ARE YOU TALKING ABOUT?!
MY CLOTHES? YOU MEAN JUST MY TOP, RIGHT?
? ??
UM... WELL, ACTUALLY...
I SAID EVERY-THING!! SO TAKE IT ALL OFF! HURRY UP!!
WHAAAAAT ?!
NOW, QUIT DAWD-LING!
WAIT! STOP!!
WHAT'S THIS ALL ABOUT?!
I SAID STRIP !!
NEVER MIND THAT. HERE ...
HEY !!
SPLSH
SLOOSH
SO MUCH FOR THAT TRICK.
Augh!! The talis-man!!
OH NO... THE TALIS-MAN!
Huh? The what??

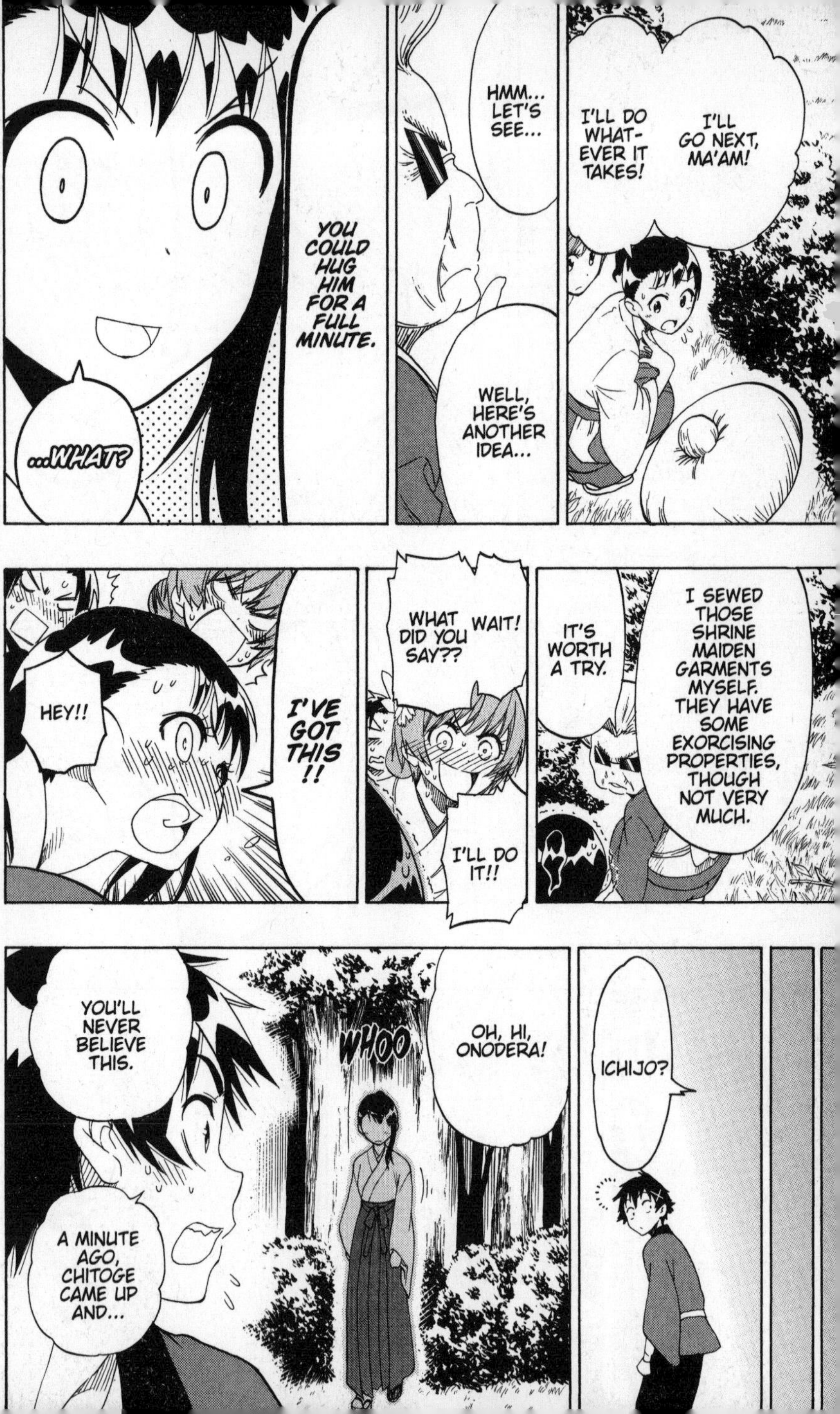
I'LL GO NEXT, MA'AM!
I'LL DO WHATEVER IT TAKES!
HMM... LET'S SEE...
WELL, HERE'S ANOTHER IDEA...
YOU COULD HUG HIM FOR A FULL MINUTE.
...WHAT?
I SEWED THOSE SHRINE MAIDEN GARMENTS MYSELF. THEY HAVE SOME EXORCISING PROPERTIES, THOUGH NOT VERY MUCH.
IT'S WORTH A TRY.
WAIT!
WHAT DID YOU SAY??
I'LL DO IT!!
I'VE GOT THIS!!
HEY!!
ICHIJO?
OH, HI, ONODERA!
WHOO
YOU'LL NEVER BELIEVE THIS.
A MINUTE AGO, CHITOGE CAME UP AND...

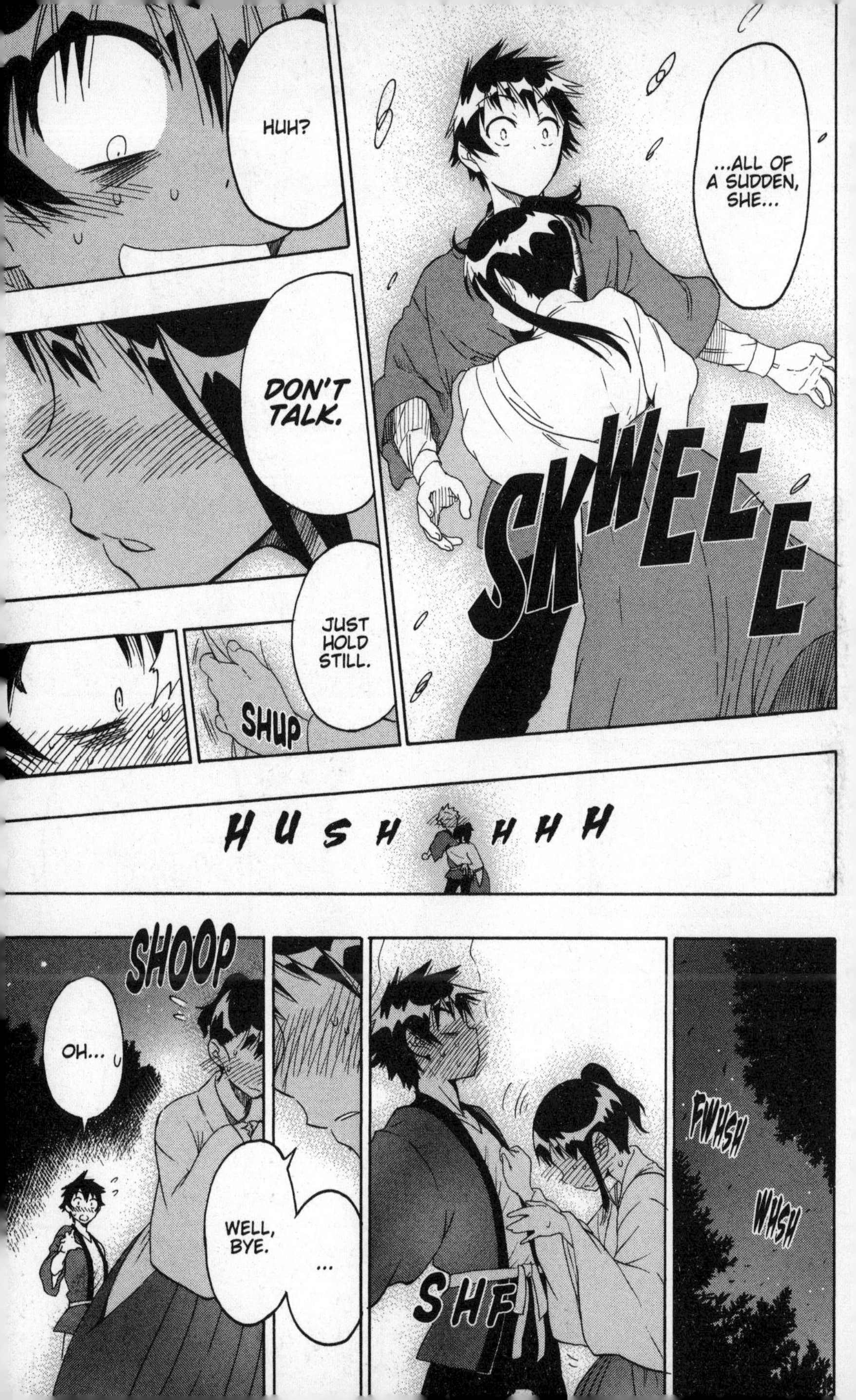

...ALL OF A SUDDEN, SHE...
SKWEEE
HUH?
DON'T TALK.
JUST HOLD STILL.
SHUP
HUSH HHH
FWHSH
WHSH
...
SHF
WELL, BYE.
SHOOP
OH...

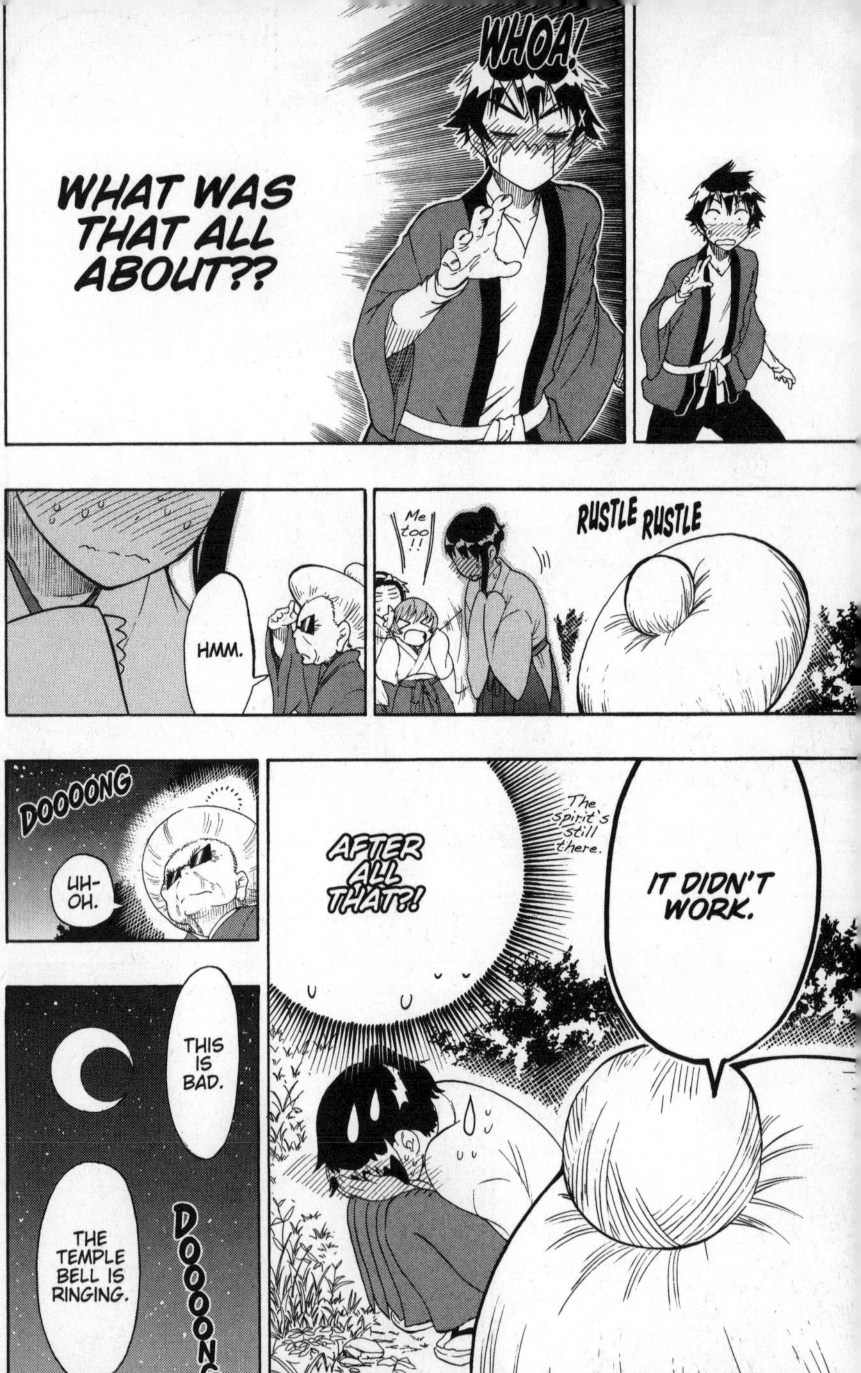
WHOA!
WHAT WAS THAT ALL ABOUT??
RUSTLE RUSTLE
Me too!!
HMM.
IT DIDN'T WORK.
The spirit's still there.
AFTER ALL THAT?!
DOOOONG
UH-OH.
THIS IS BAD.
THE TEMPLE BELL IS RINGING.
DOOOONG

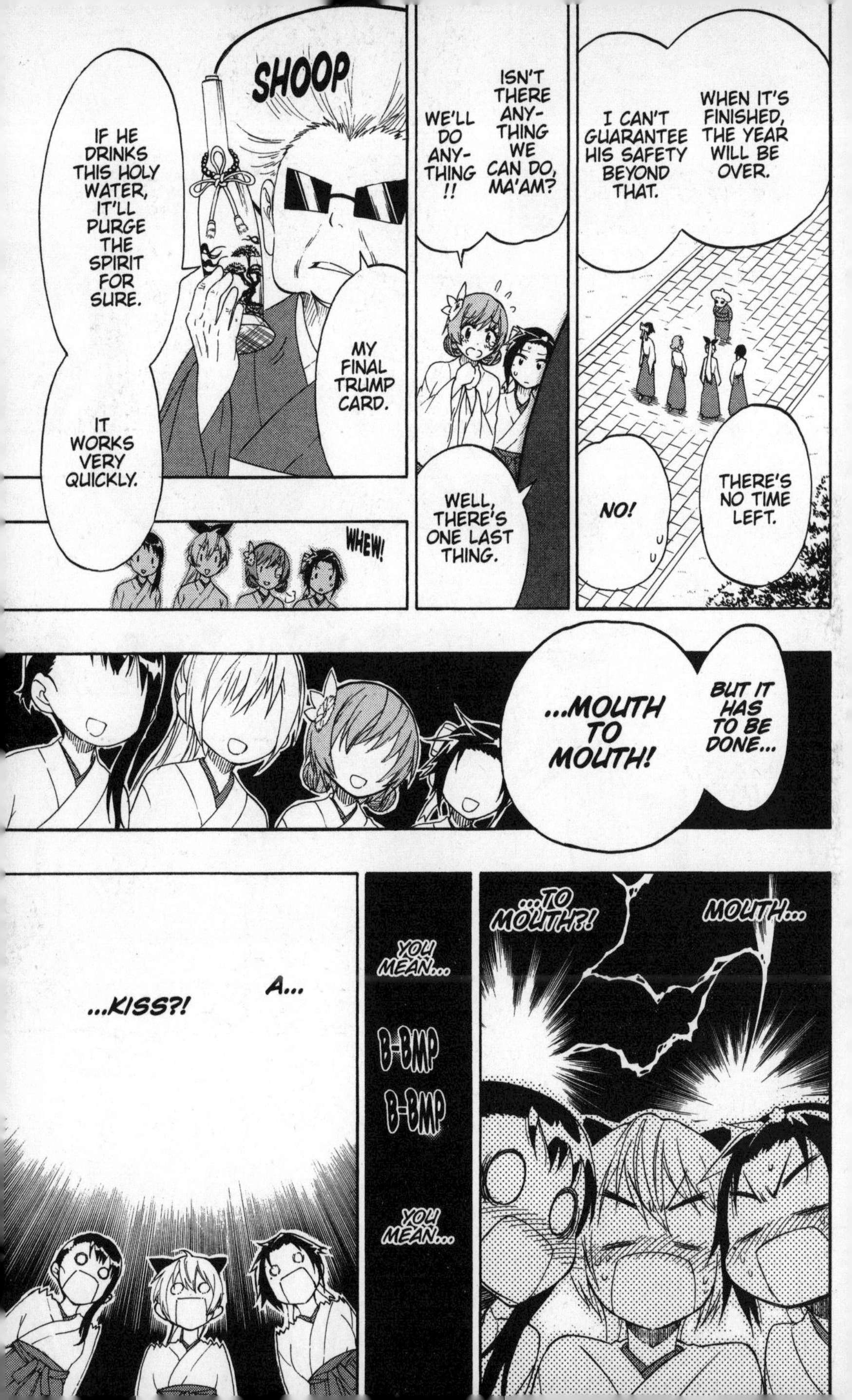
WHEN IT'S FINISHED, THE YEAR WILL BE OVER.
I CAN'T GUARANTEE HIS SAFETY BEYOND THAT.
THERE'S NO TIME LEFT.
NO!
ISN'T THERE ANYTHING WE CAN DO, MA'AM?
WE'LL DO ANYTHING!!
WELL, THERE'S ONE LAST THING.
SHOOP
MY FINAL TRUMP CARD.
IF HE DRINKS THIS HOLY WATER, IT'LL PURGE THE SPIRIT FOR SURE.
IT WORKS VERY QUICKLY.
WHEW!
BUT IT HAS TO BE DONE...
...MOUTH TO MOUTH!
MOUTH...
...TO MOUTH?!
YOU MEAN...
B-BMP
B-BMP
YOU MEAN...
A...
...KISS?!

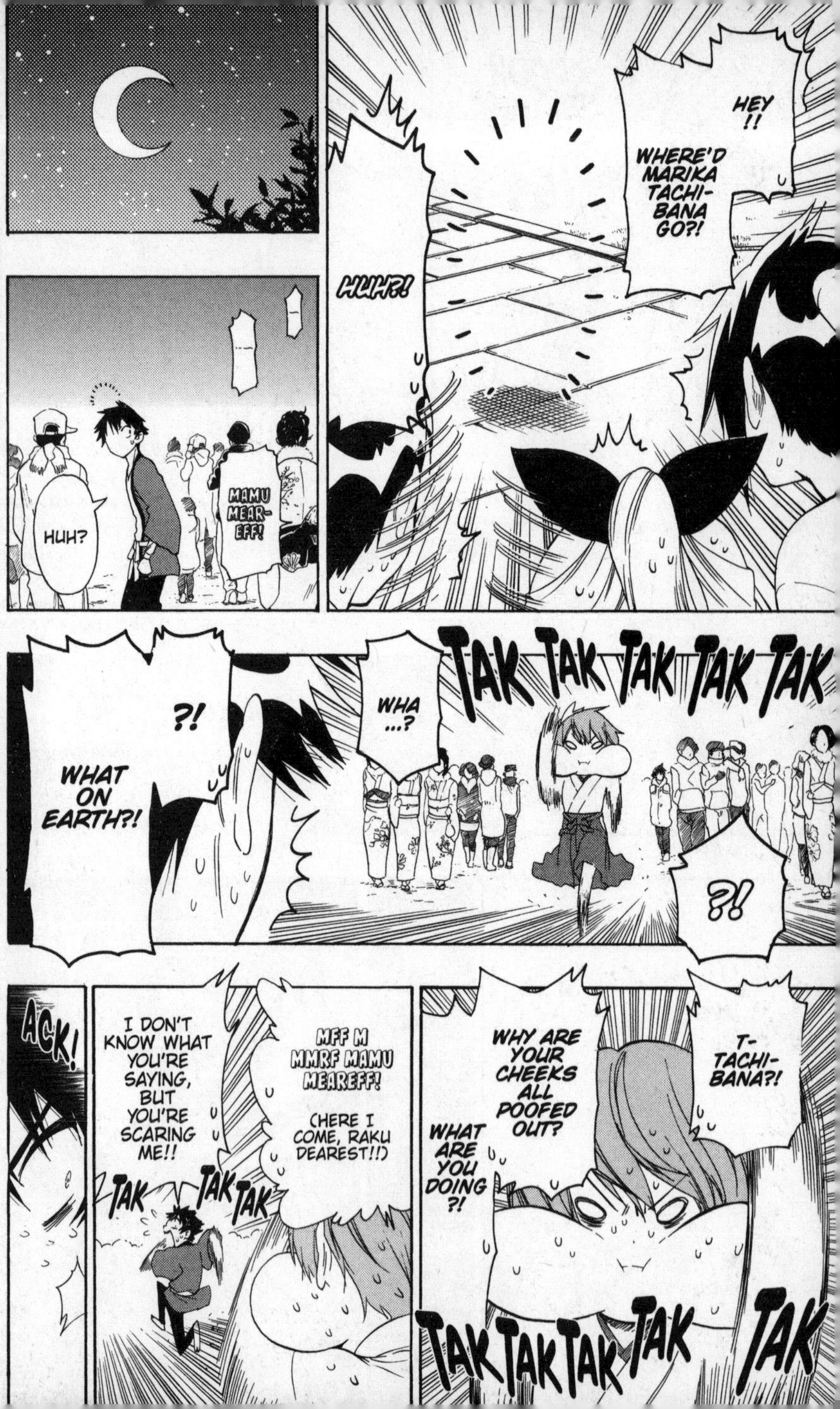
HEY!!
WHERE'D MARIKA TACHIBANA GO?!
HUH?!
HUH?
MAMU MEAR-EFF!
TAK TAK TAK TAK TAK
?!
WHA...?
?! WHAT ON EARTH?!
T-TACHIBANA?!
WHY ARE YOUR CHEEKS ALL POOFED OUT?
WHAT ARE YOU DOING?!
TAK TAK TAK TAK TAK
MFF M MMRF MAMU MEAREFF!
(HERE I COME, RAKU DEAREST!!)
I DON'T KNOW WHAT YOU'RE SAYING, BUT YOU'RE SCARING ME!!
TAK TAK TAK
ACK!

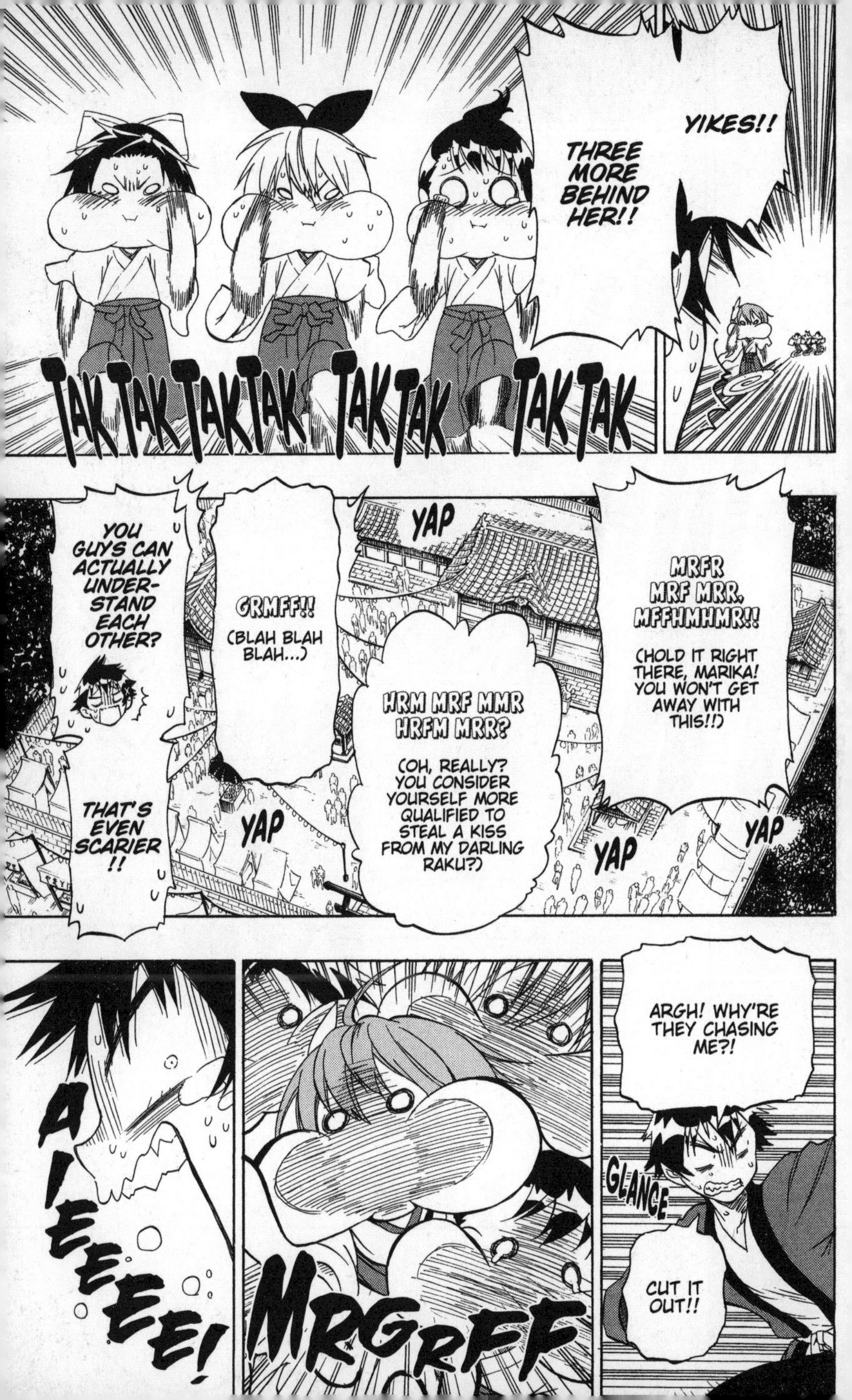
YIKES!!
THREE MORE BEHIND HER!!
TAK TAK TAK TAK TAK TAK TAK TAK
MRFR MRF MRR, MFFHMHMR!!
(HOLD IT RIGHT THERE, MARIKA! YOU WON'T GET AWAY WITH THIS!!)
YAP
YAP
HRM MRF MMR HRFM MRR?
(OH, REALLY? YOU CONSIDER YOURSELF MORE QUALIFIED TO STEAL A KISS FROM MY DARLING RAKU?)
YAP
GRMFF!!
(BLAH BLAH BLAH...)
YAP
YOU GUYS CAN ACTUALLY UNDER-STAND EACH OTHER?
THAT'S EVEN SCARIER!!
ARGH! WHY'RE THEY CHASING ME?!
GLANCE
CUT IT OUT!!
MRGRFF
AIEEEEE!

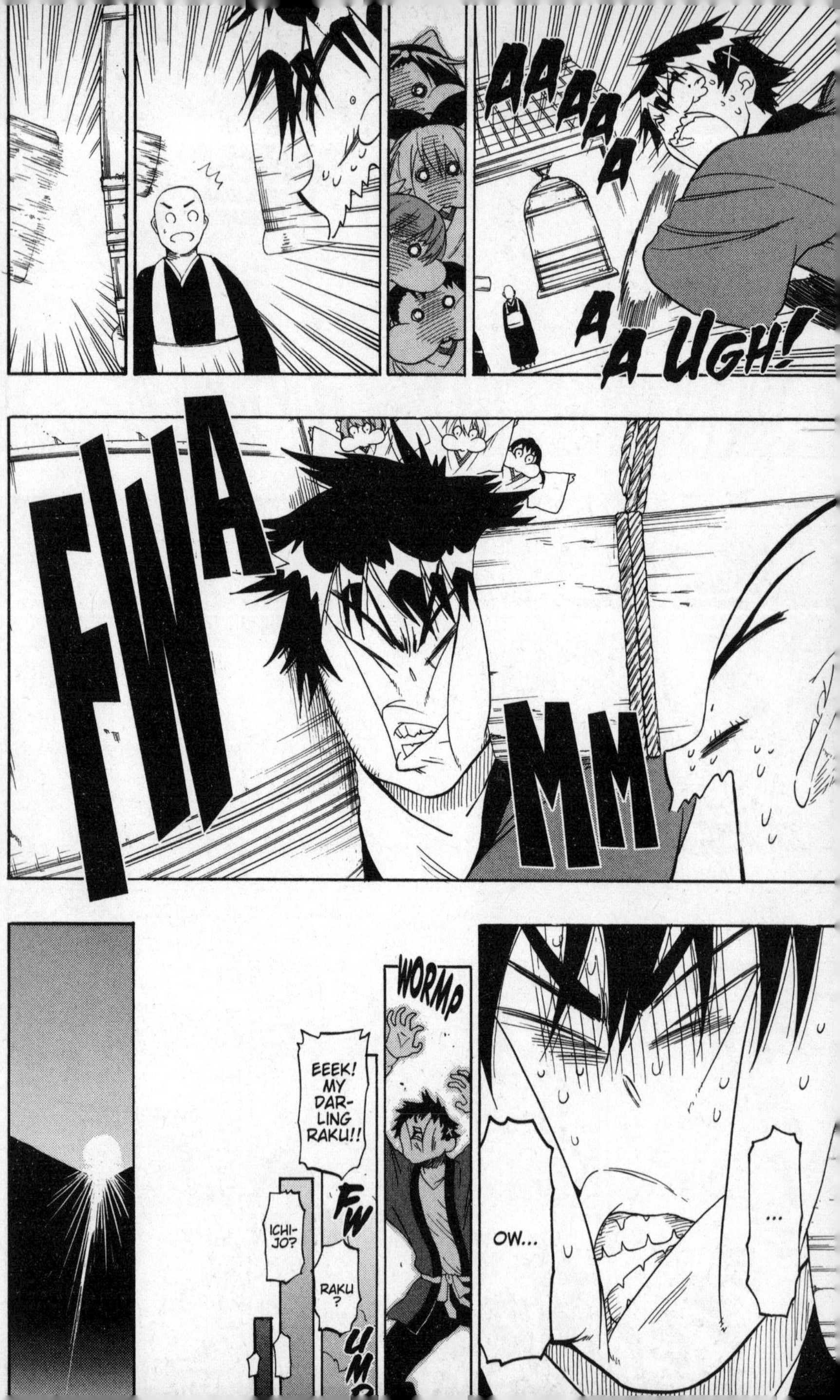
AAAAAAAAUGH!
FWAMM
...
OW...
WORMP
EEEK! MY DARLING RAKU!!
FW
ICHIJO?
RAKU?
UM

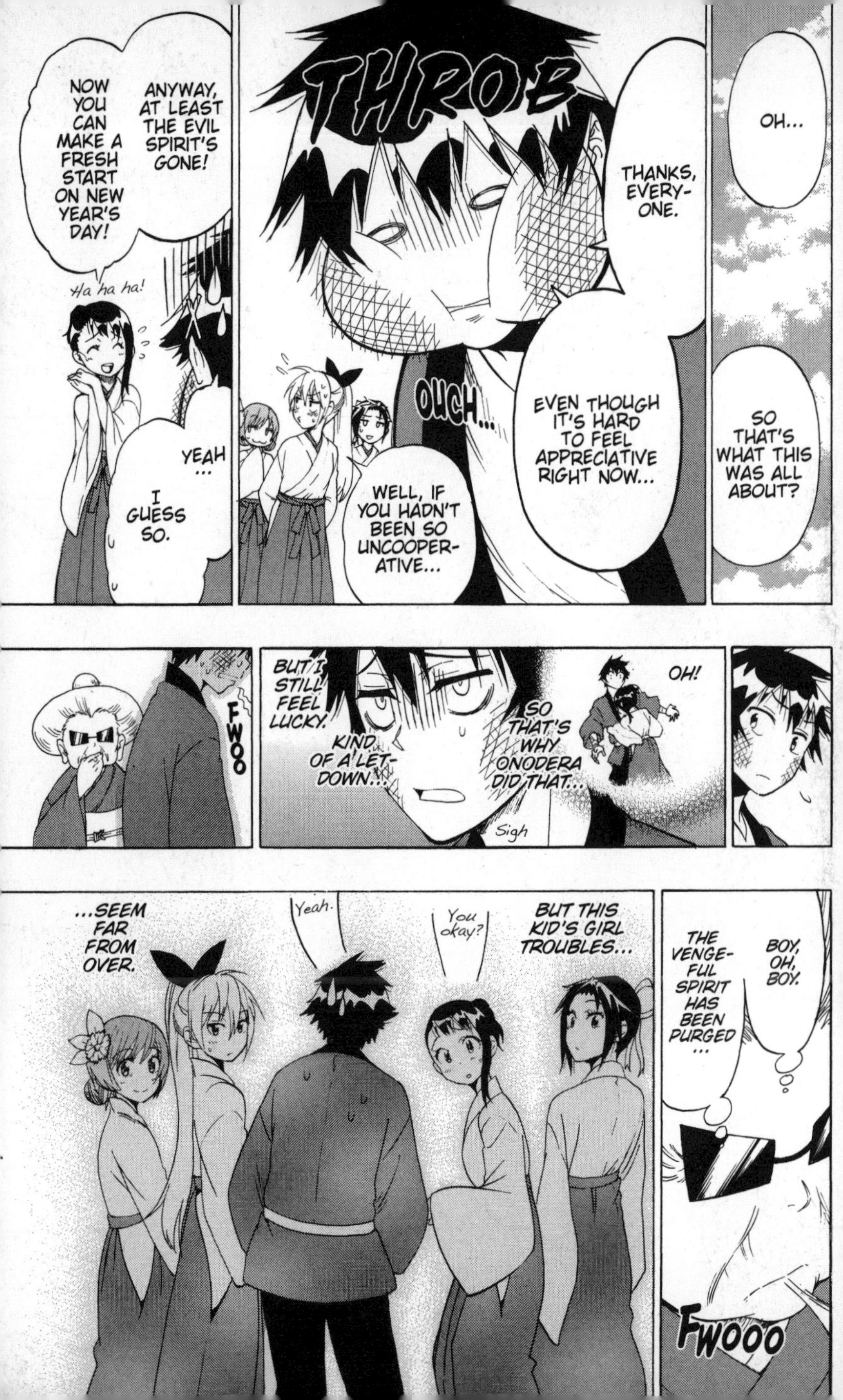
OH...
SO THAT'S WHAT THIS WAS ALL ABOUT?
THROB
THANKS, EVERY-ONE.
EVEN THOUGH IT'S HARD TO FEEL APPRECIATIVE RIGHT NOW...
OUCH...
WELL, IF YOU HADN'T BEEN SO UNCOOPER-ATIVE...
ANYWAY, AT LEAST THE EVIL SPIRIT'S GONE!
NOW YOU CAN MAKE A FRESH START ON NEW YEAR'S DAY!
Ha ha ha!
YEAH... I GUESS SO.
OH!
SO THAT'S WHY ONODERA DID THAT...
BUT I STILL FEEL LUCKY.
KIND OF A LET-DOWN...
Sigh
FWOO
BOY, OH, BOY.
THE VENGE-FUL SPIRIT HAS BEEN PURGED...
FWOOO
BUT THIS KID'S GIRL TROUBLES...
You okay?
Yeah.
...SEEM FAR FROM OVER.

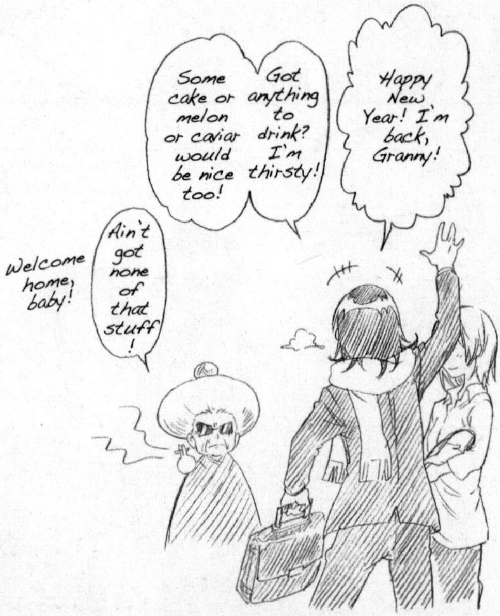
Happy New Year! I'm back, Granny!
Got anything to drink? I'm thirsty!
Some cake or melon or caviar would be nice too!
Ain't got none of that stuff!
Welcome home, baby!

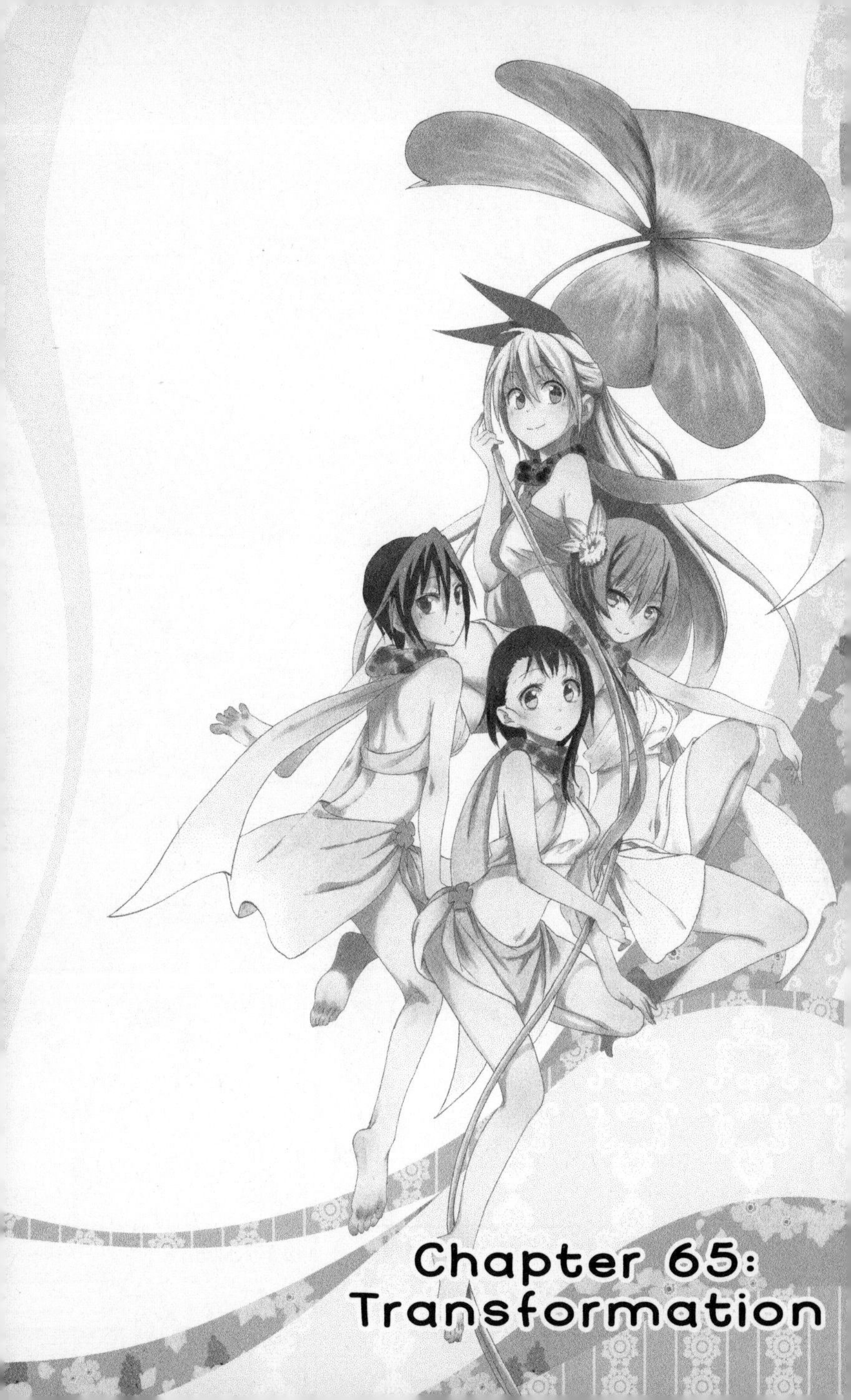

# Chapter 65: Transformation

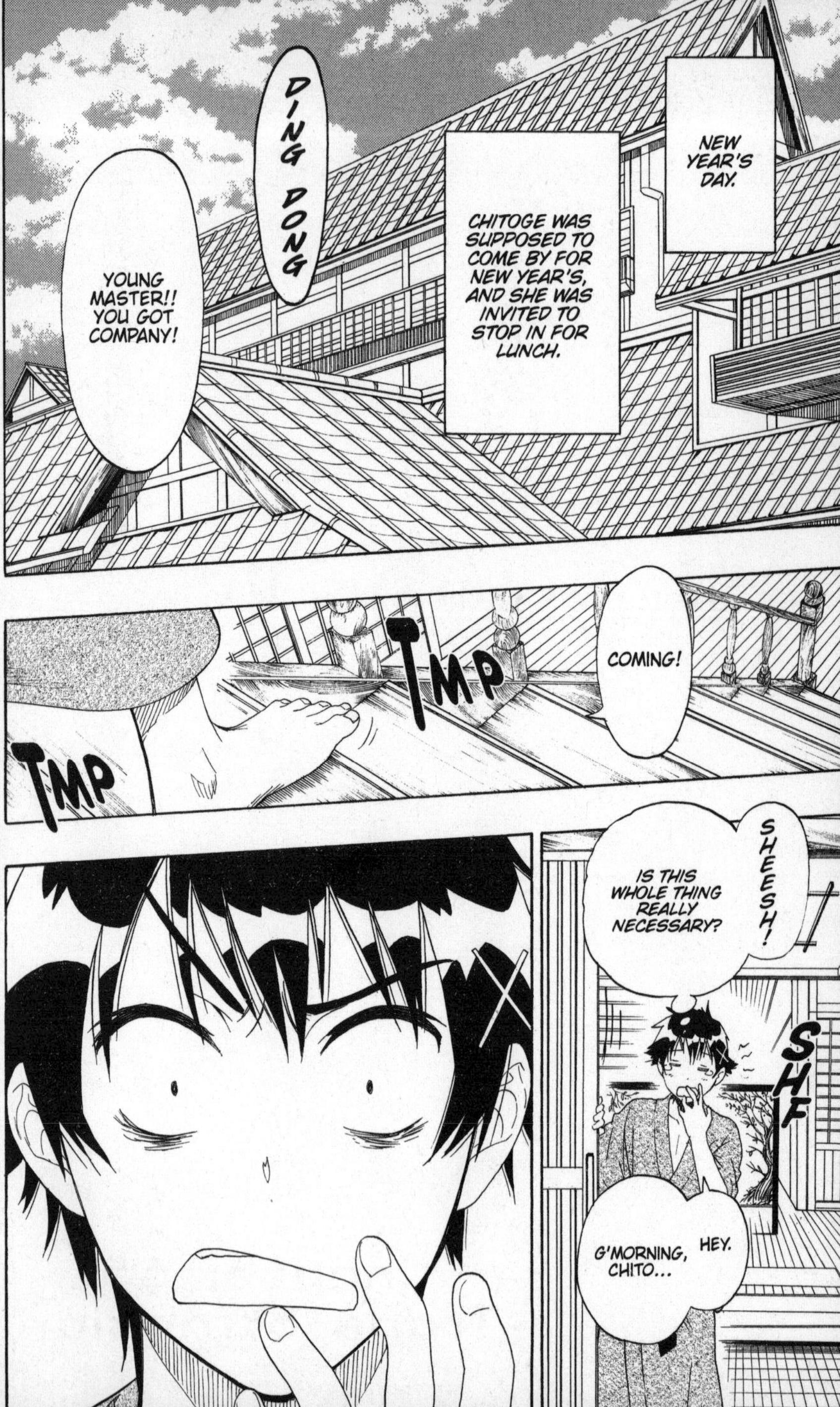
NEW YEAR'S DAY.
CHITOGE WAS SUPPOSED TO COME BY FOR NEW YEAR'S, AND SHE WAS INVITED TO STOP IN FOR LUNCH.
DING DONG
YOUNG MASTER!! YOU GOT COMPANY!
COMING!
TMP
TMP
SHEESH!
IS THIS WHOLE THING REALLY NECESSARY?
SHF
HEY.
G'MORNING, CHITO...

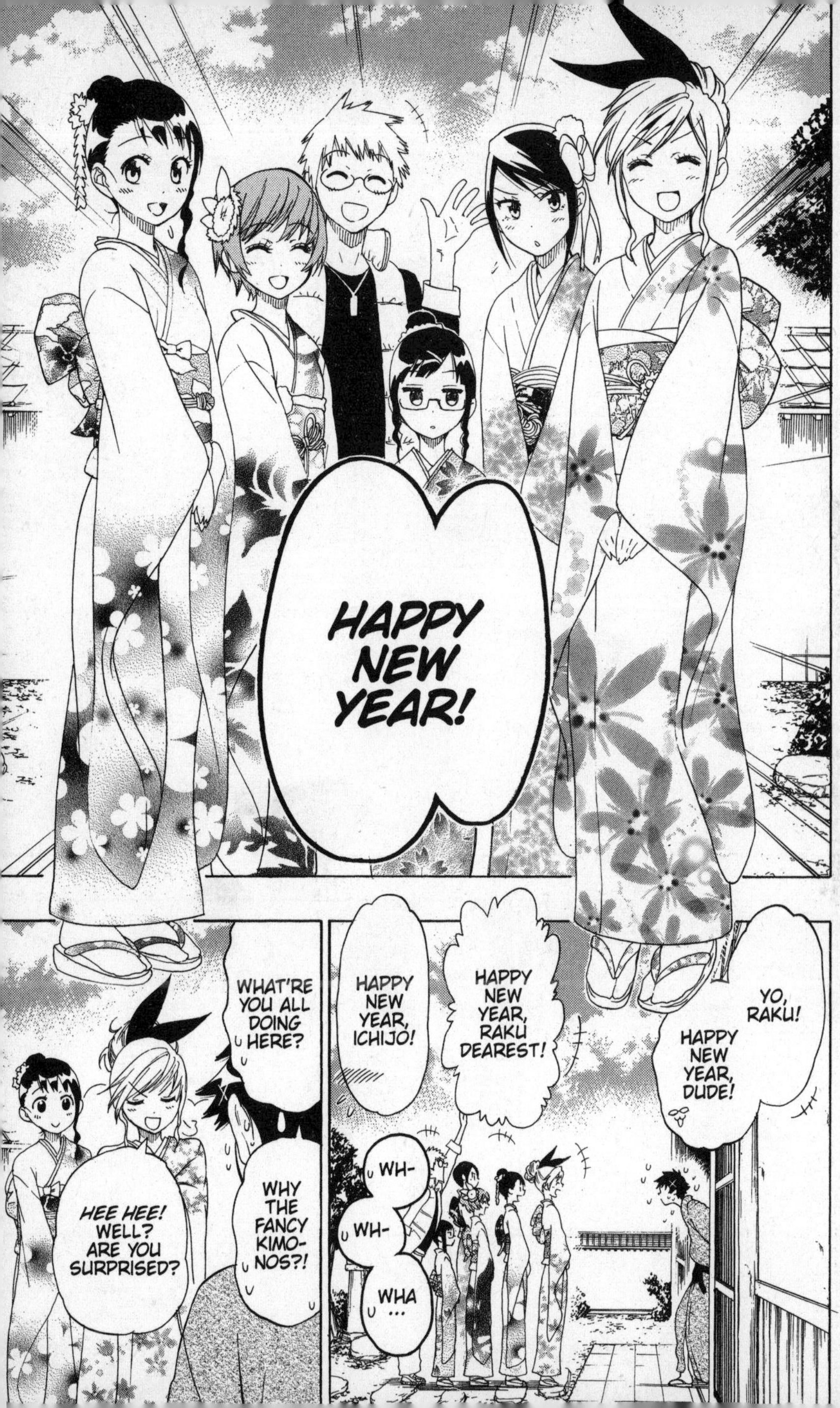
HAPPY NEW YEAR!
YO, RAKU!
HAPPY NEW YEAR, DUDE!
HAPPY NEW YEAR, RAKU DEAREST!
HAPPY NEW YEAR, ICHIJO!
WH-
WH-
WHA ...
WHAT'RE YOU ALL DOING HERE?
WHY THE FANCY KIMO-NOS?!
HEE HEE! WELL? ARE YOU SURPRISED?

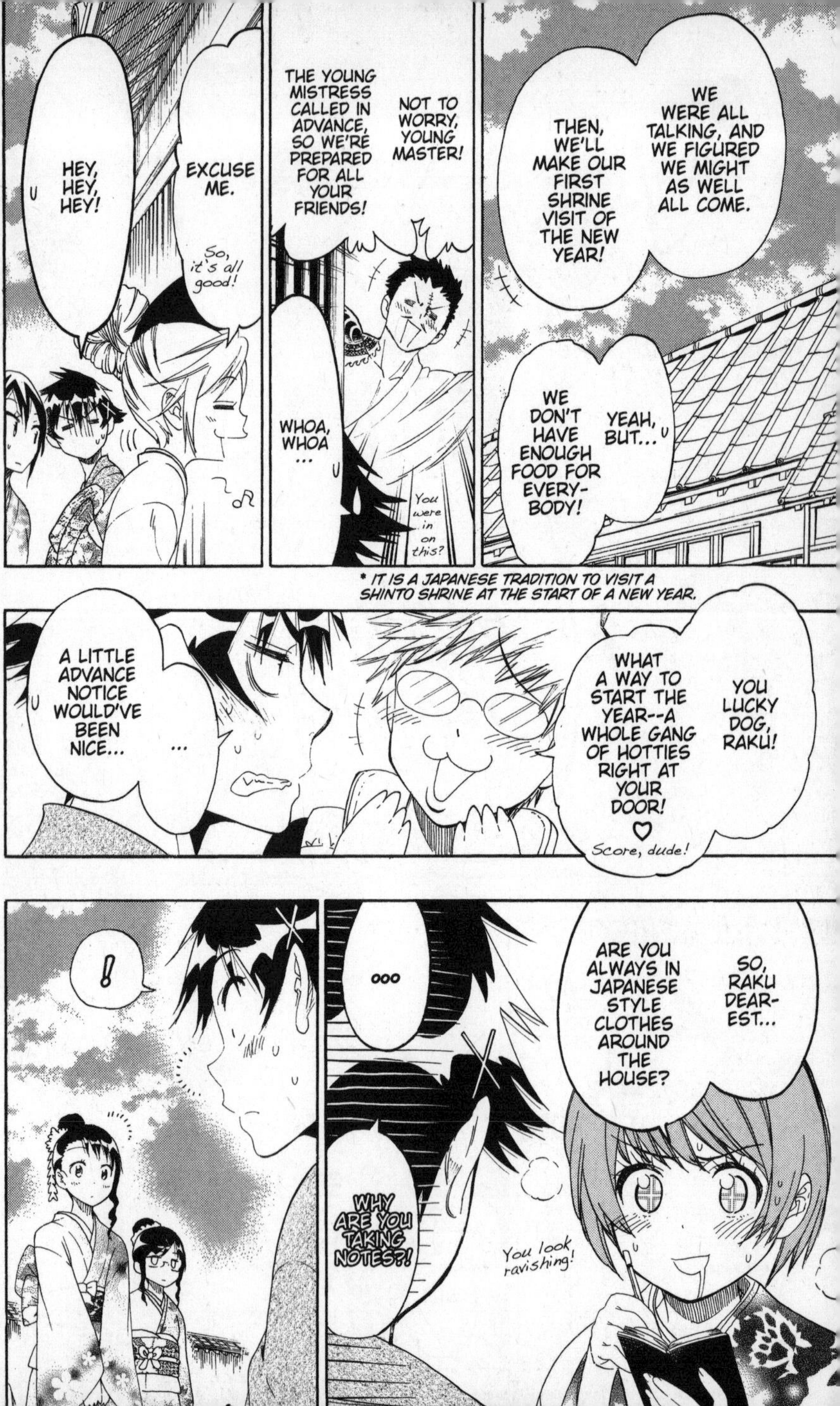
WE WERE ALL TALKING, AND WE FIGURED WE MIGHT AS WELL ALL COME.
THEN, WE'LL MAKE OUR FIRST SHRINE VISIT OF THE NEW YEAR!
YEAH, BUT...
WE DON'T HAVE ENOUGH FOOD FOR EVERY-BODY!
NOT TO WORRY, YOUNG MASTER!
THE YOUNG MISTRESS CALLED IN ADVANCE, SO WE'RE PREPARED FOR ALL YOUR FRIENDS!
WHOA, WHOA...
You were in on this?
EXCUSE ME.
So, it's all good!
HEY, HEY, HEY!
YOU LUCKY DOG, RAKU!
WHAT A WAY TO START THE YEAR--A WHOLE GANG OF HOTTIES RIGHT AT YOUR DOOR! ♡
Score, dude!
...
A LITTLE ADVANCE NOTICE WOULD'VE BEEN NICE...
SO, RAKU DEAR-EST...
ARE YOU ALWAYS IN JAPANESE STYLE CLOTHES AROUND THE HOUSE?
You look ravishing!
ooo
WHY ARE YOU TAKING NOTES?!
!

* IT IS A JAPANESE TRADITION TO VISIT A SHINTO SHRINE AT THE START OF A NEW YEAR.

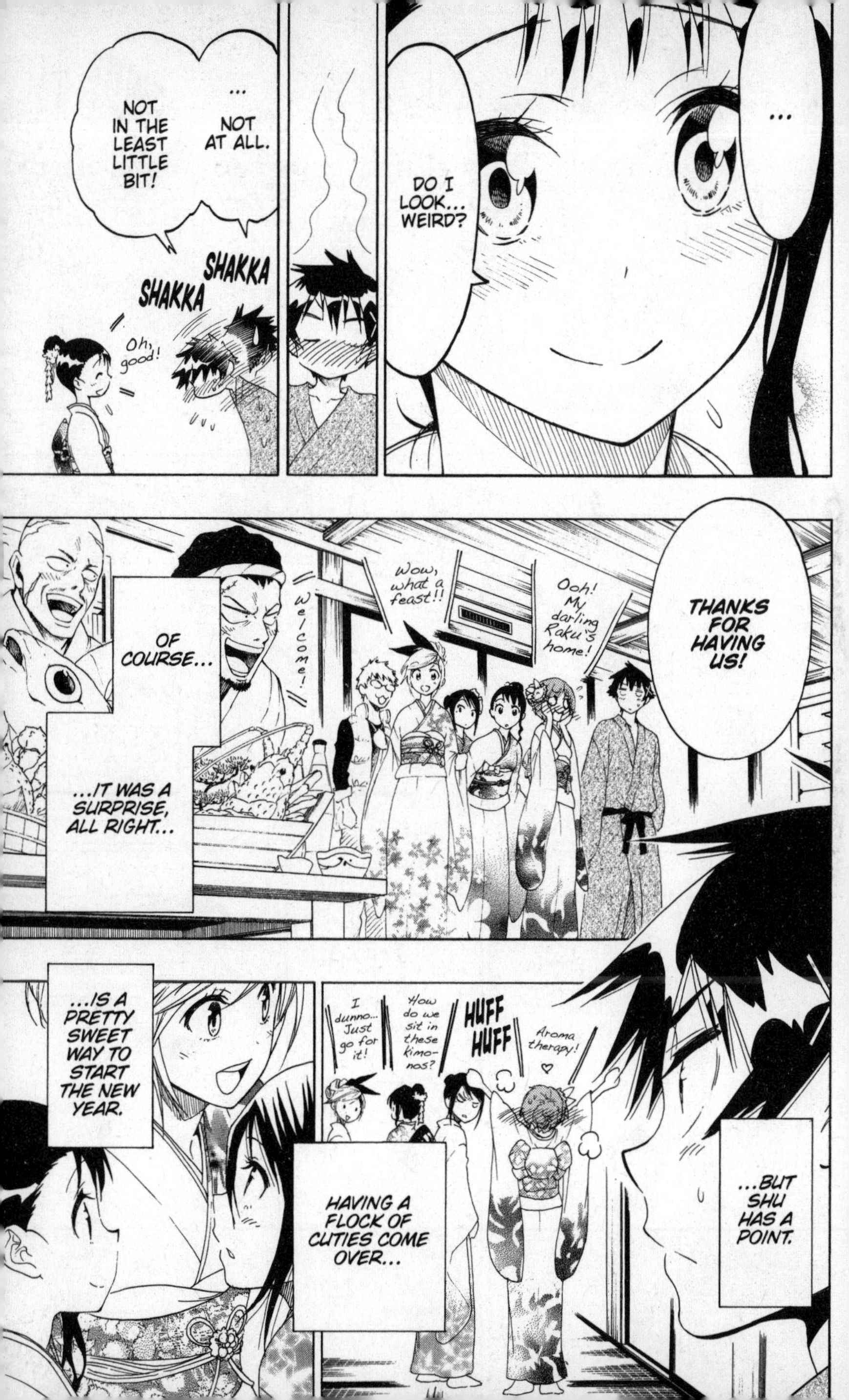
...
DO I LOOK... WEIRD?
... NOT AT ALL.
NOT IN THE LEAST LITTLE BIT!
SHAKKA
SHAKKA
Oh, good!
THANKS FOR HAVING US!
Ooh! My darling Raku's home!
Wow, what a feast!!
Welcome!
OF COURSE...
...IT WAS A SURPRISE, ALL RIGHT...
...BUT SHU HAS A POINT.
Aroma therapy!
HUFF HUFF
How do we sit in these kimonos?
I dunno... Just go for it!
HAVING A FLOCK OF CUTIES COME OVER...
...IS A PRETTY SWEET WAY TO START THE NEW YEAR.

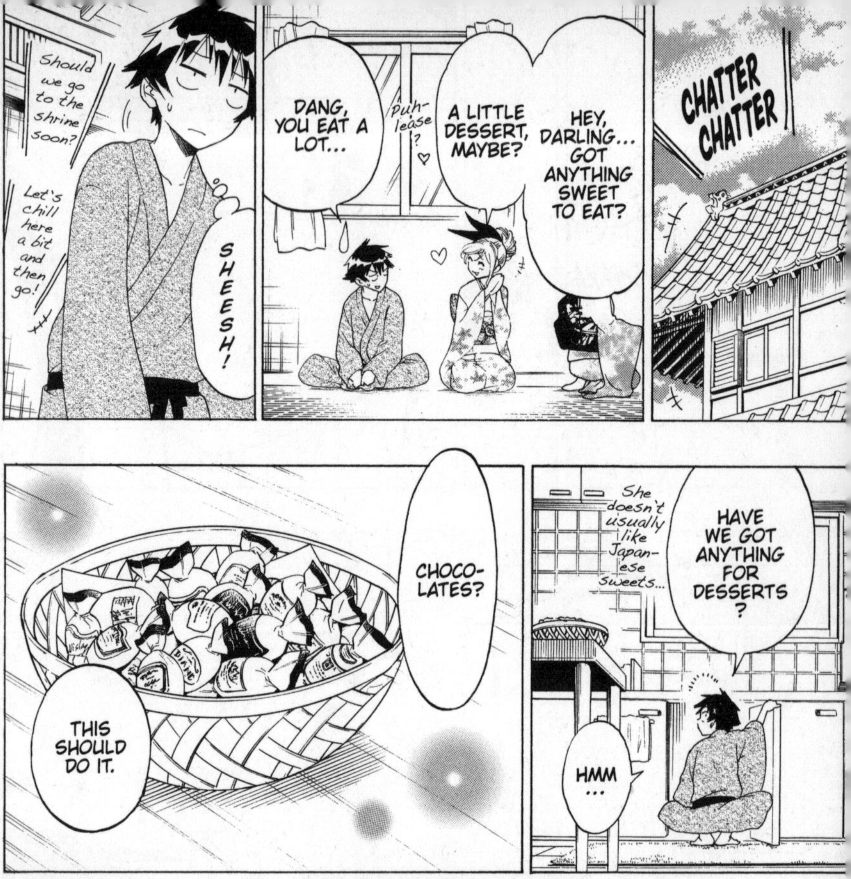
CHATTER CHATTER
HEY, DARLING... GOT ANYTHING SWEET TO EAT?
A LITTLE DESSERT, MAYBE?
Puh-lease? ♡
DANG, YOU EAT A LOT...
SHEESH!
Should we go to the shrine soon?
Let's chill here a bit and then go!
HAVE WE GOT ANYTHING FOR DESSERTS?
She doesn't usually like Japanese sweets...
HMM...
CHOCOLATES?
THIS SHOULD DO IT.

* KARUTA IS A TRADITIONAL CARD GAME PLAYED AT NEW YEAR'S.

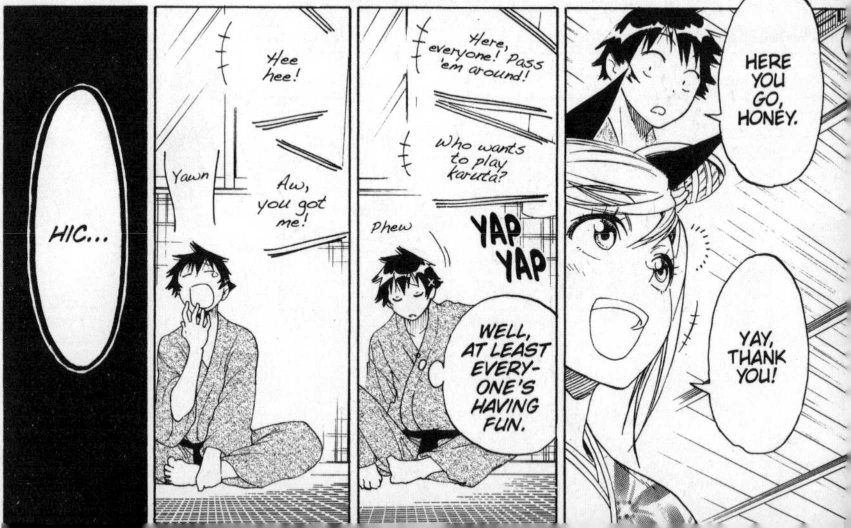
HERE YOU GO, HONEY.
YAY, THANK YOU!
Here, everyone! Pass 'em around!
Who wants to play karuta?
YAP YAP
Phew
WELL, AT LEAST EVERYONE'S HAVING FUN.
Hee hee!
Aw, you got me!
Yawn
HIC...

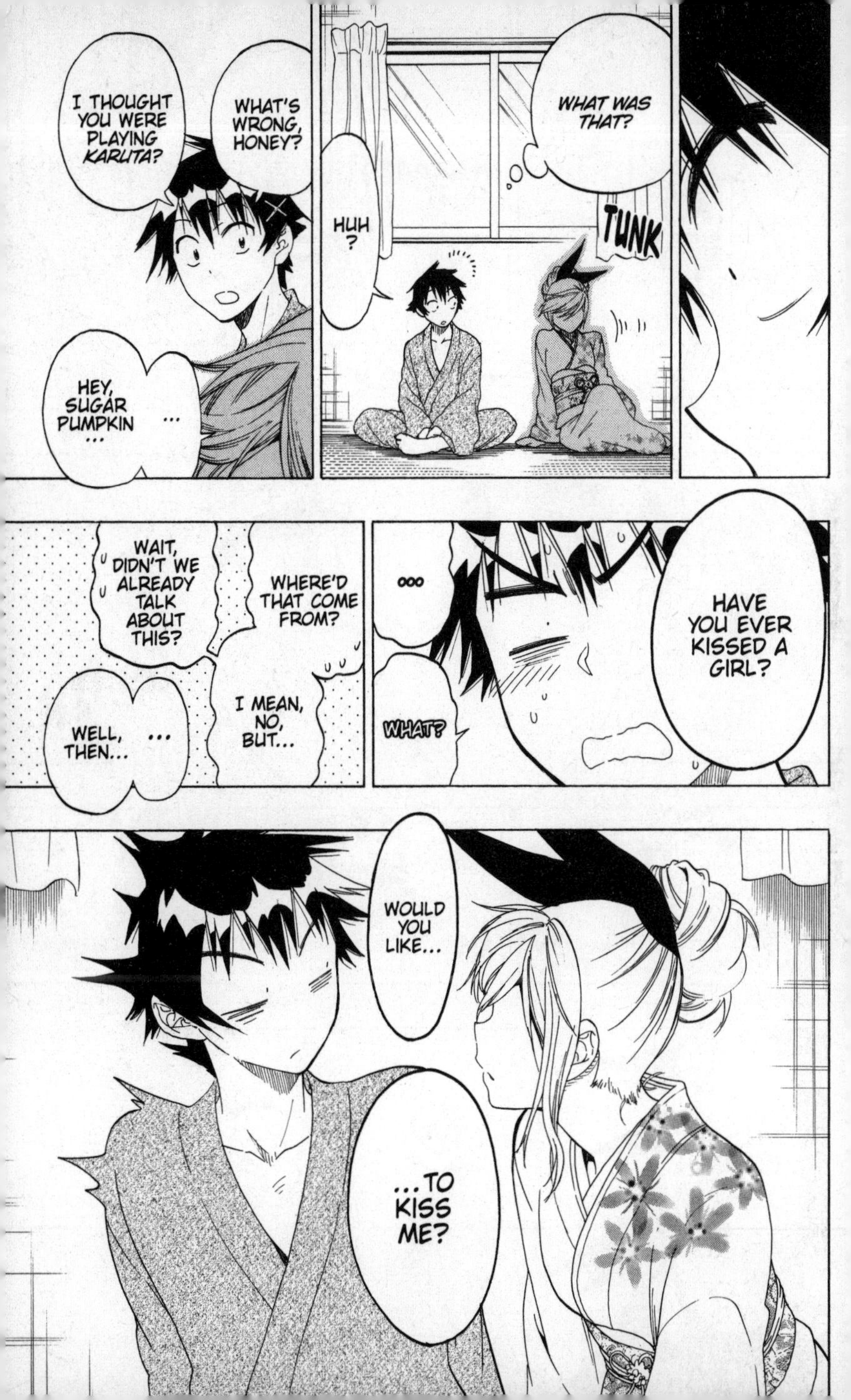
WHAT WAS THAT?
TUNK
HUH?
WHAT'S WRONG, HONEY?
I THOUGHT YOU WERE PLAYING KARUTA?
HEY, SUGAR PUMPKIN... ...
HAVE YOU EVER KISSED A GIRL?
ooo
WHAT?
WHERE'D THAT COME FROM?
WAIT, DIDN'T WE ALREADY TALK ABOUT THIS?
I MEAN, NO, BUT...
WELL, THEN... ...
WOULD YOU LIKE...
...TO KISS ME?

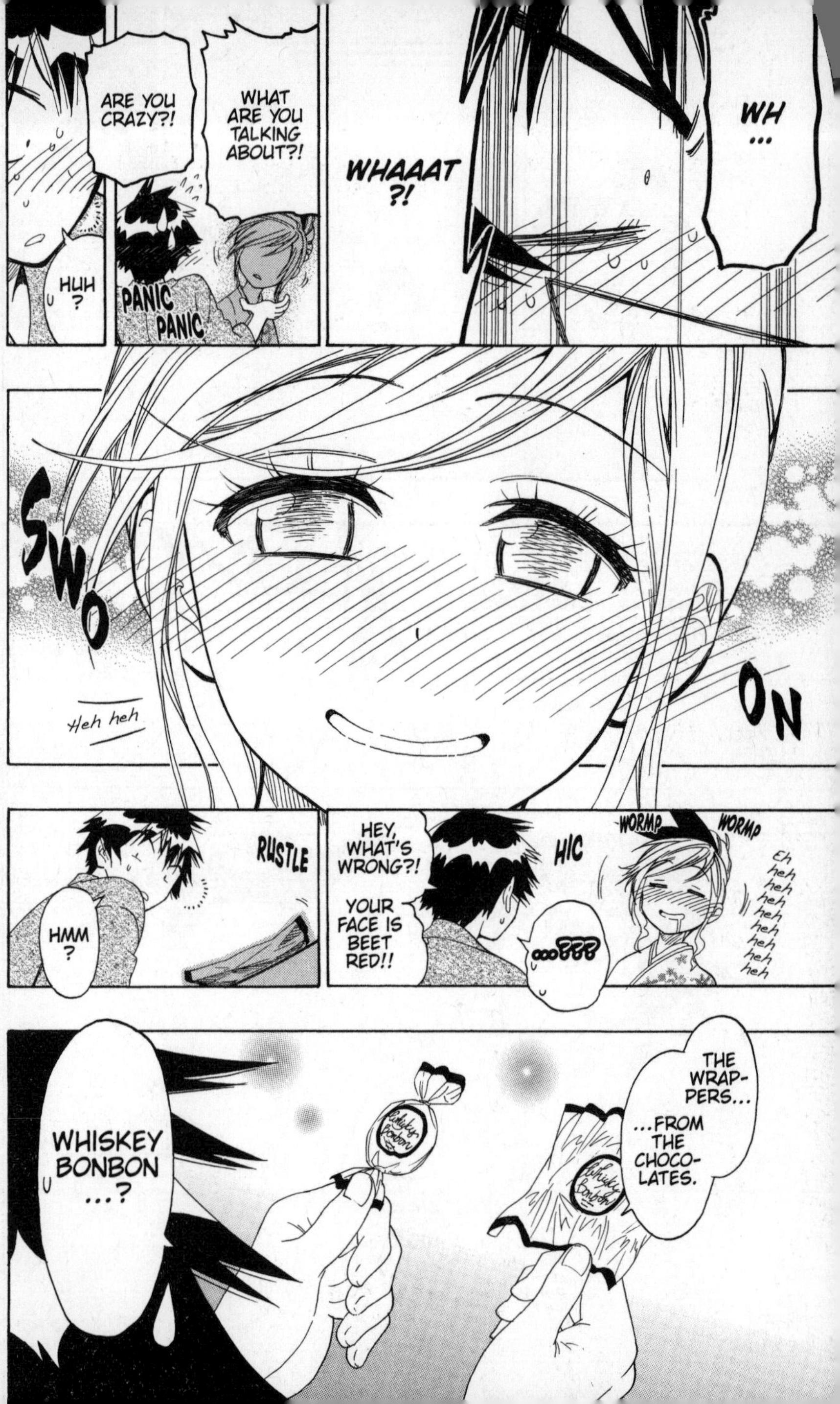
WH...
WHAAAT?!
WHAT ARE YOU TALKING ABOUT?!
ARE YOU CRAZY?!
PANIC PANIC
HUH?
SWOON
Heh heh
WORMP WORMP
Eh heh heh heh heh heh heh heh heh
HIC
HEY, WHAT'S WRONG?!
YOUR FACE IS BEET RED!!
ooo???
RUSTLE
HMM?
THE WRAPPERS...
...FROM THE CHOCOLATES.
Whisky Bonbon
Whisky Bonbon
WHISKEY BONBON...?

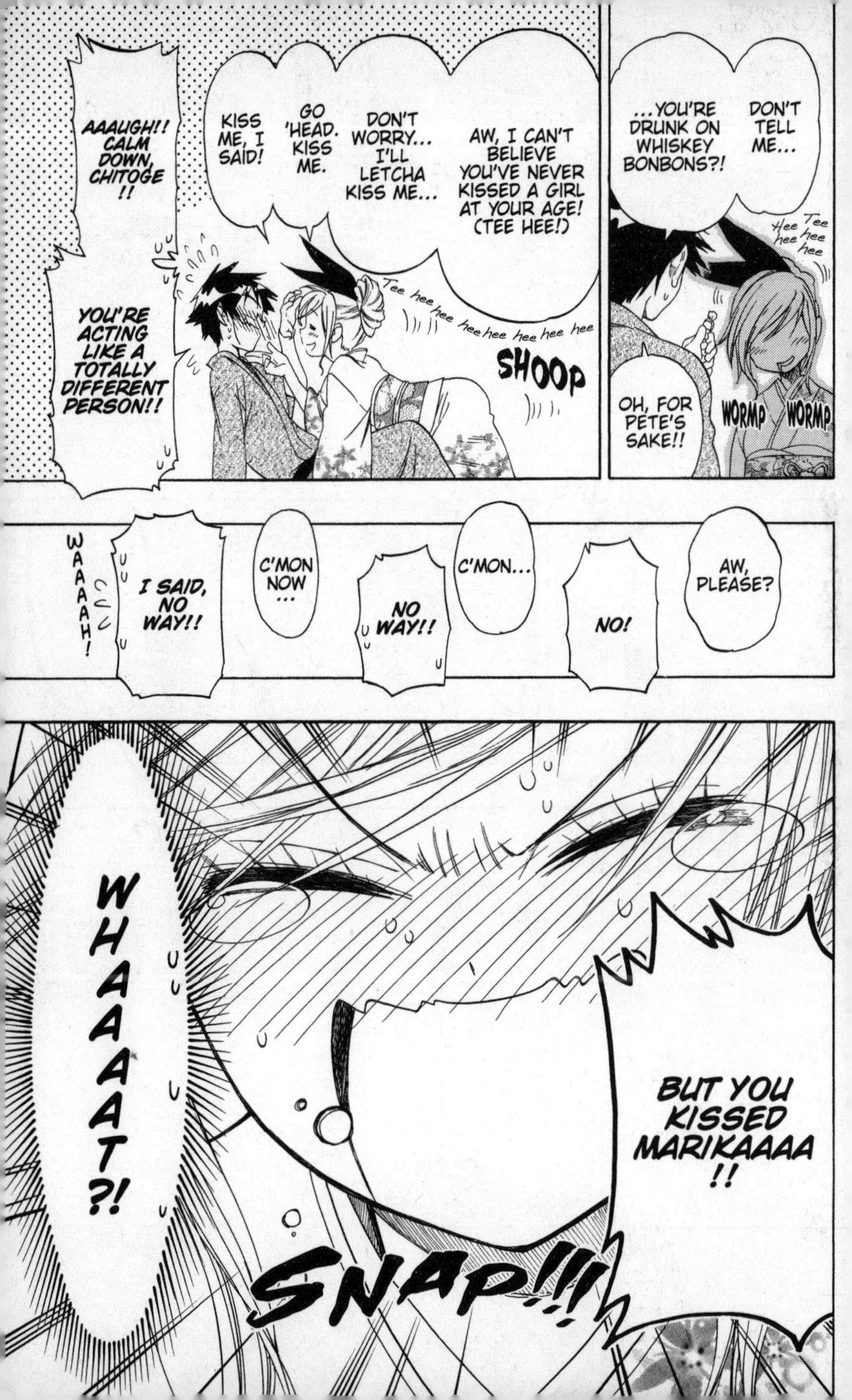
DON'T TELL ME...
...YOU'RE DRUNK ON WHISKEY BONBONS?!
Tee hee hee Hee hee hee
OH, FOR PETE'S SAKE!!
WORMP WORMP
AW, I CAN'T BELIEVE YOU'VE NEVER KISSED A GIRL AT YOUR AGE! (TEE HEE!)
DON'T WORRY... I'LL LETCHA KISS ME...
GO 'HEAD. KISS ME.
KISS ME, I SAID!
Tee hee hee hee hee hee hee hee
SHOOP
AAAUGH!! CALM DOWN, CHITOGE!!
YOU'RE ACTING LIKE A TOTALLY DIFFERENT PERSON!!
AW, PLEASE?
NO!
C'MON...
NO WAY!!
C'MON NOW...
I SAID, NO WAY!!
WAAAAAH!
BUT YOU KISSED MARIKAAAA!!
SNAP!!!
WHAAAAAT?!

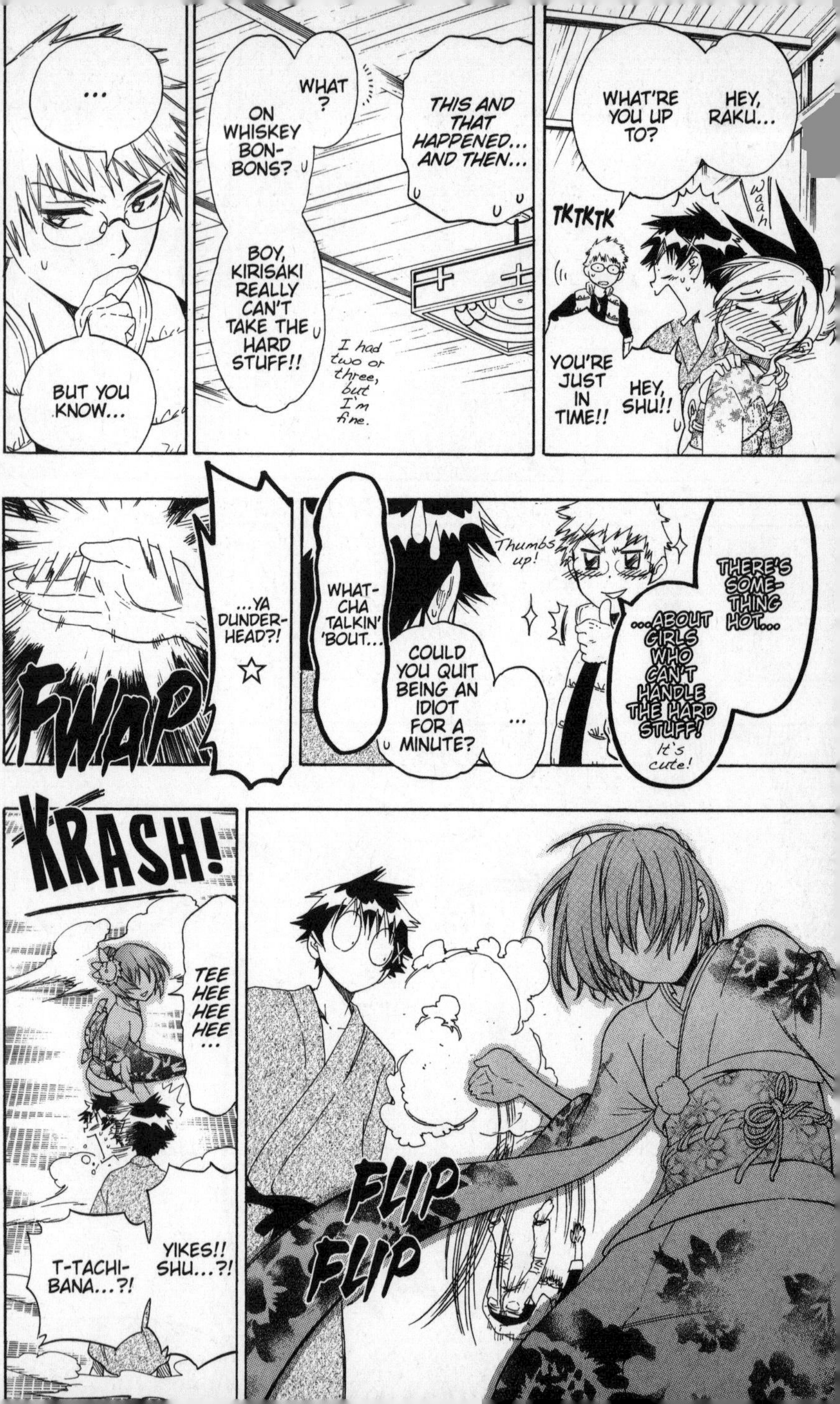
HEY, RAKU...
WHAT'RE YOU UP TO?
Waah
TKTKTK
HEY, SHU!!
YOU'RE JUST IN TIME!!
THIS AND THAT HAPPENED... AND THEN...
WHAT?
ON WHISKEY BON-BONS?
BOY, KIRISAKI REALLY CAN'T TAKE THE HARD STUFF!!
I had two or three, but I'm fine.
...
BUT YOU KNOW...
THERE'S SOMETHING HOT...
...ABOUT GIRLS WHO CAN'T HANDLE THE HARD STUFF!
It's cute!
Thumbs up!
...
COULD YOU QUIT BEING AN IDIOT FOR A MINUTE?
WHAT-CHA TALKIN' 'BOUT...
...YA DUNDER-HEAD?!
FWAP
FLIP FLIP
KRASH!
TEE HEE HEE HEE...
YIKES!! SHU...?!
T-TACHI-BANA...?!

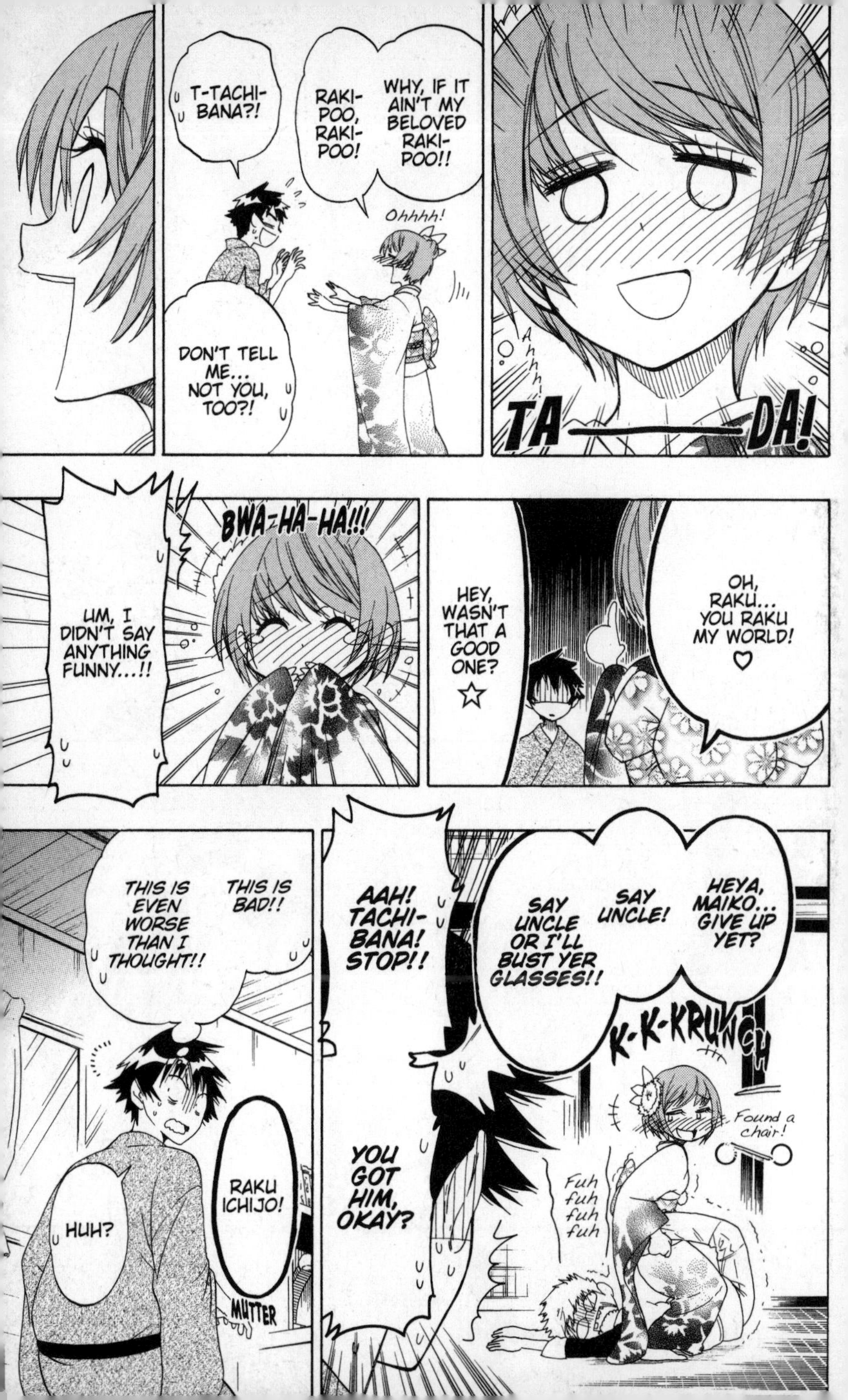
Ahhhh!
TA———DA!
WHY, IF IT AIN'T MY BELOVED RAKI-POO!!
RAKI-POO, RAKI-POO!
Ohhhh!
T-TACHI-BANA?!
DON'T TELL ME... NOT YOU, TOO?!
OH, RAKU... YOU RAKU MY WORLD! ♡
HEY, WASN'T THAT A GOOD ONE? ☆
BWA-HA-HA!!!
UM, I DIDN'T SAY ANYTHING FUNNY...!!
HEYA, MAIKO... GIVE UP YET?
SAY UNCLE!
SAY UNCLE OR I'LL BUST YER GLASSES!!
AAH! TACHI-BANA! STOP!!
K-K-KRUNCH
Found a chair!
Fuh fuh fuh fuh
YOU GOT HIM, OKAY?
THIS IS BAD!!
THIS IS EVEN WORSE THAN I THOUGHT!!
RAKU ICHIJO!
MUTTER
HUH?

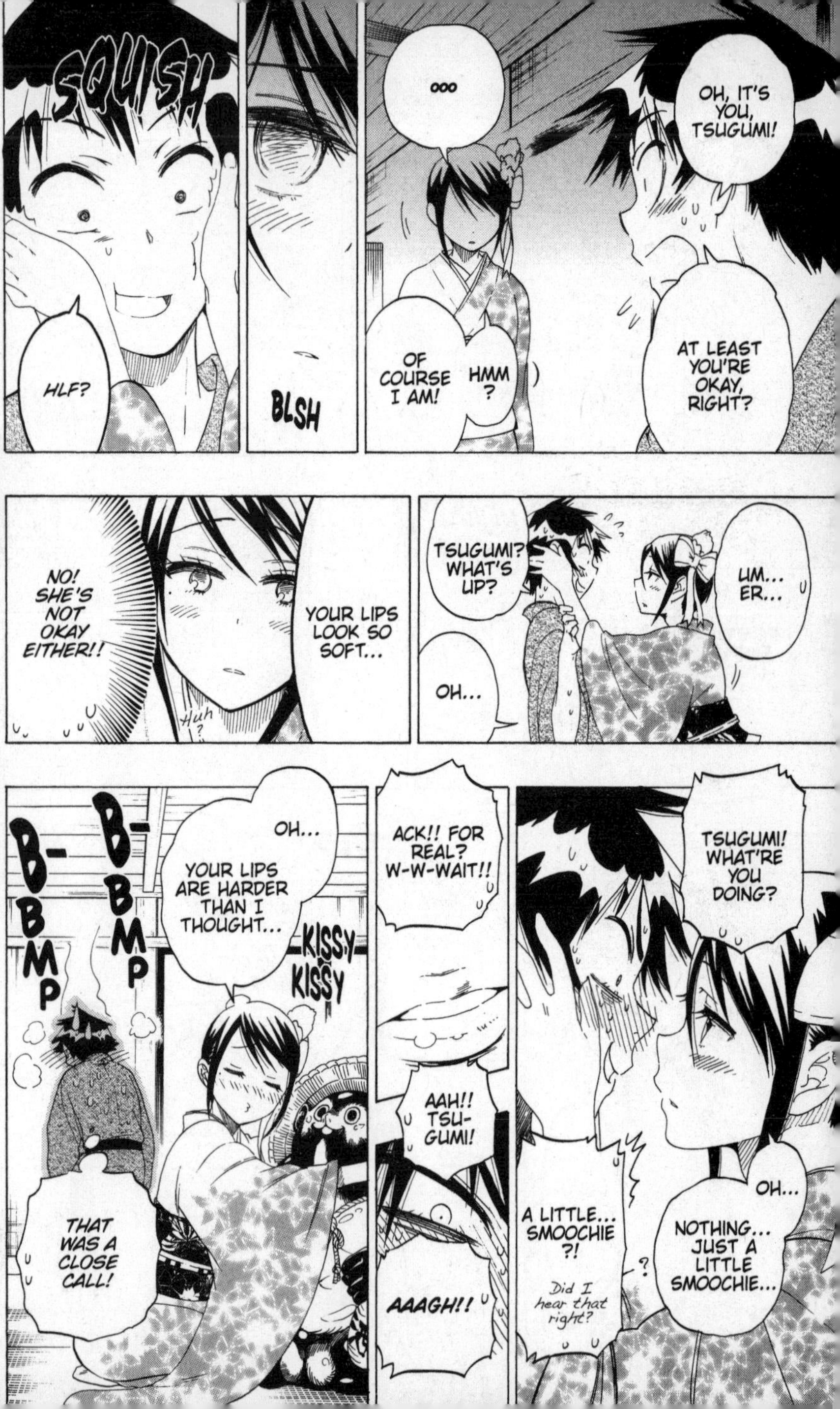
OH, IT'S YOU, TSUGUMI!
AT LEAST YOU'RE OKAY, RIGHT?
...
HMM?
OF COURSE I AM!
BLSH
SQUISH
HLF?
UM... ER...
TSUGUMI? WHAT'S UP?
OH...
YOUR LIPS LOOK SO SOFT...
NO! SHE'S NOT OKAY EITHER!!
Huh?
TSUGUMI! WHAT'RE YOU DOING?
OH...
NOTHING... JUST A LITTLE SMOOCHIE...
A LITTLE... SMOOCHIE?!
Did I hear that right?
ACK!! FOR REAL? W-W-WAIT!!
AAH!! TSU-GUMI!
AAAGH!!
OH...
YOUR LIPS ARE HARDER THAN I THOUGHT...
KISSY KISSY
B-B-BMP
B-BMP
THAT WAS A CLOSE CALL!

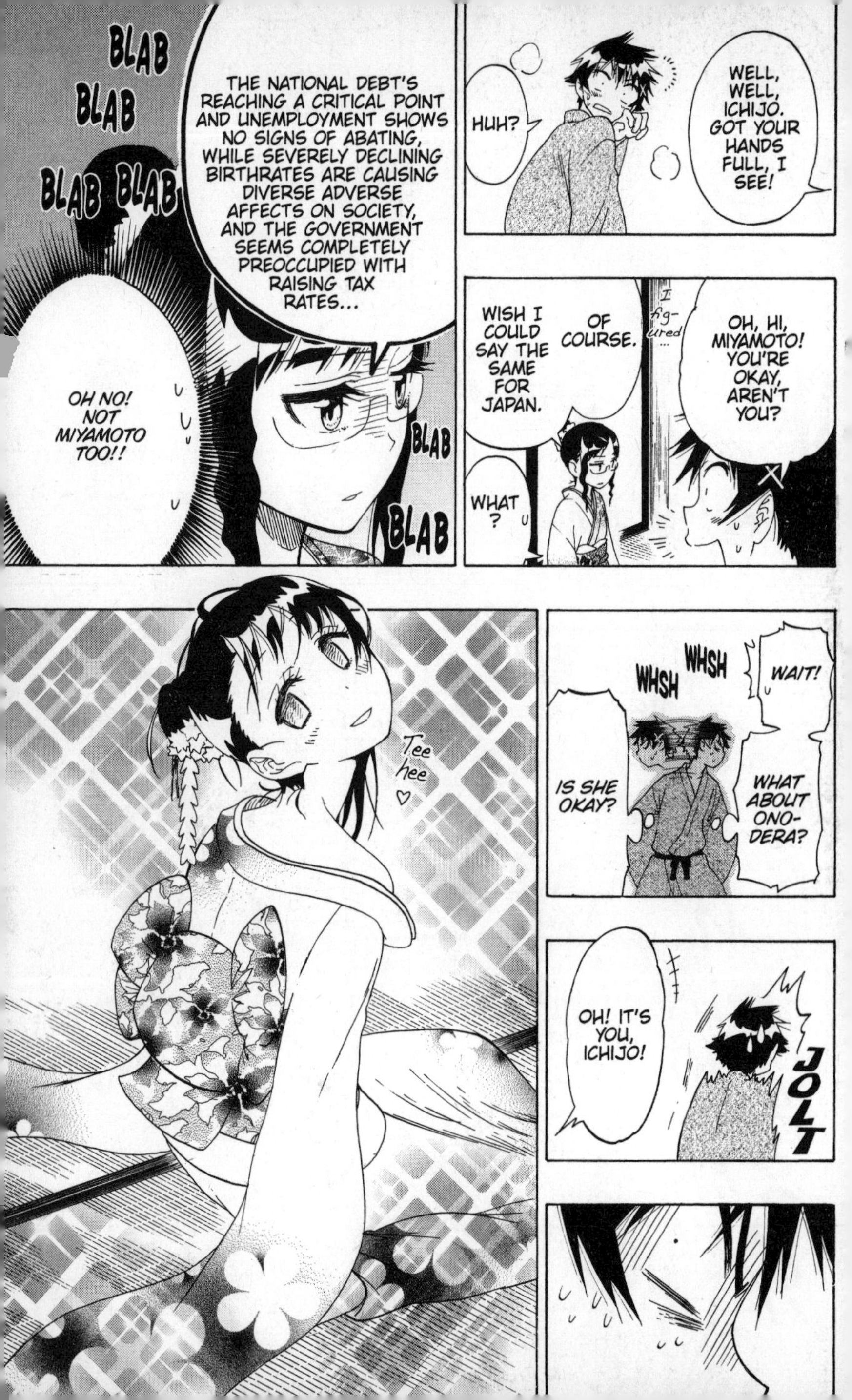

WELL, WELL, ICHIJO. GOT YOUR HANDS FULL, I SEE!
HUH?
OH, HI, MIYAMOTO! YOU'RE OKAY, AREN'T YOU?
I figured...
OF COURSE.
WISH I COULD SAY THE SAME FOR JAPAN.
WHAT?
THE NATIONAL DEBT'S REACHING A CRITICAL POINT AND UNEMPLOYMENT SHOWS NO SIGNS OF ABATING, WHILE SEVERELY DECLINING BIRTHRATES ARE CAUSING DIVERSE ADVERSE AFFECTS ON SOCIETY, AND THE GOVERNMENT SEEMS COMPLETELY PREOCCUPIED WITH RAISING TAX RATES...
BLAB BLAB BLAB BLAB
BLAB BLAB
OH NO! NOT MIYAMOTO TOO!!
WHSH WHSH
WAIT!
WHAT ABOUT ONO-DERA?
IS SHE OKAY?
OH! IT'S YOU, ICHIJO!
JOLT
Tee hee ♡

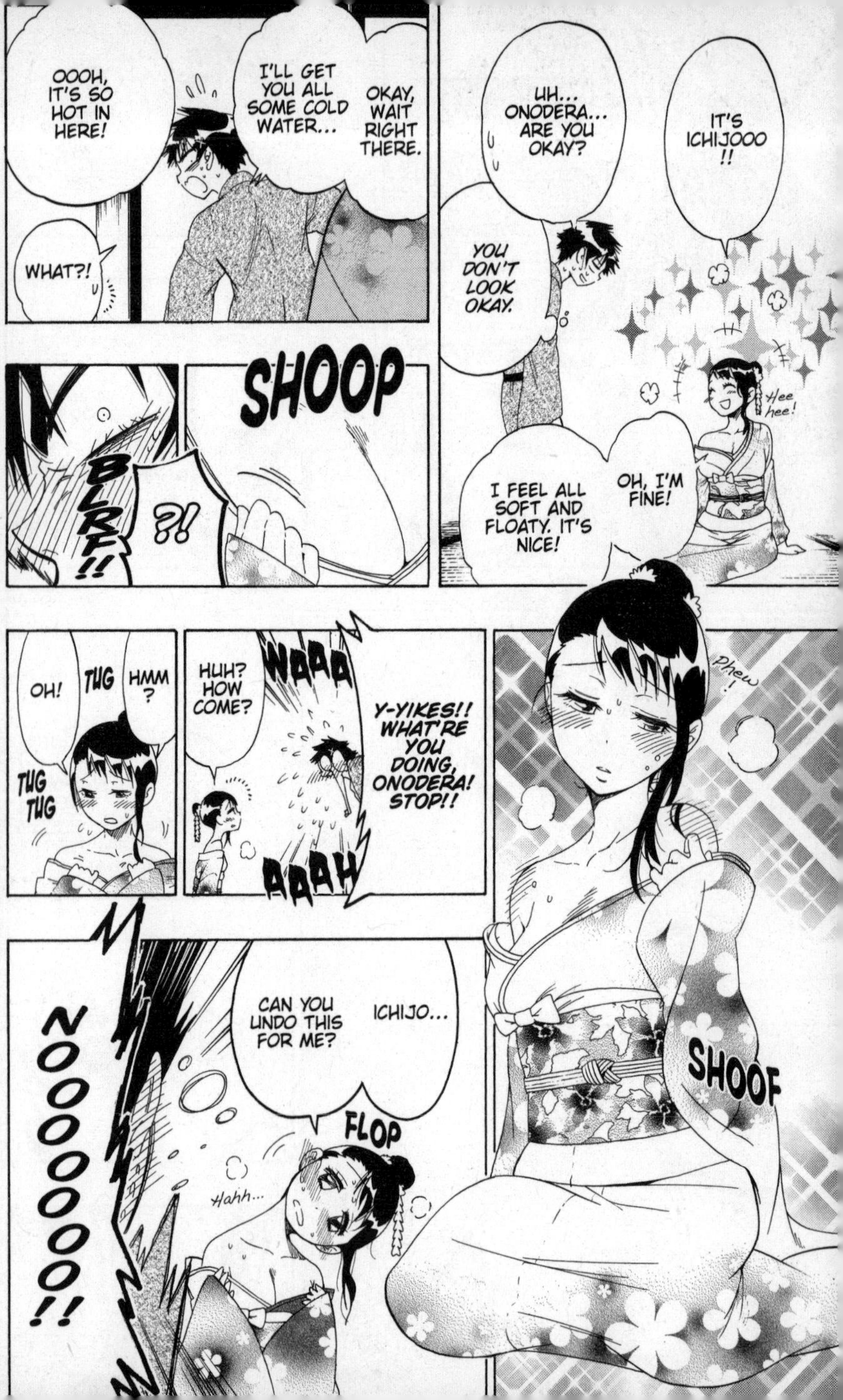
IT'S ICHIJOOO!!
UH... ONODERA... ARE YOU OKAY?
YOU DON'T LOOK OKAY.
Hee hee!
OH, I'M FINE!
I FEEL ALL SOFT AND FLOATY. IT'S NICE!
OKAY, WAIT RIGHT THERE.
I'LL GET YOU ALL SOME COLD WATER...
OOOH, IT'S SO HOT IN HERE!
WHAT?!
SHOOP
?!
BLRF!!
Phew!
SHOOF
Y-YIKES!! WHAT'RE YOU DOING, ONODERA! STOP!!
WAAA
AAAH
HUH? HOW COME?
HMM?
TUG
OH!
TUG TUG
ICHIJO...
CAN YOU UNDO THIS FOR ME?
FLOP
Hahh...
NOOOOOOOOO!!

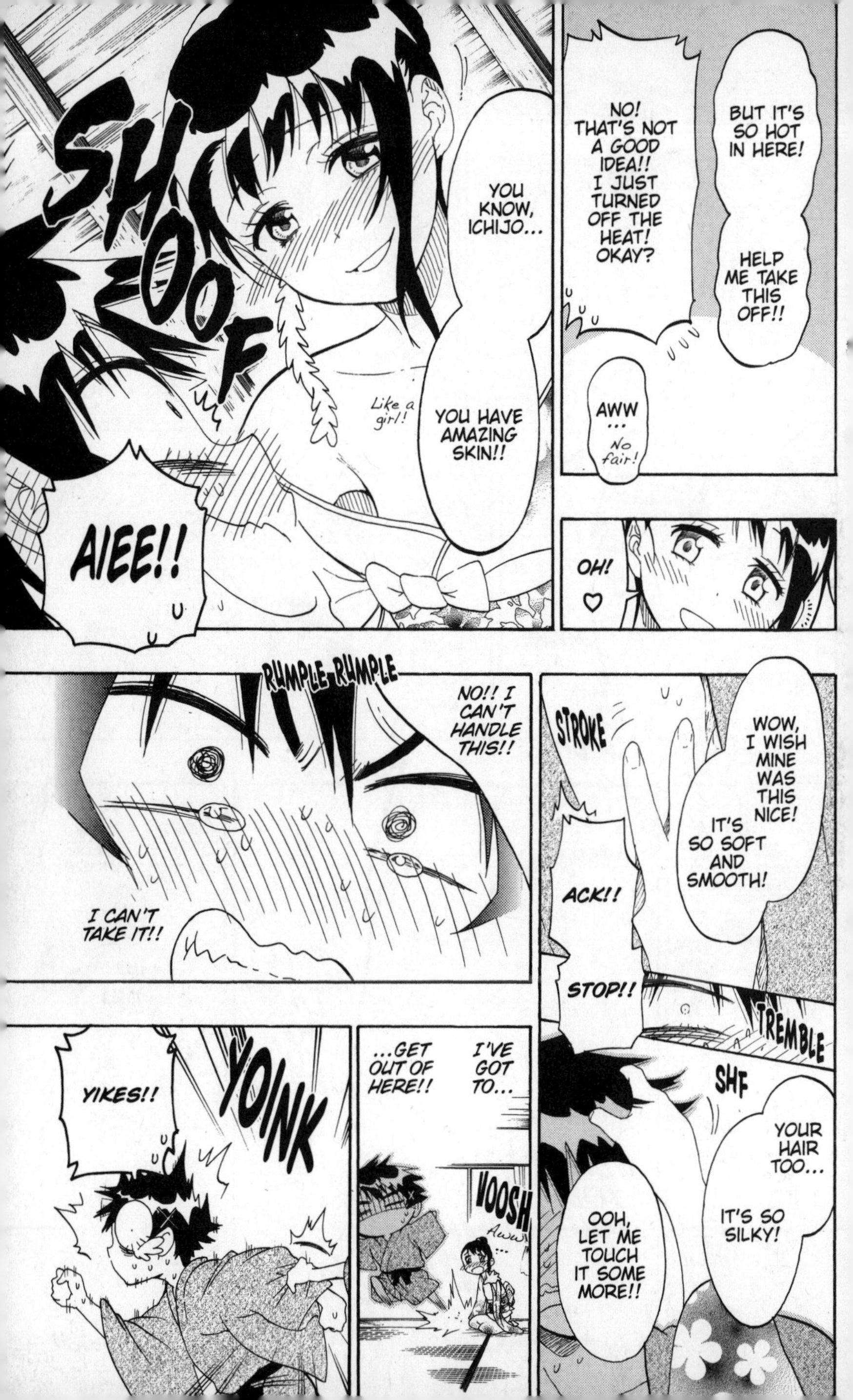
BUT IT'S SO HOT IN HERE!
HELP ME TAKE THIS OFF!!
NO! THAT'S NOT A GOOD IDEA!! I JUST TURNED OFF THE HEAT! OKAY?
AWW...
No fair!
OH! ♡
YOU KNOW, ICHIJO...
YOU HAVE AMAZING SKIN!!
Like a girl!
SHOOF
AIEE!!
WOW, I WISH MINE WAS THIS NICE!
IT'S SO SOFT AND SMOOTH!
STROKE
ACK!!
STOP!!
TREMBLE
SHF
YOUR HAIR TOO...
IT'S SO SILKY!
OOH, LET ME TOUCH IT SOME MORE!!
RUMPLE RUMPLE
NO!! I CAN'T HANDLE THIS!!
I CAN'T TAKE IT!!
I'VE GOT TO...
...GET OUT OF HERE!!
VOOSH
Aww...
YOINK
YIKES!!

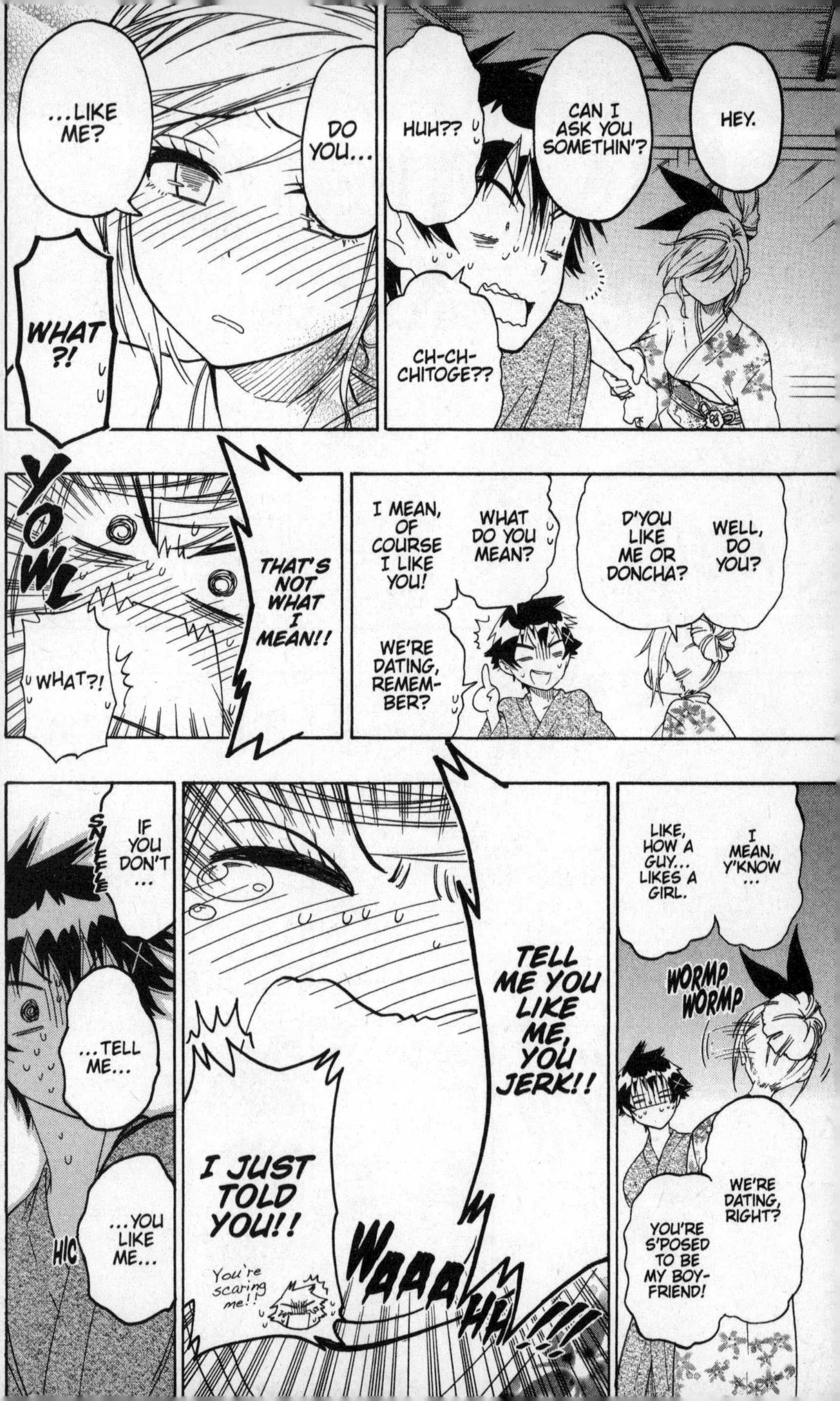
HEY.
CAN I ASK YOU SOMETHIN'?
HUH??
CH-CH-CHITOGE??
DO YOU...
...LIKE ME?
WHAT?!
WELL, DO YOU?
D'YOU LIKE ME OR DONCHA?
WHAT DO YOU MEAN?
I MEAN, OF COURSE I LIKE YOU!
WE'RE DATING, REMEMBER?
THAT'S NOT WHAT I MEAN!!
YOWL
WHAT?!
I MEAN, Y'KNOW...
LIKE, HOW A GUY... LIKES A GIRL.
WORMP WORMP
WE'RE DATING, RIGHT?
YOU'RE S'POSED TO BE MY BOY-FRIEND!
TELL ME YOU LIKE ME, YOU JERK!!
I JUST TOLD YOU!!
WAAAAH!!!
You're scaring me!!
SNIFFLE
IF YOU DON'T...
...TELL ME...
...YOU LIKE ME...
HIC

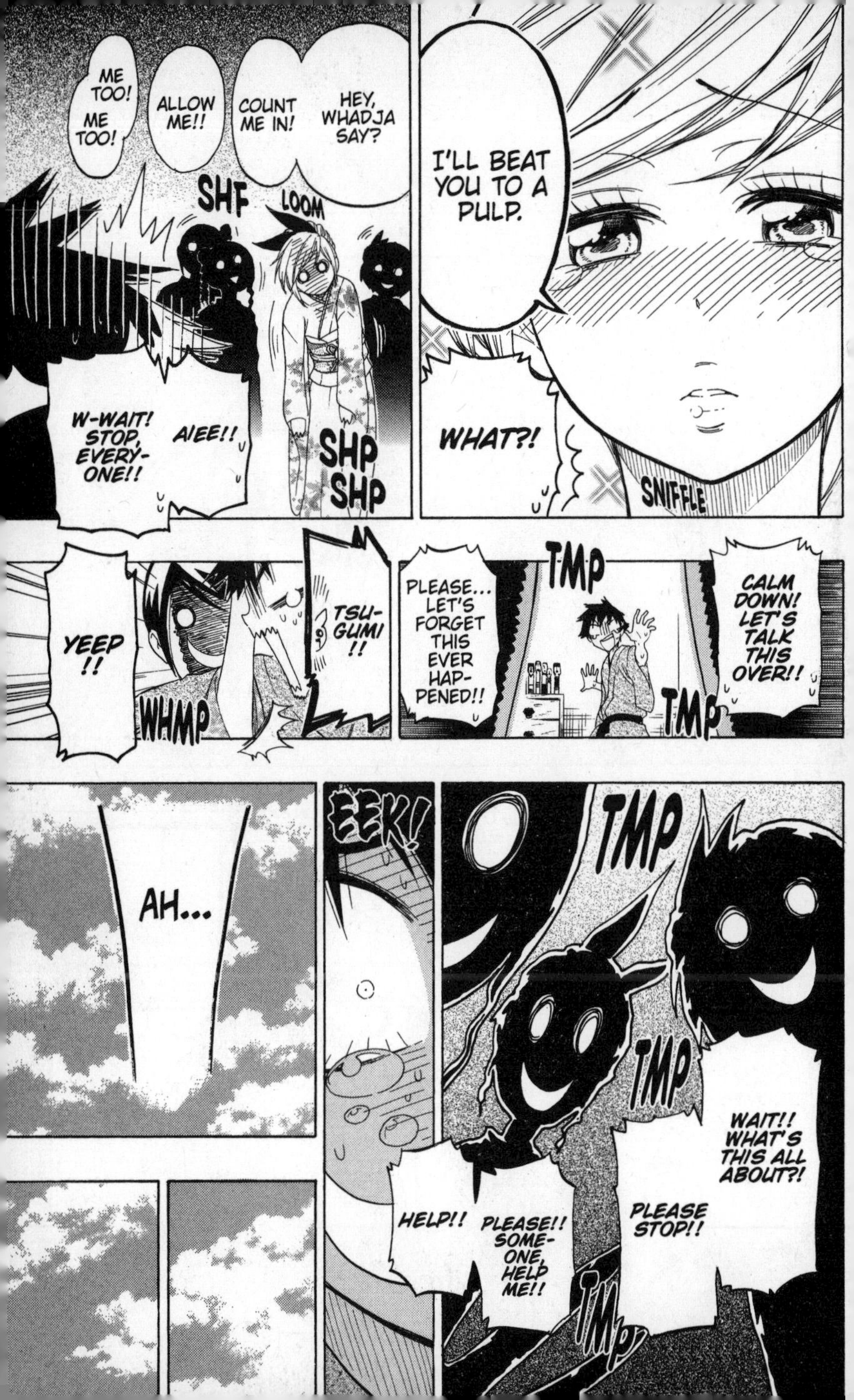
I'LL BEAT YOU TO A PULP.
SNIFFLE
WHAT?!
HEY, WHADJA SAY?
LOOM
COUNT ME IN!
SHF
ALLOW ME!!
ME TOO! ME TOO!
AIEE!!
SHP SHP
W-WAIT! STOP, EVERYONE!!
CALM DOWN! LET'S TALK THIS OVER!!
TMP
TMP
PLEASE... LET'S FORGET THIS EVER HAPPENED!!
TSU-GUMI!!
YEEP!!
WHMP
TMP
WAIT!! WHAT'S THIS ALL ABOUT?!
TMP
PLEASE STOP!!
TMP
EEK!
PLEASE!! SOMEONE, HELP ME!!
HELP!!
AH...

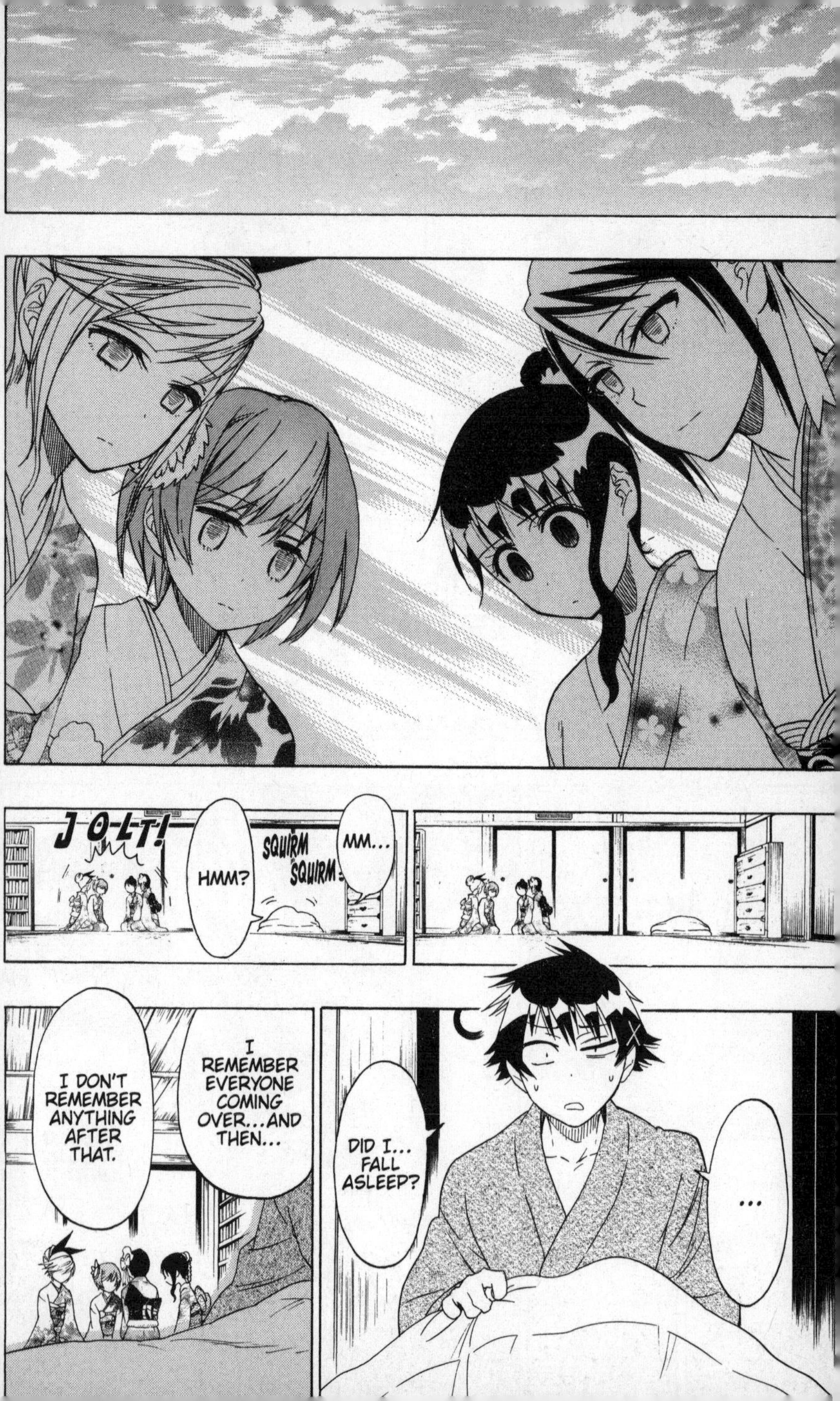
MM...
SQUIRM SQUIRM
HMM?
J-O-L-T!
...
DID I... FALL ASLEEP?
I REMEMBER EVERYONE COMING OVER...AND THEN...
I DON'T REMEMBER ANYTHING AFTER THAT.

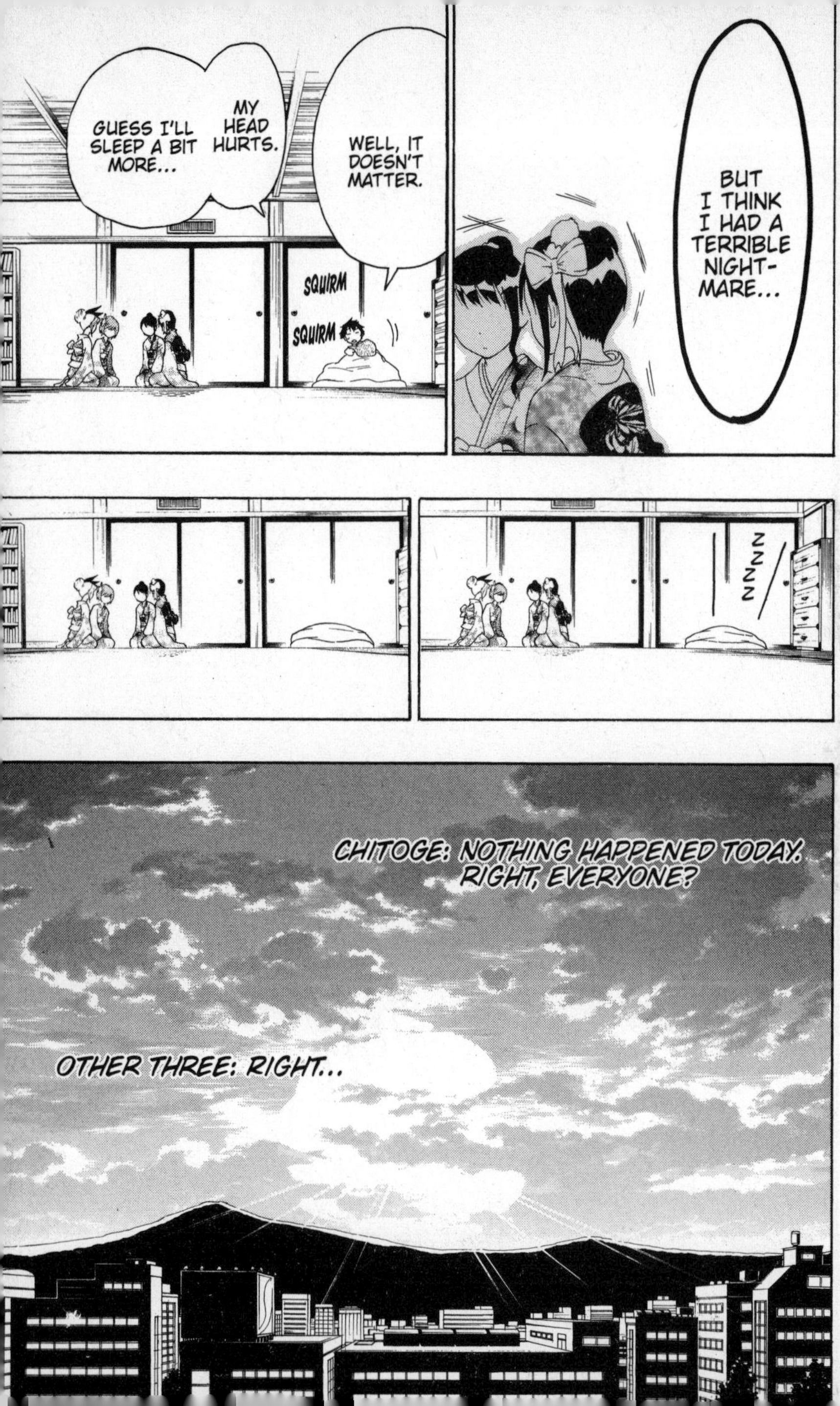
BUT I THINK I HAD A TERRIBLE NIGHT-MARE...
WELL, IT DOESN'T MATTER.
SQUIRM
SQUIRM
MY HEAD HURTS.
GUESS I'LL SLEEP A BIT MORE...
ZZZZ
CHITOGE: NOTHING HAPPENED TODAY. RIGHT, EVERYONE?
OTHER THREE: RIGHT...

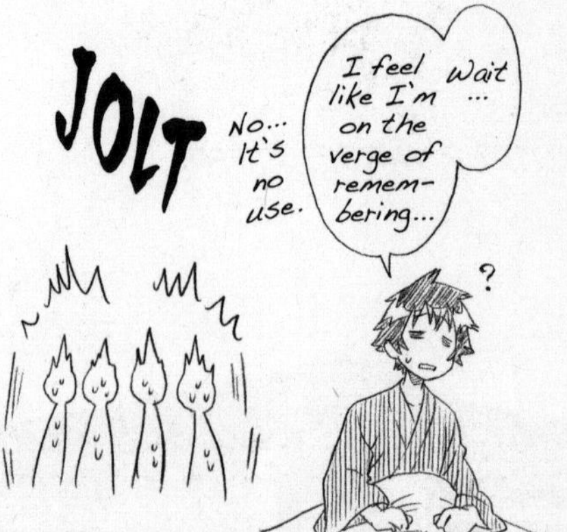
Wait...
I feel like I'm on the verge of remem-bering...
No... It's no use.
JOLT

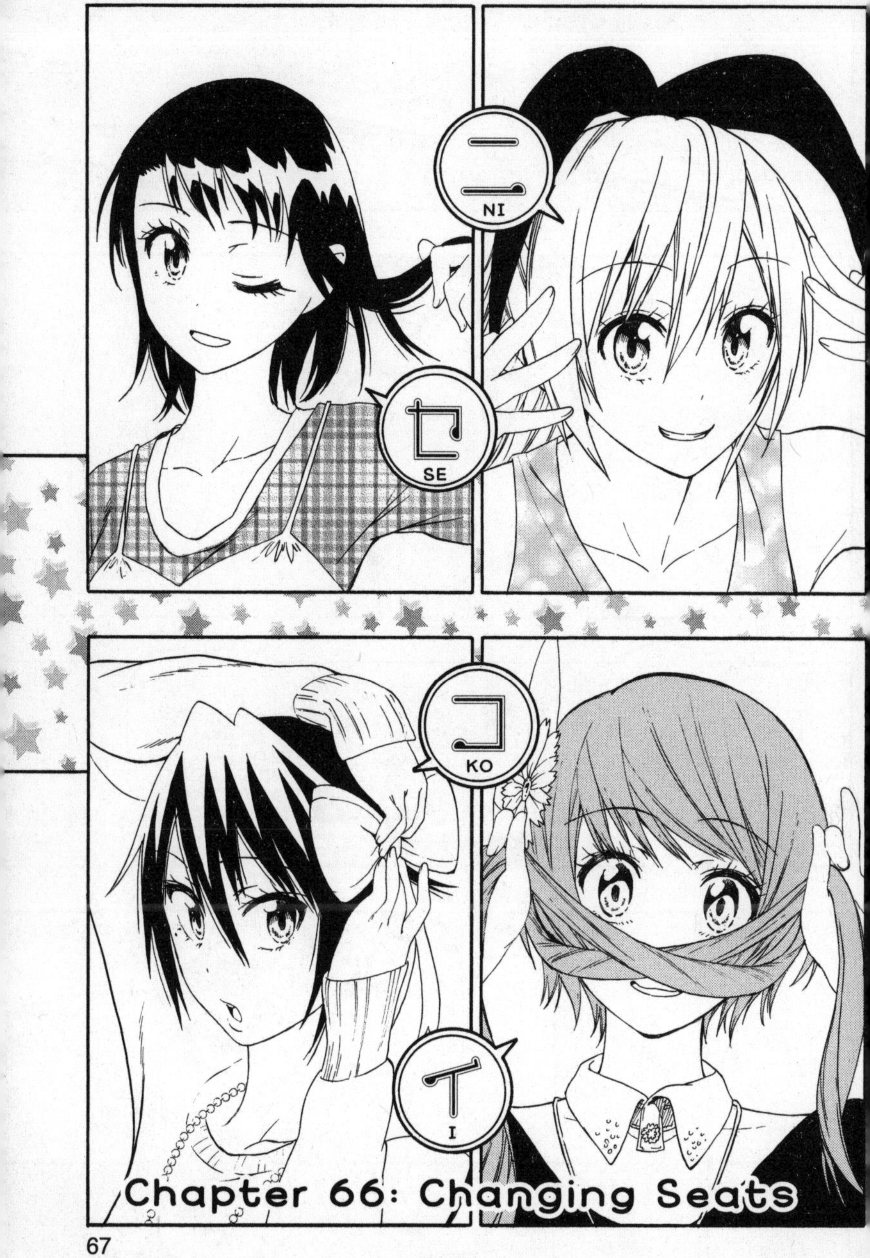
ニ
NI
セ
SE
コ
KO
イ
I

# Chapter 66: Changing Seats

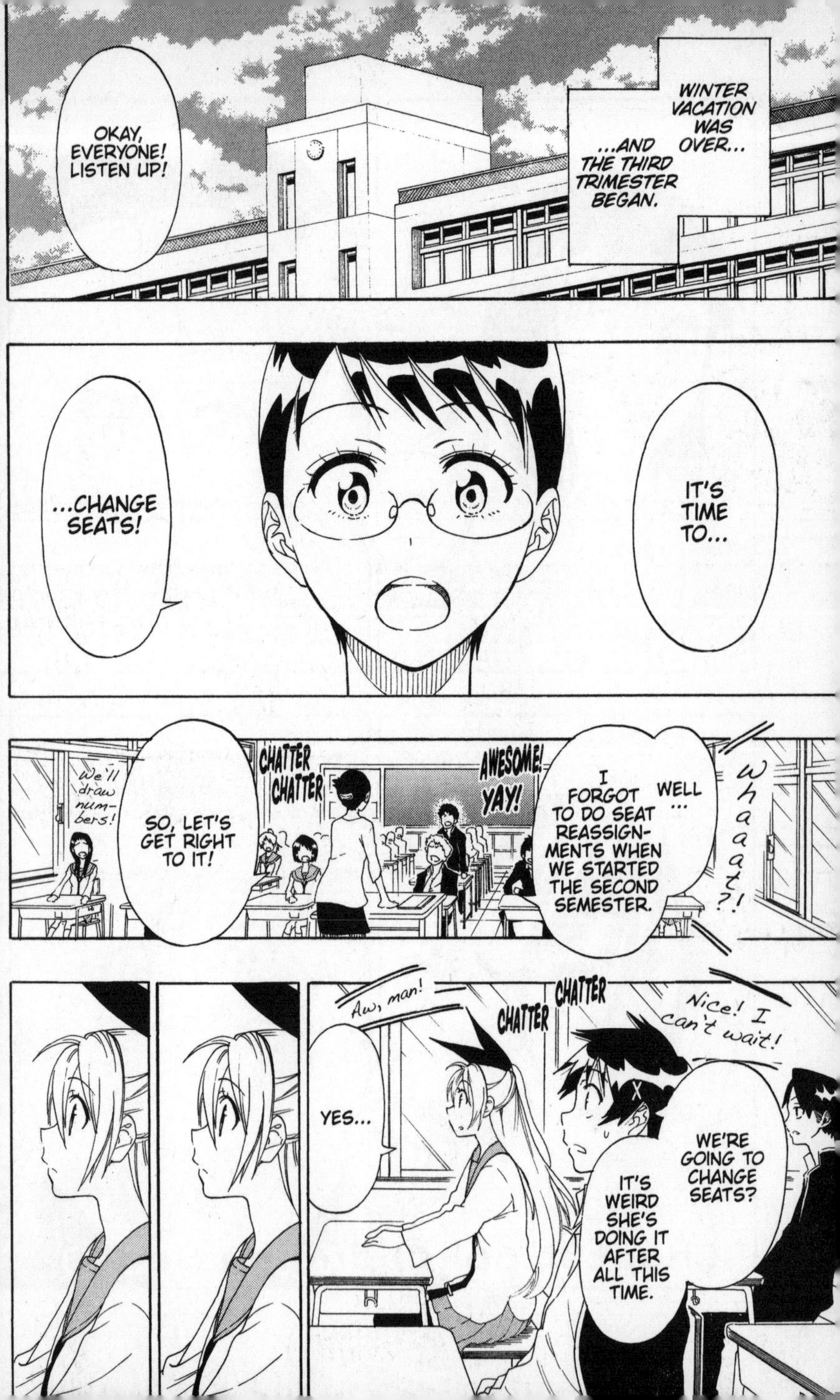
WINTER VACATION WAS OVER...
...AND THE THIRD TRIMESTER BEGAN.
OKAY, EVERYONE! LISTEN UP!
IT'S TIME TO...
...CHANGE SEATS!
Whaaat?!
WELL... I FORGOT TO DO SEAT REASSIGN- MENTS WHEN WE STARTED THE SECOND SEMESTER.
AWESOME! YAY!
CHATTER CHATTER
SO, LET'S GET RIGHT TO IT!
We'll draw num- bers!
Nice! I can't wait!
WE'RE GOING TO CHANGE SEATS?
IT'S WEIRD SHE'S DOING IT AFTER ALL THIS TIME.
CHATTER CHATTER
Aw, man!
YES...

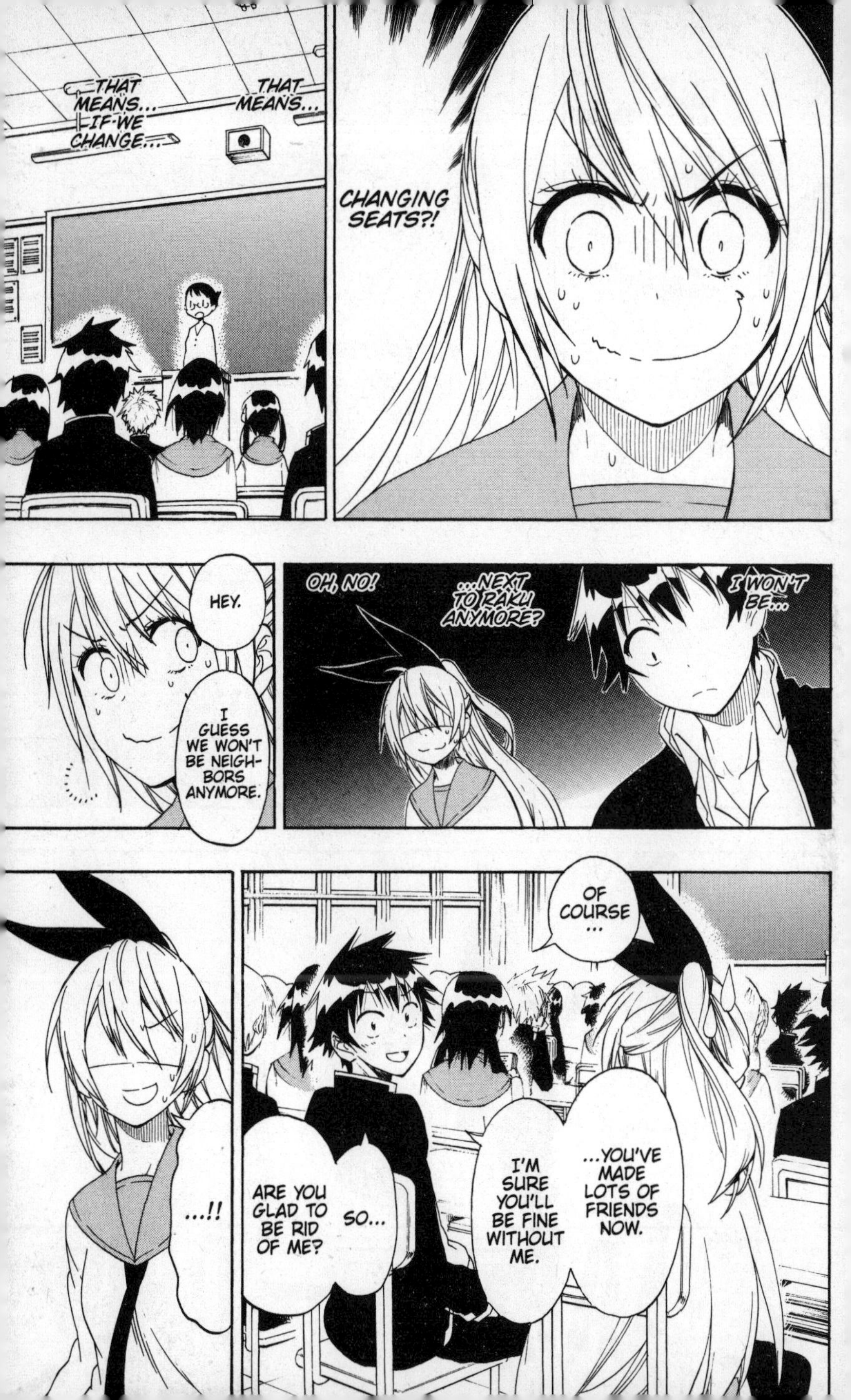
CHANGING SEATS?!
THAT MEANS...
THAT MEANS... IF WE CHANGE...
I WON'T BE...
...NEXT TO RAKU ANYMORE?
OH, NO!
HEY.
I GUESS WE WON'T BE NEIGHBORS ANYMORE.
OF COURSE...
...YOU'VE MADE LOTS OF FRIENDS NOW.
I'M SURE YOU'LL BE FINE WITHOUT ME.
SO...
ARE YOU GLAD TO BE RID OF ME?
...!!

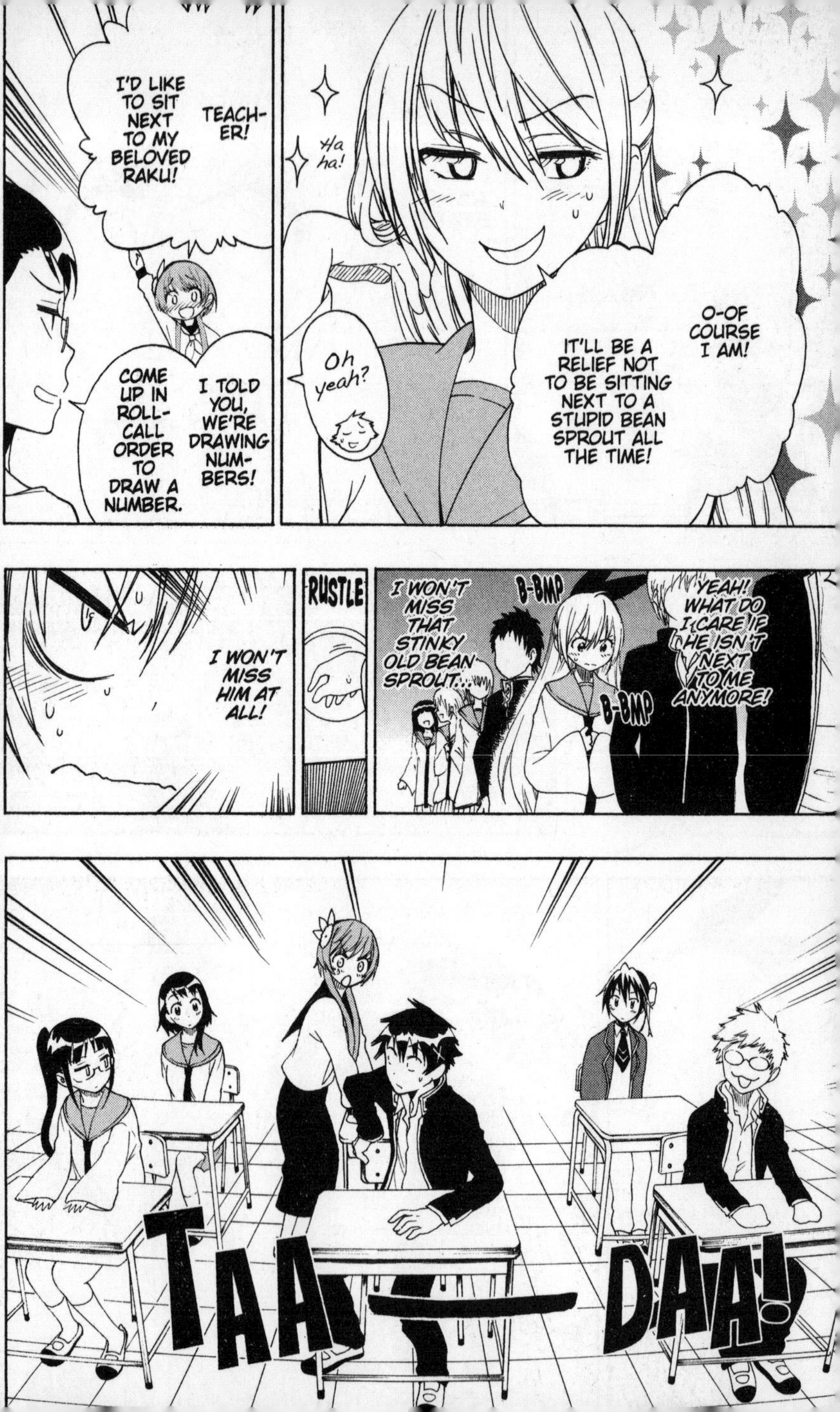
O-OF COURSE I AM!
IT'LL BE A RELIEF NOT TO BE SITTING NEXT TO A STUPID BEAN SPROUT ALL THE TIME!
Ha ha!
Oh yeah?
TEACHER!
I'D LIKE TO SIT NEXT TO MY BELOVED RAKU!
I TOLD YOU, WE'RE DRAWING NUMBERS!
COME UP IN ROLL-CALL ORDER TO DRAW A NUMBER.
YEAH! WHAT DO I CARE IF HE ISN'T NEXT TO ME ANYMORE!
B-BMP
B-BMP
I WON'T MISS THAT STINKY OLD BEAN SPROUT...
RUSTLE
I WON'T MISS HIM AT ALL!
TAA—DAA!

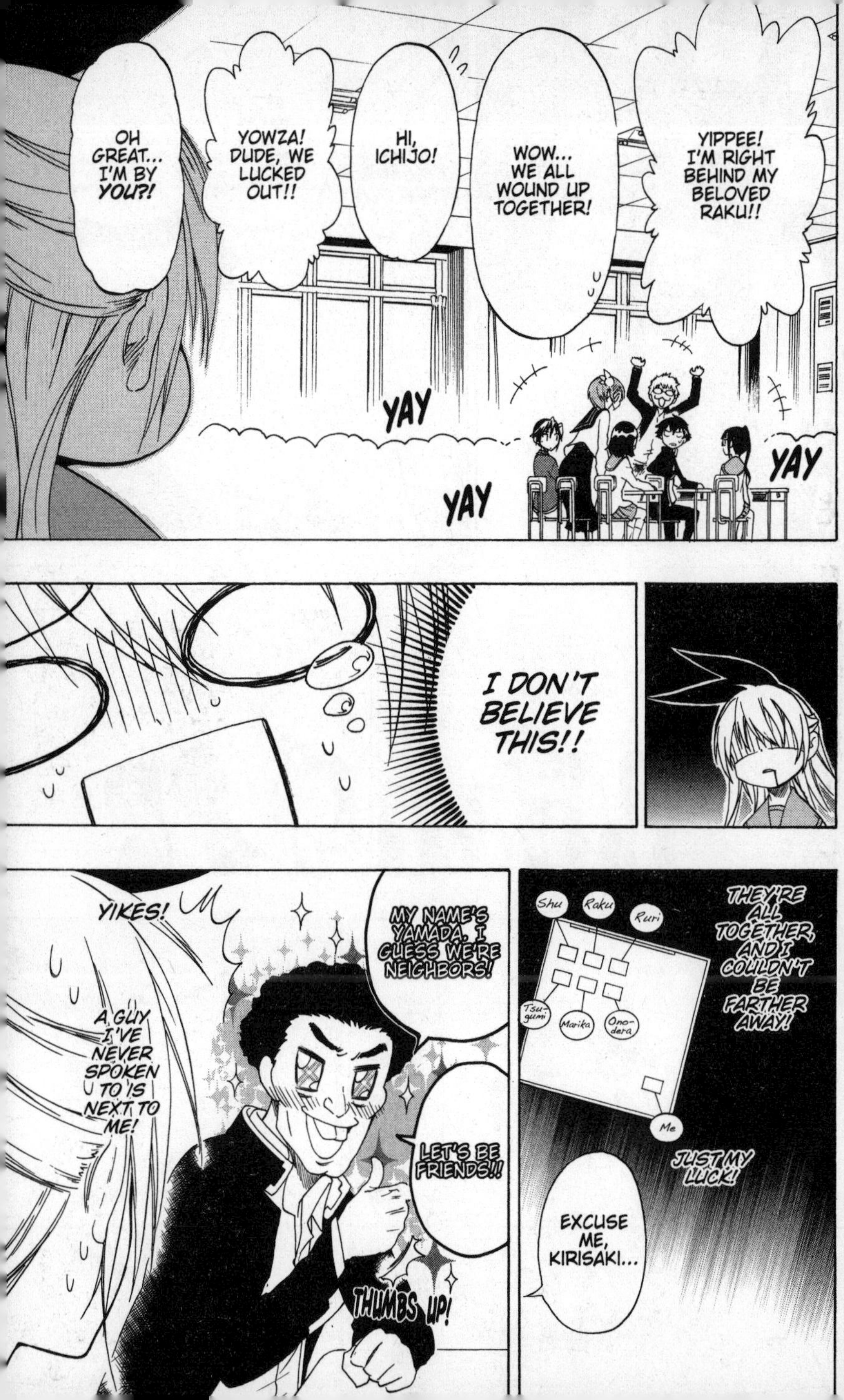
YIPPEE! I'M RIGHT BEHIND MY BELOVED RAKU!!
WOW... WE ALL WOUND UP TOGETHER!
HI, ICHIJO!
YOWZA! DUDE, WE LUCKED OUT!!
OH GREAT... I'M BY YOU?!
YAY
YAY
YAY
I DON'T BELIEVE THIS!!
THEY'RE ALL TOGETHER, AND I COULDN'T BE FARTHER AWAY!
Shu
Raku
Ruri
Tsu-gumi
Marika
Ono-dera
Me
JUST MY LUCK!
EXCUSE ME, KIRISAKI...
MY NAME'S YAMADA. I GUESS WE'RE NEIGHBORS!
YIKES!
LET'S BE FRIENDS!!
A GUY I'VE NEVER SPOKEN TO IS NEXT TO ME!
THUMBS UP!

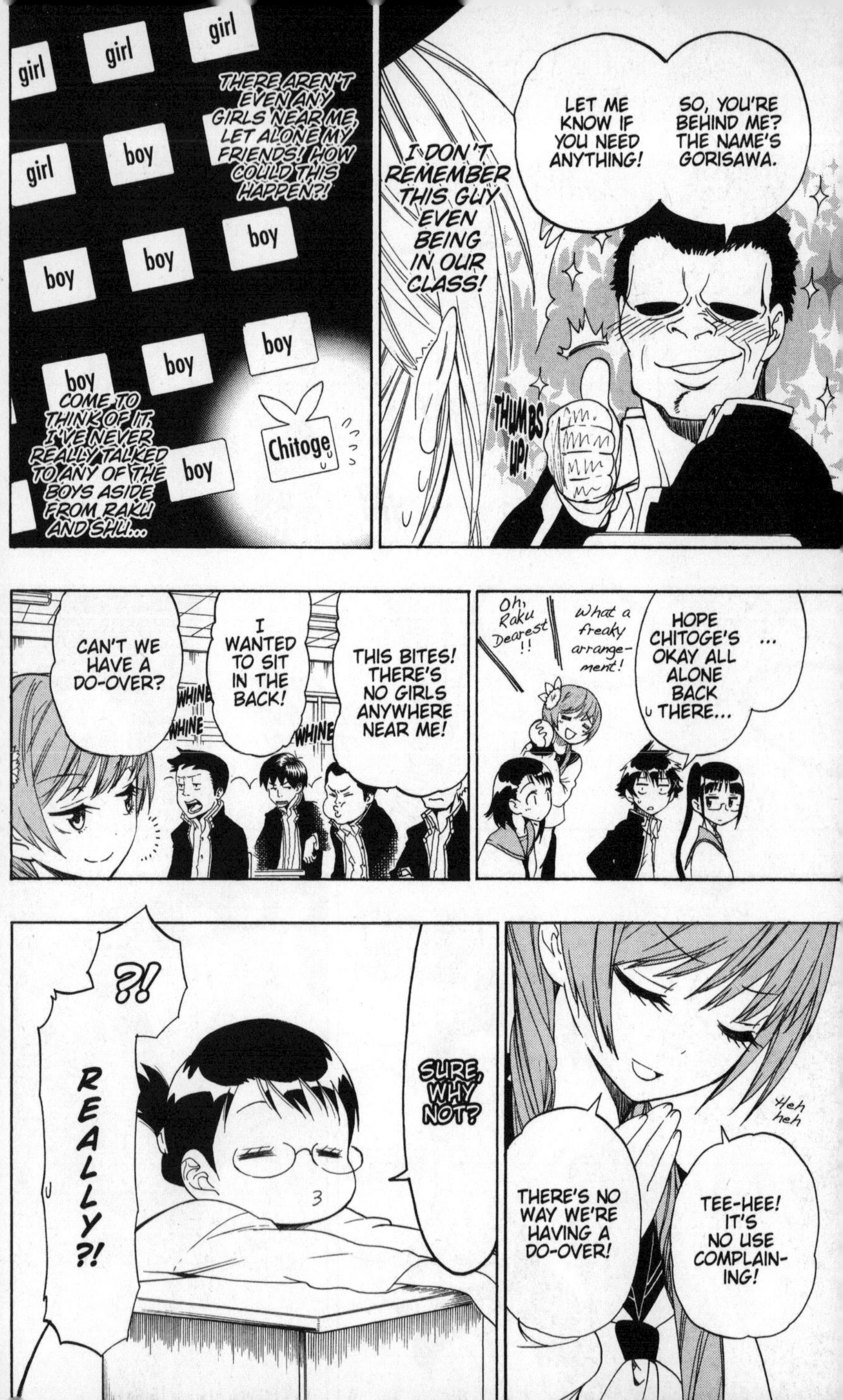
SO, YOU'RE BEHIND ME? THE NAME'S GORISAWA.
LET ME KNOW IF YOU NEED ANYTHING!
THUMBS UP!
I DON'T REMEMBER THIS GUY EVEN BEING IN OUR CLASS!
THERE AREN'T EVEN ANY GIRLS NEAR ME, LET ALONE MY FRIENDS! HOW COULD THIS HAPPEN?!
girl
girl
girl
girl
boy
boy
boy
boy
boy
boy
boy
boy
Chitoge
COME TO THINK OF IT, I'VE NEVER REALLY TALKED TO ANY OF THE BOYS ASIDE FROM RAKU AND SHU...
HOPE CHITOGE'S OKAY ALL ALONE BACK THERE...
...
What a freaky arrangement!
Oh, Raku Dearest!!
THIS BITES! THERE'S NO GIRLS ANYWHERE NEAR ME!
WHINE
I WANTED TO SIT IN THE BACK!
WHINE
WHINE
CAN'T WE HAVE A DO-OVER?
TEE-HEE! IT'S NO USE COMPLAINING!
THERE'S NO WAY WE'RE HAVING A DO-OVER!
Heh heh
SURE, WHY NOT?
?!
REALLY?!

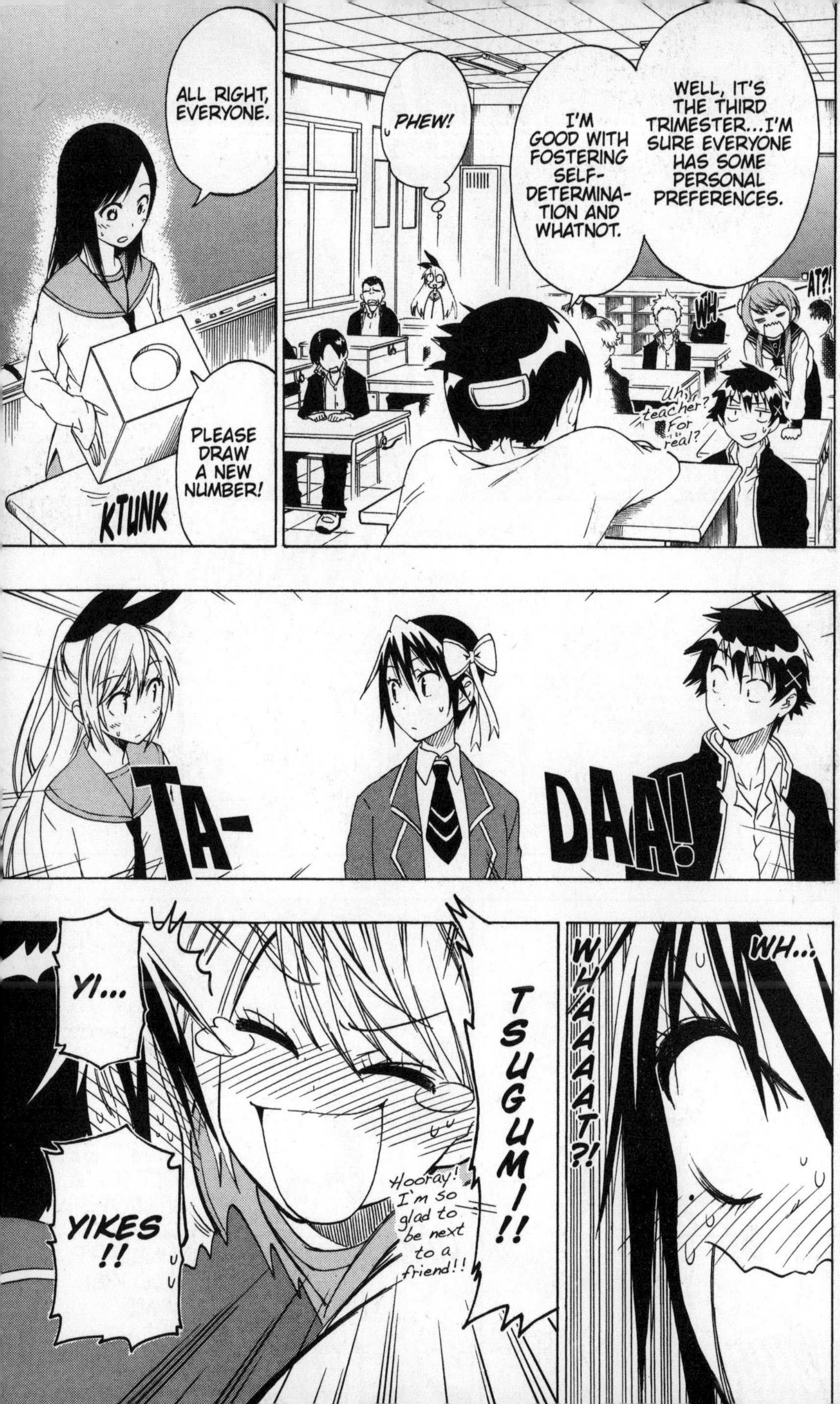
WELL, IT'S THE THIRD TRIMESTER...I'M SURE EVERYONE HAS SOME PERSONAL PREFERENCES.
I'M GOOD WITH FOSTERING SELF-DETERMINATION AND WHATNOT.
AT?!
WH
PHEW!
Uh, teacher? For real?
ALL RIGHT, EVERYONE.
PLEASE DRAW A NEW NUMBER!
KTUNK
TA-
DAA!
WH...
WHAAAAAT?!
TSUGUMI!!
Hooray! I'm so glad to be next to a friend!!
YI...
YIKES!!

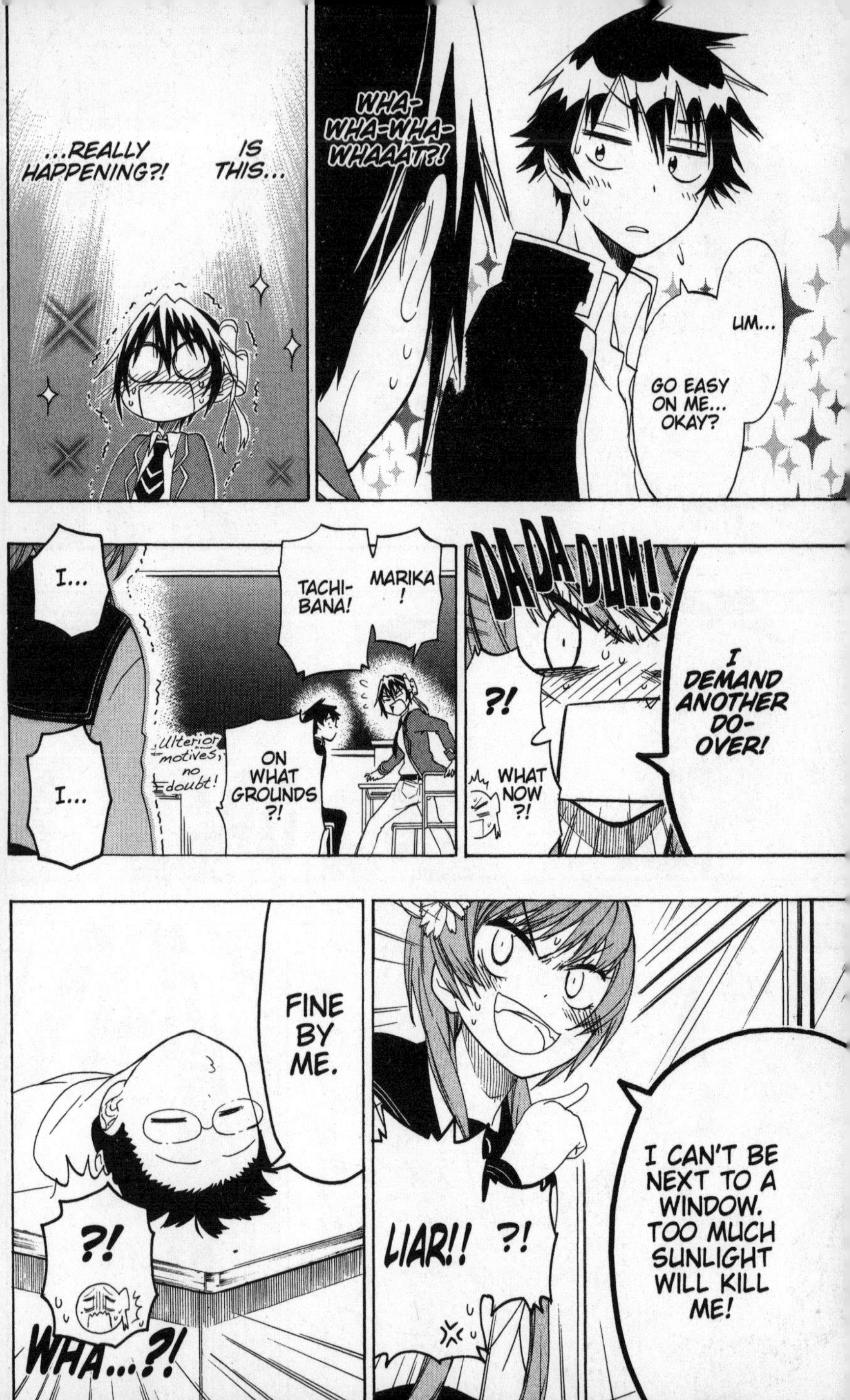
UM...
GO EASY ON ME... OKAY?
WHA-WHA-WHA-WHAAAT?!
IS THIS...
...REALLY HAPPENING?!
DA DA DUM!
I DEMAND ANOTHER DO-OVER!
?!
WHAT NOW?!
MARIKA!
TACHIBANA!
ON WHAT GROUNDS?!
Ulterior motives, no doubt!
I...
I...
I CAN'T BE NEXT TO A WINDOW. TOO MUCH SUNLIGHT WILL KILL ME!
?!
LIAR!!
FINE BY ME.
?!
WHA...?!

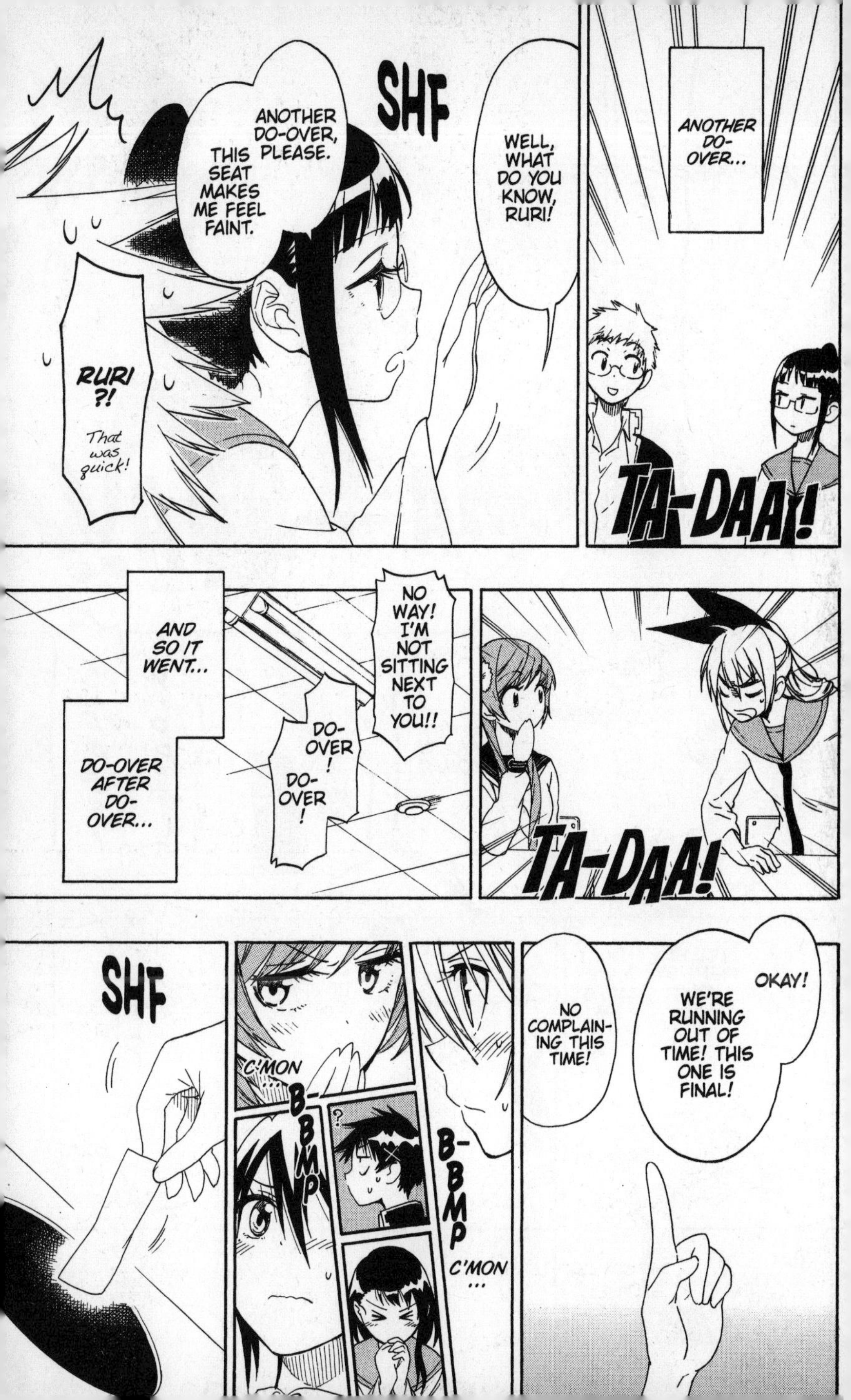
ANOTHER DO-OVER...
TA-DAA!
WELL, WHAT DO YOU KNOW, RURI!
SHF
ANOTHER DO-OVER, PLEASE. THIS SEAT MAKES ME FEEL FAINT.
RURI?!
That was quick!
TA-DAA!
NO WAY! I'M NOT SITTING NEXT TO YOU!!
AND SO IT WENT...
DO-OVER! DO-OVER!
DO-OVER AFTER DO-OVER...
OKAY! WE'RE RUNNING OUT OF TIME! THIS ONE IS FINAL!
NO COMPLAINING THIS TIME!
B-BBMP
C'MON...
C'MON...
B-BBMP
SHF

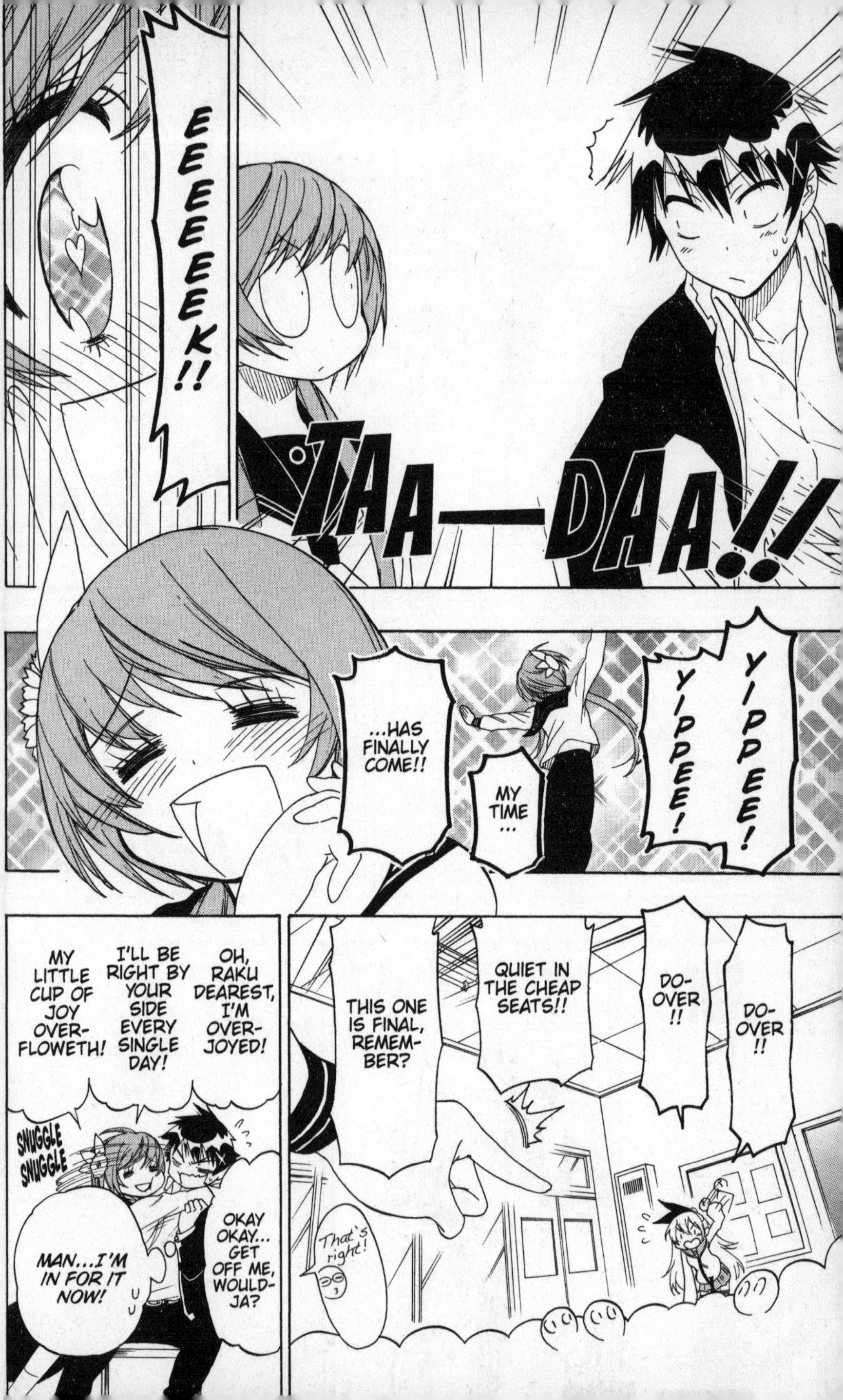

TAA—DAA!!
EEEEEEEK!!
YIPPEE! YIPPEE!
MY TIME...
...HAS FINALLY COME!!
DO-OVER!!
DO-OVER!!
QUIET IN THE CHEAP SEATS!!
THIS ONE IS FINAL, REMEMBER?
That's right!
OH, RAKU DEAREST, I'M OVERJOYED!
I'LL BE RIGHT BY YOUR SIDE EVERY SINGLE DAY!
MY LITTLE CUP OF JOY OVERFLOWETH!
SNUGGLE SNUGGLE
OKAY OKAY... GET OFF ME, WOULDJA?
MAN...I'M IN FOR IT NOW!

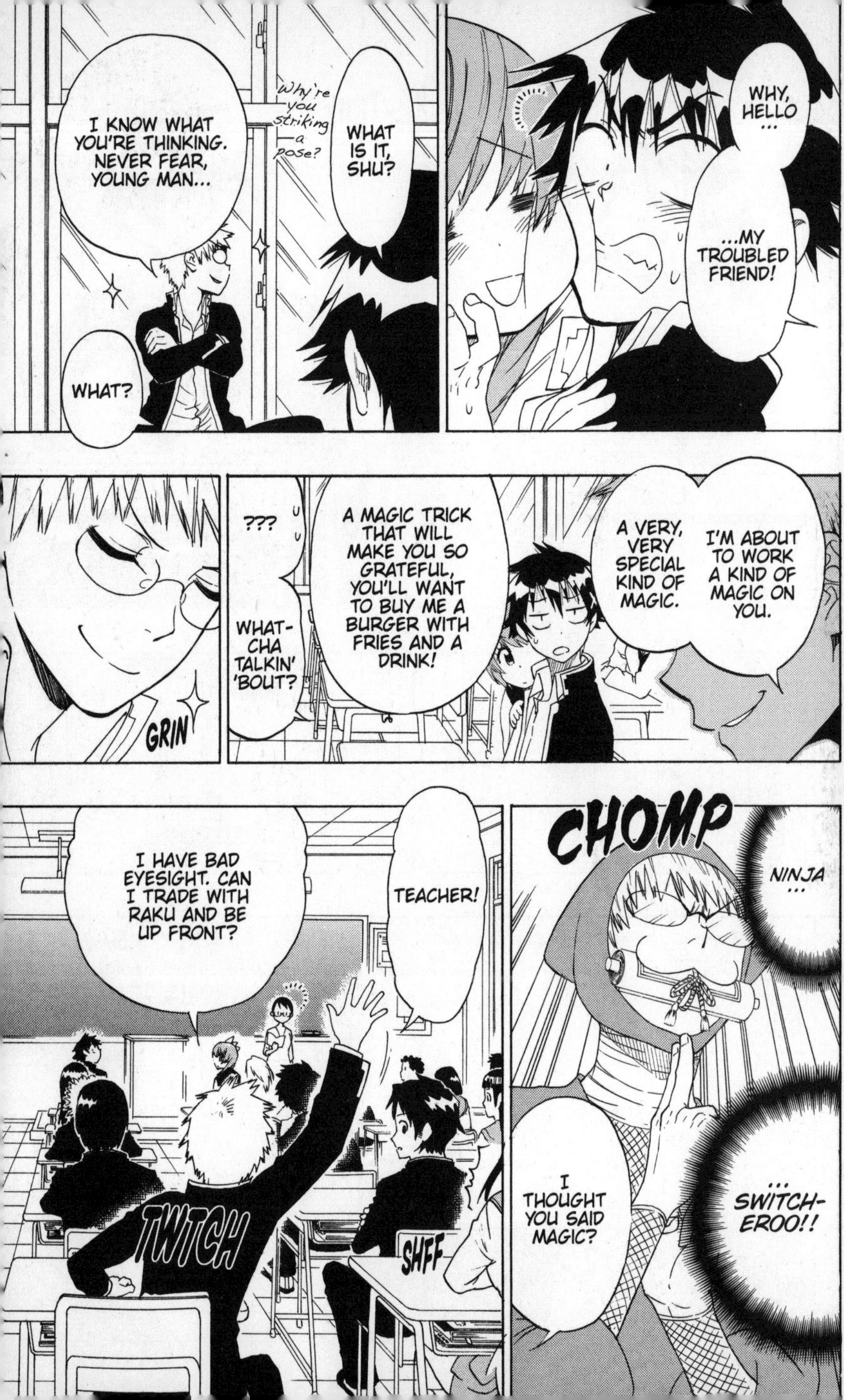
WHY, HELLO...
...MY TROUBLED FRIEND!
WHAT IS IT, SHU?
Why're you striking a pose?
I KNOW WHAT YOU'RE THINKING. NEVER FEAR, YOUNG MAN...
WHAT?
I'M ABOUT TO WORK A KIND OF MAGIC ON YOU.
A VERY, VERY SPECIAL KIND OF MAGIC.
A MAGIC TRICK THAT WILL MAKE YOU SO GRATEFUL, YOU'LL WANT TO BUY ME A BURGER WITH FRIES AND A DRINK!
???
WHAT-CHA TALKIN' 'BOUT?
GRIN
CHOMP
NINJA...
...SWITCH-EROO!!
I THOUGHT YOU SAID MAGIC?
TEACHER!
I HAVE BAD EYESIGHT. CAN I TRADE WITH RAKU AND BE UP FRONT?
TWITCH
SHFF

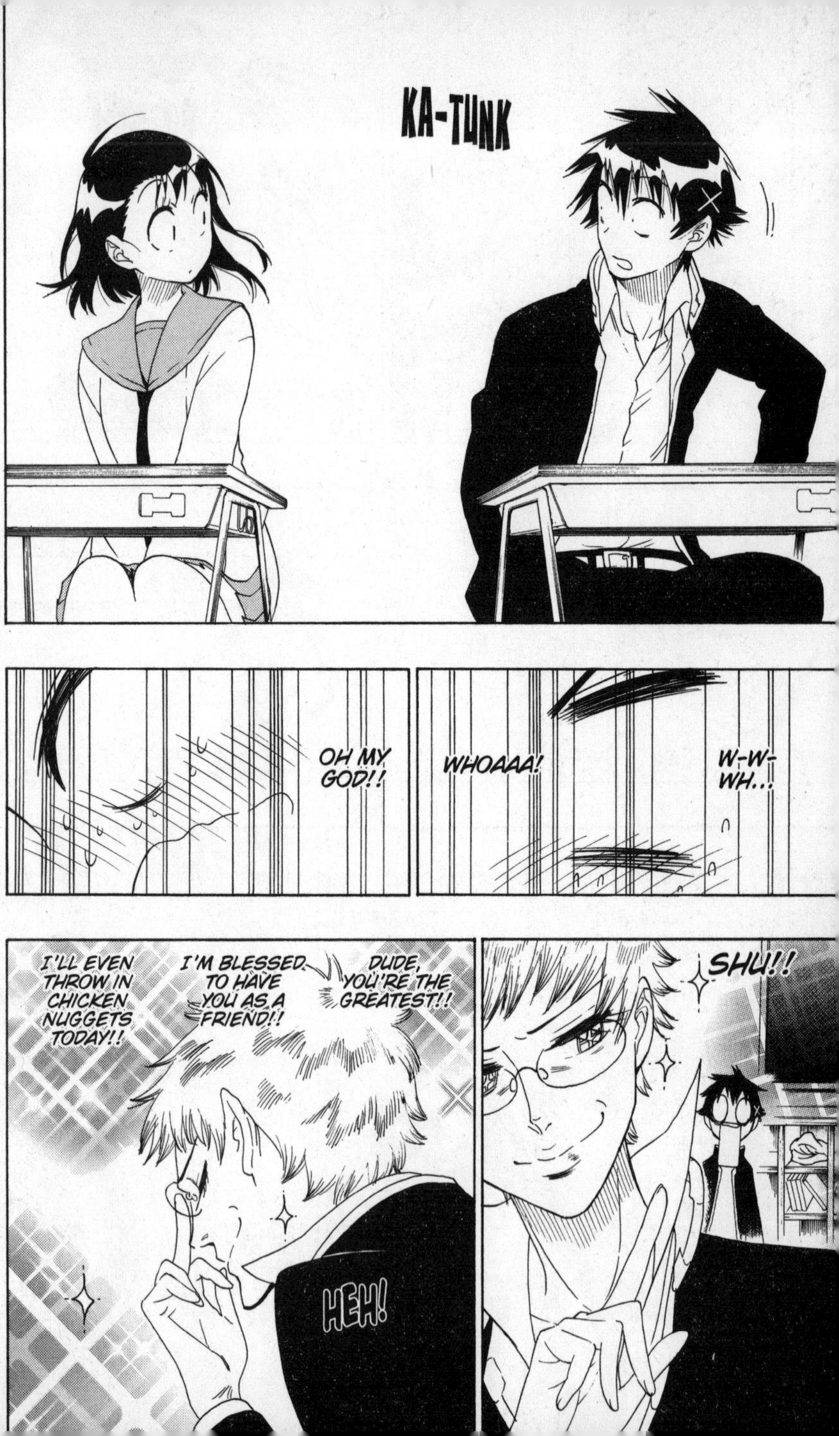
KA-TUNK
W-W-WH...
WHOAAA!
OH MY GOD!!
SHU!!
DUDE, YOU'RE THE GREATEST!!
I'M BLESSED TO HAVE YOU AS A FRIEND!!
I'LL EVEN THROW IN CHICKEN NUGGETS TODAY!!
HEH!

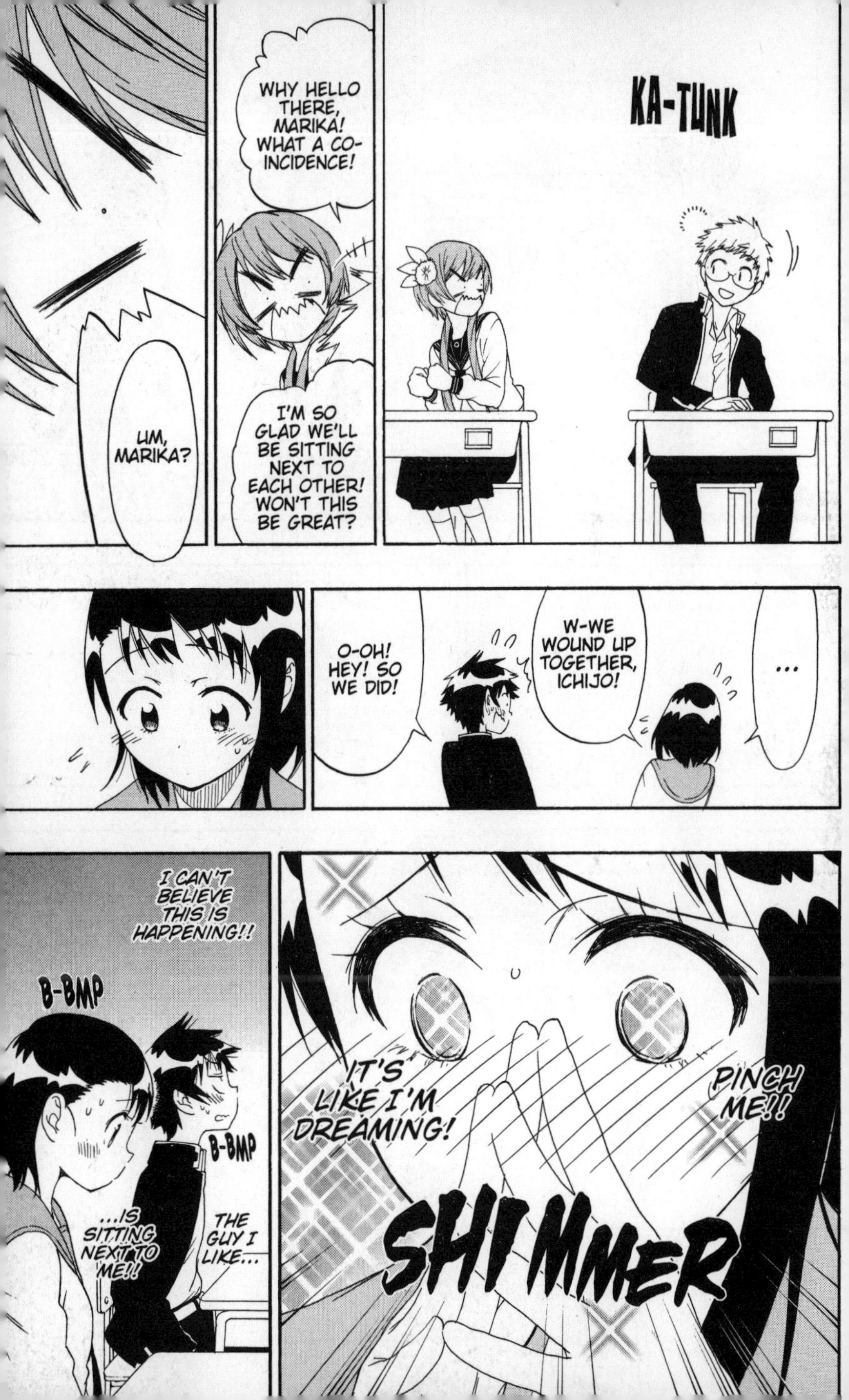
KA-TUNK
WHY HELLO THERE, MARIKA! WHAT A CO-INCIDENCE!
I'M SO GLAD WE'LL BE SITTING NEXT TO EACH OTHER! WON'T THIS BE GREAT?
UM, MARIKA?
...
W-WE WOUND UP TOGETHER, ICHIJO!
O-OH! HEY! SO WE DID!
PINCH ME!!
IT'S LIKE I'M DREAMING!
SHIMMER
I CAN'T BELIEVE THIS IS HAPPENING!!
B-BMP
B-BMP
THE GUY I LIKE...
...IS SITTING NEXT TO ME!!

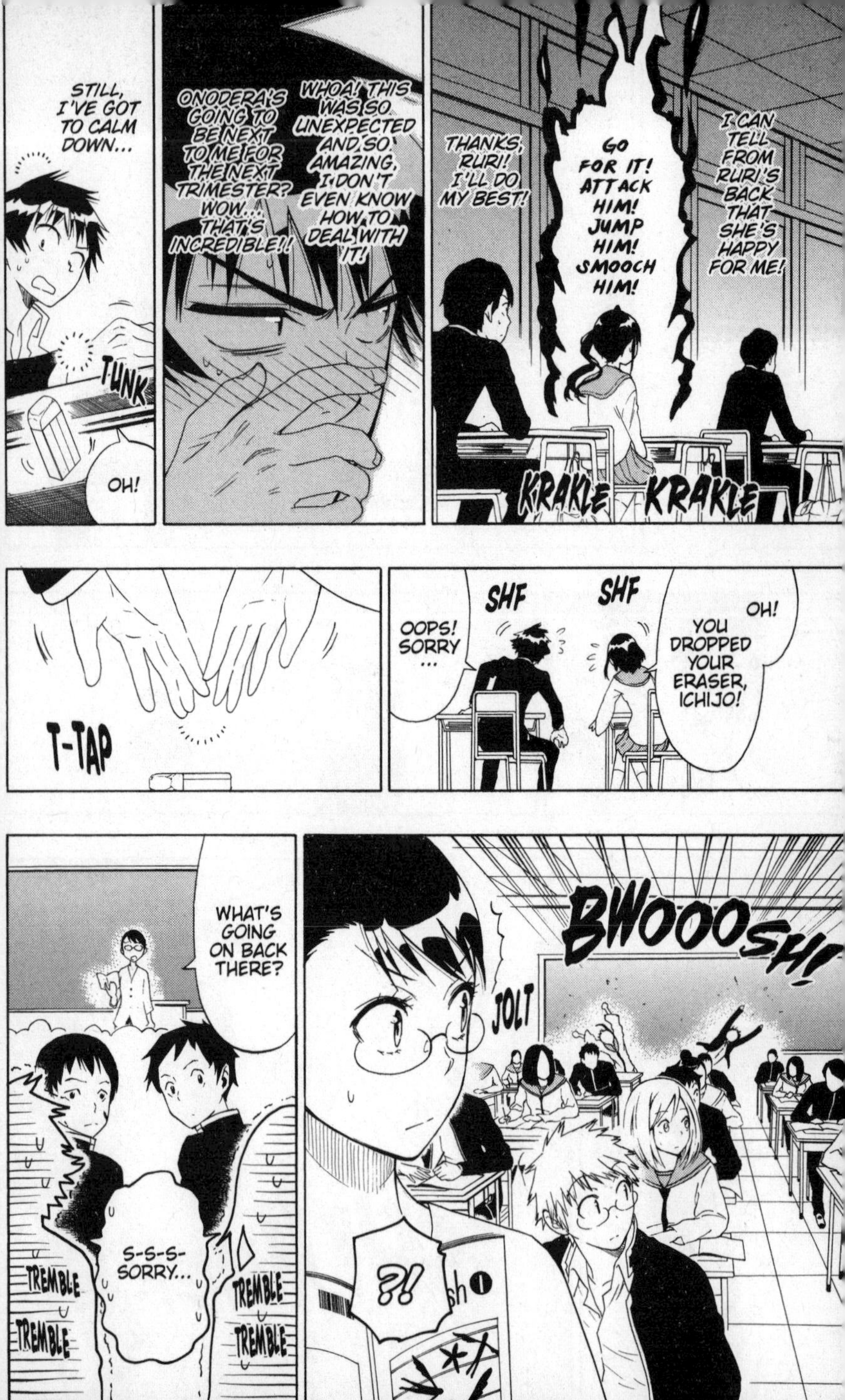
I CAN TELL FROM RURI'S BACK THAT SHE'S HAPPY FOR ME!
GO FOR IT! ATTACK HIM! JUMP HIM! SMOOCH HIM!
THANKS, RURI! I'LL DO MY BEST!
KRAKLE KRAKLE
WHOA! THIS WAS SO UNEXPECTED AND SO AMAZING, I DON'T EVEN KNOW HOW TO DEAL WITH IT!
ONODERA'S GOING TO BE NEXT TO ME FOR THE NEXT TRIMESTER? WOW... THAT'S INCREDIBLE!!
STILL, I'VE GOT TO CALM DOWN...
TUNK
OH!
OH! YOU DROPPED YOUR ERASER, ICHIJO!
SHF
SHF
OOPS! SORRY...
T-TAP
BWOOOSH!
JOLT
?!
WHAT'S GOING ON BACK THERE?
S-S-S-SORRY...
TREMBLE
TREMBLE
TREMBLE
TREMBLE

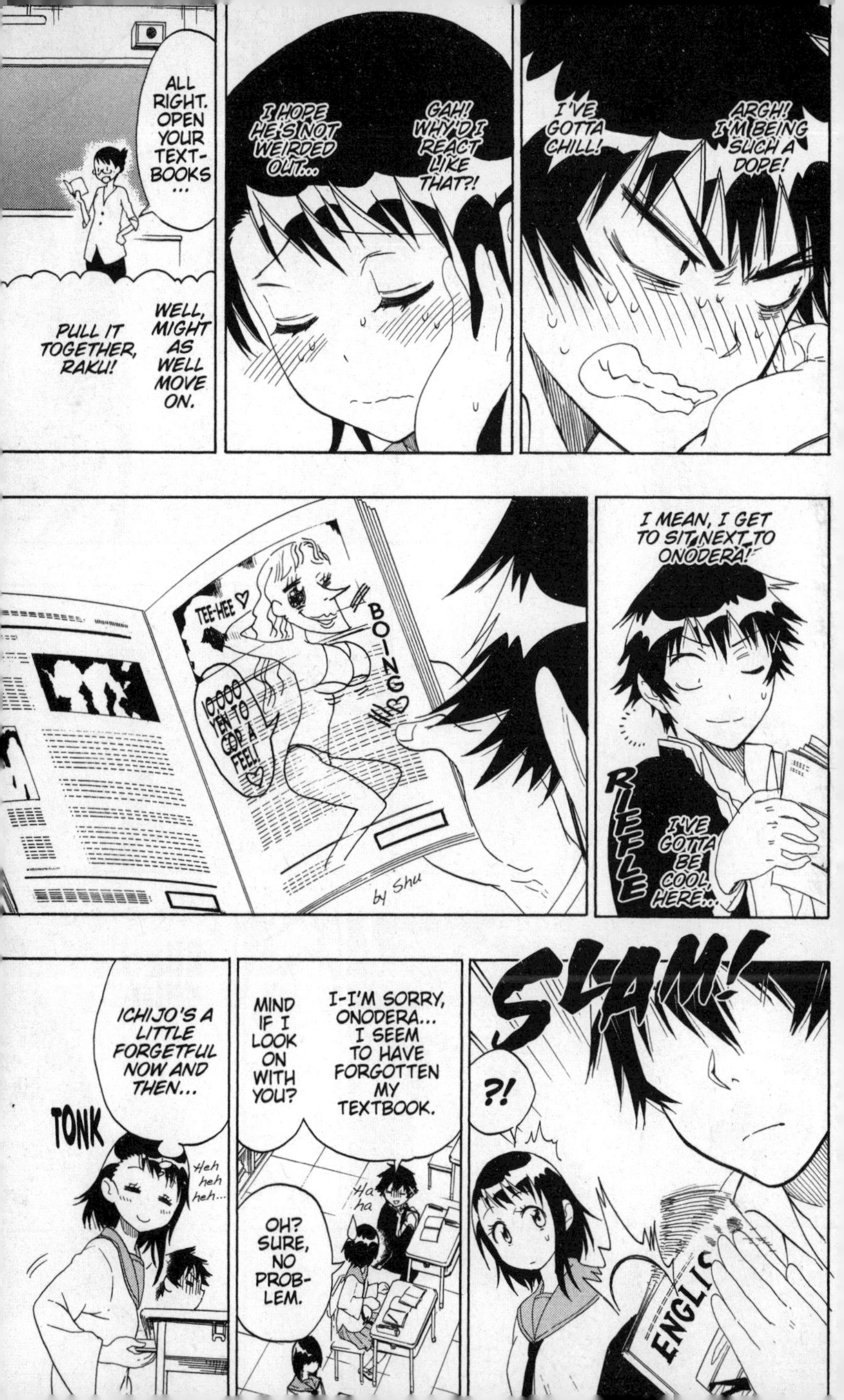
ARGH! I'M BEING SUCH A DOPE!
I'VE GOTTA CHILL!
GAH! WHY'D I REACT LIKE THAT?!
I HOPE HE'S NOT WEIRDED OUT...
ALL RIGHT. OPEN YOUR TEXT-BOOKS...
WELL, MIGHT AS WELL MOVE ON.
PULL IT TOGETHER, RAKU!
I MEAN, I GET TO SIT NEXT TO ONODERA!
RIFFLE
I'VE GOTTA BE COOL, HERE...
BOING ♡
TEE-HEE ♡
10,000 YEN TO COP A FEEL! ♡
by Shu
SLAM!
?!
ENGLIS
I-I'M SORRY, ONODERA... I SEEM TO HAVE FORGOTTEN MY TEXTBOOK.
MIND IF I LOOK ON WITH YOU?
Ha ha
OH? SURE, NO PROBLEM.
ICHIJO'S A LITTLE FORGETFUL NOW AND THEN...
TONK
Heh heh heh...

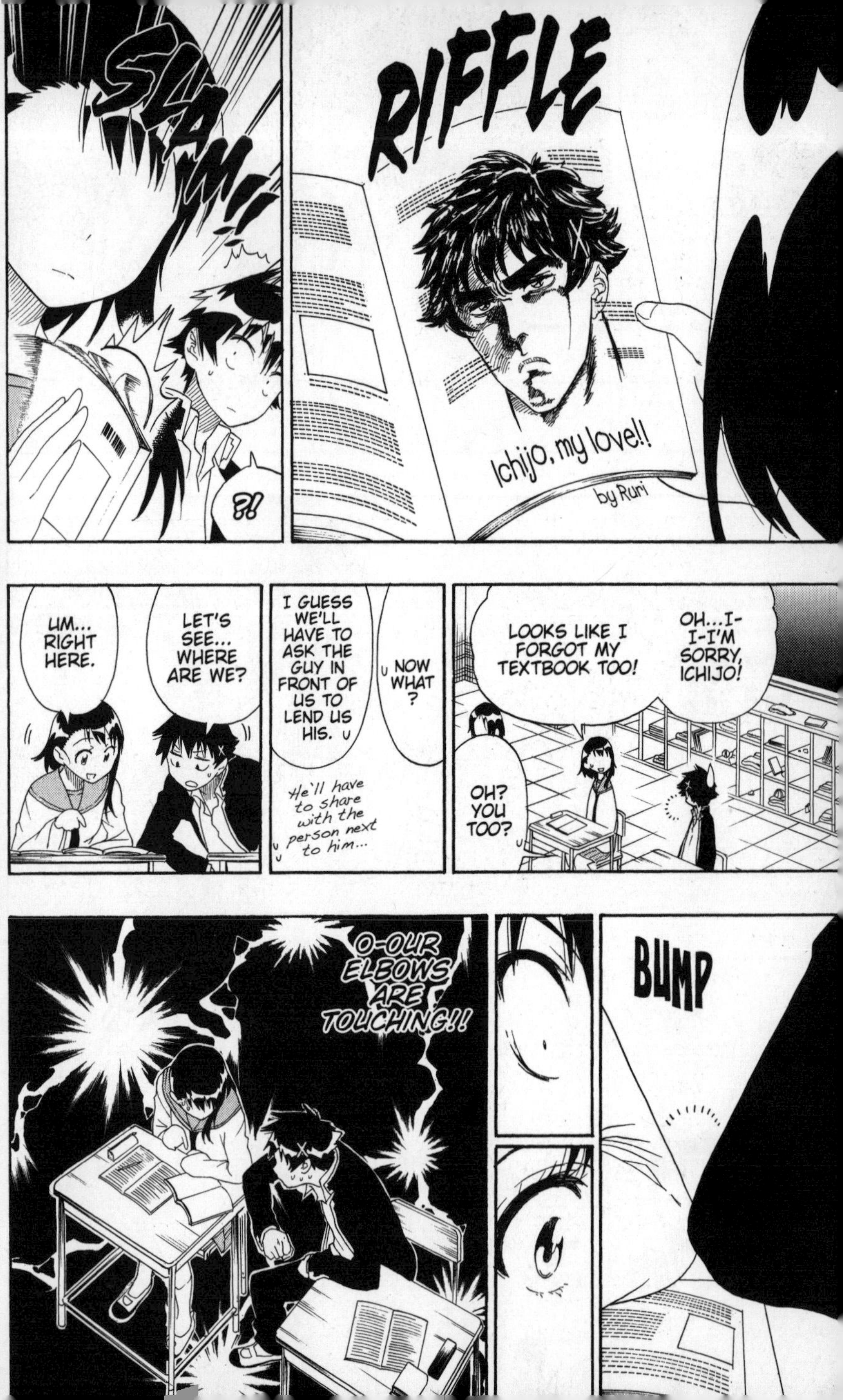
RIFFLE
Ichijo, my love!!
by Ruri
SLAM!!
?!
OH...I- I-I'M SORRY, ICHIJO!
LOOKS LIKE I FORGOT MY TEXTBOOK TOO!
OH? YOU TOO?
NOW WHAT?
I GUESS WE'LL HAVE TO ASK THE GUY IN FRONT OF US TO LEND US HIS.
He'll have to share with the person next to him...
LET'S SEE... WHERE ARE WE?
UM... RIGHT HERE.
BUMP
O-OUR ELBOWS ARE TOUCHING!!

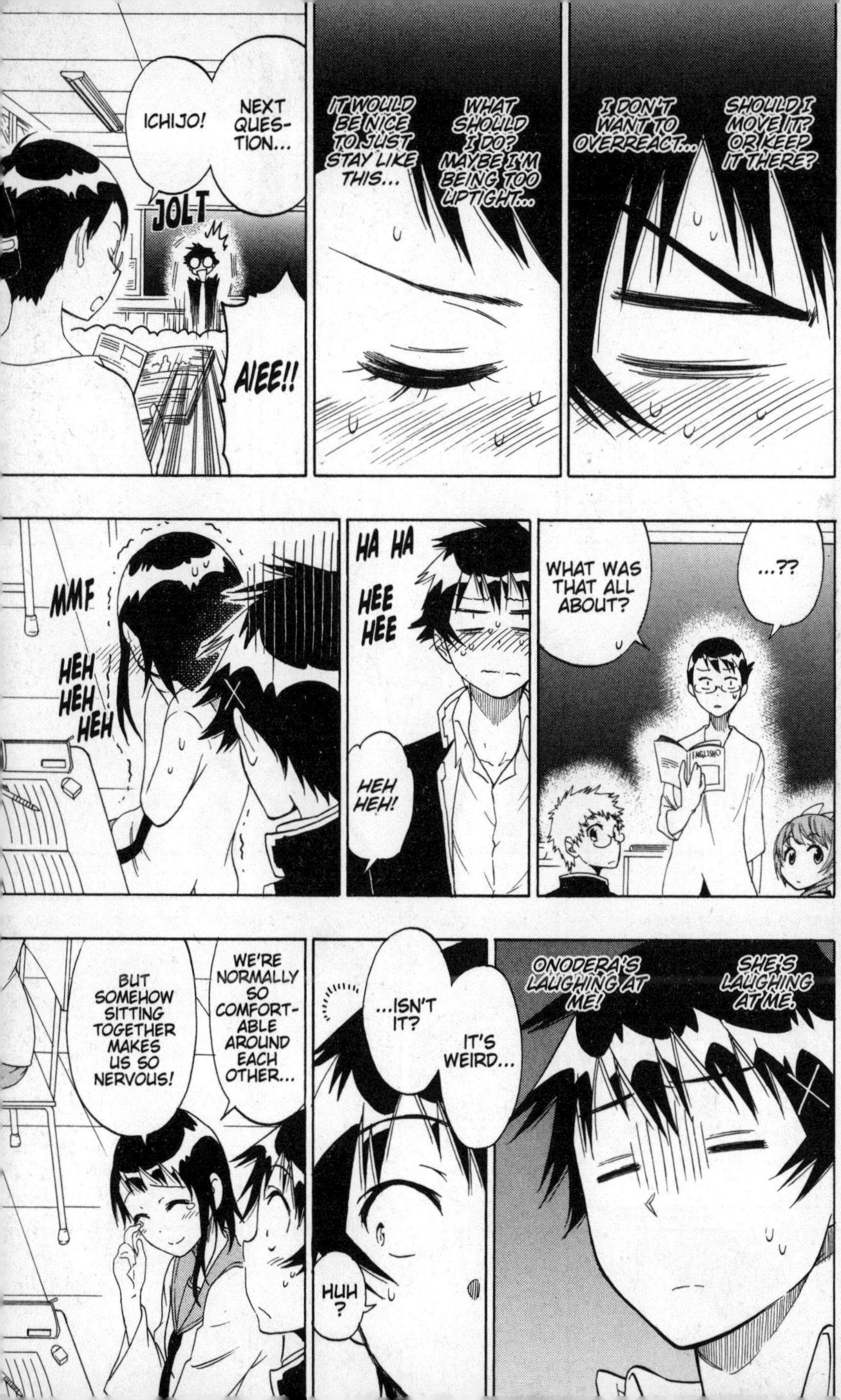
SHOULD I MOVE IT? OR KEEP IT THERE?
I DON'T WANT TO OVERREACT...
WHAT SHOULD I DO? MAYBE I'M BEING TOO UPTIGHT...
IT WOULD BE NICE TO JUST STAY LIKE THIS...
NEXT QUESTION...
ICHIJO!
JOLT
AIEE!!
...??
WHAT WAS THAT ALL ABOUT?
HA HA
HEE HEE
HEH HEH!
MMF
HEH HEH HEH
SHE'S LAUGHING AT ME.
ONODERA'S LAUGHING AT ME!
IT'S WEIRD...
...ISN'T IT?
HUH?
WE'RE NORMALLY SO COMFORTABLE AROUND EACH OTHER...
BUT SOMEHOW SITTING TOGETHER MAKES US SO NERVOUS!

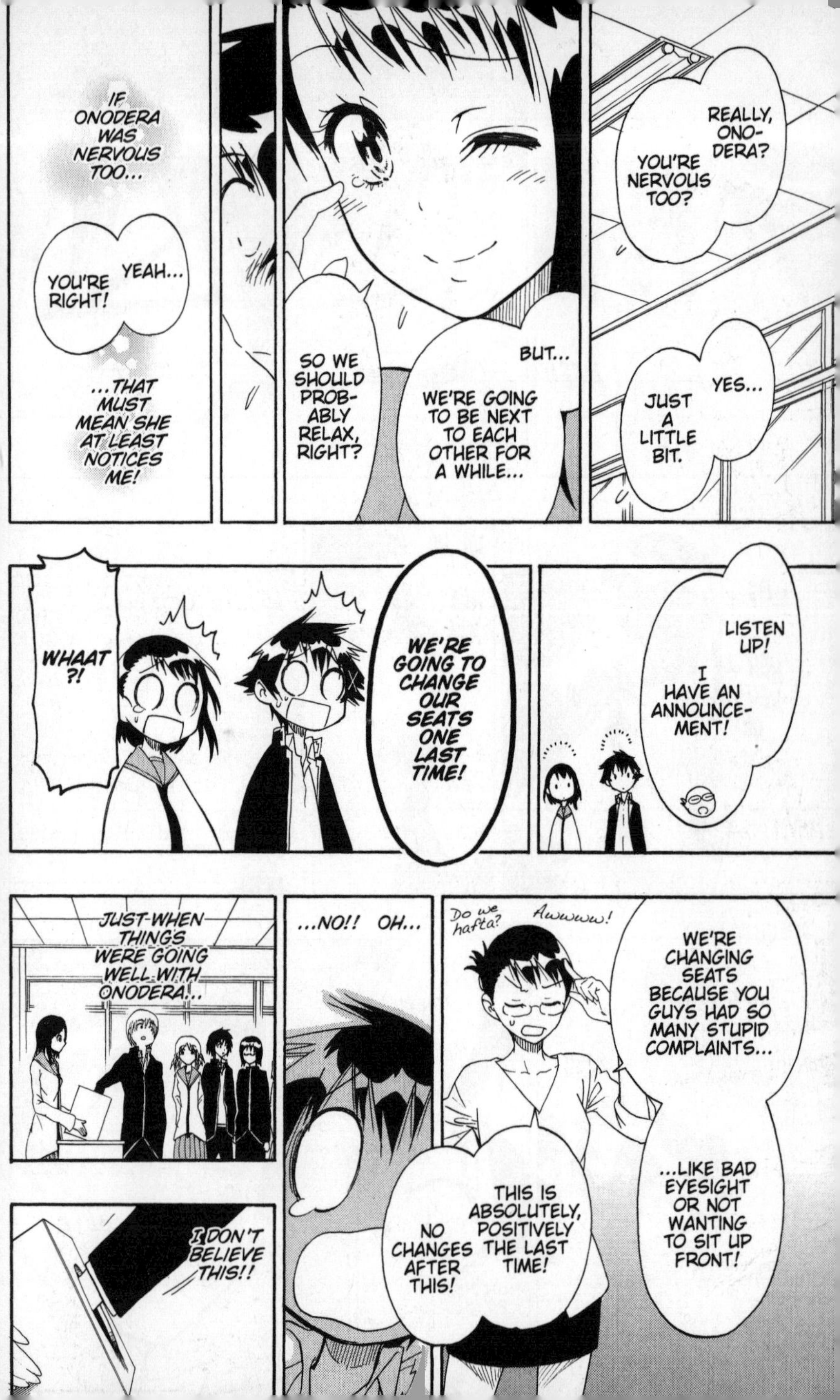
REALLY, ONO-DERA? YOU'RE NERVOUS TOO?
YES... JUST A LITTLE BIT.
BUT... WE'RE GOING TO BE NEXT TO EACH OTHER FOR A WHILE...
SO WE SHOULD PROB-ABLY RELAX, RIGHT?
IF ONODERA WAS NERVOUS TOO...
YEAH... YOU'RE RIGHT!
...THAT MUST MEAN SHE AT LEAST NOTICES ME!
LISTEN UP! I HAVE AN ANNOUNCE-MENT!
WE'RE GOING TO CHANGE OUR SEATS ONE LAST TIME!
WHAAT ?!
Awwww!
Do we hafta?
WE'RE CHANGING SEATS BECAUSE YOU GUYS HAD SO MANY STUPID COMPLAINTS...
...LIKE BAD EYESIGHT OR NOT WANTING TO SIT UP FRONT!
THIS IS ABSOLUTELY, POSITIVELY THE LAST TIME! NO CHANGES AFTER THIS!
OH...
...NO!!
JUST WHEN THINGS WERE GOING WELL WITH ONODERA...
I DON'T BELIEVE THIS!!

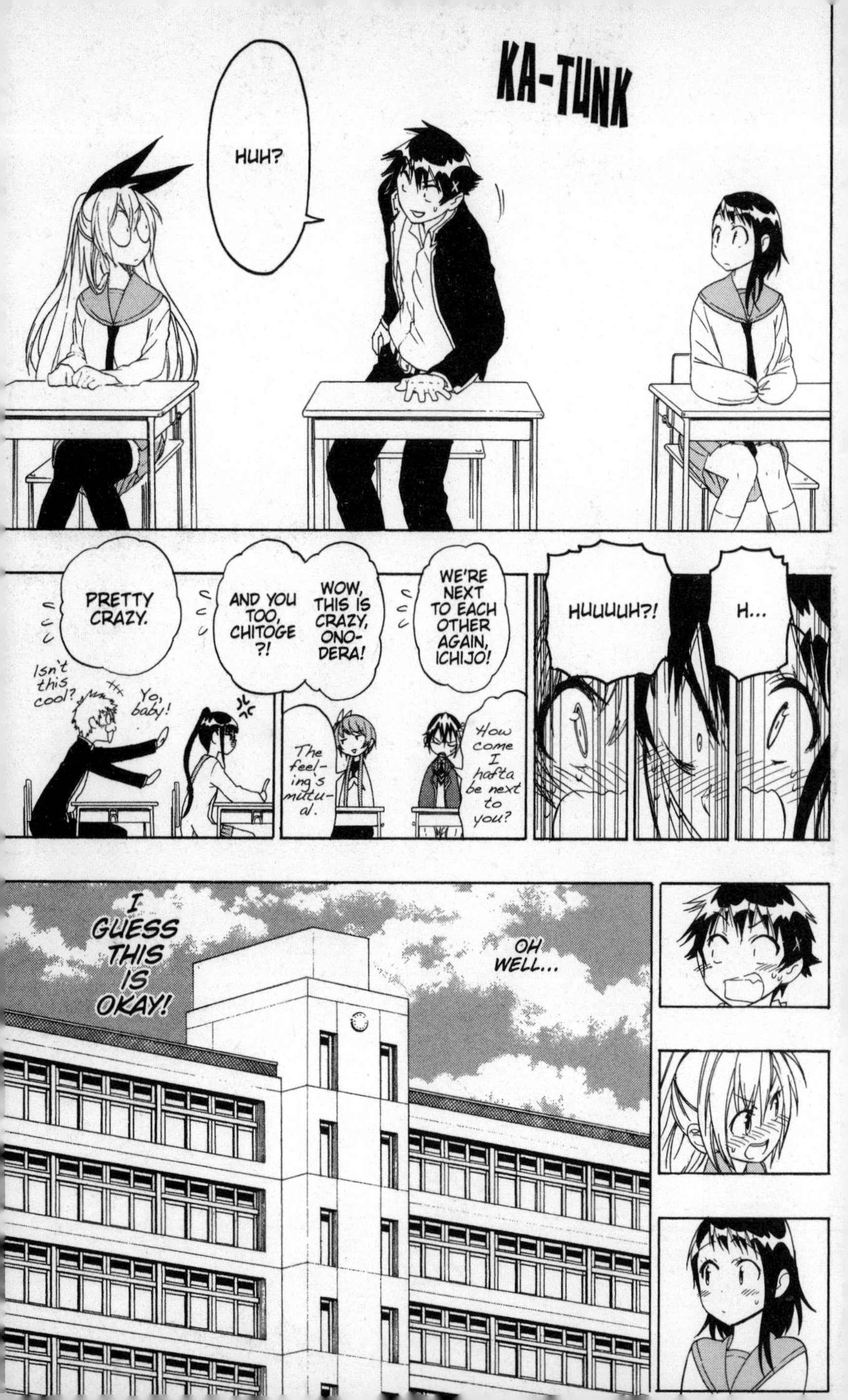
KA-TUNK
HUH?
H...
HUUUUH?!
WE'RE NEXT TO EACH OTHER AGAIN, ICHIJO!
WOW, THIS IS CRAZY, ONODERA!
How come I hafta be next to you?
The feel-ing's mutu-al.
AND YOU TOO, CHITOGE?!
PRETTY CRAZY.
Yo, baby!
Isn't this cool?
OH WELL...
I GUESS THIS IS OKAY!

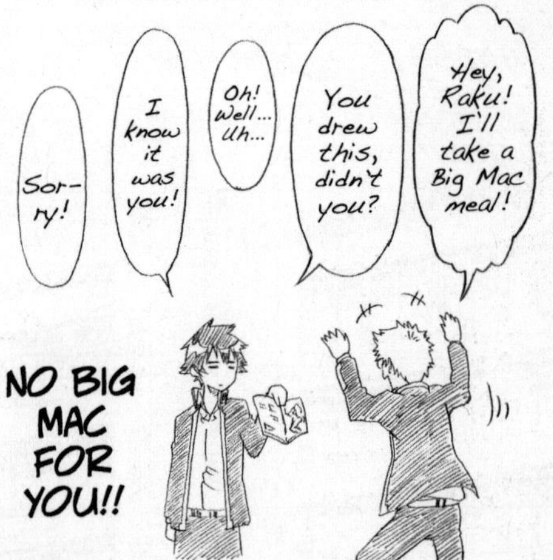
Hey, Raku! I'll take a Big Mac meal!
You drew this, didn't you?
Oh! Well... Uh...
I know it was you!
Sor-ry!
NO BIG MAC FOR YOU!!

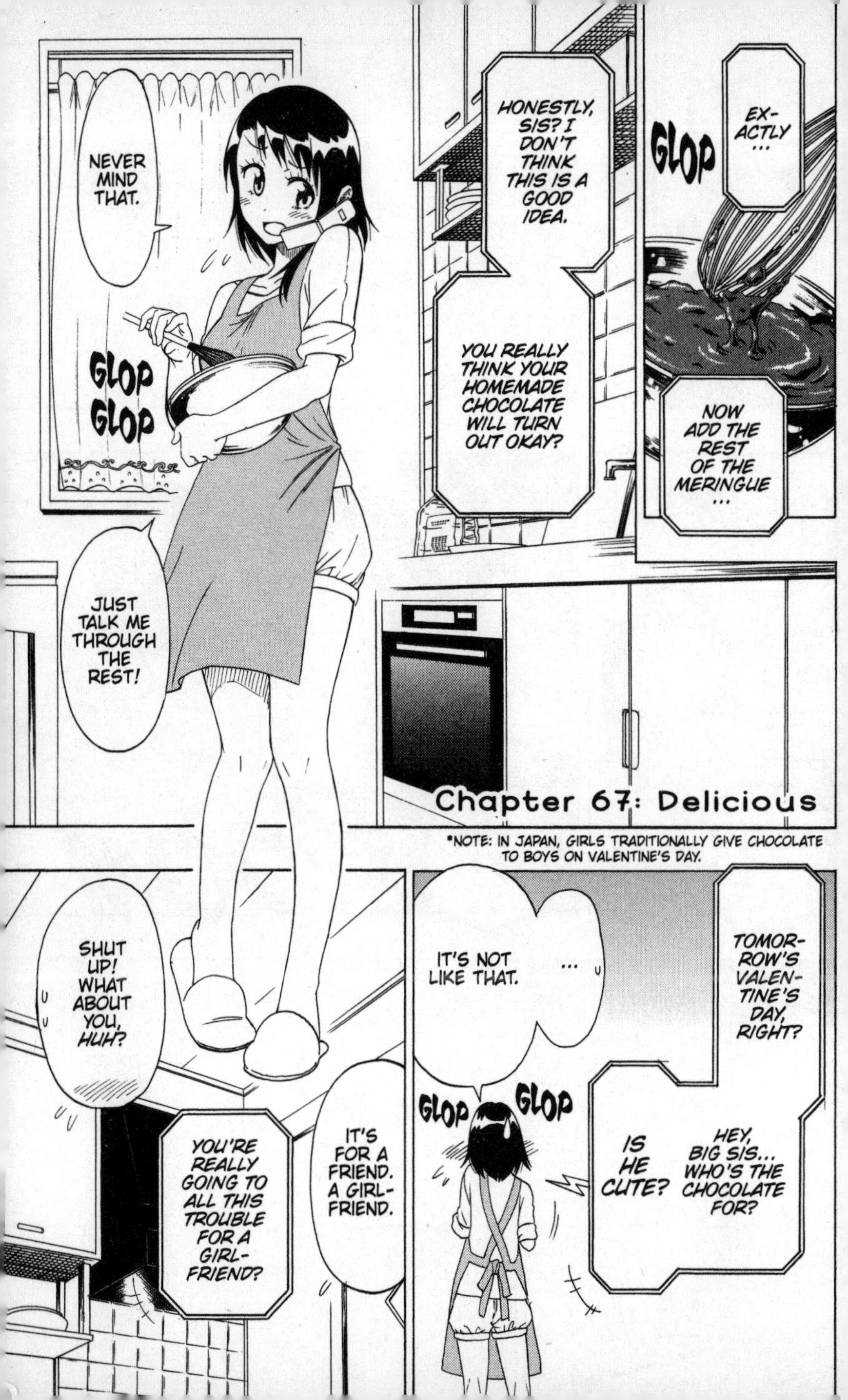
EX-ACTLY...
GLOP
NOW ADD THE REST OF THE MERINGUE...
HONESTLY, SIS? I DON'T THINK THIS IS A GOOD IDEA.
YOU REALLY THINK YOUR HOMEMADE CHOCOLATE WILL TURN OUT OKAY?
NEVER MIND THAT.
GLOP GLOP
JUST TALK ME THROUGH THE REST!
Chapter 67: Delicious
*NOTE: IN JAPAN, GIRLS TRADITIONALLY GIVE CHOCOLATE TO BOYS ON VALENTINE'S DAY.
TOMORROW'S VALENTINE'S DAY, RIGHT?
HEY, BIG SIS... WHO'S THE CHOCOLATE FOR?
IS HE CUTE?
...
IT'S NOT LIKE THAT.
GLOP
GLOP
IT'S FOR A FRIEND. A GIRLFRIEND.
YOU'RE REALLY GOING TO ALL THIS TROUBLE FOR A GIRLFRIEND?
SHUT UP! WHAT ABOUT YOU, HUH?

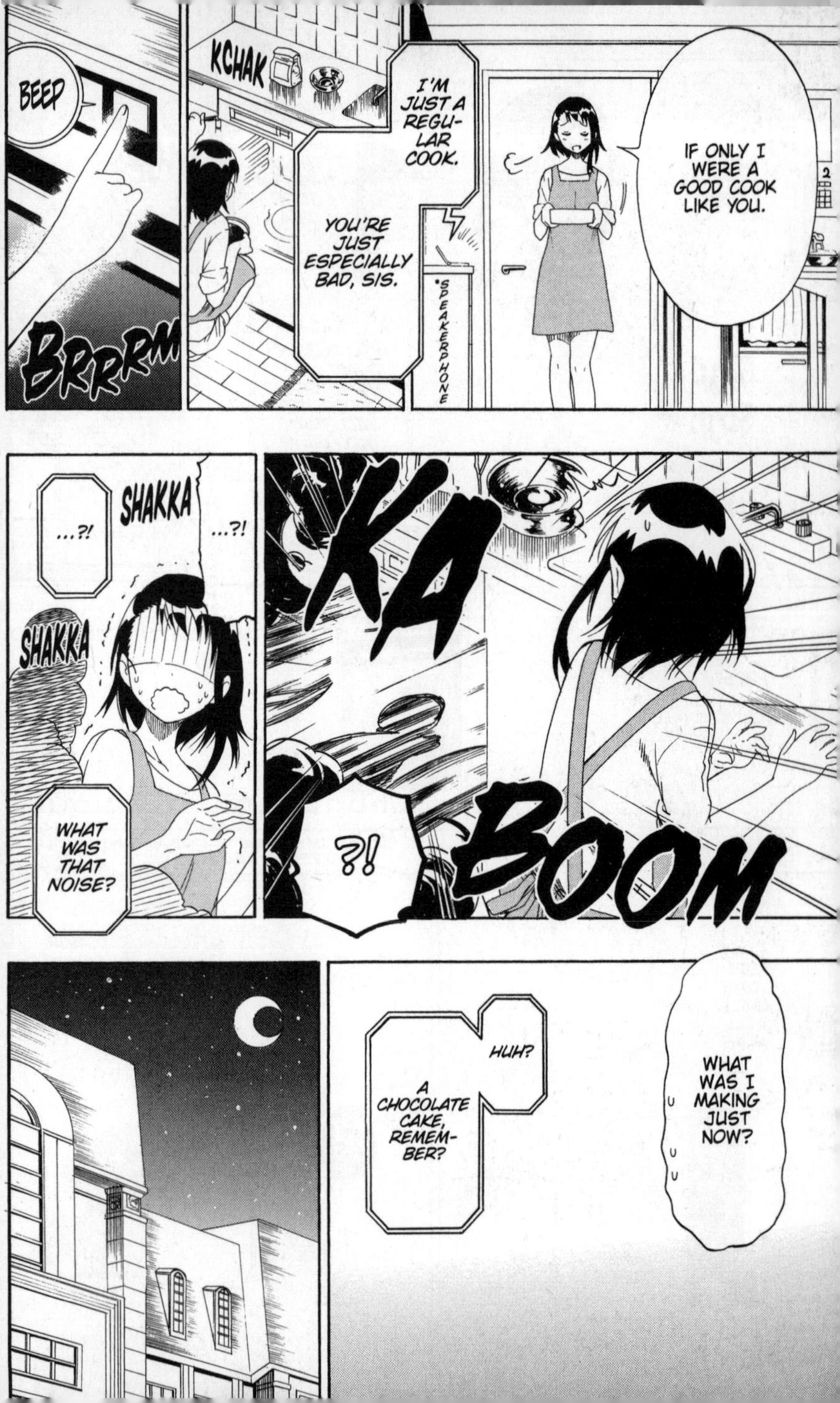
IF ONLY I WERE A GOOD COOK LIKE YOU.
KCHAK
I'M JUST A REGULAR COOK.
YOU'RE JUST ESPECIALLY BAD, SIS.
*SPEAKERPHONE
BEEP
BRRRM
KA
BOOM
?!
...?!
SHAKKA
...?!
SHAKKA
WHAT WAS THAT NOISE?
WHAT WAS I MAKING JUST NOW?
HUH?
A CHOCOLATE CAKE, REMEMBER?

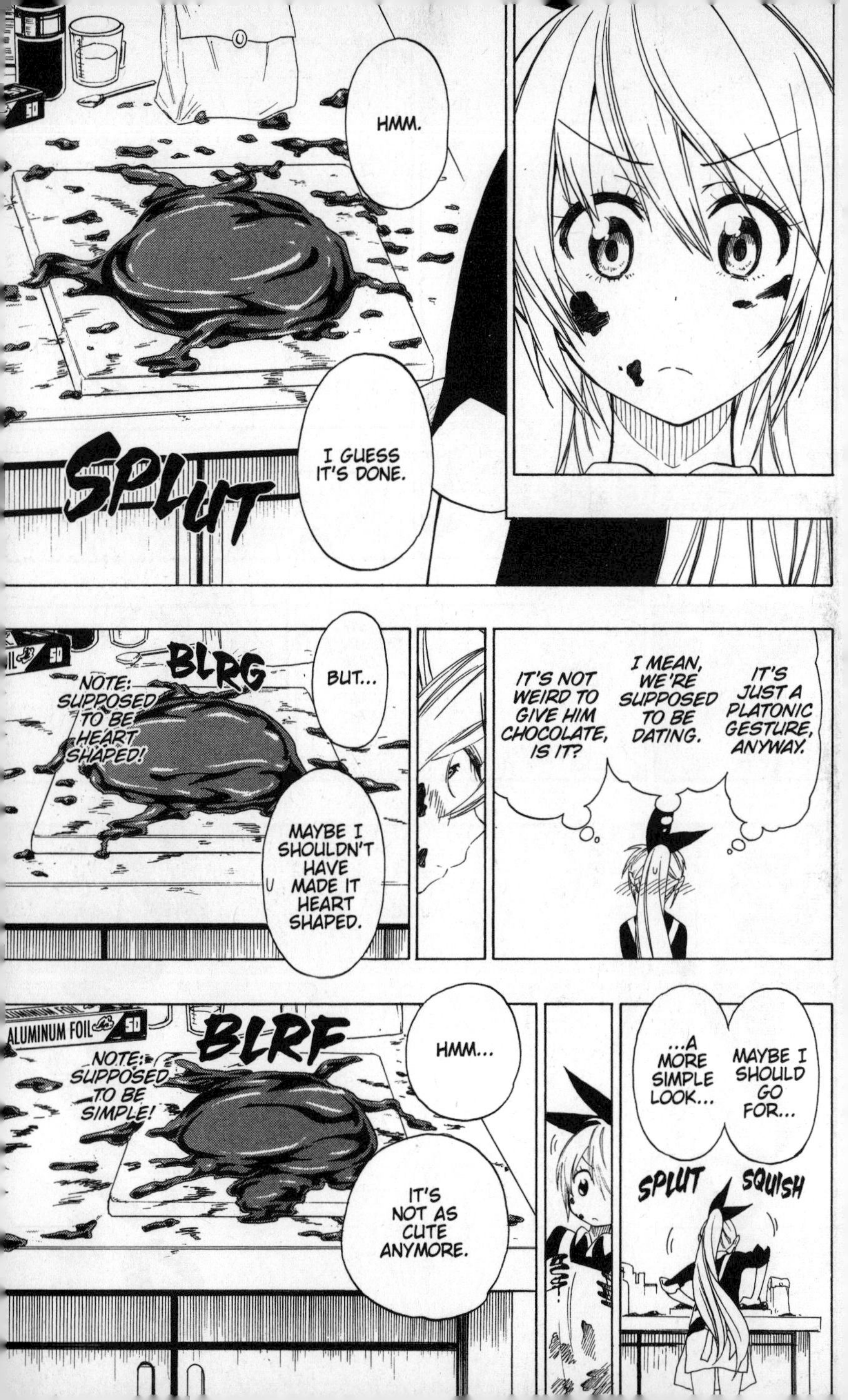
HMM.
I GUESS IT'S DONE.
SPLUT
IT'S JUST A PLATONIC GESTURE, ANYWAY.
I MEAN, WE'RE SUPPOSED TO BE DATING.
IT'S NOT WEIRD TO GIVE HIM CHOCOLATE, IS IT?
BUT...
BLRG
NOTE: SUPPOSED TO BE HEART SHAPED!
MAYBE I SHOULDN'T HAVE MADE IT HEART SHAPED.
MAYBE I SHOULD GO FOR...
...A MORE SIMPLE LOOK...
SQUISH
SPLUT
HMM...
BLRF
ALUMINUM FOIL
50
NOTE: SUPPOSED TO BE SIMPLE!
IT'S NOT AS CUTE ANYMORE.

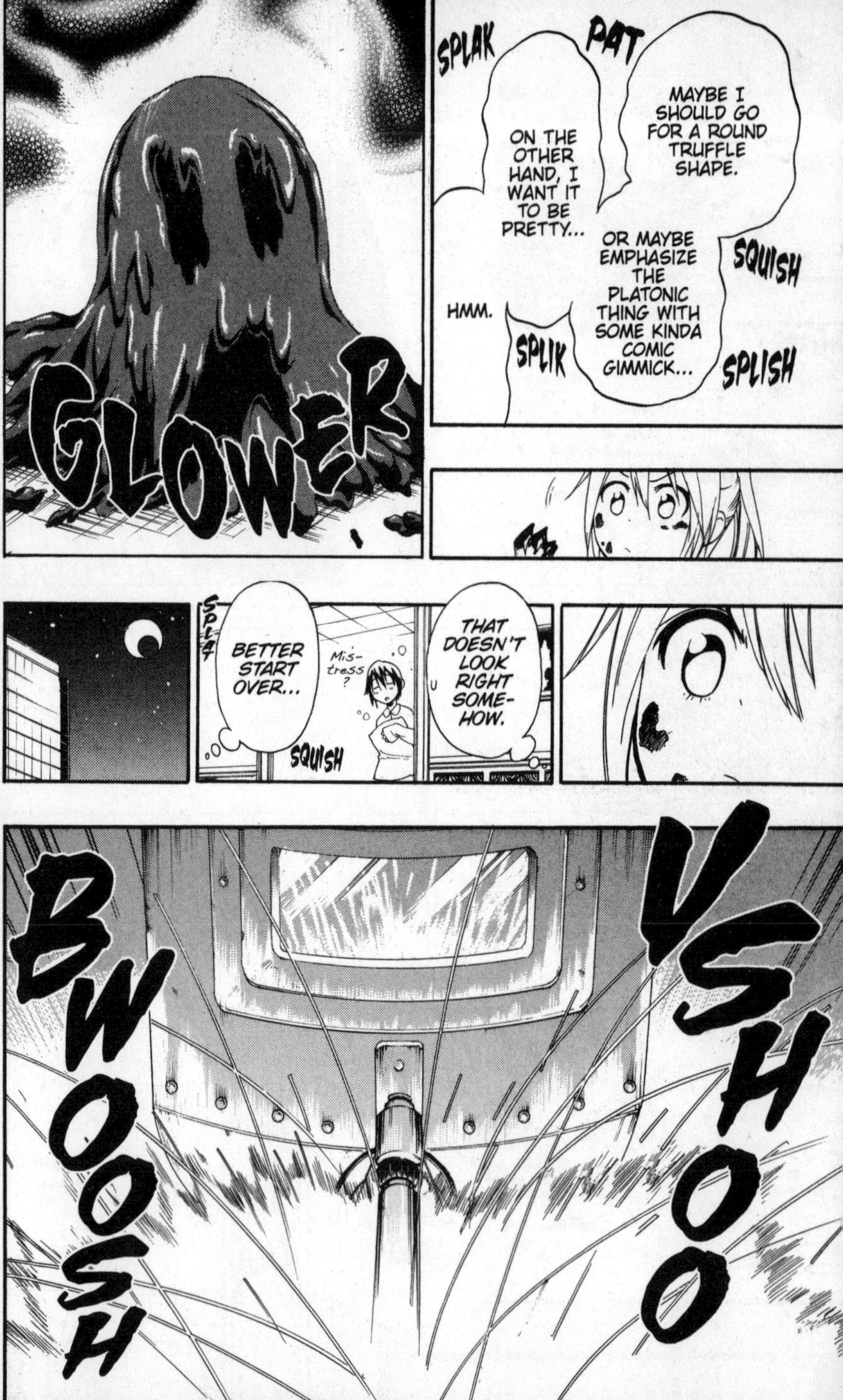
PAT
MAYBE I SHOULD GO FOR A ROUND TRUFFLE SHAPE.
SPLAK
ON THE OTHER HAND, I WANT IT TO BE PRETTY...
SQUISH
OR MAYBE EMPHASIZE THE PLATONIC THING WITH SOME KINDA COMIC GIMMICK...
SPLISH
SPLIK
HMM.
GLOWER
THAT DOESN'T LOOK RIGHT SOMEHOW.
Mis-tress?
BETTER START OVER...
SQUISH
VSHOOO
BWOOOSH

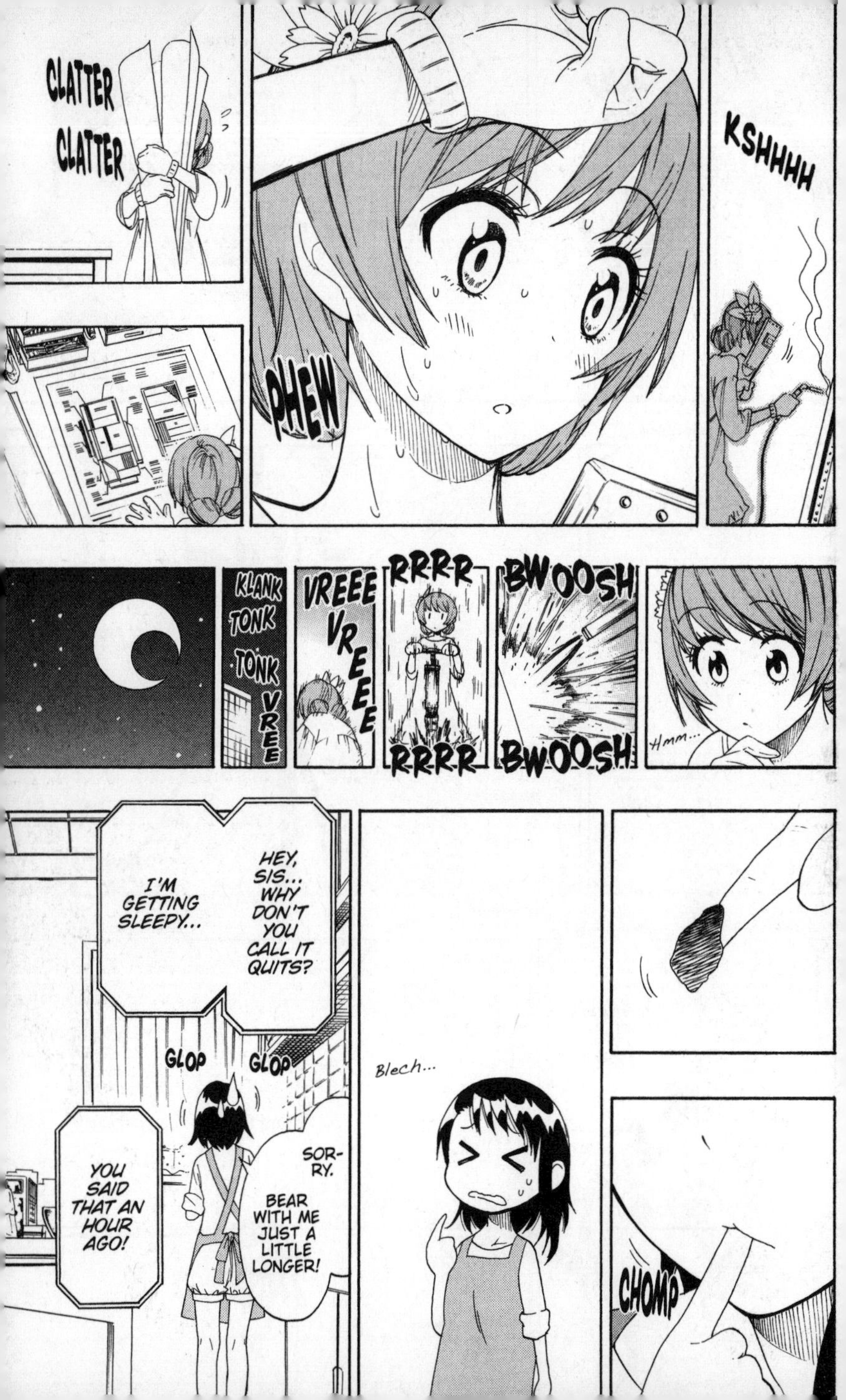
KSHHHH
PHEW
CLATTER
CLATTER
Hmm...
BWOOSH
BWOOSH
RRRR
RRRR
VREEE
VREEE
KLANK
TONK
TONK
VREE
CHOMP
Blech...
HEY, SIS... WHY DON'T YOU CALL IT QUITS?
I'M GETTING SLEEPY...
GLOP
GLOP
SORRY. BEAR WITH ME JUST A LITTLE LONGER!
YOU SAID THAT AN HOUR AGO!

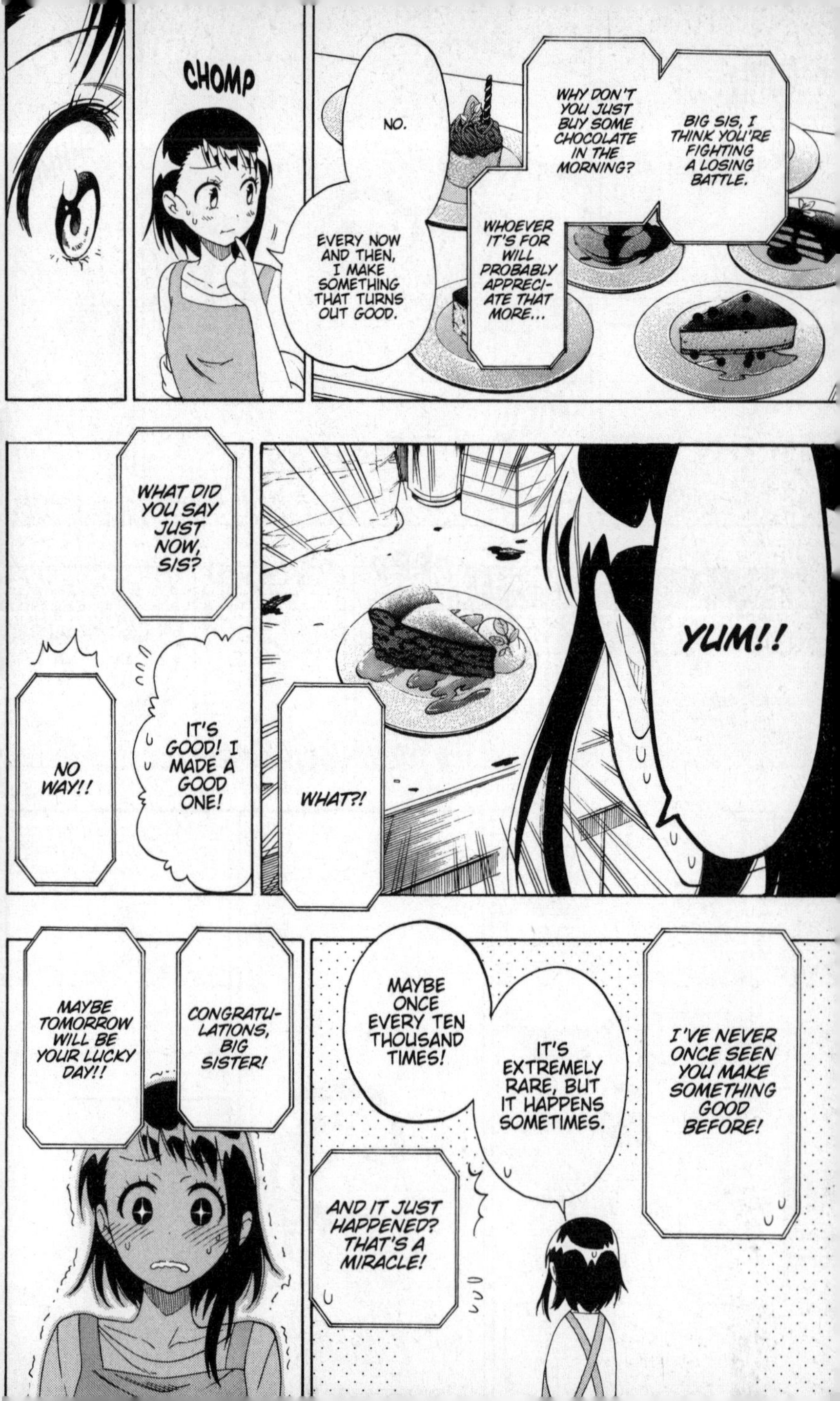
BIG SIS, I THINK YOU'RE FIGHTING A LOSING BATTLE.
WHY DON'T YOU JUST BUY SOME CHOCOLATE IN THE MORNING?
WHOEVER IT'S FOR WILL PROBABLY APPRECIATE THAT MORE...
NO.
EVERY NOW AND THEN, I MAKE SOMETHING THAT TURNS OUT GOOD.
CHOMP
YUM!!
WHAT?!
WHAT DID YOU SAY JUST NOW, SIS?
IT'S GOOD! I MADE A GOOD ONE!
NO WAY!!
I'VE NEVER ONCE SEEN YOU MAKE SOMETHING GOOD BEFORE!
IT'S EXTREMELY RARE, BUT IT HAPPENS SOMETIMES.
MAYBE ONCE EVERY TEN THOUSAND TIMES!
AND IT JUST HAPPENED? THAT'S A MIRACLE!
CONGRATULATIONS, BIG SISTER!
MAYBE TOMORROW WILL BE YOUR LUCKY DAY!!

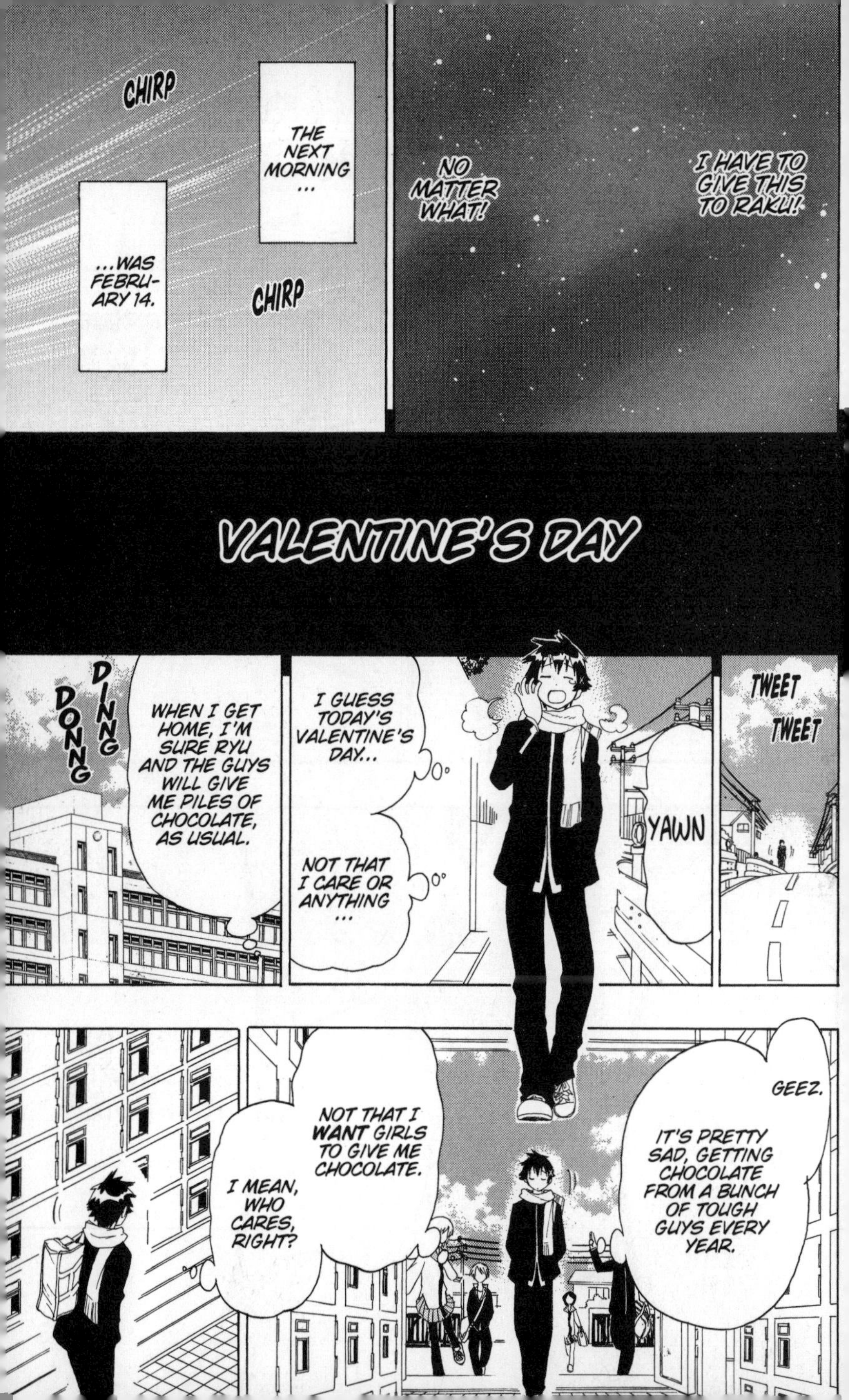
I HAVE TO GIVE THIS TO RAKU!
NO MATTER WHAT!
THE NEXT MORNING...
CHIRP
...WAS FEBRU-ARY 14.
CHIRP
VALENTINE'S DAY
TWEET
TWEET
YAWN
I GUESS TODAY'S VALENTINE'S DAY...
NOT THAT I CARE OR ANYTHING...
DING
DONG
WHEN I GET HOME, I'M SURE RYU AND THE GUYS WILL GIVE ME PILES OF CHOCOLATE, AS USUAL.
GEEZ.
IT'S PRETTY SAD, GETTING CHOCOLATE FROM A BUNCH OF TOUGH GUYS EVERY YEAR.
NOT THAT I WANT GIRLS TO GIVE ME CHOCOLATE.
I MEAN, WHO CARES, RIGHT?

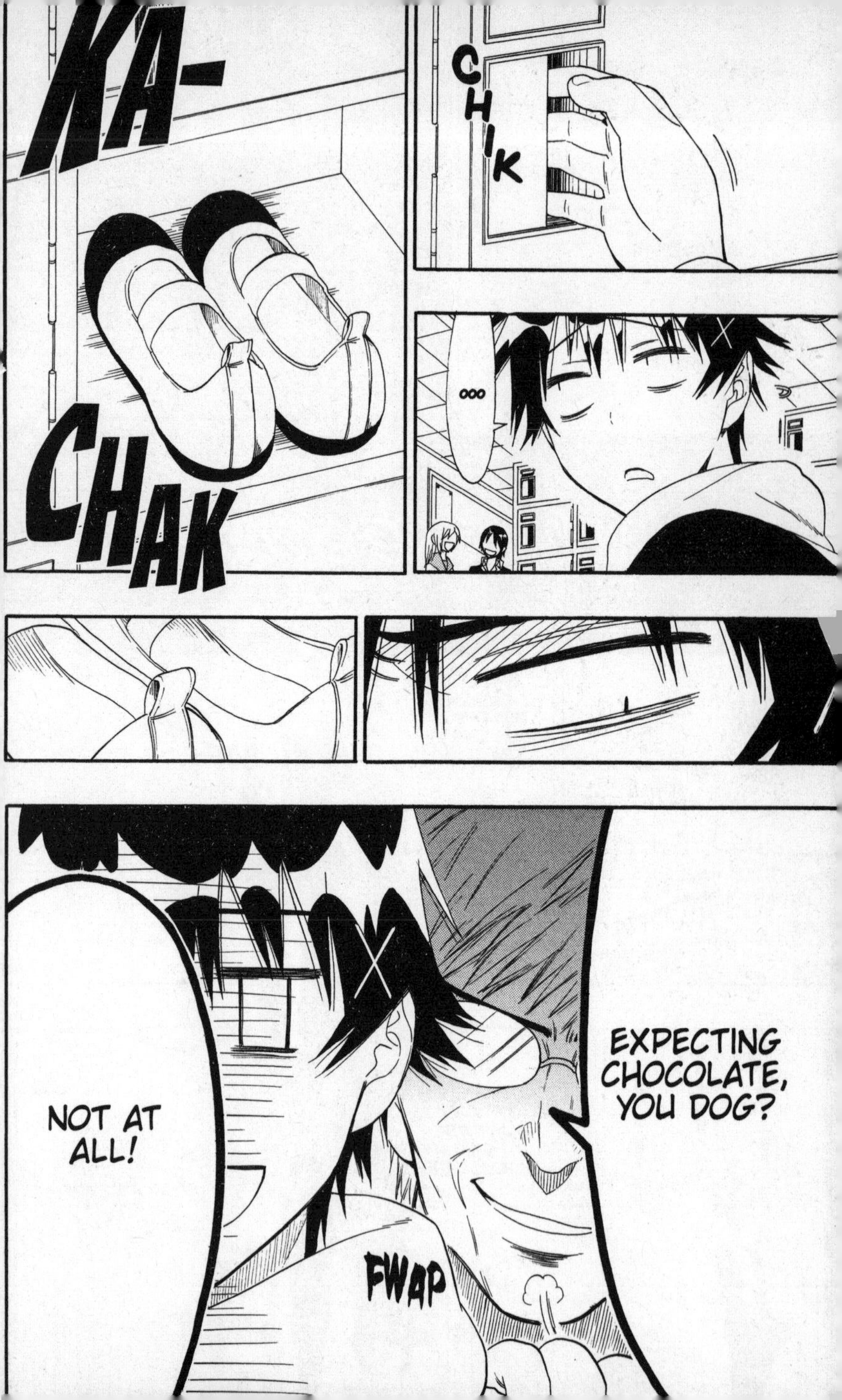
CHIK
...
KA-CHAK
EXPECTING CHOCOLATE, YOU DOG?
NOT AT ALL!
FWAP

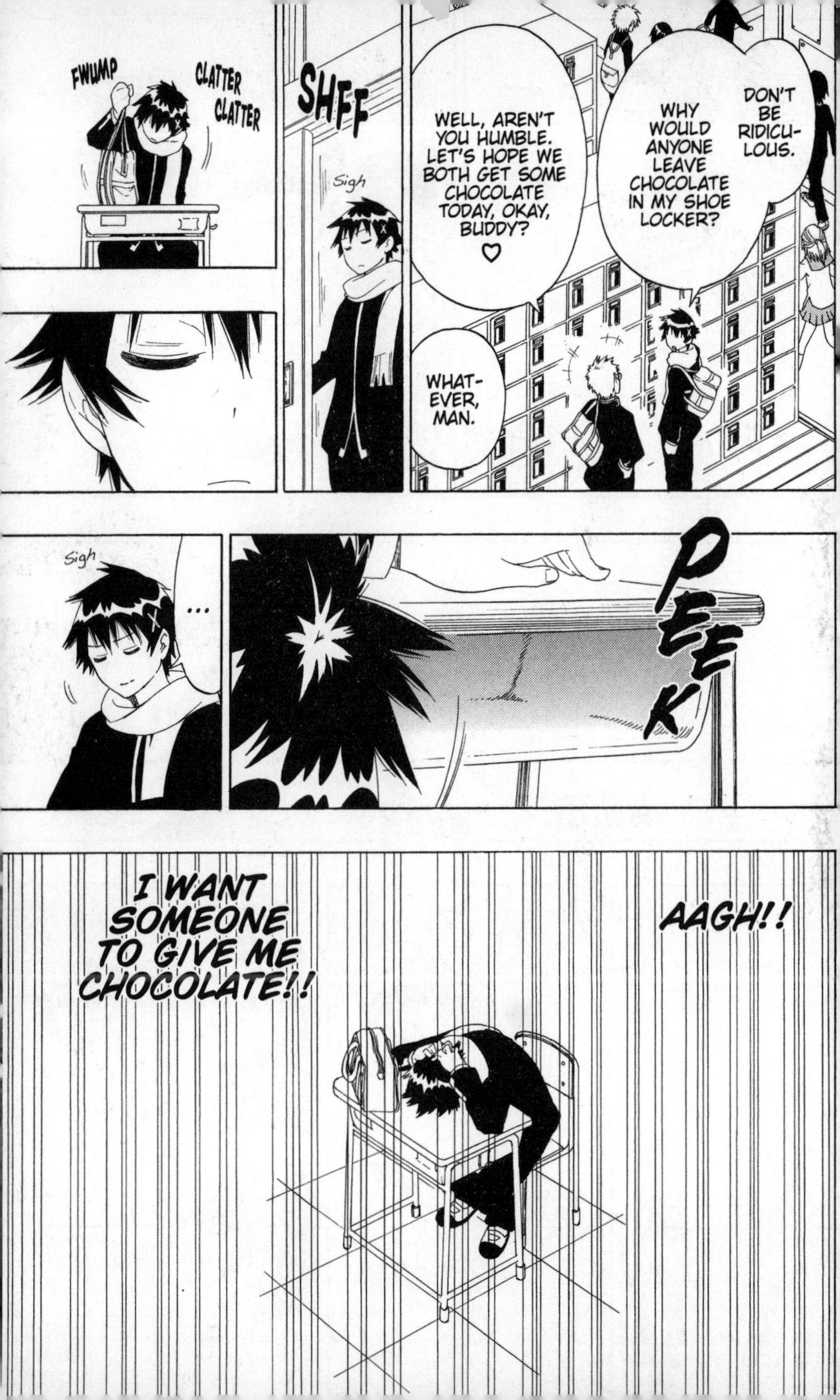
DON'T BE RIDICULOUS.
WHY WOULD ANYONE LEAVE CHOCOLATE IN MY SHOE LOCKER?
WELL, AREN'T YOU HUMBLE. LET'S HOPE WE BOTH GET SOME CHOCOLATE TODAY, OKAY, BUDDY? ♡
WHAT-EVER, MAN.
SHFF
Sigh
CLATTER CLATTER
FWUMP
PEEK
...
Sigh
AAGH!!
I WANT SOMEONE TO GIVE ME CHOCOLATE!!

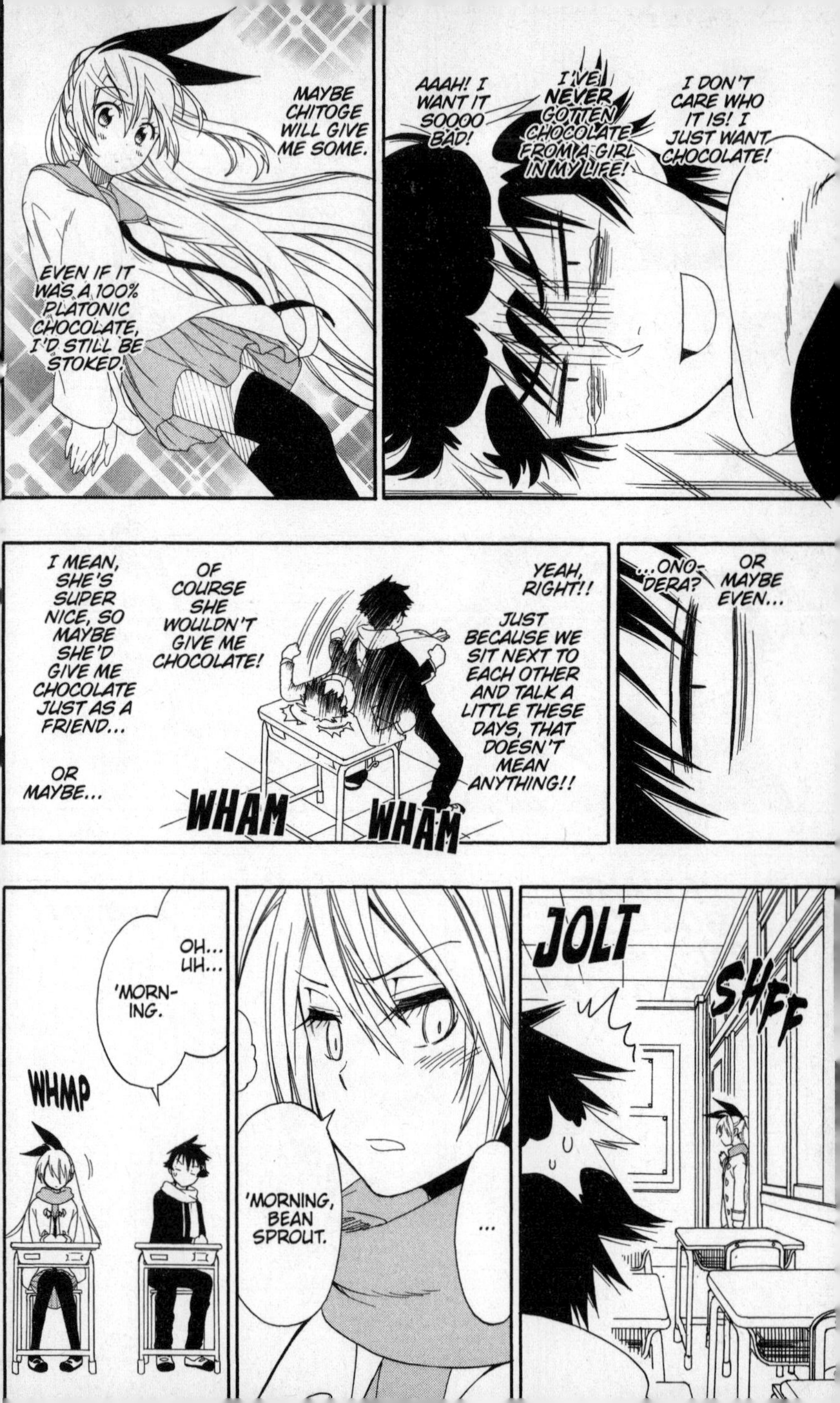
I DON'T CARE WHO IT IS! I JUST WANT CHOCOLATE!
I'VE NEVER GOTTEN CHOCOLATE FROM A GIRL IN MY LIFE!
AAAH! I WANT IT SOOOO BAD!
MAYBE CHITOGE WILL GIVE ME SOME.
EVEN IF IT WAS A 100% PLATONIC CHOCOLATE, I'D STILL BE STOKED.
OR MAYBE EVEN...
...ONO-DERA?
YEAH, RIGHT!!
JUST BECAUSE WE SIT NEXT TO EACH OTHER AND TALK A LITTLE THESE DAYS, THAT DOESN'T MEAN ANYTHING!!
WHAM
WHAM
OF COURSE SHE WOULDN'T GIVE ME CHOCOLATE!
I MEAN, SHE'S SUPER NICE, SO MAYBE SHE'D GIVE ME CHOCOLATE JUST AS A FRIEND...
OR MAYBE...
JOLT
SHFF
...
'MORNING, BEAN SPROUT.
OH... UH...
'MORN-ING.
WHMP

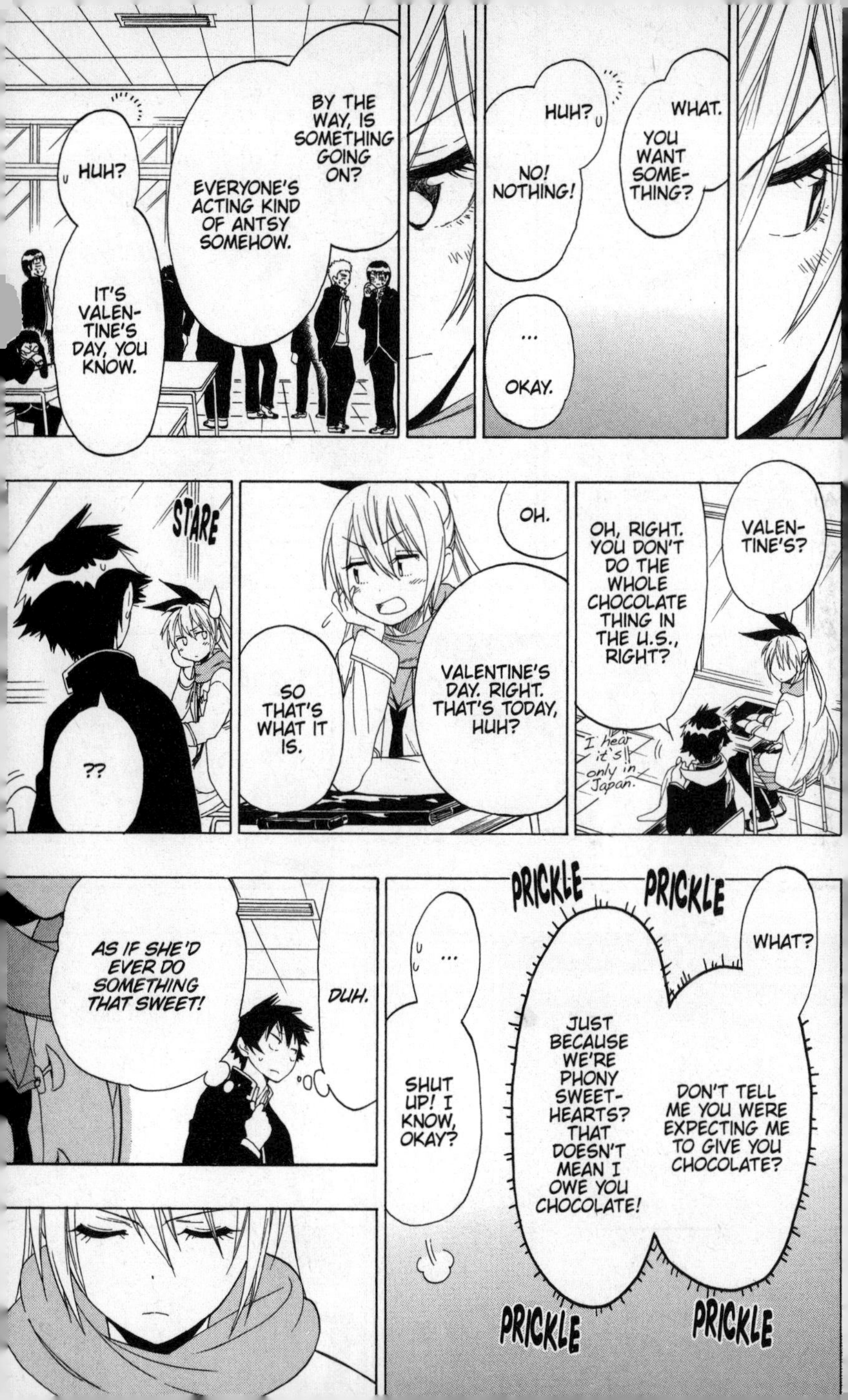
WHAT.
YOU WANT SOMETHING?
HUH?
NO! NOTHING!
...
OKAY.
BY THE WAY, IS SOMETHING GOING ON?
EVERYONE'S ACTING KIND OF ANTSY SOMEHOW.
HUH?
IT'S VALENTINE'S DAY, YOU KNOW.
VALENTINE'S?
OH, RIGHT. YOU DON'T DO THE WHOLE CHOCOLATE THING IN THE U.S., RIGHT?
I hear it's only in Japan.
OH.
VALENTINE'S DAY. RIGHT. THAT'S TODAY, HUH?
SO THAT'S WHAT IT IS.
STARE
??
PRICKLE
PRICKLE
WHAT?
DON'T TELL ME YOU WERE EXPECTING ME TO GIVE YOU CHOCOLATE?
JUST BECAUSE WE'RE PHONY SWEETHEARTS? THAT DOESN'T MEAN I OWE YOU CHOCOLATE!
PRICKLE
PRICKLE
...
SHUT UP! I KNOW, OKAY?
DUH.
AS IF SHE'D EVER DO SOMETHING THAT SWEET!

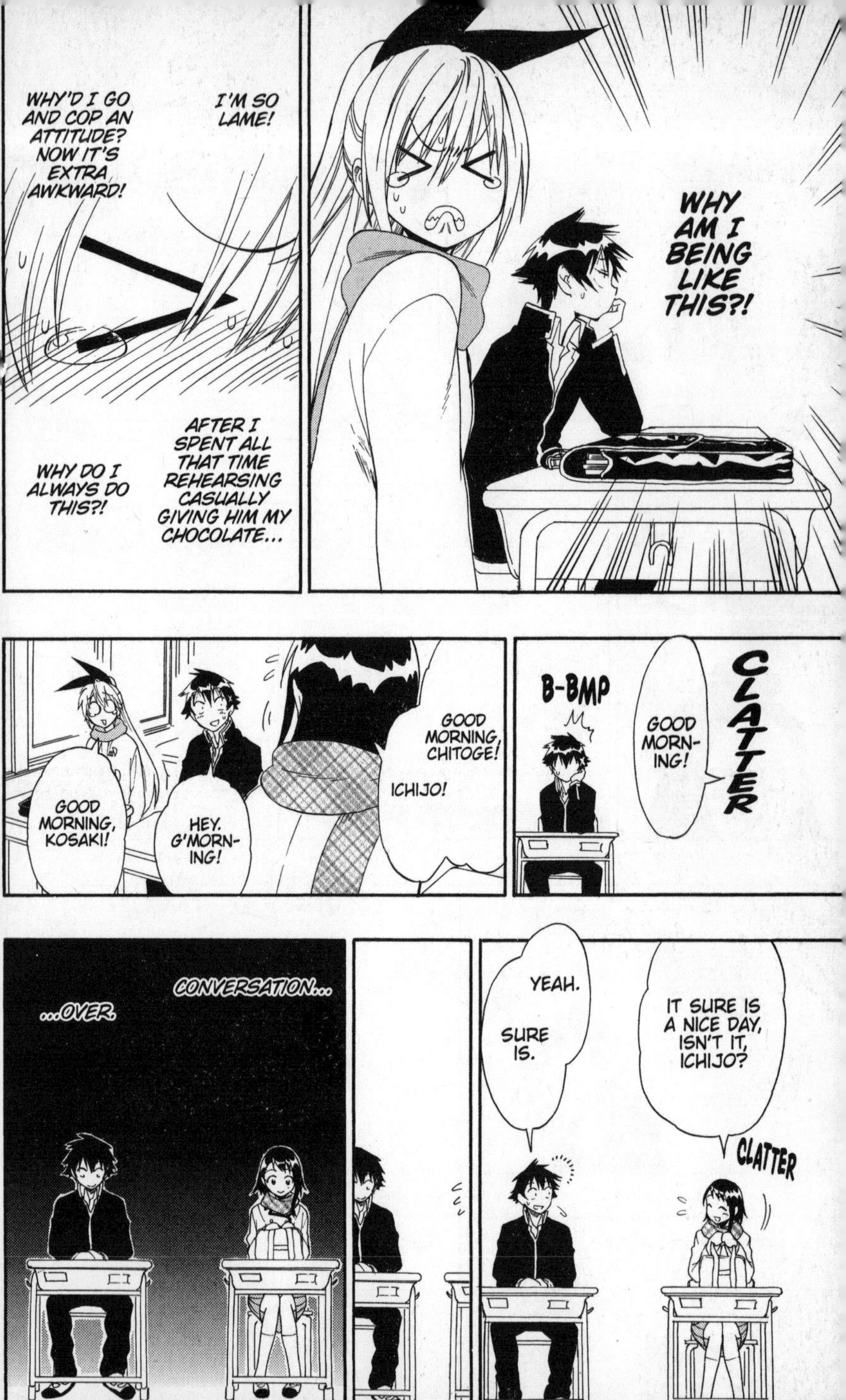
WHY AM I BEING LIKE THIS?!
I'M SO LAME!
WHY'D I GO AND COP AN ATTITUDE? NOW IT'S EXTRA AWKWARD!
AFTER I SPENT ALL THAT TIME REHEARSING CASUALLY GIVING HIM MY CHOCOLATE...
WHY DO I ALWAYS DO THIS?!
CLATTER
GOOD MORN-ING!
B-BMP
GOOD MORNING, CHITOGE!
ICHIJO!
HEY. G'MORN-ING!
GOOD MORNING, KOSAKI!
IT SURE IS A NICE DAY, ISN'T IT, ICHIJO?
CLATTER
YEAH.
SURE IS.
CONVERSATION...
...OVER.

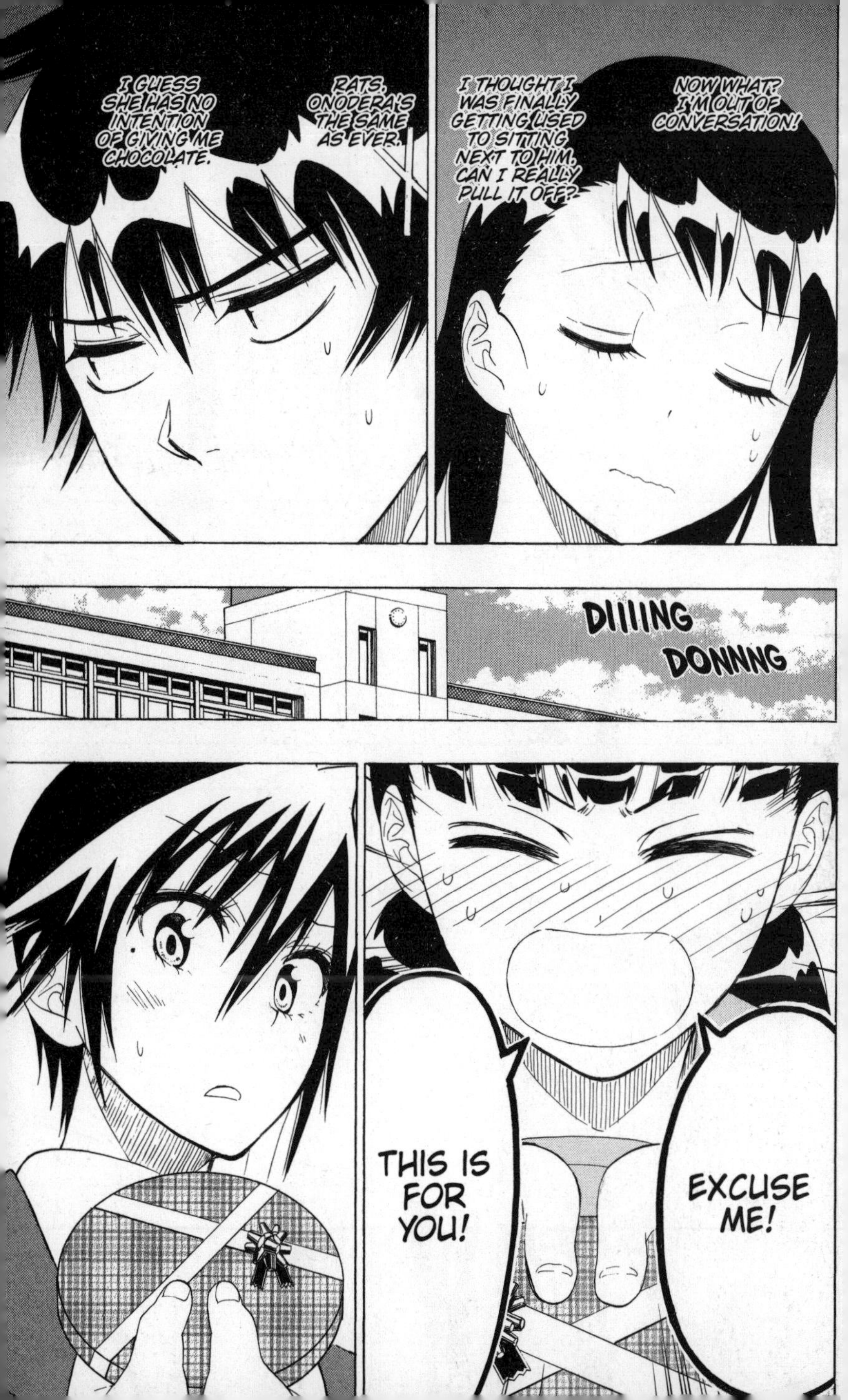
NOW WHAT? I'M OUT OF CONVERSATION!
I THOUGHT I WAS FINALLY GETTING USED TO SITTING NEXT TO HIM. CAN I REALLY PULL IT OFF?
RATS, ONODERA'S THE SAME AS EVER.
I GUESS SHE HAS NO INTENTION OF GIVING ME CHOCOLATE.
DIIIING
DONNNG
EXCUSE ME!
THIS IS FOR YOU!

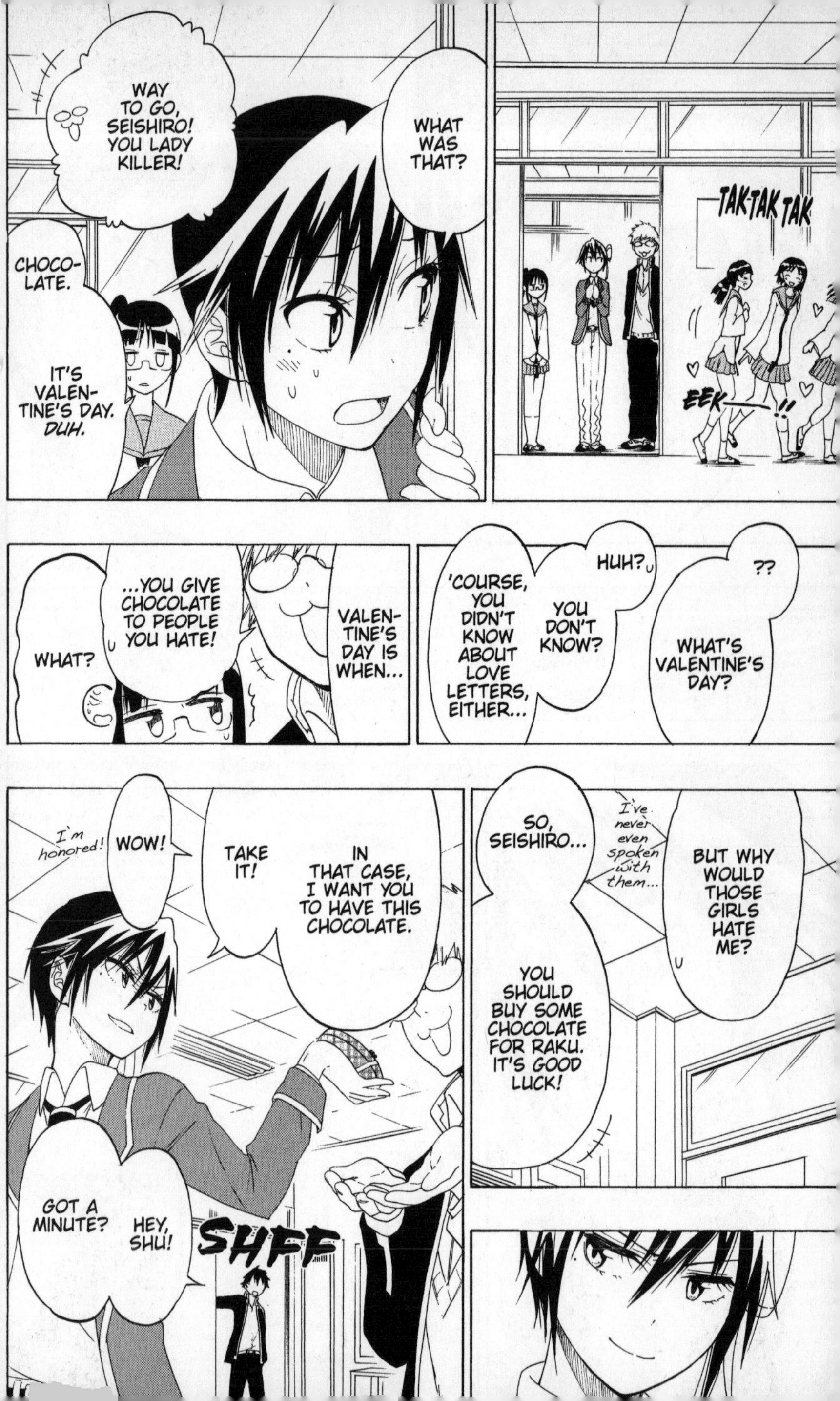
TAK-TAK TAK
EEK!!
WHAT WAS THAT?
WAY TO GO, SEISHIRO! YOU LADY KILLER!
CHOCOLATE.
IT'S VALENTINE'S DAY. DUH.
??
WHAT'S VALENTINE'S DAY?
HUH?
YOU DON'T KNOW?
'COURSE, YOU DIDN'T KNOW ABOUT LOVE LETTERS, EITHER...
VALENTINE'S DAY IS WHEN...
...YOU GIVE CHOCOLATE TO PEOPLE YOU HATE!
WHAT?
BUT WHY WOULD THOSE GIRLS HATE ME?
I've never even spoken with them...
SO, SEISHIRO...
YOU SHOULD BUY SOME CHOCOLATE FOR RAKU. IT'S GOOD LUCK!
IN THAT CASE, I WANT YOU TO HAVE THIS CHOCOLATE.
TAKE IT!
WOW!
I'm honored!
HEY, SHU!
GOT A MINUTE?
SHFF

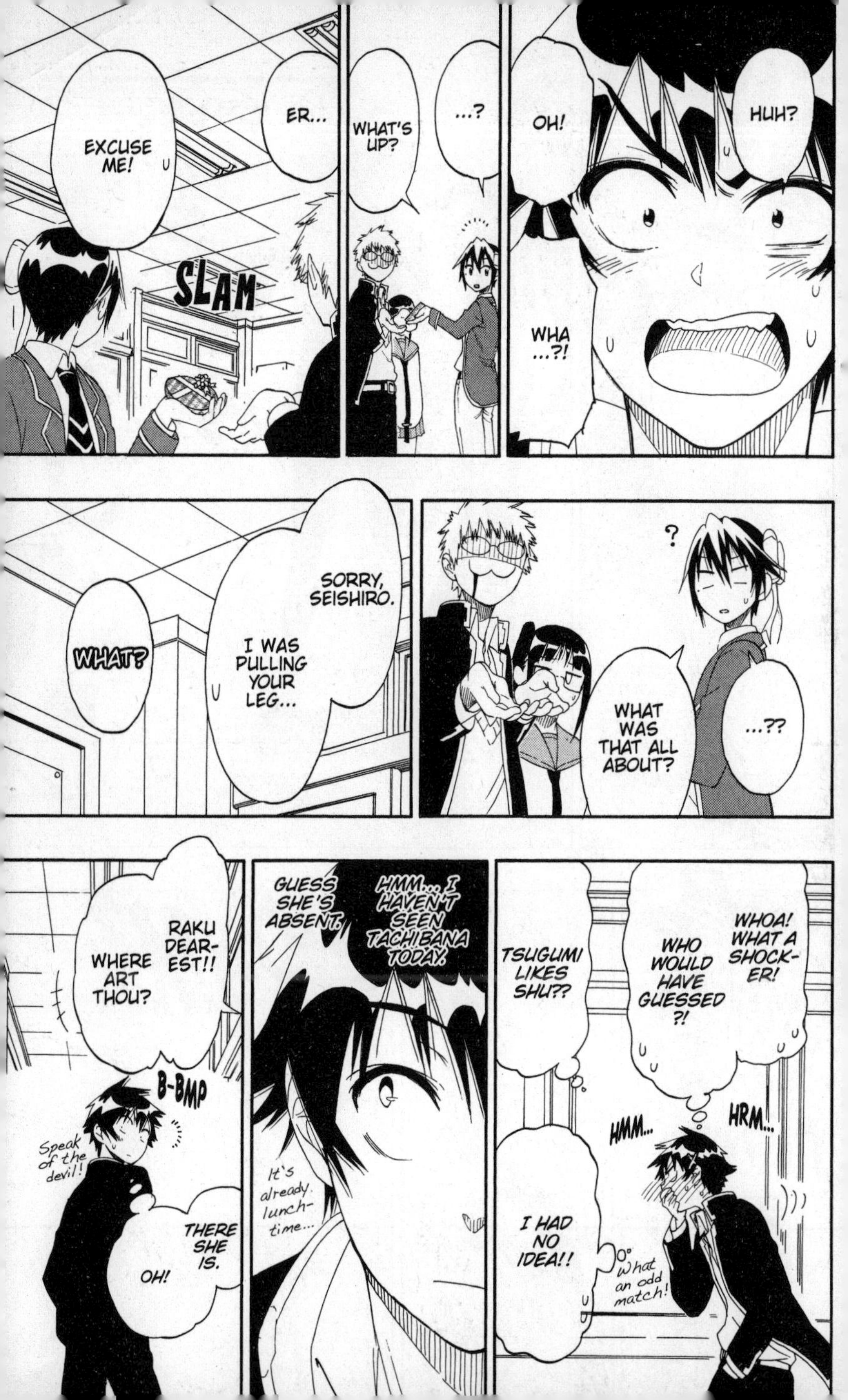
HUH?
OH!
WHA...?!
...?
WHAT'S UP?
ER...
EXCUSE ME!
SLAM
?
...??
WHAT WAS THAT ALL ABOUT?
SORRY, SEISHIRO.
I WAS PULLING YOUR LEG...
WHAT?
WHOA! WHAT A SHOCKER!
WHO WOULD HAVE GUESSED?!
TSUGUMI LIKES SHU??
HRM...
HMM...
I HAD NO IDEA!!
What an odd match!
HMM... I HAVEN'T SEEN TACHIBANA TODAY.
GUESS SHE'S ABSENT.
It's already lunchtime...
RAKU DEAREST!!
WHERE ART THOU?
B-BMP
Speak of the devil!
THERE SHE IS.
OH!

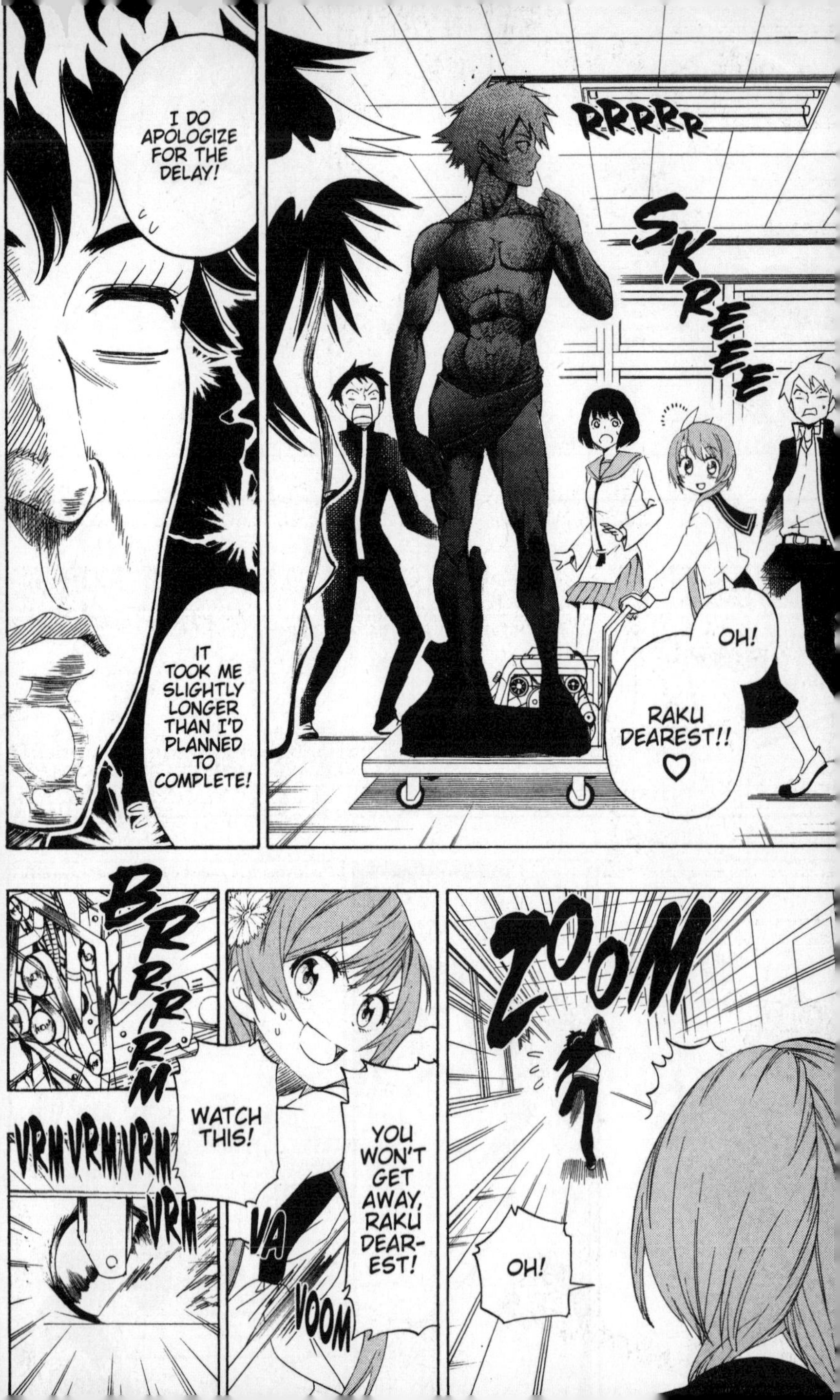
RRRRR
SKREEE
OH!
RAKU DEAREST!! ♡
I DO APOLOGIZE FOR THE DELAY!
IT TOOK ME SLIGHTLY LONGER THAN I'D PLANNED TO COMPLETE!
ZOOM
OH!
WATCH THIS!
YOU WON'T GET AWAY, RAKU DEAR-EST!
VA VOOM
BRRRRM
VRMVRMVRM
VRM

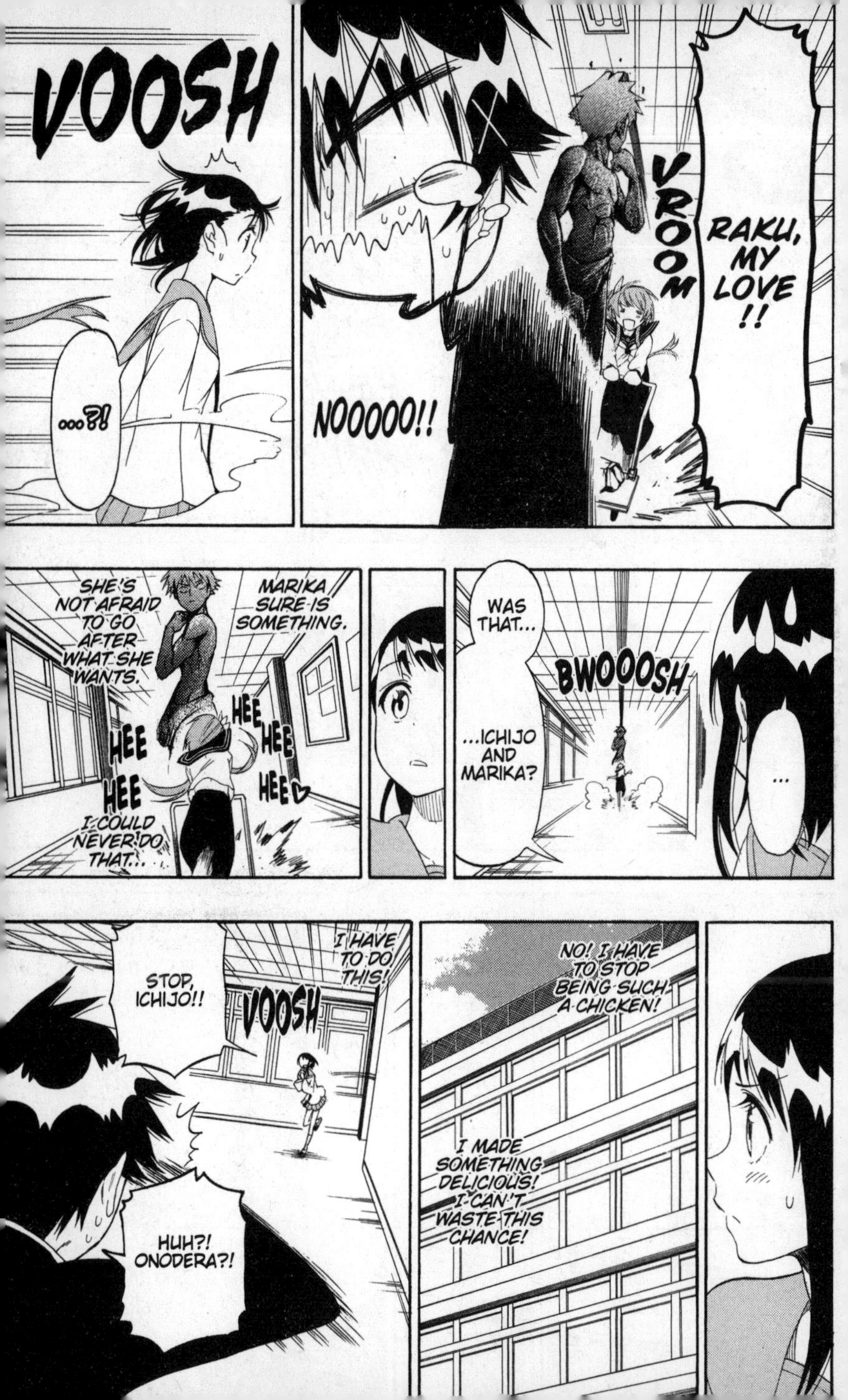
RAKU, MY LOVE!!
VROOM
NOOOOO!!
VOOSH
...?!
...
WAS THAT...
BWOOOSH
...ICHIJO AND MARIKA?
MARIKA SURE IS SOMETHING.
SHE'S NOT AFRAID TO GO AFTER WHAT SHE WANTS.
HEE HEE HEE HEE HEE
I COULD NEVER DO THAT...
NO! I HAVE TO STOP BEING SUCH A CHICKEN!
I MADE SOMETHING DELICIOUS! I CAN'T WASTE THIS CHANCE!
I HAVE TO DO THIS!
VOOSH
STOP, ICHIJO!!
HUH?! ONODERA?!

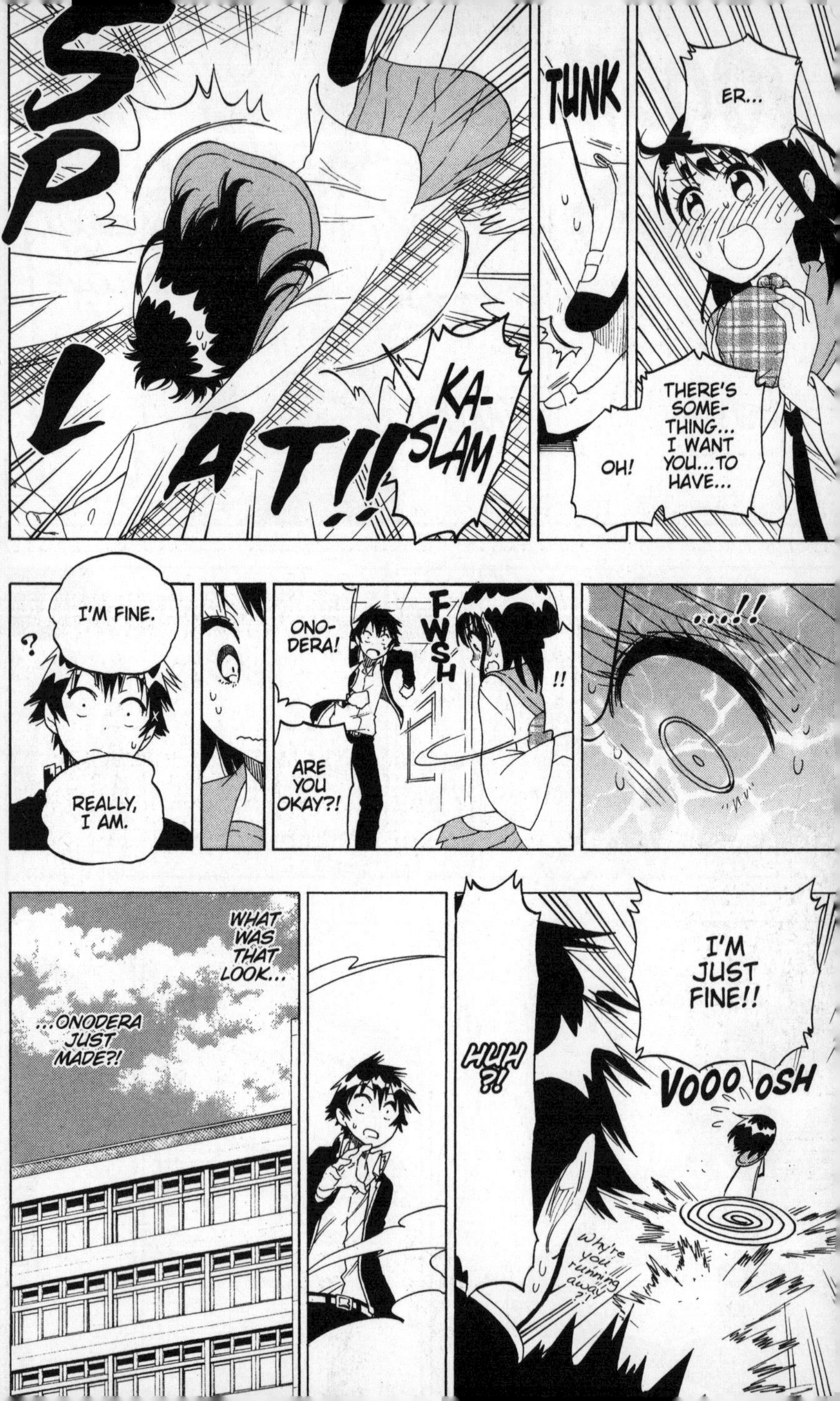
ER...
THERE'S SOME-THING... I WANT YOU...TO HAVE...
TUNK
OH!
SPLAT!!
KA-SLAM
...!!
FWSH
!!
ONO-DERA!
ARE YOU OKAY?!
I'M FINE.
?
REALLY, I AM.
I'M JUST FINE!!
VOOO OSH
Why're you running away?!
HUH?!
WHAT WAS THAT LOOK...
...ONODERA JUST MADE?!

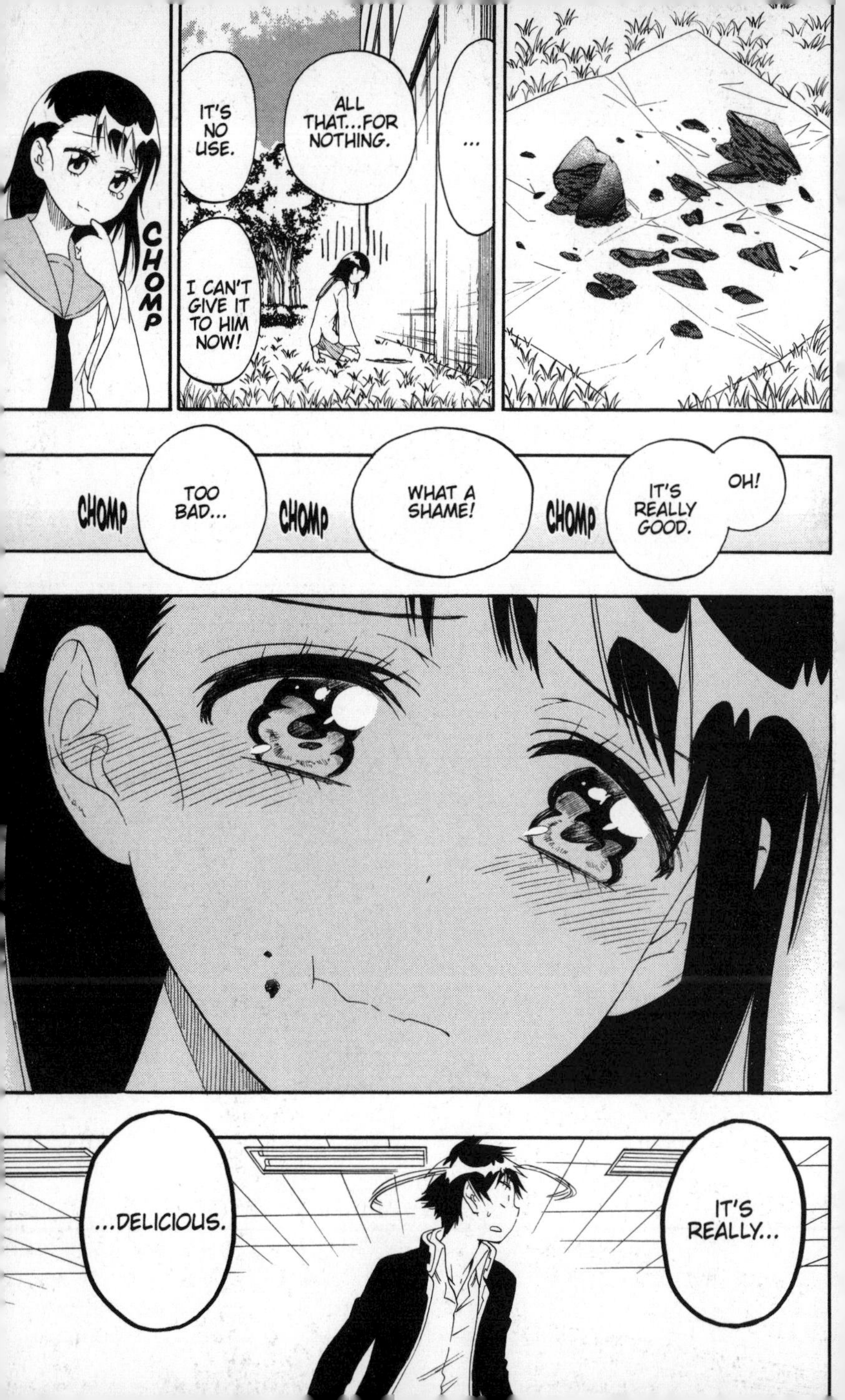
...
ALL THAT...FOR NOTHING.
IT'S NO USE.
I CAN'T GIVE IT TO HIM NOW!
CHOMP
OH!
IT'S REALLY GOOD.
CHOMP
WHAT A SHAME!
CHOMP
TOO BAD...
CHOMP
IT'S REALLY...
...DELICIOUS.

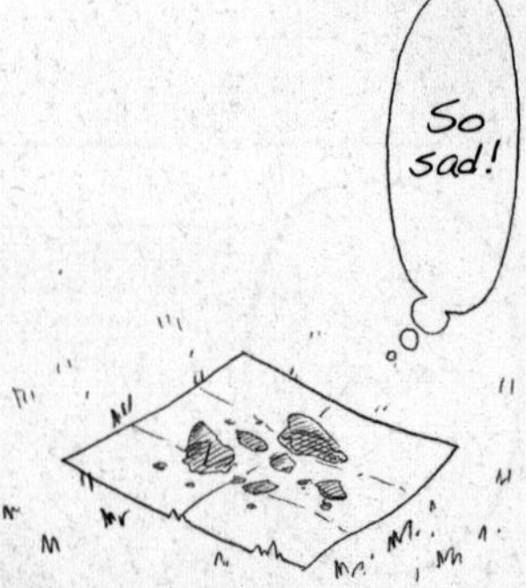
So sad!

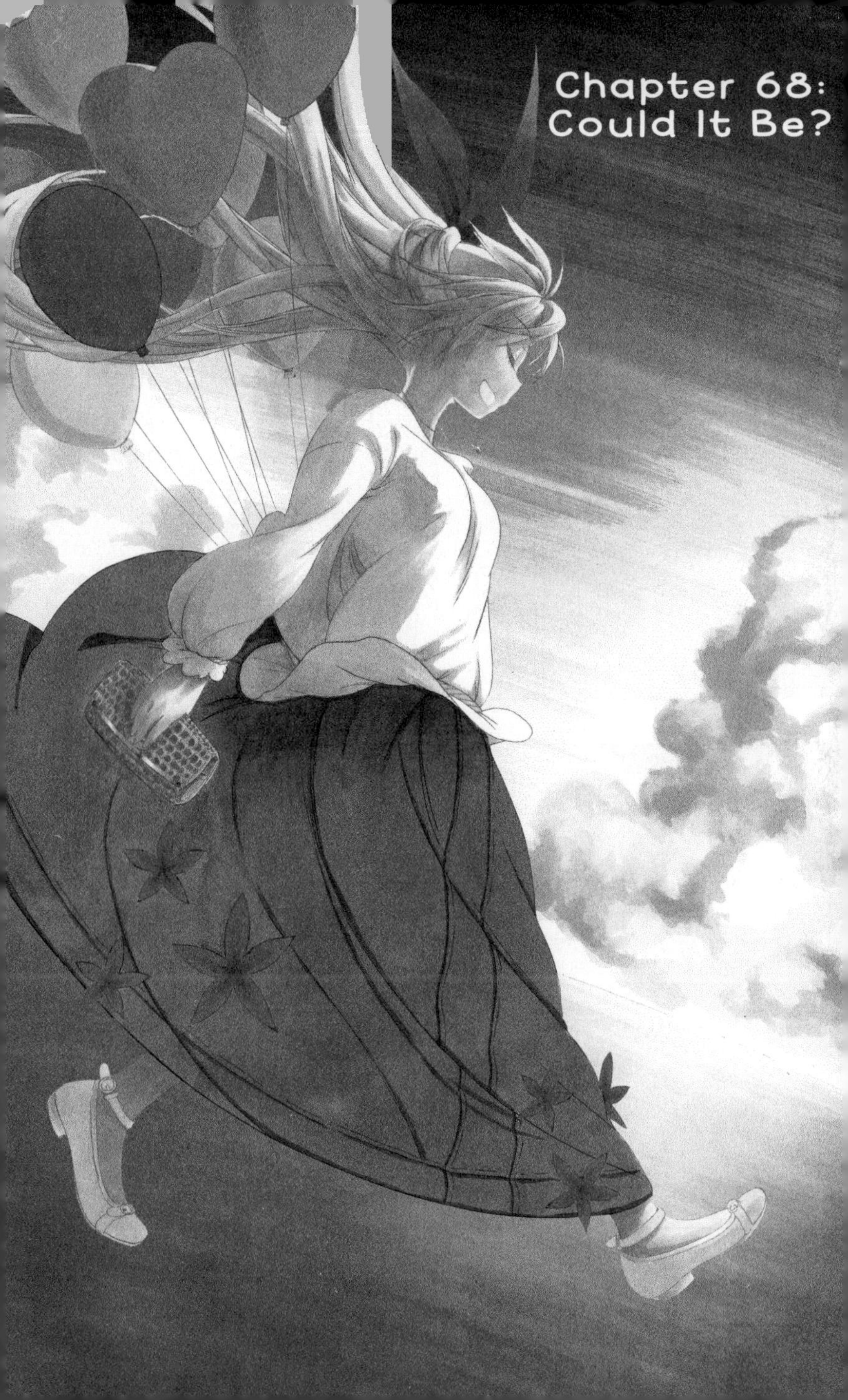
Chapter 68:
Could It Be?

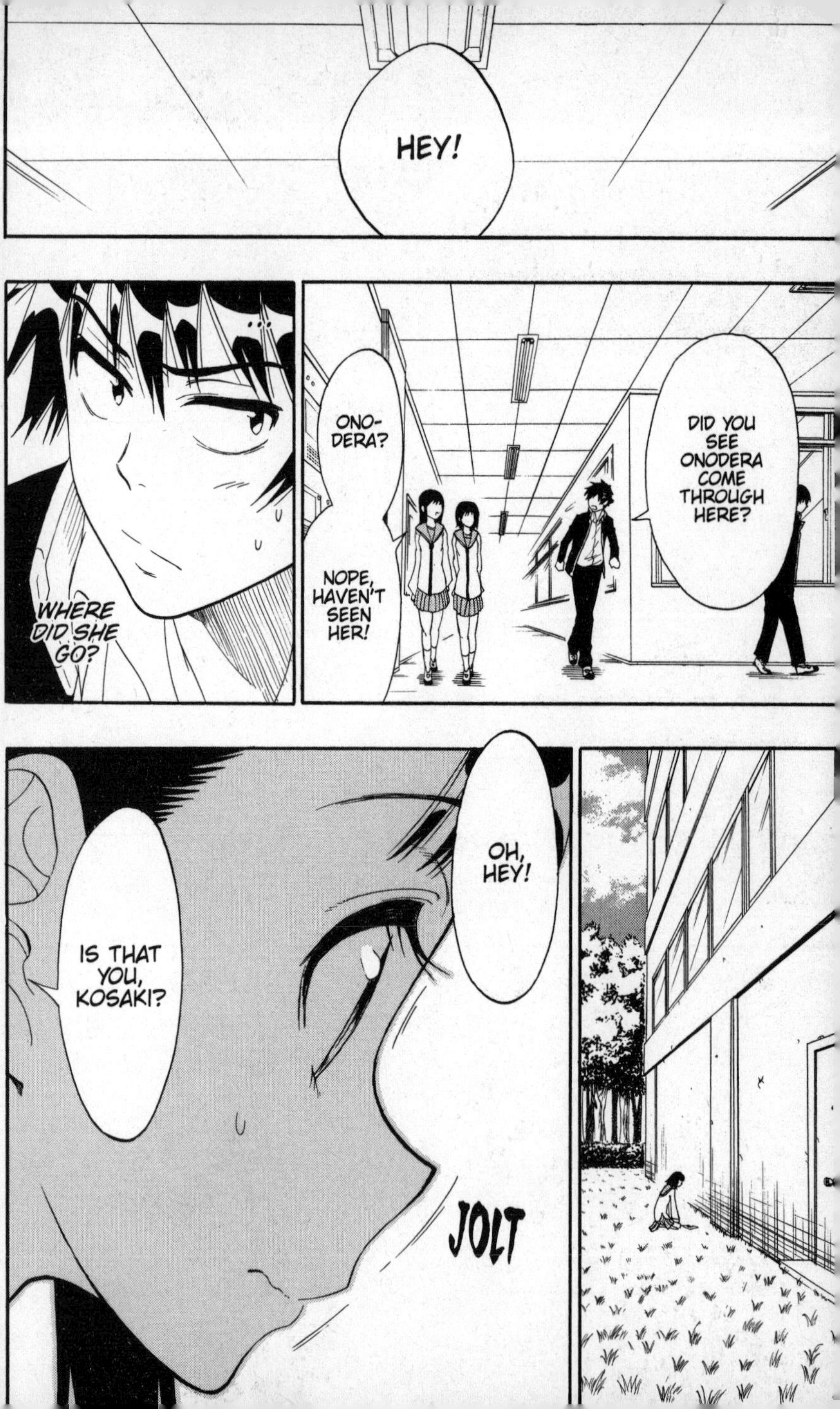
HEY!
DID YOU SEE ONODERA COME THROUGH HERE?
ONO-DERA?
NOPE, HAVEN'T SEEN HER!
...
WHERE DID SHE GO?
OH, HEY!
IS THAT YOU, KOSAKI?
JOLT

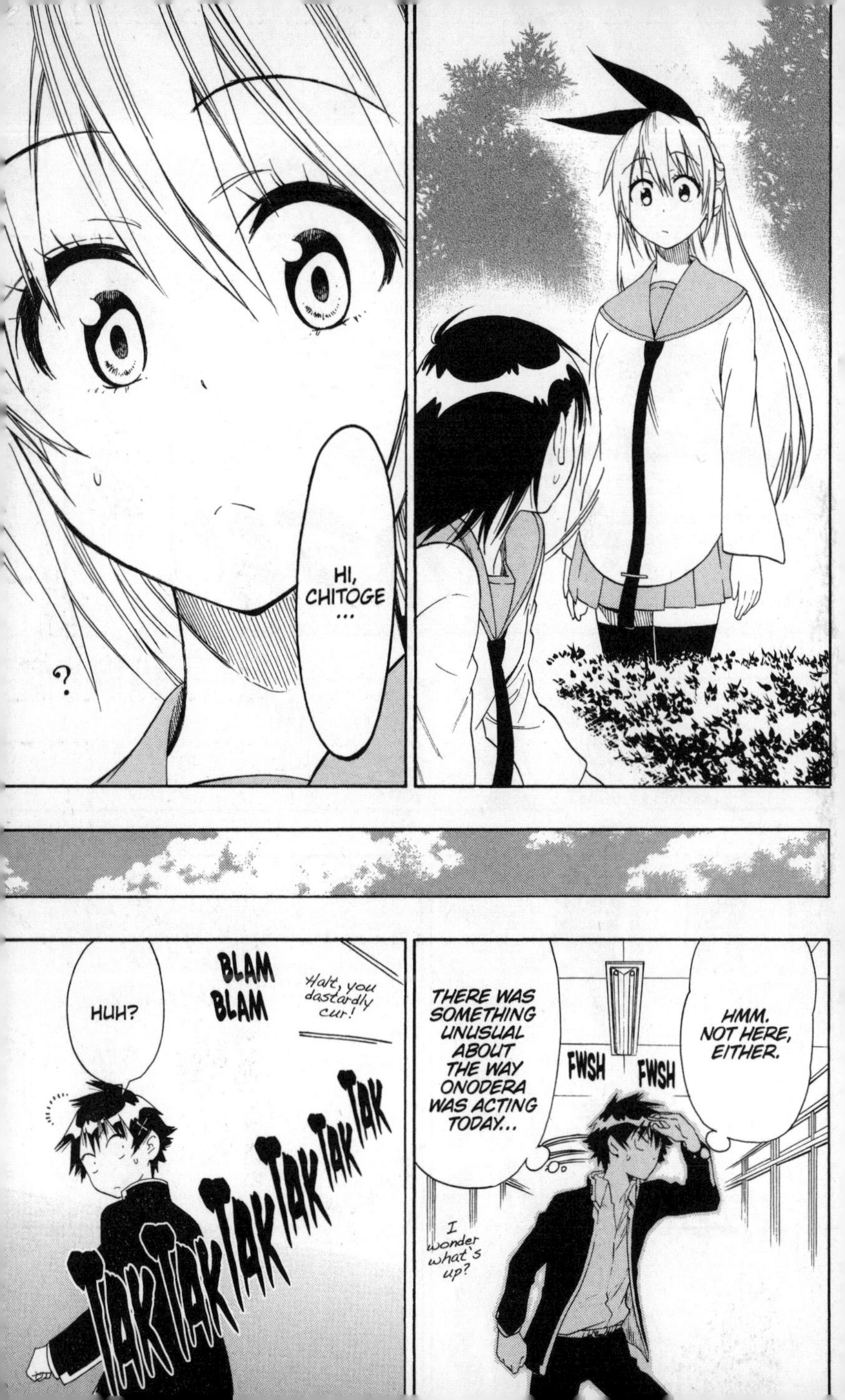
HI, CHITOGE...
?
HMM. NOT HERE, EITHER.
FWSH FWSH
THERE WAS SOMETHING UNUSUAL ABOUT THE WAY ONODERA WAS ACTING TODAY...
I wonder what's up?
Halt, you dastardly cur!
BLAM BLAM
HUH?
TAK TAK TAK TAK TAK TAK

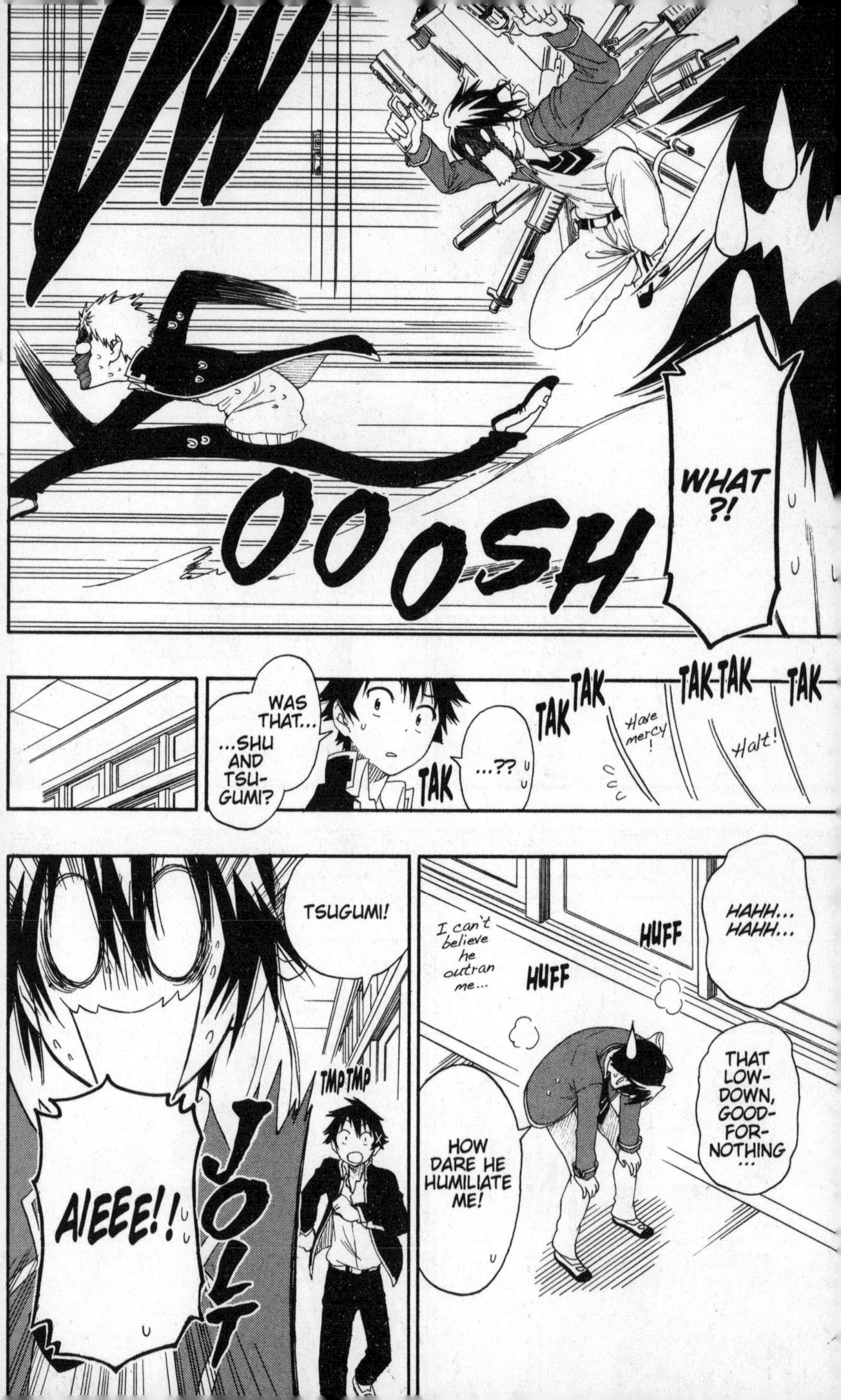
WHAT?!
OOOSH
TAK TAK-TAK TAK
Halt!
Have mercy!
TAK TAK
TAK
...??
WAS THAT... ...SHU AND TSUGUMI?
HAHH... HAHH...
HUFF
HUFF
I can't believe he outran me...
THAT LOW-DOWN, GOOD-FOR-NOTHING...
HOW DARE HE HUMILIATE ME!
TSUGUMI!
TMP TMP
JOLT
AIEEE!!

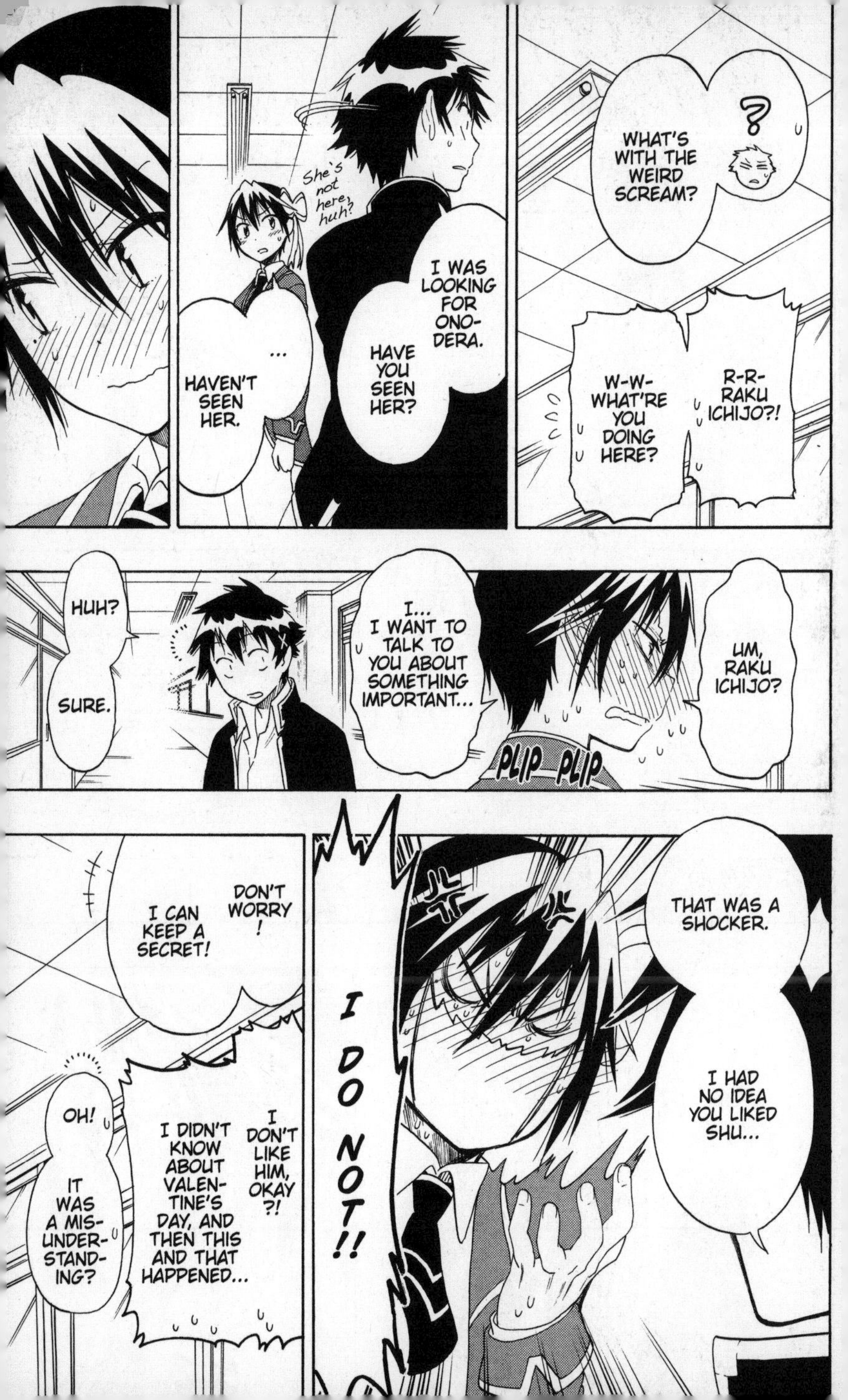
WHAT'S WITH THE WEIRD SCREAM?
R-R-RAKU ICHIJO?!
W-W-WHAT'RE YOU DOING HERE?
I WAS LOOKING FOR ONODERA.
HAVE YOU SEEN HER?
She's not here, huh?
...
HAVEN'T SEEN HER.
UM, RAKU ICHIJO?
I... I WANT TO TALK TO YOU ABOUT SOMETHING IMPORTANT...
PLIP PLIP
HUH?
SURE.
THAT WAS A SHOCKER.
I HAD NO IDEA YOU LIKED SHU...
I DO NOT!!
DON'T WORRY!
I CAN KEEP A SECRET!
I DON'T LIKE HIM, OKAY?!
I DIDN'T KNOW ABOUT VALENTINE'S DAY, AND THEN THIS AND THAT HAPPENED...
OH!
IT WAS A MISUNDERSTANDING?

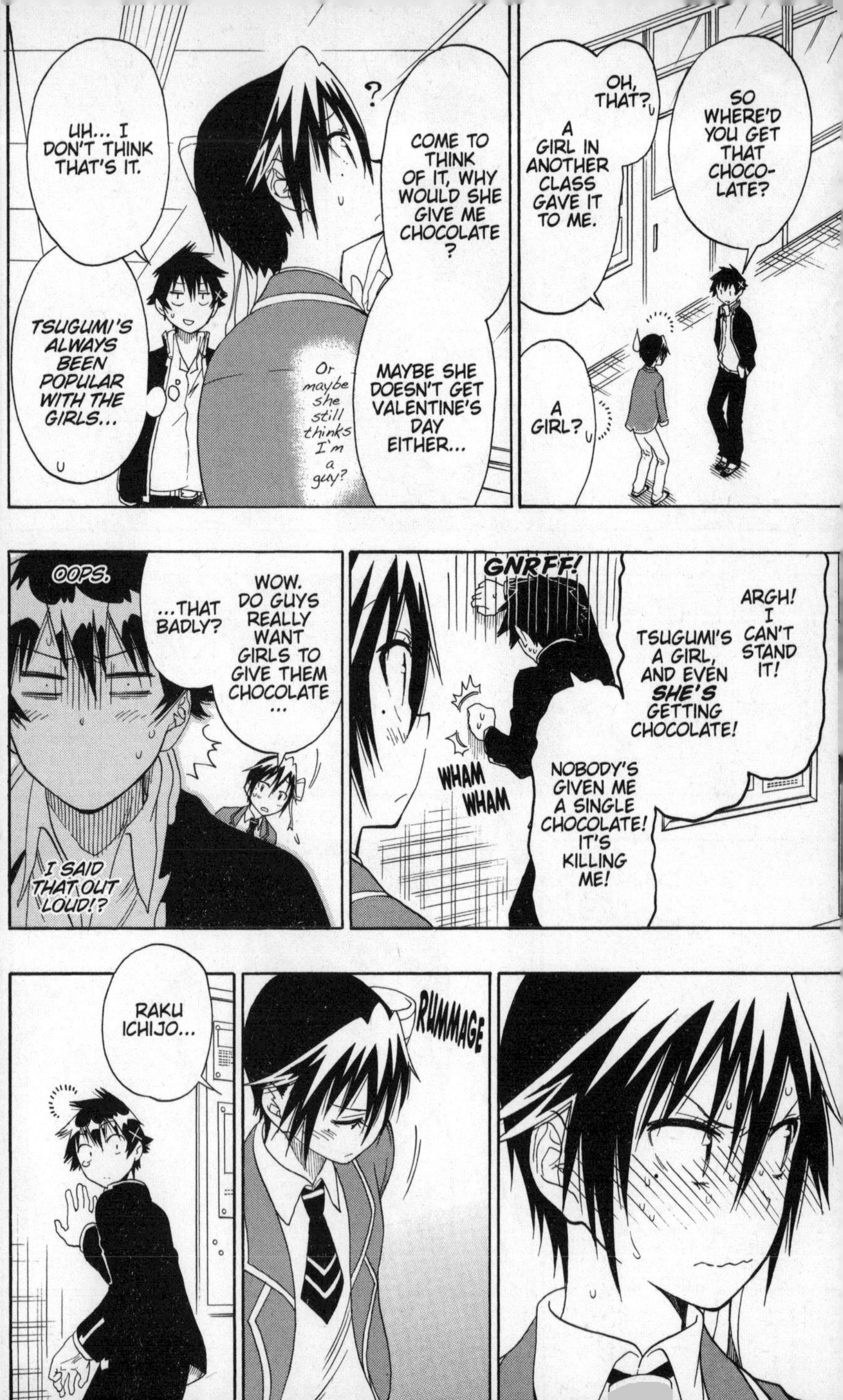
SO WHERE'D YOU GET THAT CHOCOLATE?
OH, THAT?
A GIRL IN ANOTHER CLASS GAVE IT TO ME.
A GIRL?
COME TO THINK OF IT, WHY WOULD SHE GIVE ME CHOCOLATE?
MAYBE SHE DOESN'T GET VALENTINE'S DAY EITHER...
Or maybe she still thinks I'm a guy?
UH... I DON'T THINK THAT'S IT.
TSUGUMI'S ALWAYS BEEN POPULAR WITH THE GIRLS...
GNRFF!
ARGH! I CAN'T STAND IT!
TSUGUMI'S A GIRL, AND EVEN SHE'S GETTING CHOCOLATE!
NOBODY'S GIVEN ME A SINGLE CHOCOLATE! IT'S KILLING ME!
WHAM WHAM
WOW. DO GUYS REALLY WANT GIRLS TO GIVE THEM CHOCOLATE...
...THAT BADLY?
OOPS.
I SAID THAT OUT LOUD!?
RUMMAGE
RAKU ICHIJO...

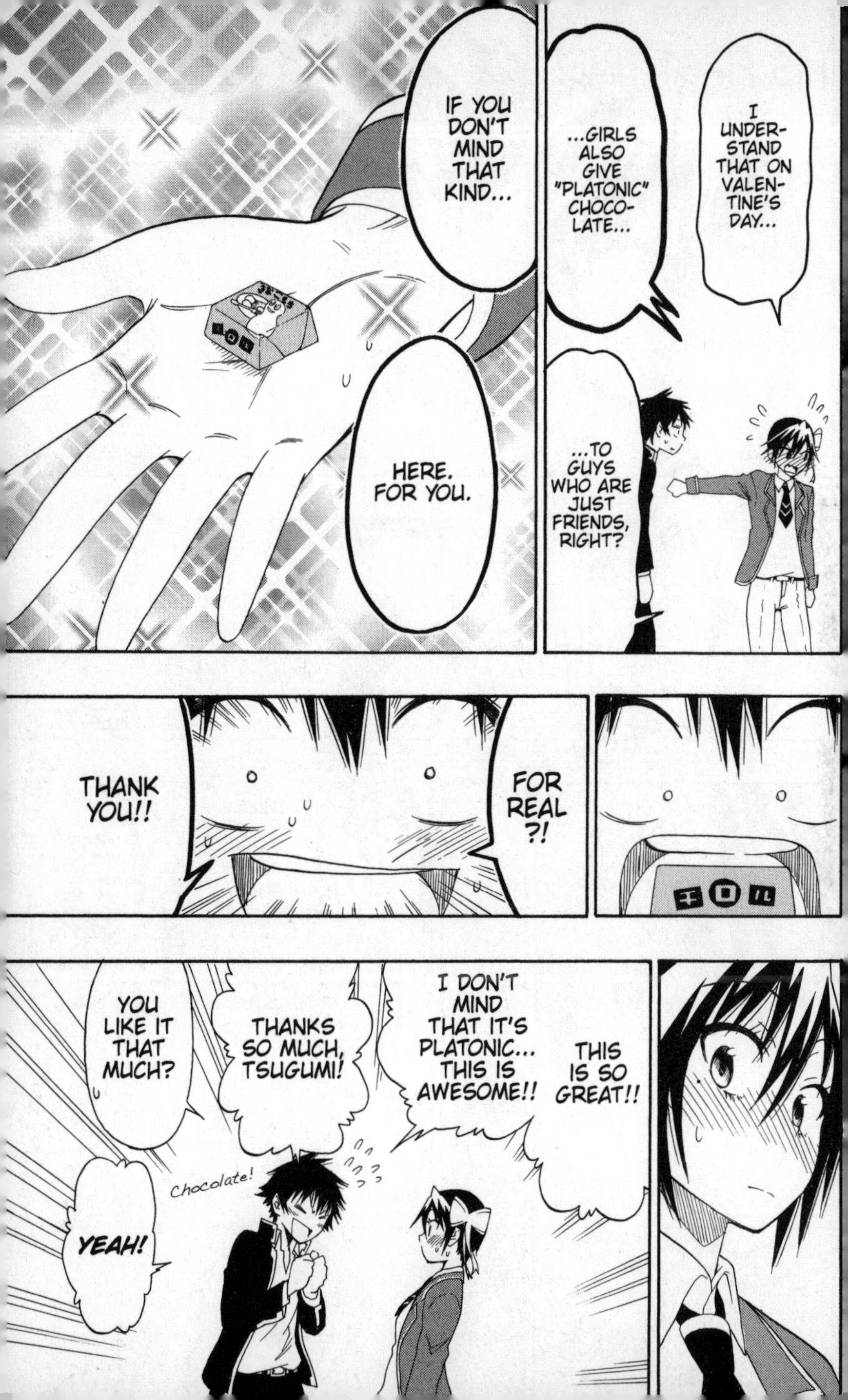
I UNDERSTAND THAT ON VALENTINE'S DAY...
...GIRLS ALSO GIVE "PLATONIC" CHOCOLATE...
...TO GUYS WHO ARE JUST FRIENDS, RIGHT?
IF YOU DON'T MIND THAT KIND...
HERE. FOR YOU.
FOR REAL?!
THANK YOU!!
THIS IS SO GREAT!!
I DON'T MIND THAT IT'S PLATONIC... THIS IS AWESOME!!
THANKS SO MUCH, TSUGUMI!
YOU LIKE IT THAT MUCH?
Chocolate!
YEAH!

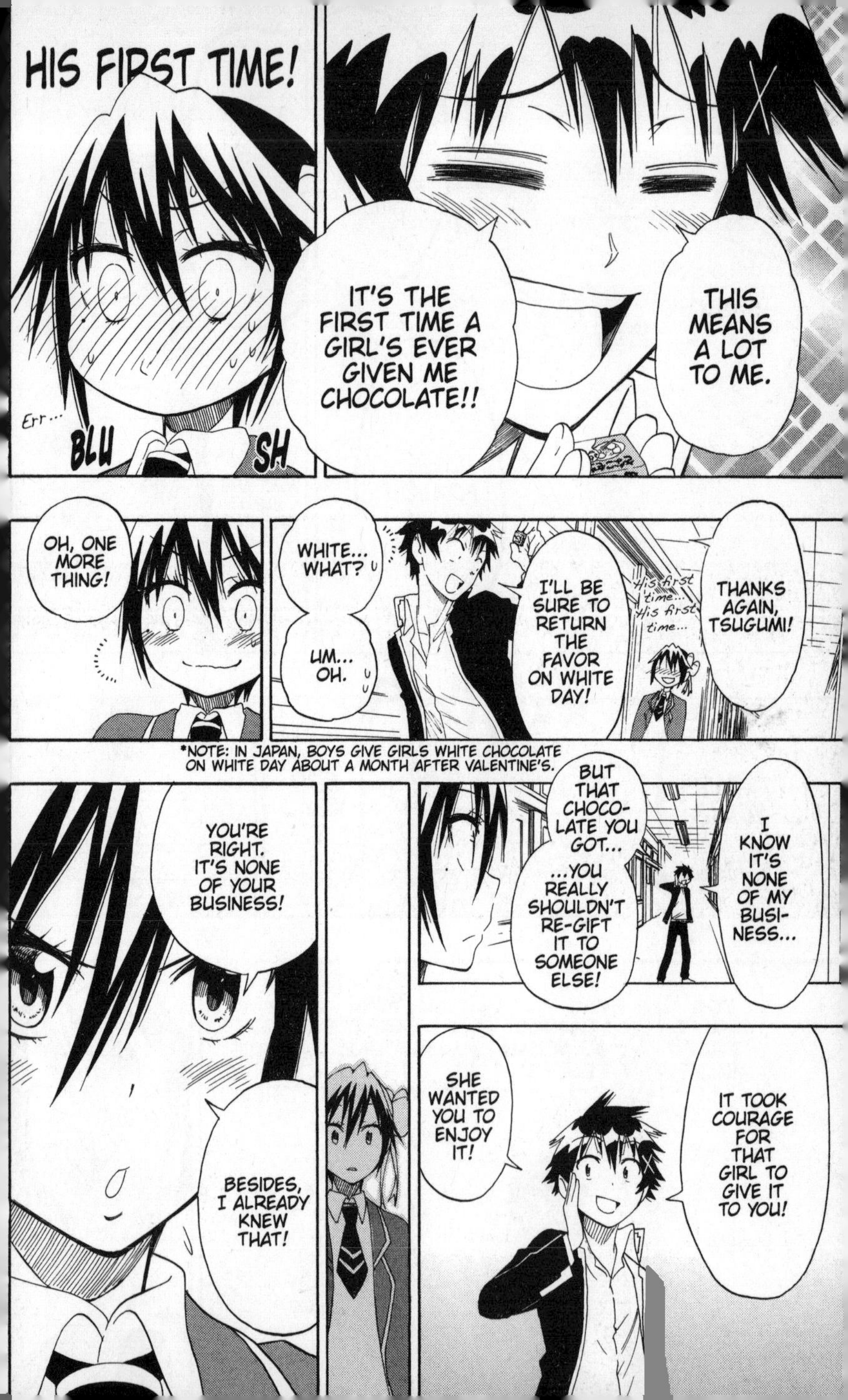
THIS MEANS A LOT TO ME.
IT'S THE FIRST TIME A GIRL'S EVER GIVEN ME CHOCOLATE!!
HIS FIRST TIME!
Err...
BLUSH
THANKS AGAIN, TSUGUMI!
His first time... His first time...
I'LL BE SURE TO RETURN THE FAVOR ON WHITE DAY!
WHITE... WHAT?
UM... OH.
OH, ONE MORE THING!
*NOTE: IN JAPAN, BOYS GIVE GIRLS WHITE CHOCOLATE ON WHITE DAY ABOUT A MONTH AFTER VALENTINE'S.
I KNOW IT'S NONE OF MY BUSINESS...
BUT THAT CHOCOLATE YOU GOT...
...YOU REALLY SHOULDN'T RE-GIFT IT TO SOMEONE ELSE!
IT TOOK COURAGE FOR THAT GIRL TO GIVE IT TO YOU!
SHE WANTED YOU TO ENJOY IT!
YOU'RE RIGHT. IT'S NONE OF YOUR BUSINESS!
BESIDES, I ALREADY KNEW THAT!

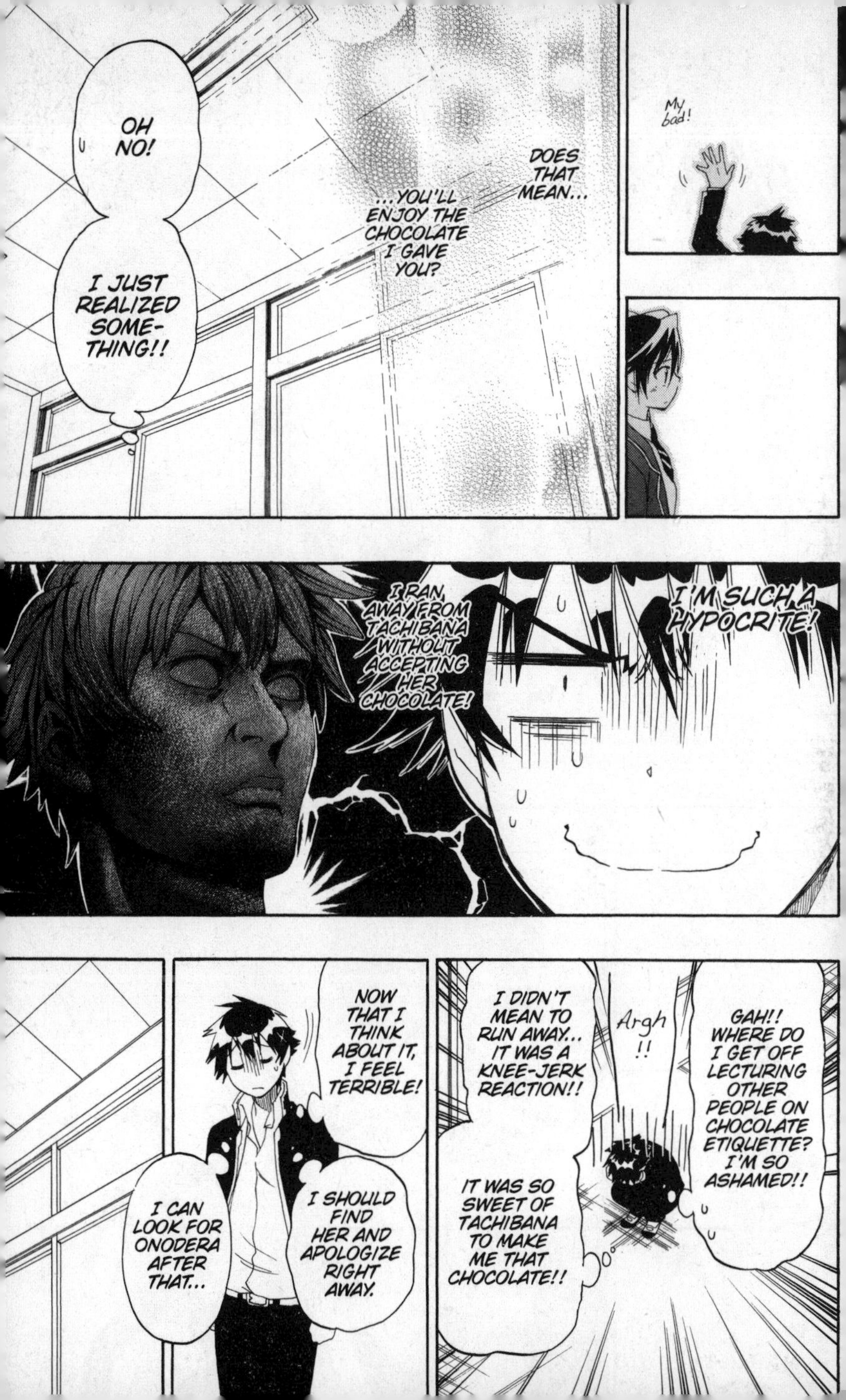
My bad!
DOES THAT MEAN...
...YOU'LL ENJOY THE CHOCOLATE I GAVE YOU?
OH NO!
I JUST REALIZED SOME-THING!!
I'M SUCH A HYPOCRITE!
I RAN AWAY FROM TACHIBANA WITHOUT ACCEPTING HER CHOCOLATE!
GAH!! WHERE DO I GET OFF LECTURING OTHER PEOPLE ON CHOCOLATE ETIQUETTE? I'M SO ASHAMED!!
Argh!!
I DIDN'T MEAN TO RUN AWAY... IT WAS A KNEE-JERK REACTION!!
IT WAS SO SWEET OF TACHIBANA TO MAKE ME THAT CHOCOLATE!!
NOW THAT I THINK ABOUT IT, I FEEL TERRIBLE!
I SHOULD FIND HER AND APOLOGIZE RIGHT AWAY.
I CAN LOOK FOR ONODERA AFTER THAT...

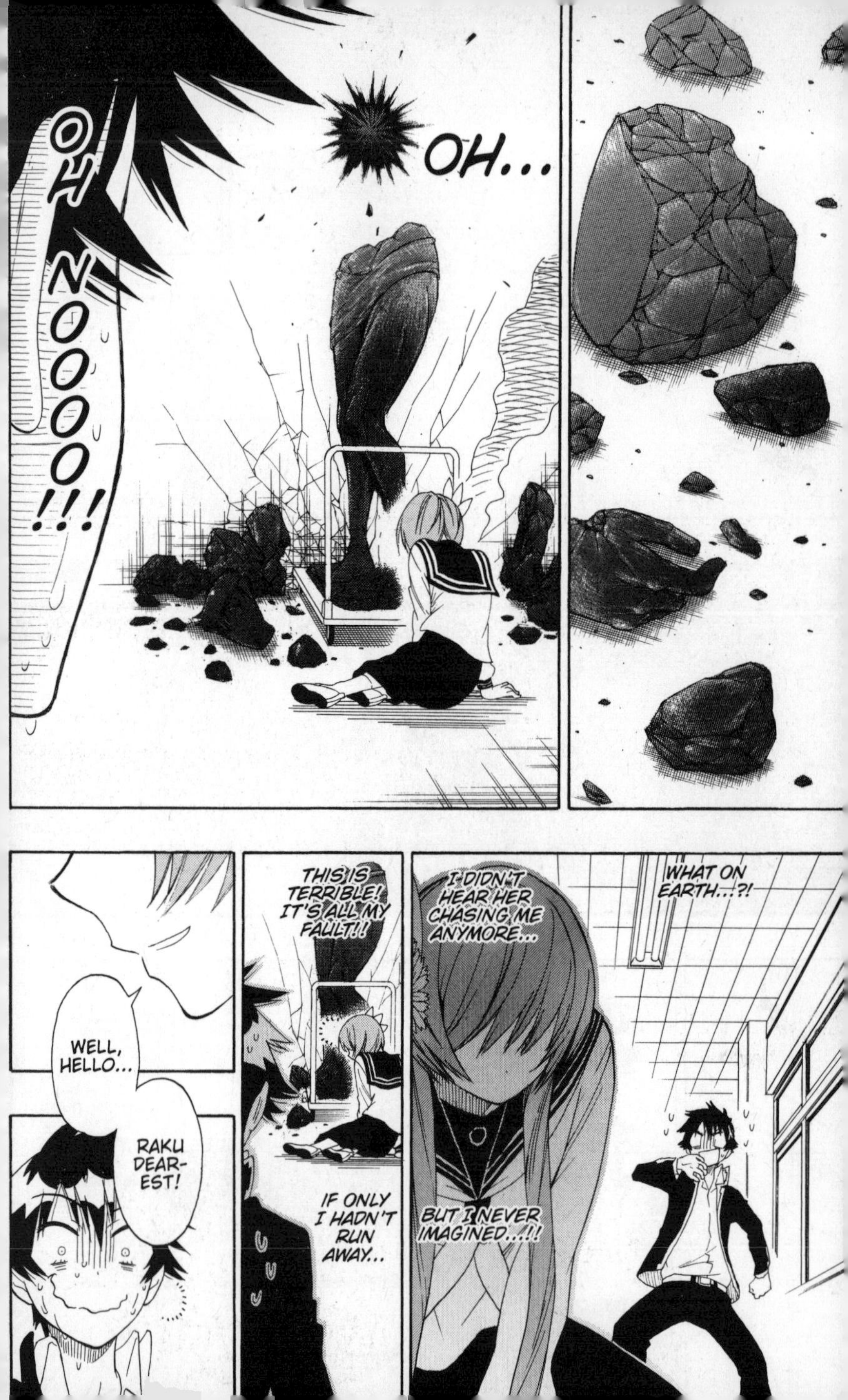
OH...
OH NOOOOO!!!
WHAT ON EARTH...?!
I DIDN'T HEAR HER CHASING ME ANYMORE...
BUT I NEVER IMAGINED...!!
THIS IS TERRIBLE! IT'S ALL MY FAULT!!
IF ONLY I HADN'T RUN AWAY...
WELL, HELLO...
RAKU DEAREST!

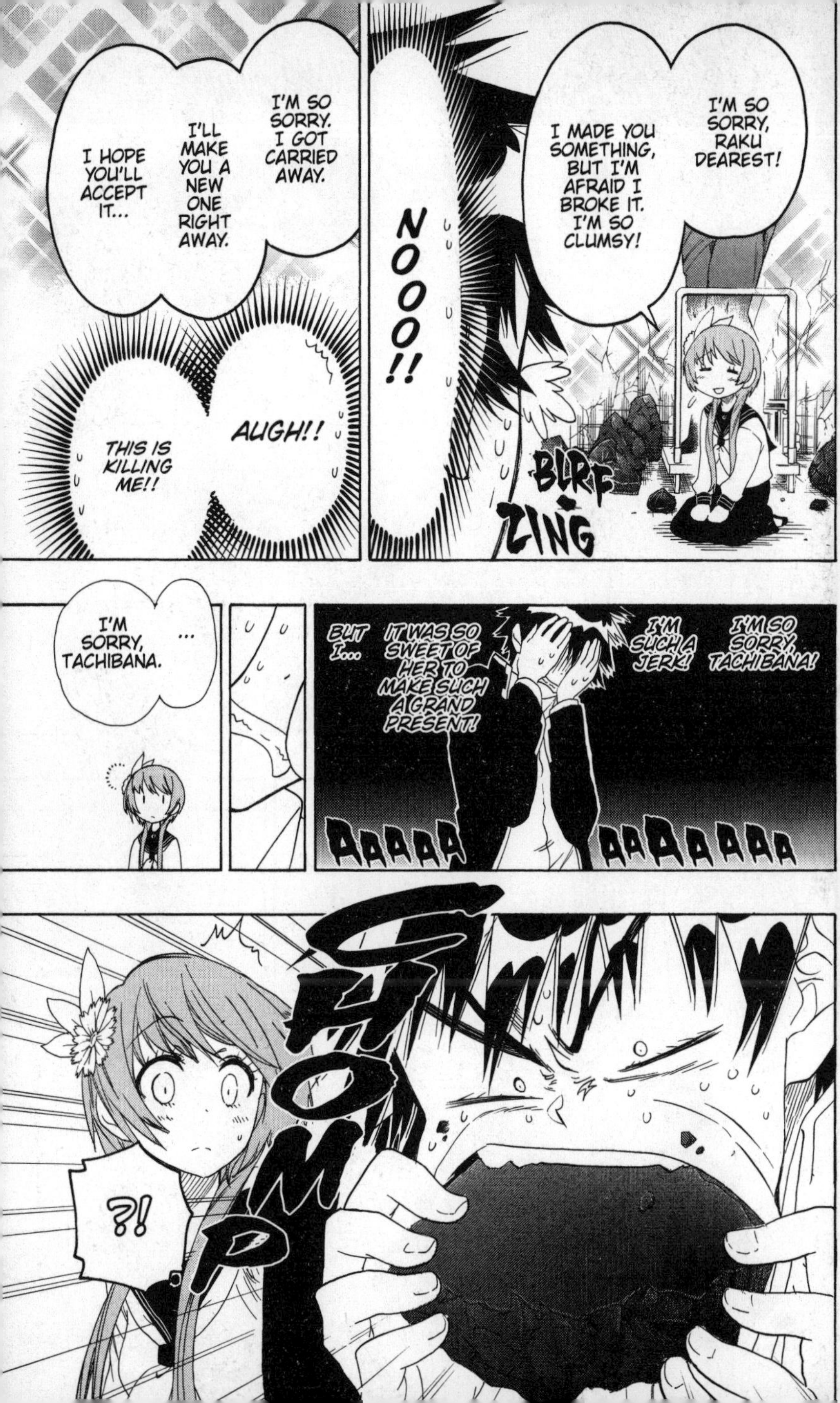
I'M SO SORRY, RAKU DEAREST!
I MADE YOU SOMETHING, BUT I'M AFRAID I BROKE IT. I'M SO CLUMSY!
NOOOO!!
BLRF
ZING
I'M SO SORRY. I GOT CARRIED AWAY.
I'LL MAKE YOU A NEW ONE RIGHT AWAY.
I HOPE YOU'LL ACCEPT IT...
AUGH!!
THIS IS KILLING ME!!
I'M SO SORRY, TACHIBANA!
I'M SUCH A JERK!
IT WAS SO SWEET OF HER TO MAKE SUCH A GRAND PRESENT!
BUT I...
AAAAAAA
AAAAA
...
I'M SORRY, TACHIBANA.
CHOMP
?!

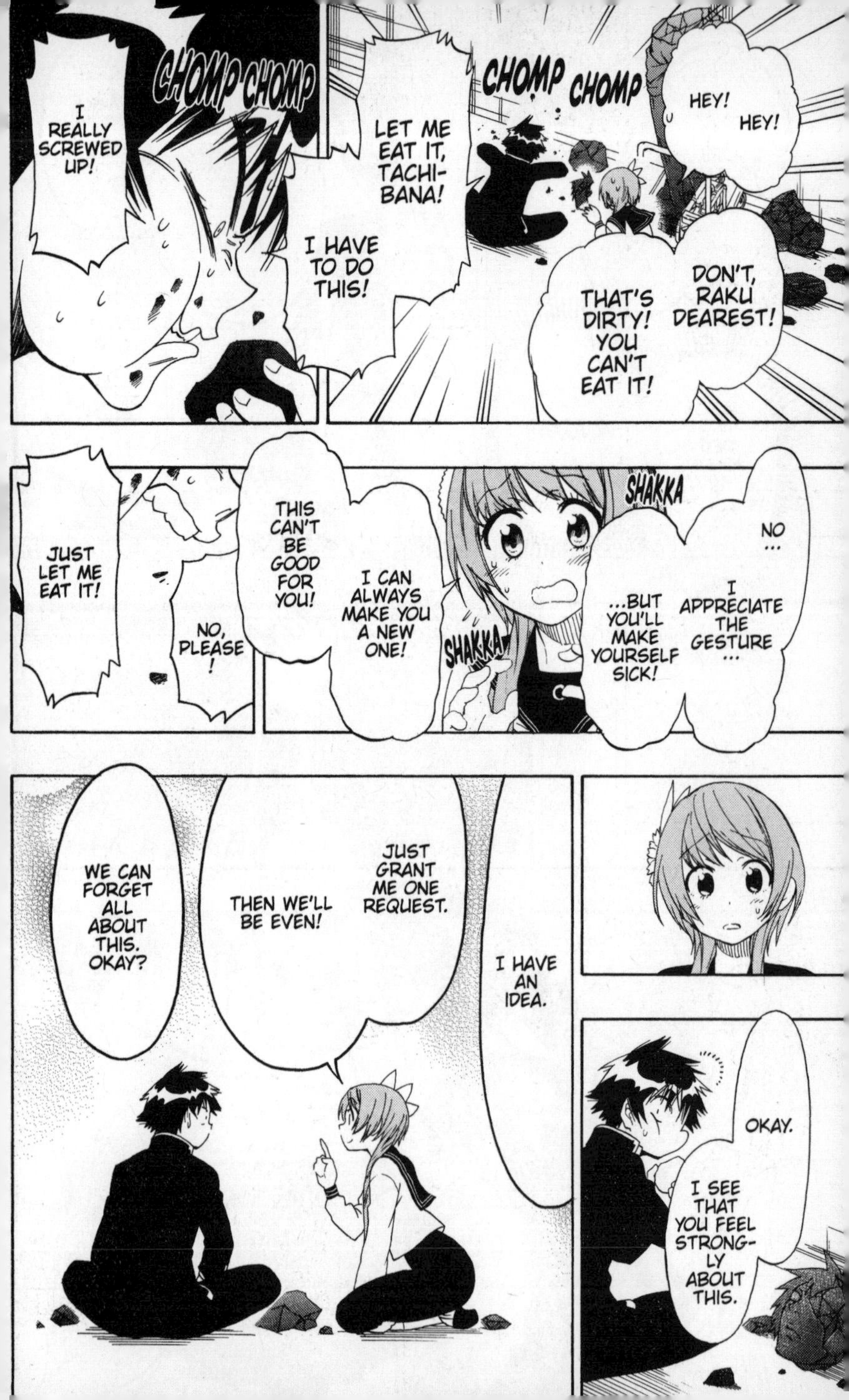
CHOMP CHOMP
HEY! HEY!
DON'T, RAKU DEAREST!
THAT'S DIRTY! YOU CAN'T EAT IT!
LET ME EAT IT, TACHIBANA!
I HAVE TO DO THIS!
CHOMP CHOMP
I REALLY SCREWED UP!
SHAKKA
NO... I APPRECIATE THE GESTURE...
...BUT YOU'LL MAKE YOURSELF SICK!
SHAKKA
I CAN ALWAYS MAKE YOU A NEW ONE!
THIS CAN'T BE GOOD FOR YOU!
NO, PLEASE!
JUST LET ME EAT IT!
OKAY.
I SEE THAT YOU FEEL STRONG-LY ABOUT THIS.
I HAVE AN IDEA.
JUST GRANT ME ONE REQUEST.
THEN WE'LL BE EVEN!
WE CAN FORGET ALL ABOUT THIS. OKAY?

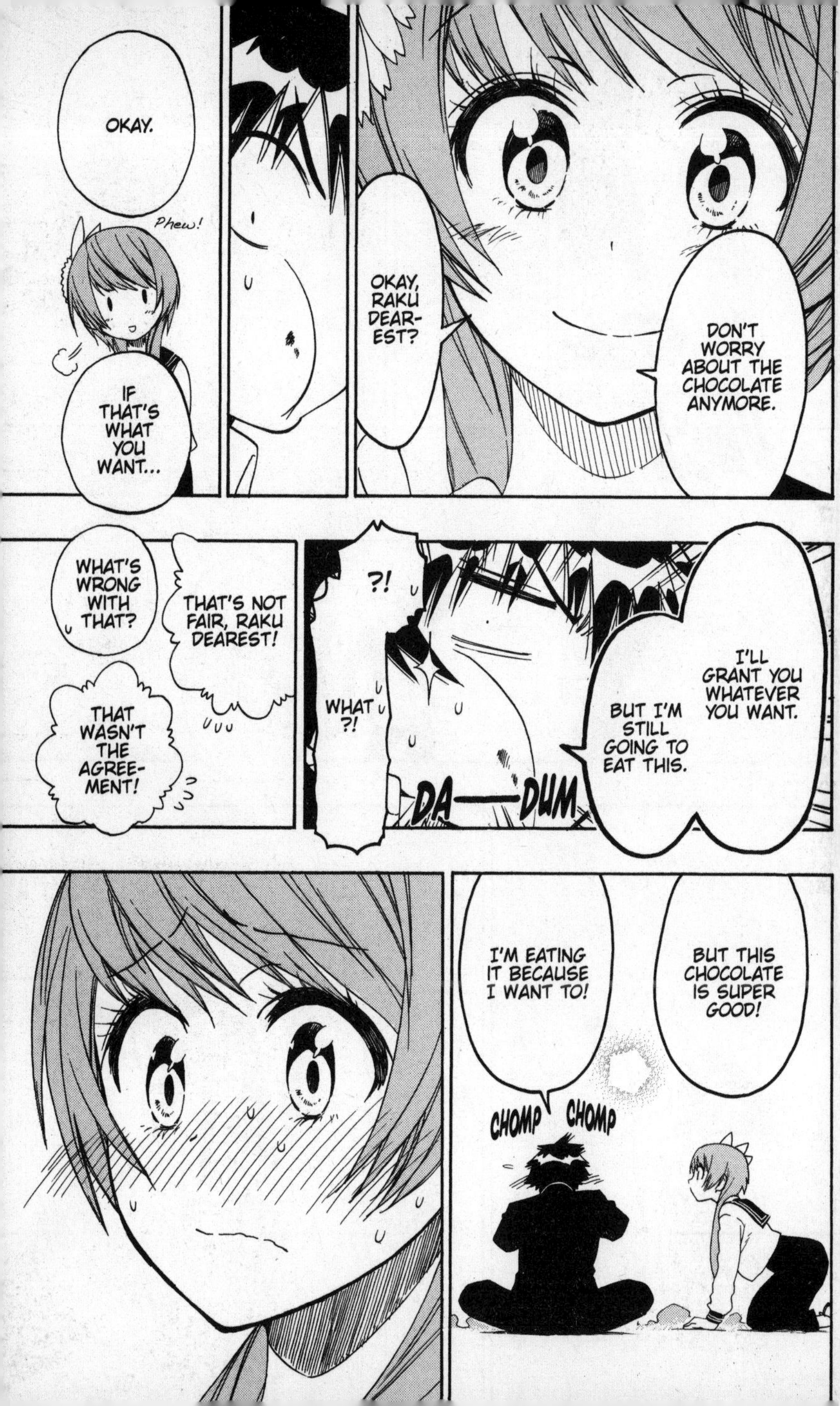
DON'T WORRY ABOUT THE CHOCOLATE ANYMORE.
OKAY, RAKU DEAREST?
OKAY.
Phew!
IF THAT'S WHAT YOU WANT...
I'LL GRANT YOU WHATEVER YOU WANT.
BUT I'M STILL GOING TO EAT THIS.
DA—DUM
?!
WHAT ?!
THAT'S NOT FAIR, RAKU DEAREST!
WHAT'S WRONG WITH THAT?
THAT WASN'T THE AGREEMENT!
BUT THIS CHOCOLATE IS SUPER GOOD!
I'M EATING IT BECAUSE I WANT TO!
CHOMP CHOMP

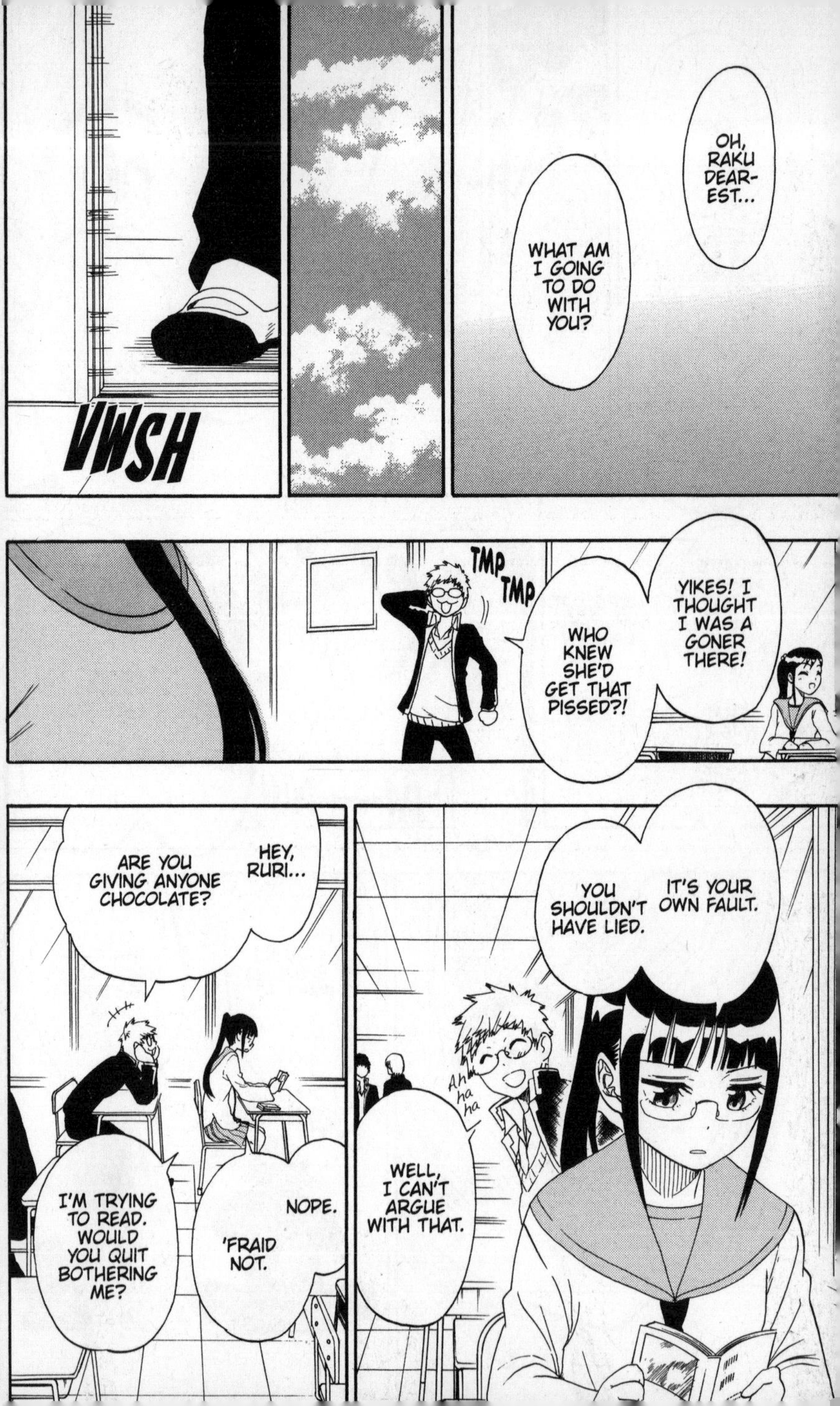
OH, RAKU DEAREST...
WHAT AM I GOING TO DO WITH YOU?
VWSH
TMP TMP
YIKES! I THOUGHT I WAS A GONER THERE!
WHO KNEW SHE'D GET THAT PISSED?!
IT'S YOUR OWN FAULT.
YOU SHOULDN'T HAVE LIED.
Ah ha ha
WELL, I CAN'T ARGUE WITH THAT.
HEY, RURI...
ARE YOU GIVING ANYONE CHOCOLATE?
NOPE.
'FRAID NOT.
I'M TRYING TO READ. WOULD YOU QUIT BOTHERING ME?

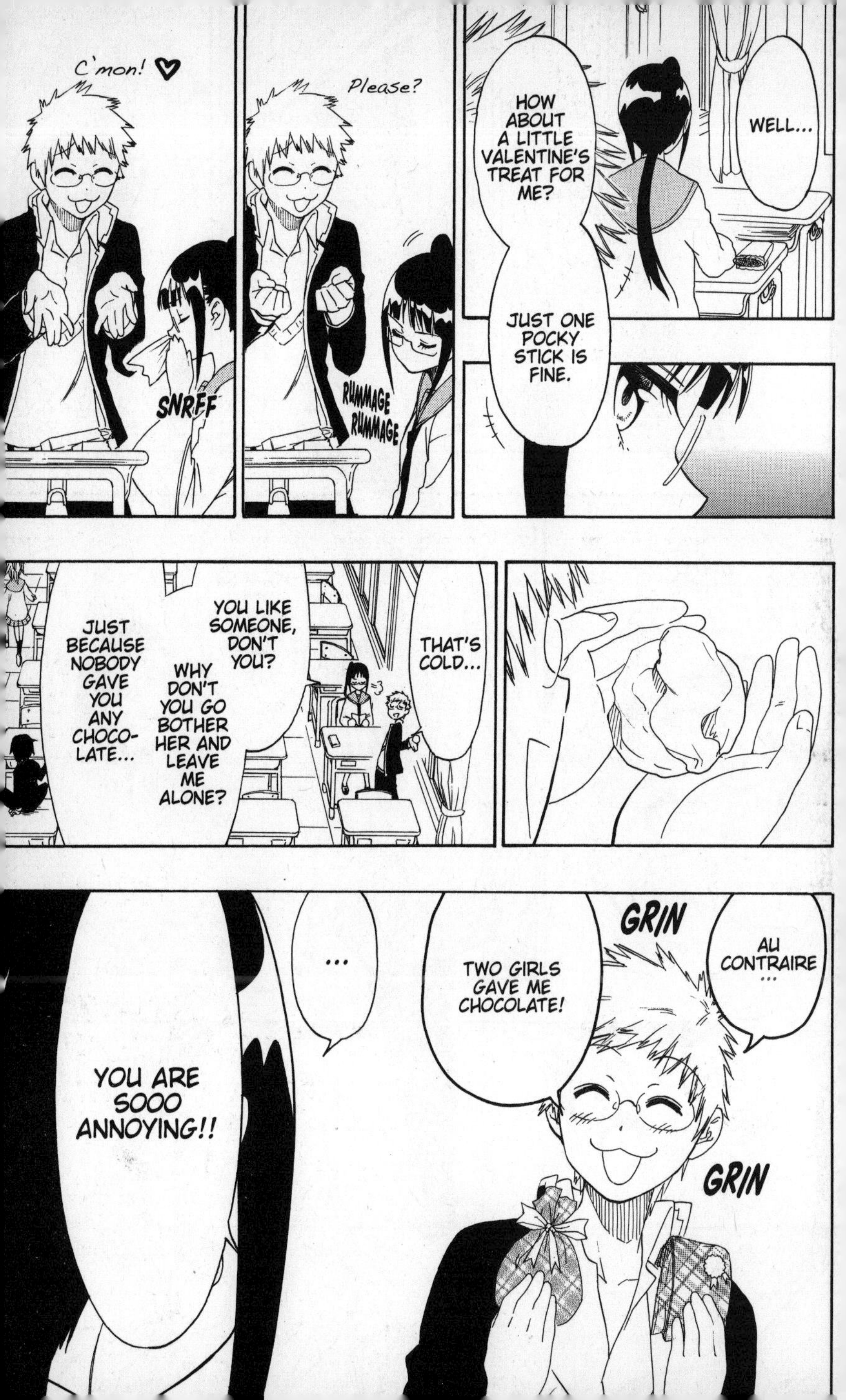
WELL...
HOW ABOUT A LITTLE VALENTINE'S TREAT FOR ME?
JUST ONE POCKY STICK IS FINE.
Please?
RUMMAGE RUMMAGE
C'mon! ♥
SNRFF
THAT'S COLD...
YOU LIKE SOMEONE, DON'T YOU?
WHY DON'T YOU GO BOTHER HER AND LEAVE ME ALONE?
JUST BECAUSE NOBODY GAVE YOU ANY CHOCO-LATE...
AU CONTRAIRE ...
GRIN
TWO GIRLS GAVE ME CHOCOLATE!
GRIN
...
YOU ARE SOOO ANNOYING!!

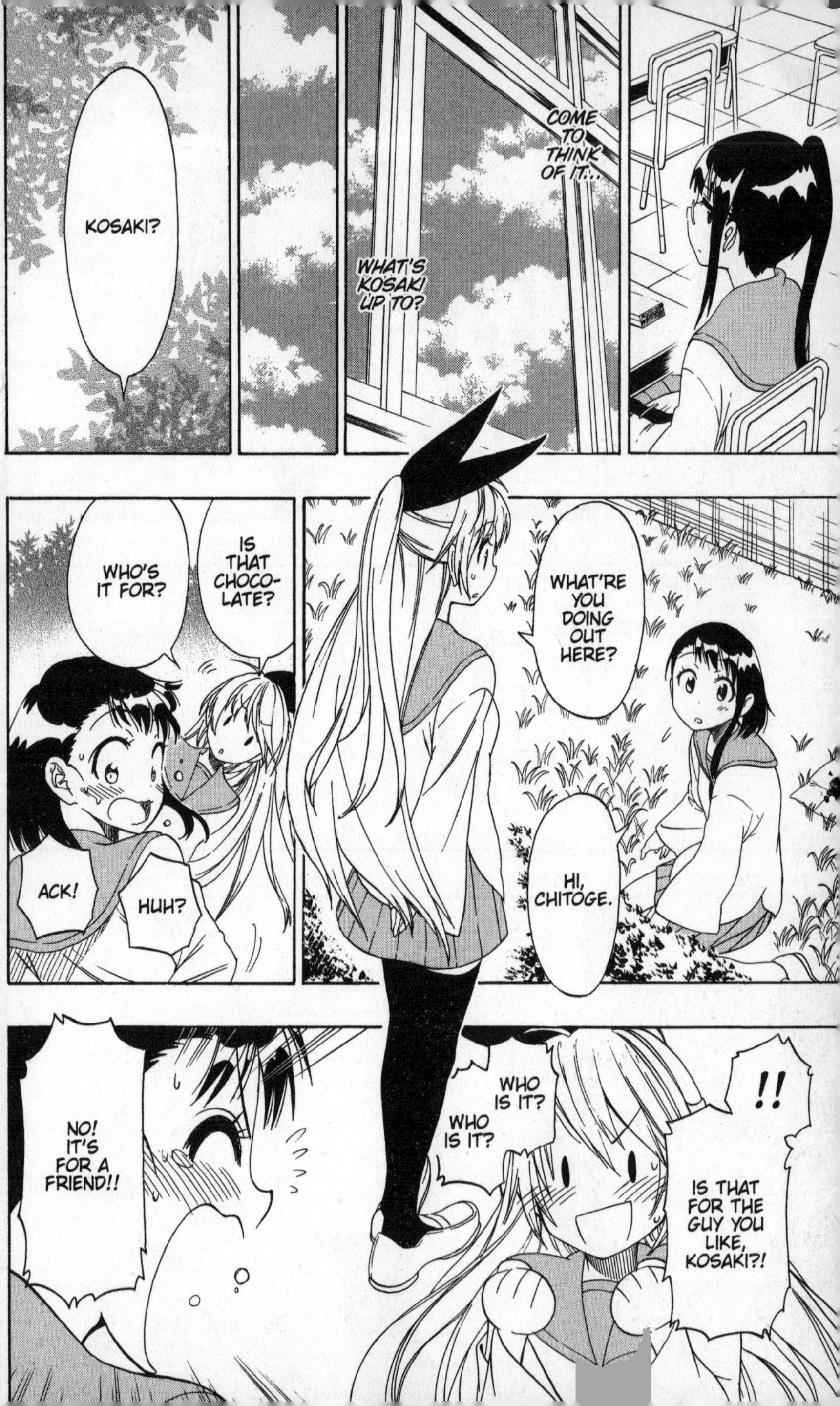
COME TO THINK OF IT...
WHAT'S KOSAKI UP TO?
KOSAKI?
WHAT'RE YOU DOING OUT HERE?
HI, CHITOGE.
IS THAT CHOCOLATE?
WHO'S IT FOR?
HUH?
ACK!
!!
IS THAT FOR THE GUY YOU LIKE, KOSAKI?!
WHO IS IT?
WHO IS IT?
NO! IT'S FOR A FRIEND!!

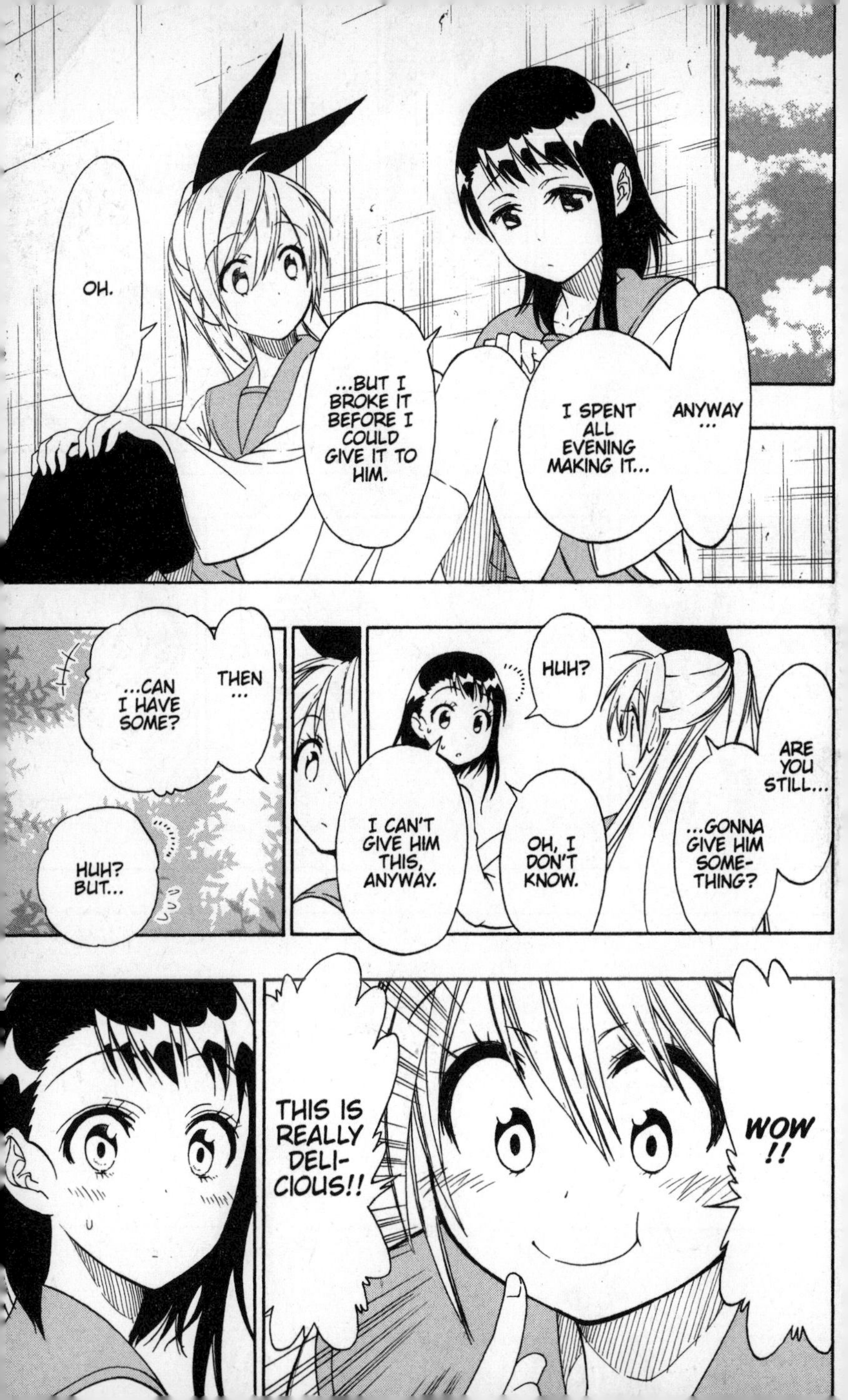
ANYWAY...
I SPENT ALL EVENING MAKING IT...
...BUT I BROKE IT BEFORE I COULD GIVE IT TO HIM.
OH.
ARE YOU STILL...
...GONNA GIVE HIM SOMETHING?
HUH?
OH, I DON'T KNOW.
I CAN'T GIVE HIM THIS, ANYWAY.
THEN...
...CAN I HAVE SOME?
HUH? BUT...
WOW!!
THIS IS REALLY DELICIOUS!!

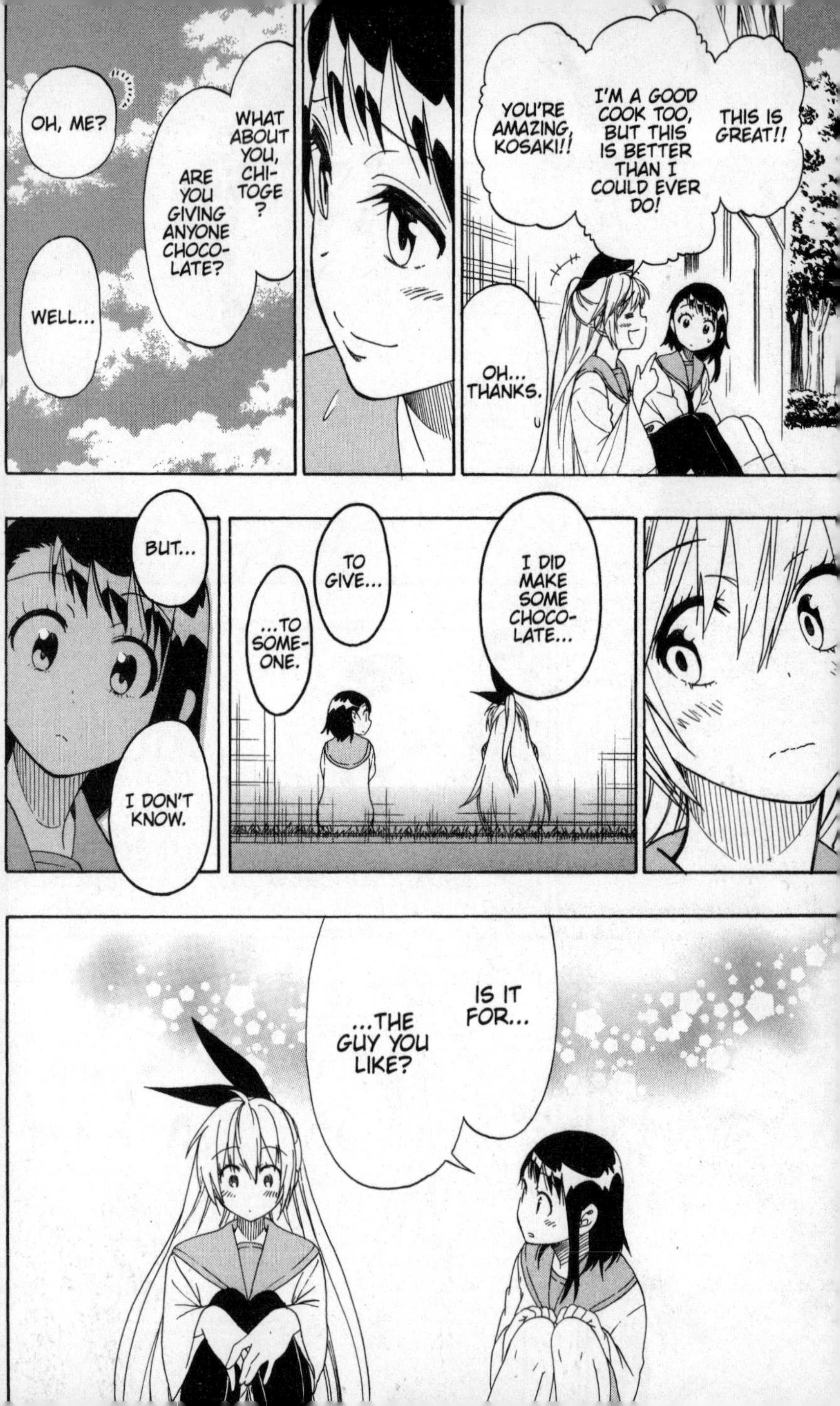
THIS IS GREAT!!
I'M A GOOD COOK TOO, BUT THIS IS BETTER THAN I COULD EVER DO!
YOU'RE AMAZING, KOSAKI!!
OH... THANKS.
WHAT ABOUT YOU, CHITOGE?
ARE YOU GIVING ANYONE CHOCOLATE?
OH, ME?
WELL...
I DID MAKE SOME CHOCOLATE...
TO GIVE...
...TO SOMEONE.
BUT...
I DON'T KNOW.
IS IT FOR...
...THE GUY YOU LIKE?

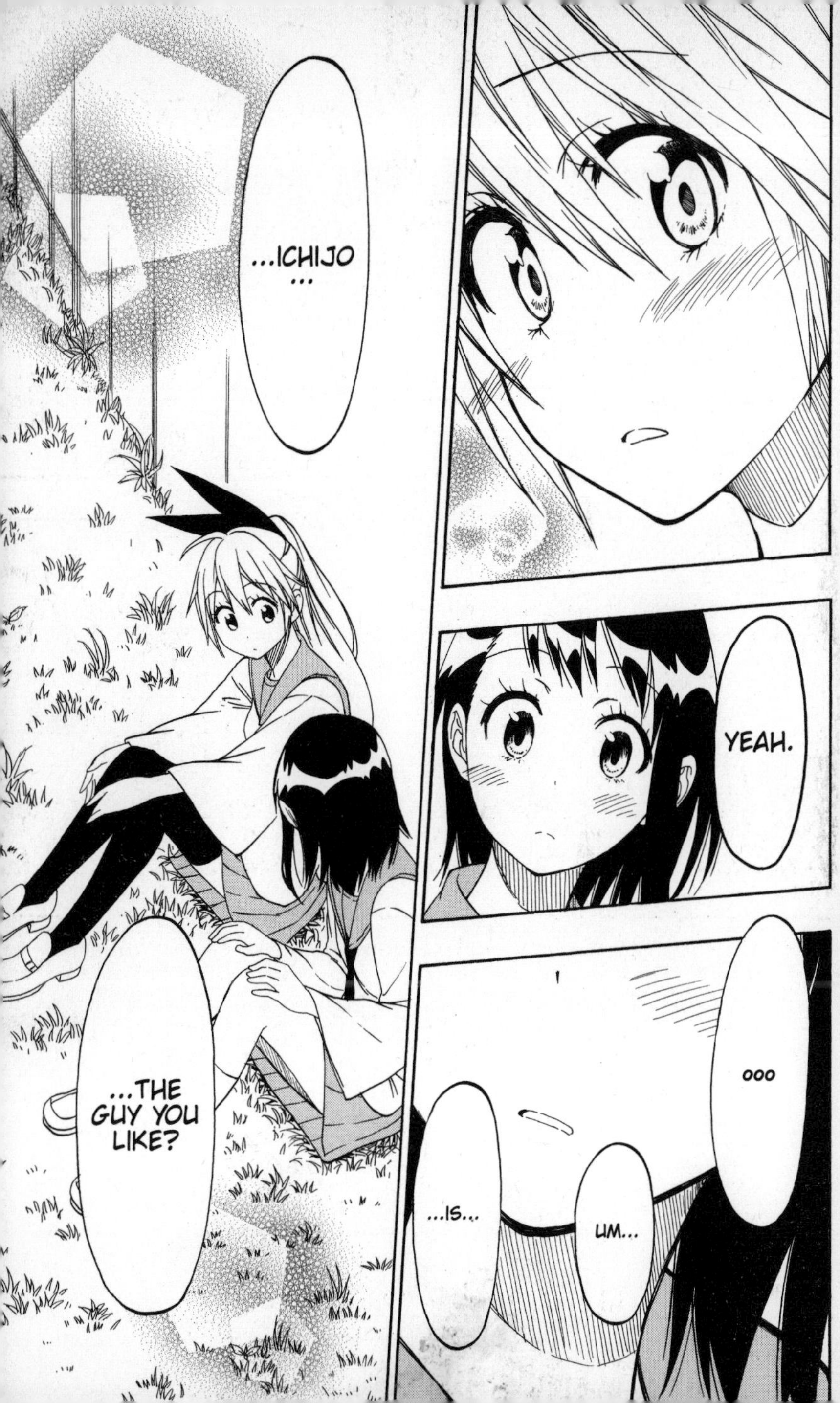
YEAH.
ooo
UM...
...IS...
...ICHIJO ...
...THE GUY YOU LIKE?

So
sad!

Sniff...

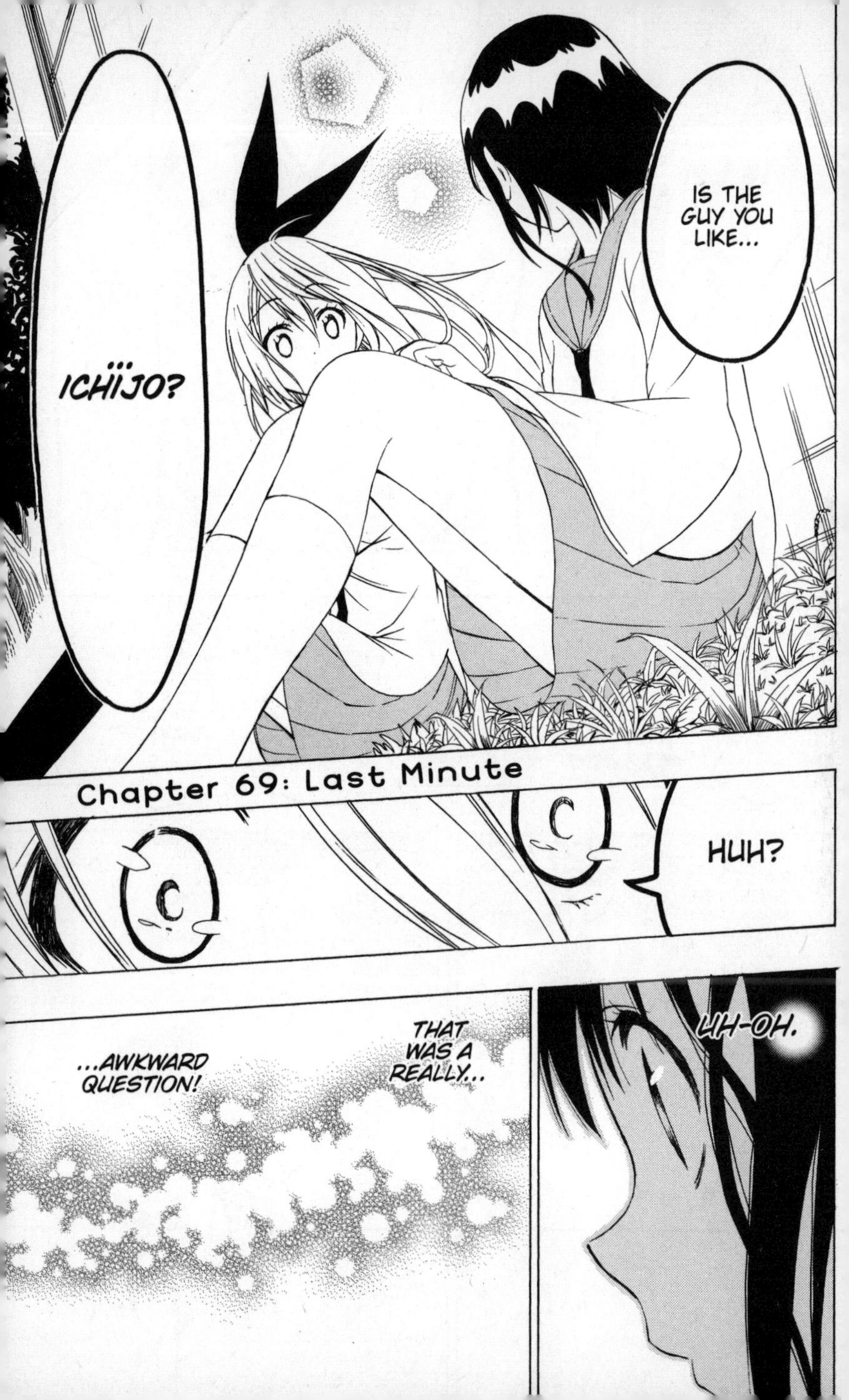
IS THE GUY YOU LIKE...
...ICHIJO?
Chapter 69: Last Minute
HUH?
UH-OH.
THAT WAS A REALLY...
...AWKWARD QUESTION!

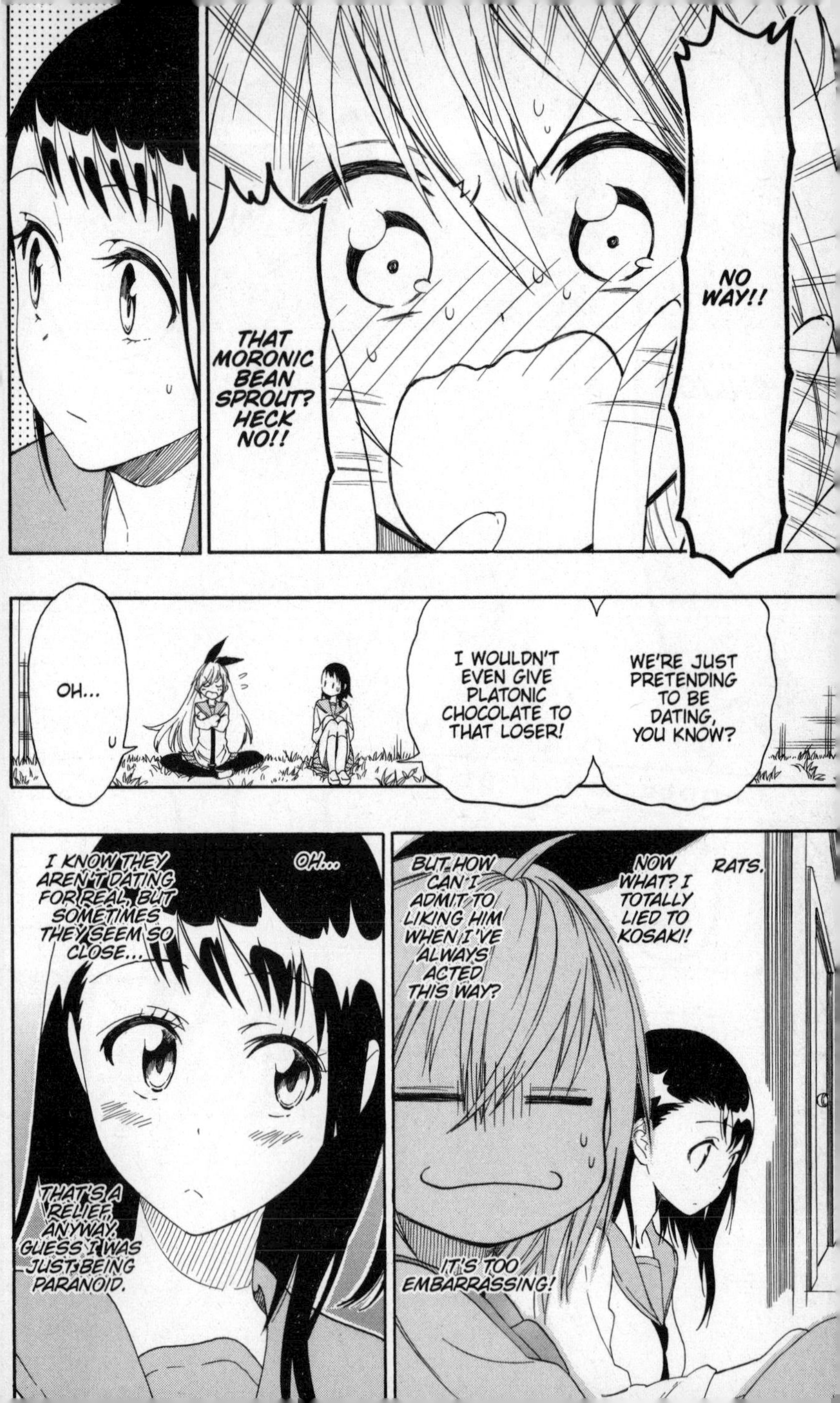
NO WAY!!
THAT MORONIC BEAN SPROUT? HECK NO!!
WE'RE JUST PRETENDING TO BE DATING, YOU KNOW?
I WOULDN'T EVEN GIVE PLATONIC CHOCOLATE TO THAT LOSER!
OH...
RATS.
NOW WHAT? I TOTALLY LIED TO KOSAKI!
BUT HOW CAN I ADMIT TO LIKING HIM WHEN I'VE ALWAYS ACTED THIS WAY?
IT'S TOO EMBARRASSING!
OH...
I KNOW THEY AREN'T DATING FOR REAL, BUT SOMETIMES THEY SEEM SO CLOSE...
THAT'S A RELIEF, ANYWAY. GUESS I WAS JUST BEING PARANOID.

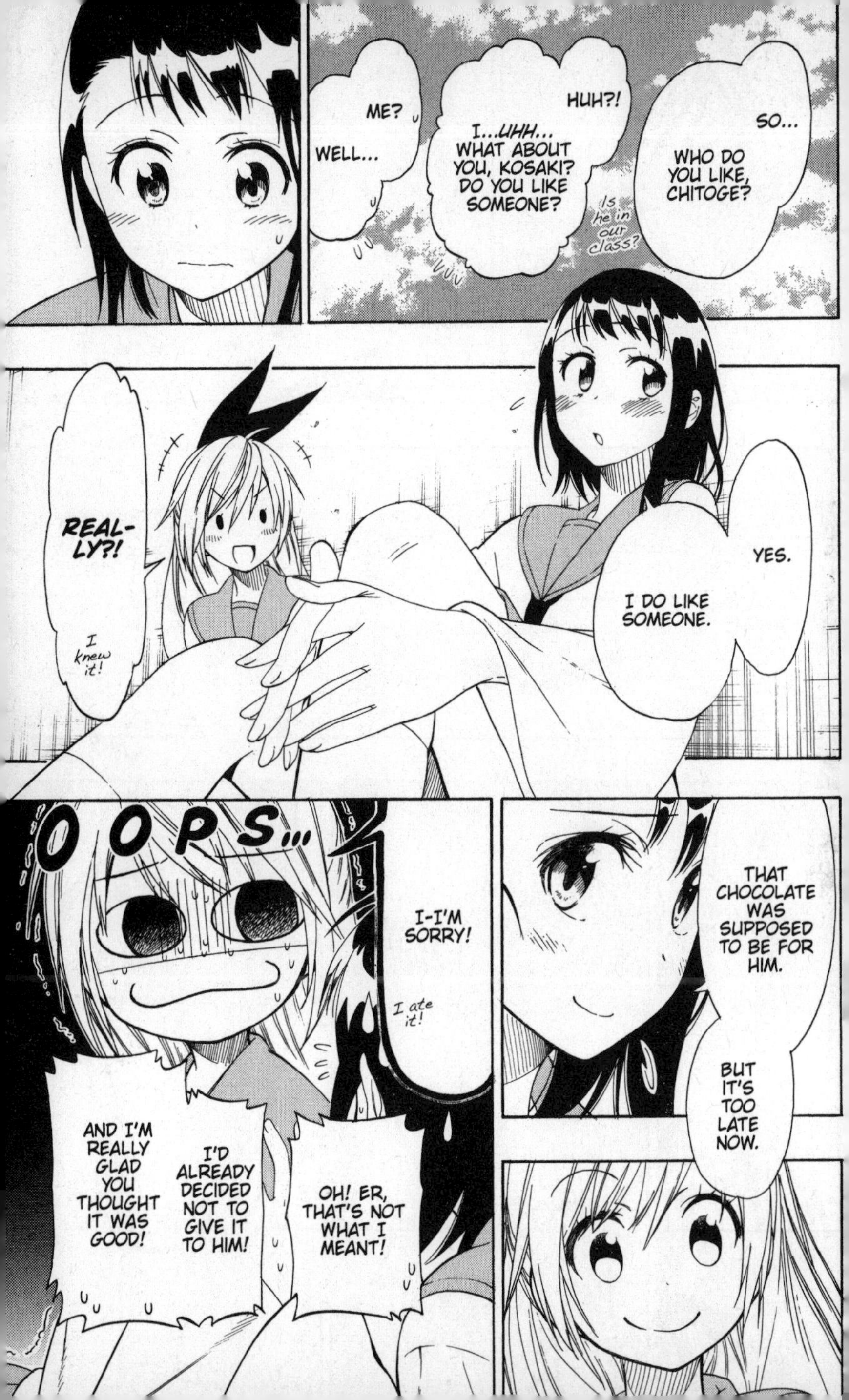
SO... WHO DO YOU LIKE, CHITOGE?
Is he in our class?
HUH?!
I...UHH... WHAT ABOUT YOU, KOSAKI? DO YOU LIKE SOMEONE?
ME? WELL...
YES. I DO LIKE SOMEONE.
REAL-LY?!
I knew it!
THAT CHOCOLATE WAS SUPPOSED TO BE FOR HIM.
BUT IT'S TOO LATE NOW.
OOPS...
I-I'M SORRY!
I ate it!
OH! ER, THAT'S NOT WHAT I MEANT!
I'D ALREADY DECIDED NOT TO GIVE IT TO HIM!
AND I'M REALLY GLAD YOU THOUGHT IT WAS GOOD!

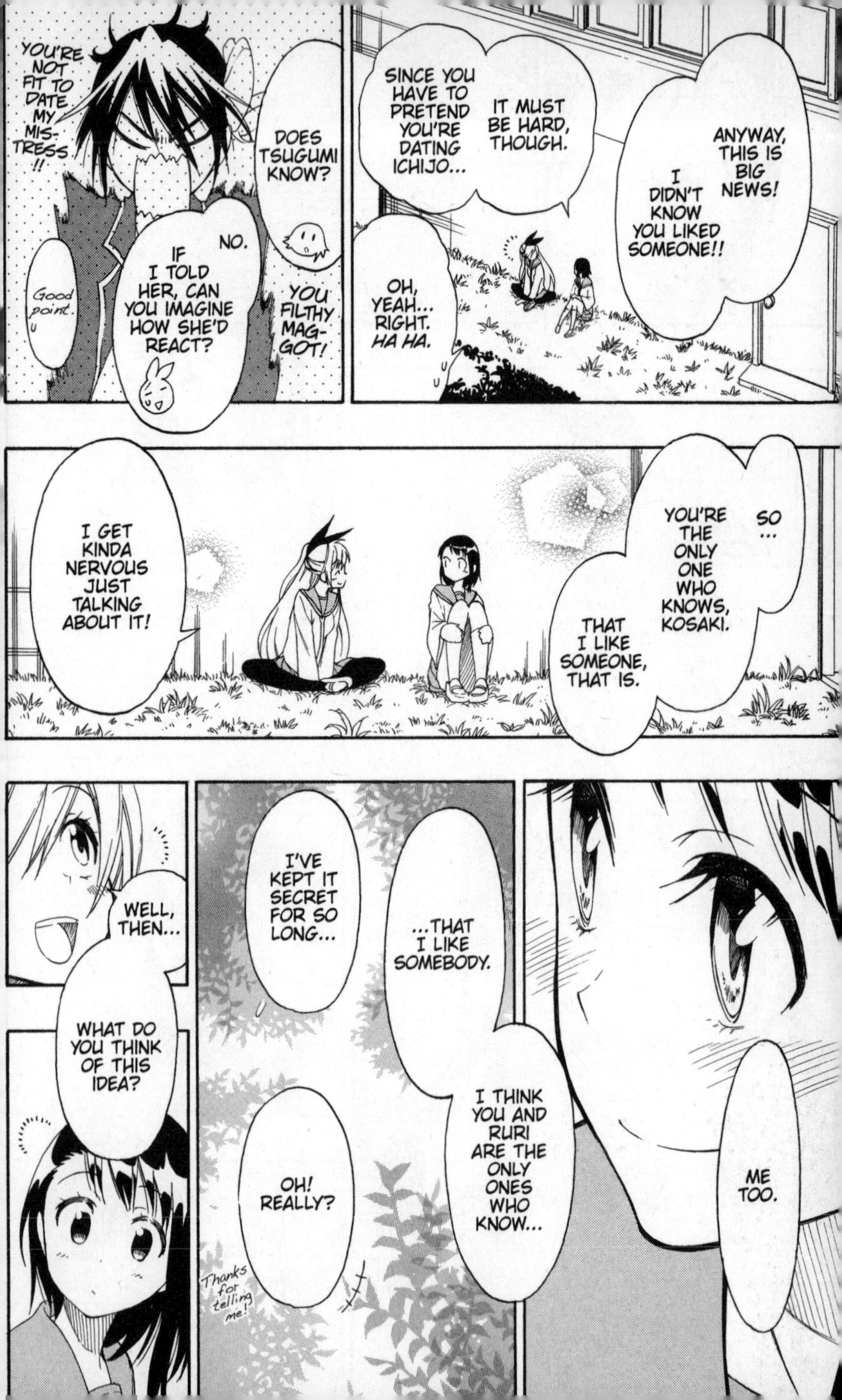
ANYWAY, THIS IS BIG NEWS!
I DIDN'T KNOW YOU LIKED SOMEONE!!
IT MUST BE HARD, THOUGH.
SINCE YOU HAVE TO PRETEND YOU'RE DATING ICHIJO...
OH, YEAH... RIGHT. HA HA.
DOES TSUGUMI KNOW?
NO.
IF I TOLD HER, CAN YOU IMAGINE HOW SHE'D REACT?
YOU FILTHY MAGGOT!
YOU'RE NOT FIT TO DATE MY MISTRESS!!
Good point.
SO...
YOU'RE THE ONLY ONE WHO KNOWS, KOSAKI.
THAT I LIKE SOMEONE, THAT IS.
I GET KINDA NERVOUS JUST TALKING ABOUT IT!
ME TOO.
I'VE KEPT IT SECRET FOR SO LONG...
...THAT I LIKE SOMEBODY.
I THINK YOU AND RURI ARE THE ONLY ONES WHO KNOW...
OH! REALLY?
Thanks for telling me!
WELL, THEN...
WHAT DO YOU THINK OF THIS IDEA?

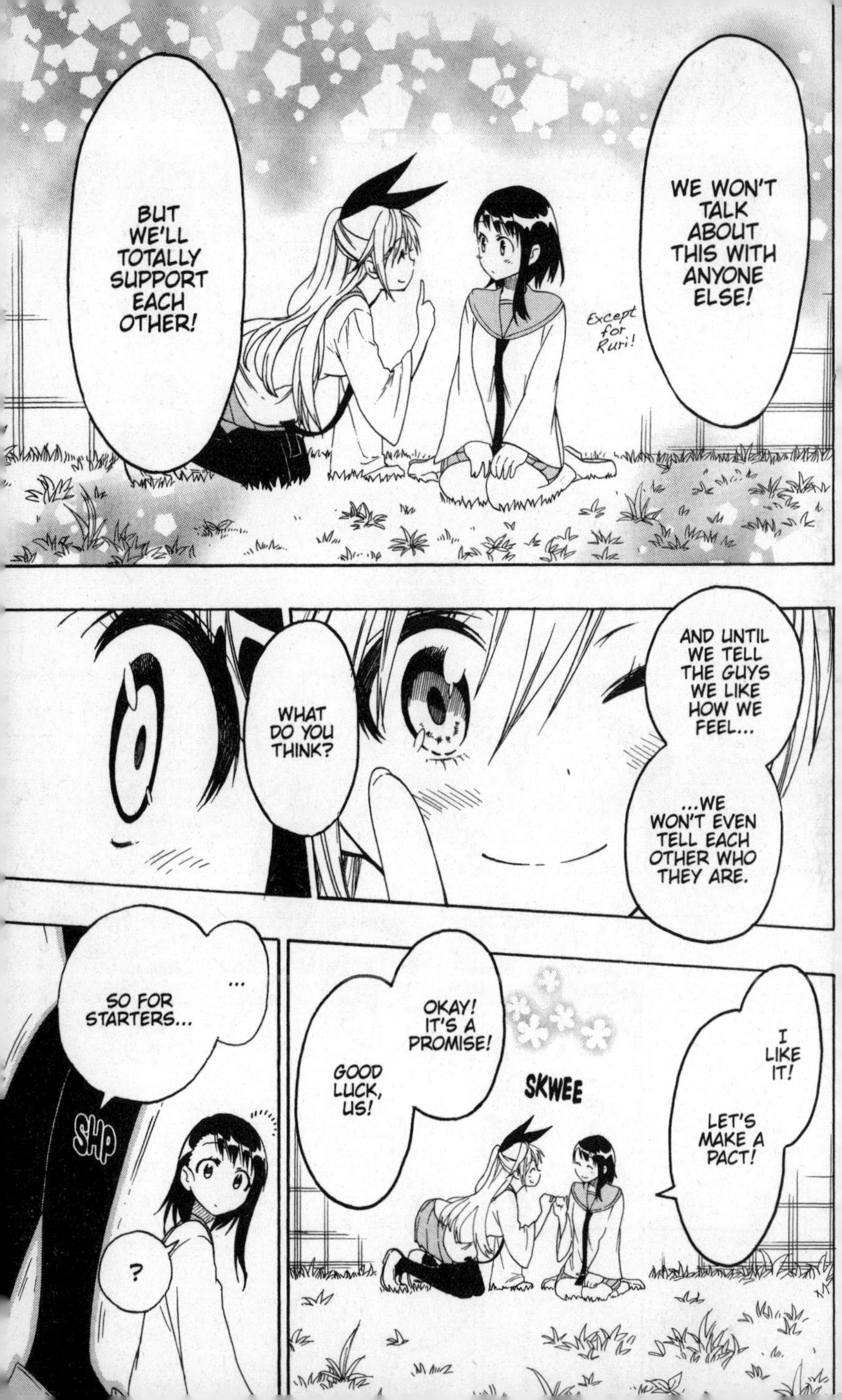
WE WON'T TALK ABOUT THIS WITH ANYONE ELSE!
Except for Ruri!
BUT WE'LL TOTALLY SUPPORT EACH OTHER!
AND UNTIL WE TELL THE GUYS WE LIKE HOW WE FEEL...
...WE WON'T EVEN TELL EACH OTHER WHO THEY ARE.
WHAT DO YOU THINK?
I LIKE IT!
LET'S MAKE A PACT!
SKWEE
OKAY! IT'S A PROMISE!
GOOD LUCK, US!
...
SO FOR STARTERS...
SHP
?

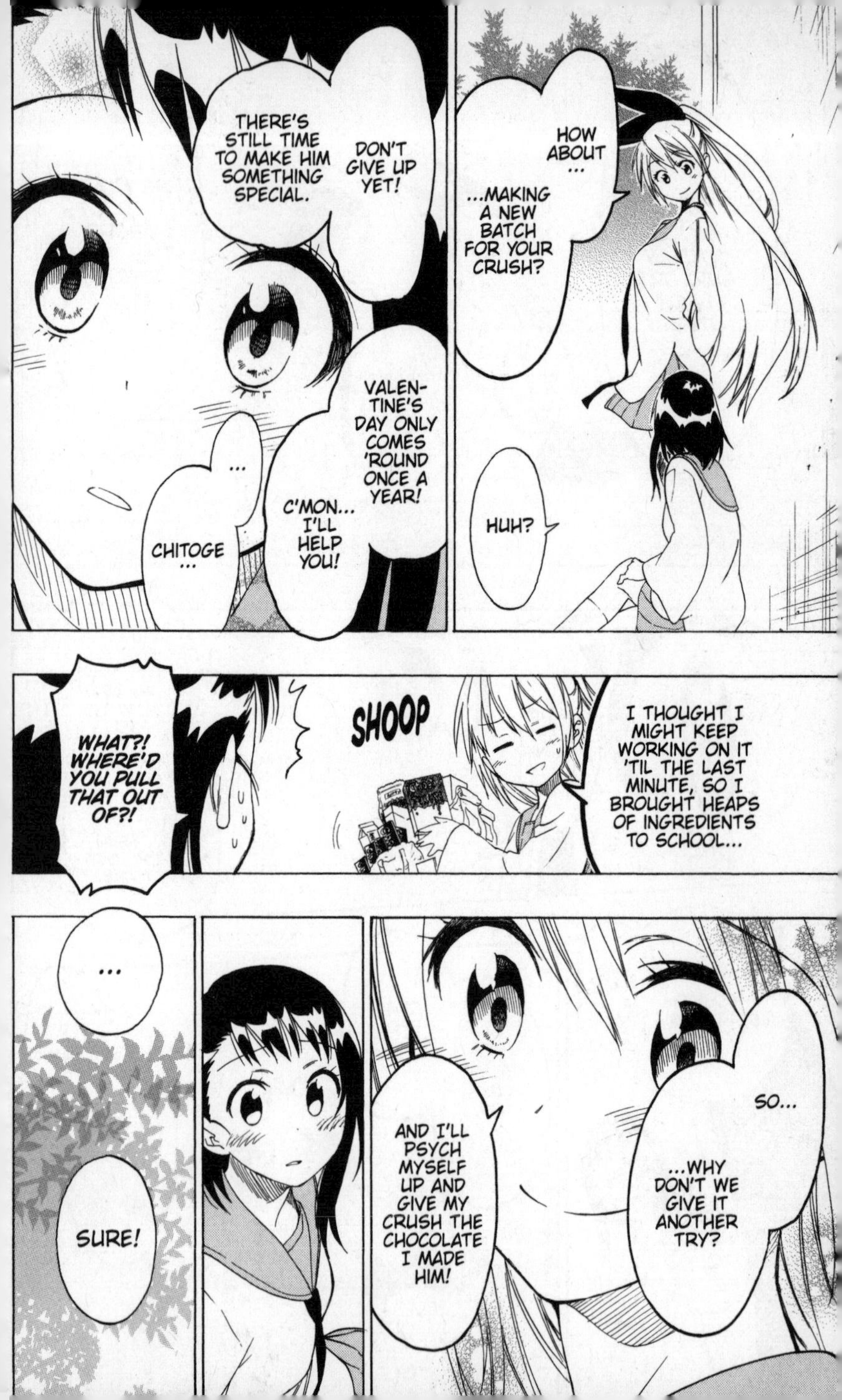
HOW ABOUT ...
...MAKING A NEW BATCH FOR YOUR CRUSH?
HUH?
DON'T GIVE UP YET!
THERE'S STILL TIME TO MAKE HIM SOMETHING SPECIAL.
VALEN-TINE'S DAY ONLY COMES 'ROUND ONCE A YEAR!
C'MON... I'LL HELP YOU!
...
CHITOGE ...
I THOUGHT I MIGHT KEEP WORKING ON IT 'TIL THE LAST MINUTE, SO I BROUGHT HEAPS OF INGREDIENTS TO SCHOOL...
SHOOP
WHAT?! WHERE'D YOU PULL THAT OUT OF?!
SO...
...WHY DON'T WE GIVE IT ANOTHER TRY?
AND I'LL PSYCH MYSELF UP AND GIVE MY CRUSH THE CHOCOLATE I MADE HIM!
...
SURE!

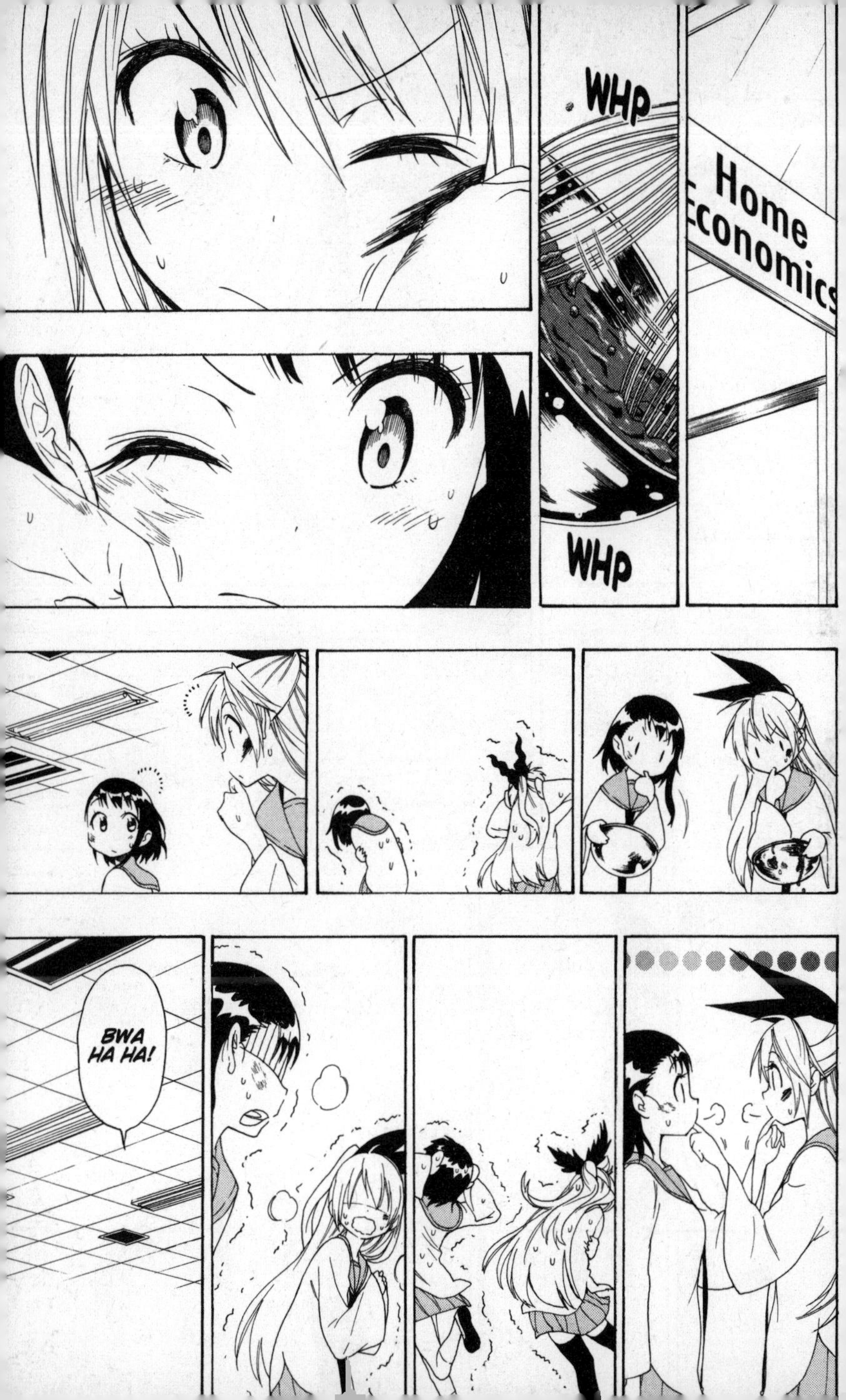
Home Economics
WHP
WHP
BWA HA HA!

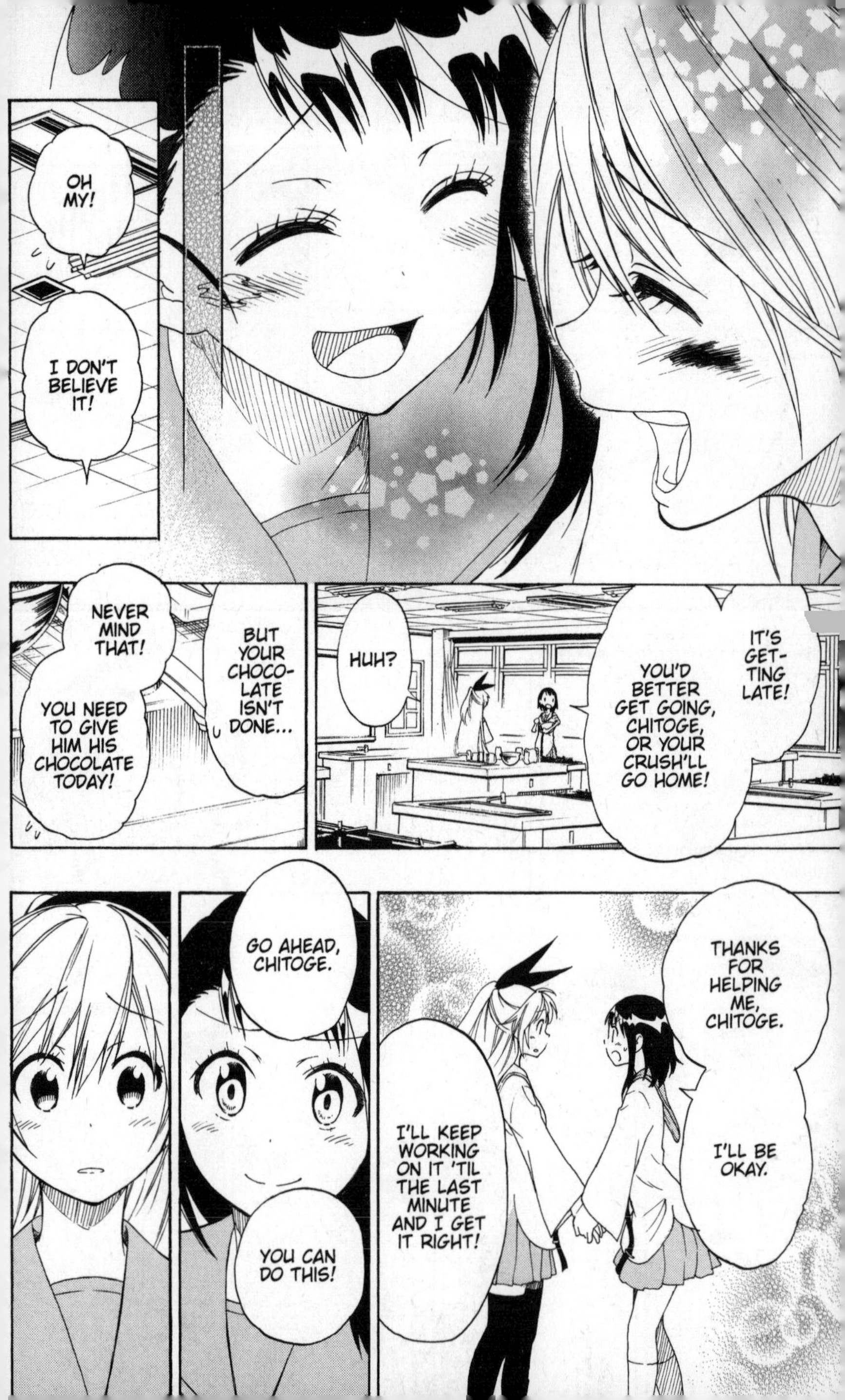
OH MY!
I DON'T BELIEVE IT!
IT'S GET-TING LATE!
YOU'D BETTER GET GOING, CHITOGE, OR YOUR CRUSH'LL GO HOME!
HUH?
BUT YOUR CHOCO-LATE ISN'T DONE...
NEVER MIND THAT!
YOU NEED TO GIVE HIM HIS CHOCOLATE TODAY!
THANKS FOR HELPING ME, CHITOGE.
I'LL BE OKAY.
I'LL KEEP WORKING ON IT 'TIL THE LAST MINUTE AND I GET IT RIGHT!
GO AHEAD, CHITOGE.
YOU CAN DO THIS!

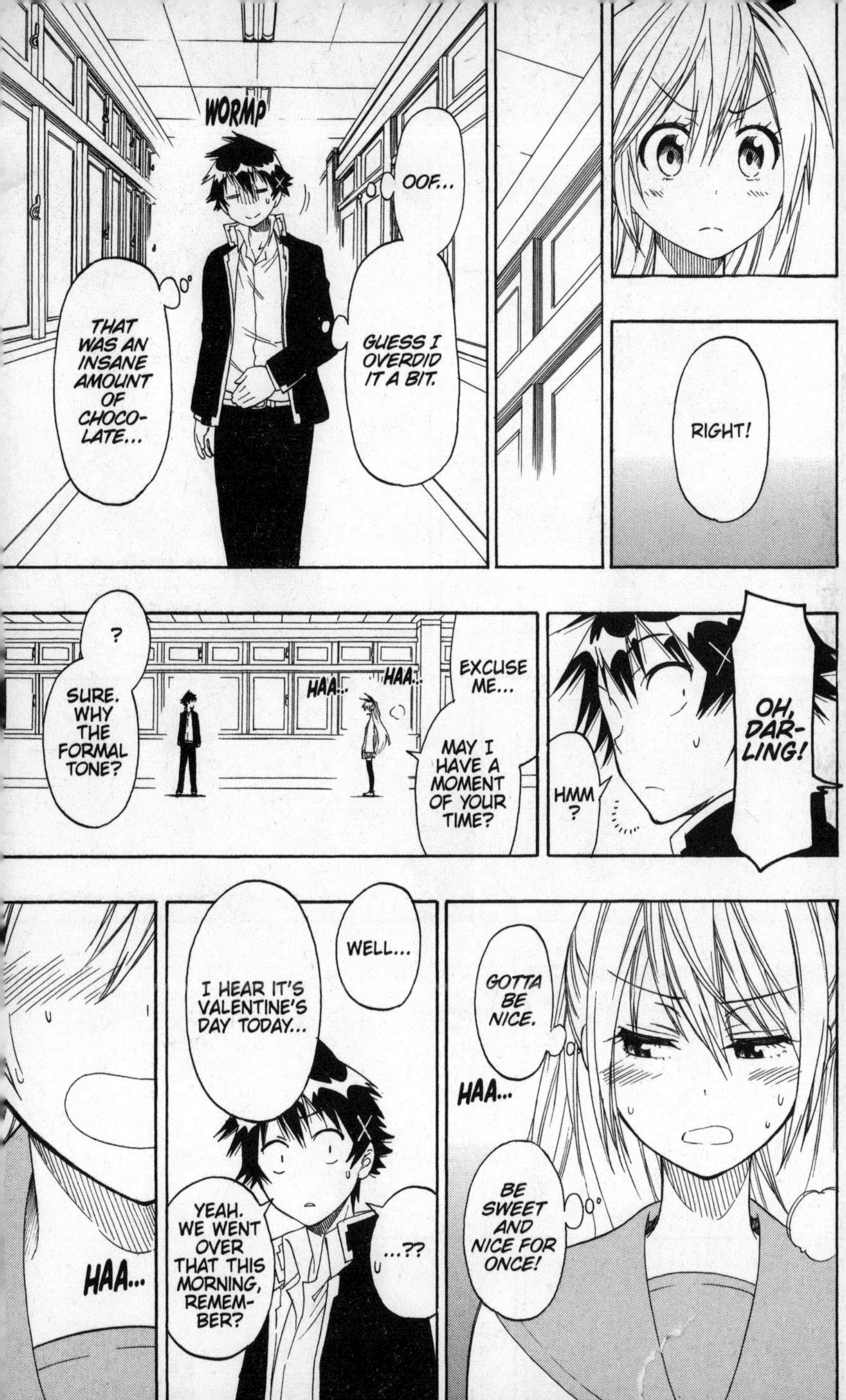
RIGHT!
WORMP
OOF...
GUESS I OVERDID IT A BIT.
THAT WAS AN INSANE AMOUNT OF CHOCOLATE...
OH, DARLING!
HMM?
EXCUSE ME...
MAY I HAVE A MOMENT OF YOUR TIME?
HAA... HAA...
?
SURE. WHY THE FORMAL TONE?
GOTTA BE NICE.
HAA...
BE SWEET AND NICE FOR ONCE!
WELL...
I HEAR IT'S VALENTINE'S DAY TODAY...
...??
YEAH. WE WENT OVER THAT THIS MORNING, REMEMBER?
HAA...

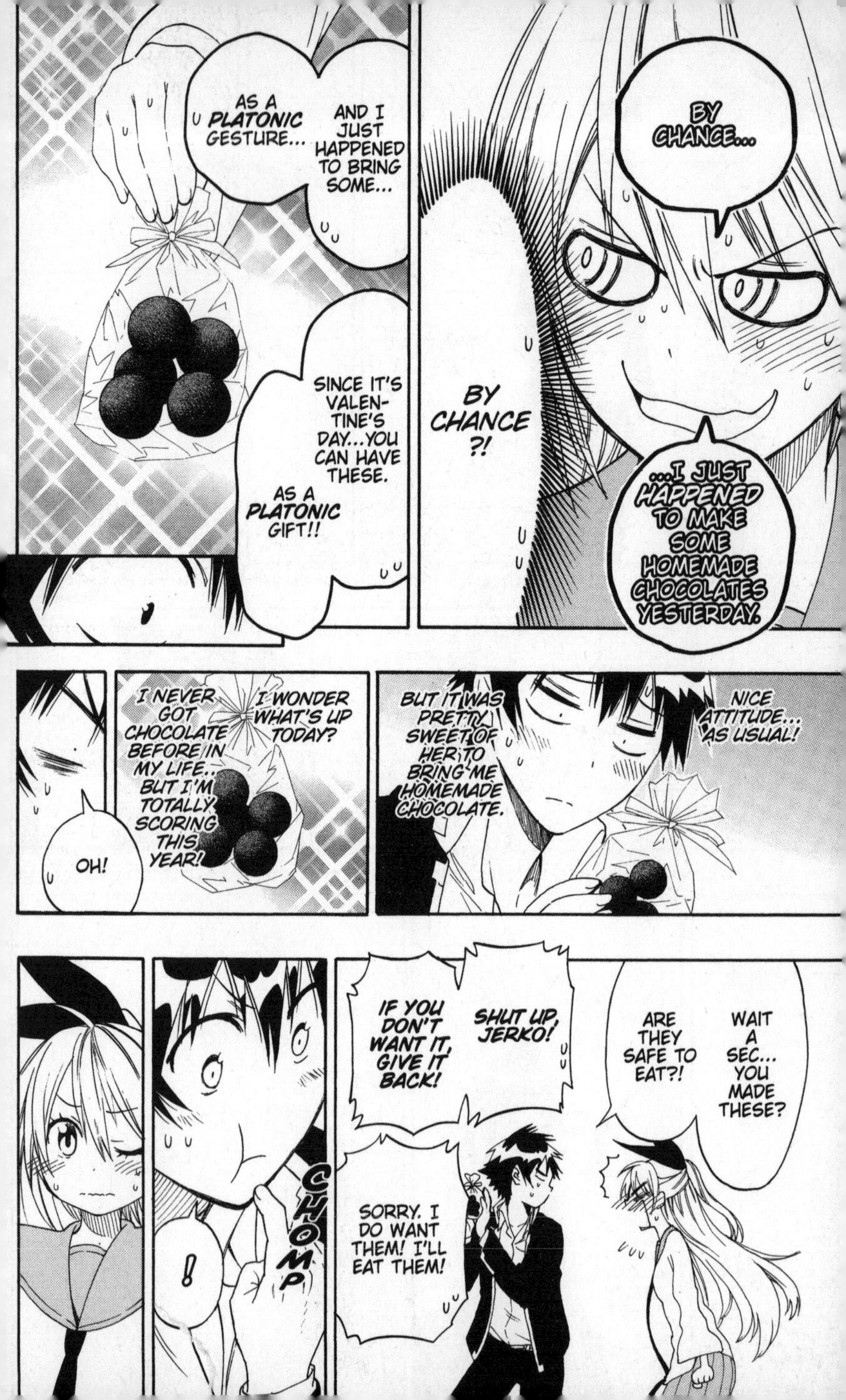
BY CHANCE...
...I JUST HAPPENED TO MAKE SOME HOMEMADE CHOCOLATES YESTERDAY.
BY CHANCE?!
AND I JUST HAPPENED TO BRING SOME...
AS A PLATONIC GESTURE...
SINCE IT'S VALEN-TINE'S DAY...YOU CAN HAVE THESE.
AS A PLATONIC GIFT!!
NICE ATTITUDE... AS USUAL!
BUT IT WAS PRETTY SWEET OF HER TO BRING ME HOMEMADE CHOCOLATE.
I WONDER WHAT'S UP TODAY?
I NEVER GOT CHOCOLATE BEFORE IN MY LIFE... BUT I'M TOTALLY SCORING THIS YEAR!
OH!
WAIT A SEC... YOU MADE THESE?
ARE THEY SAFE TO EAT?!
SHUT UP, JERKO!
IF YOU DON'T WANT IT, GIVE IT BACK!
SORRY. I DO WANT THEM! I'LL EAT THEM!
CHOMP
!

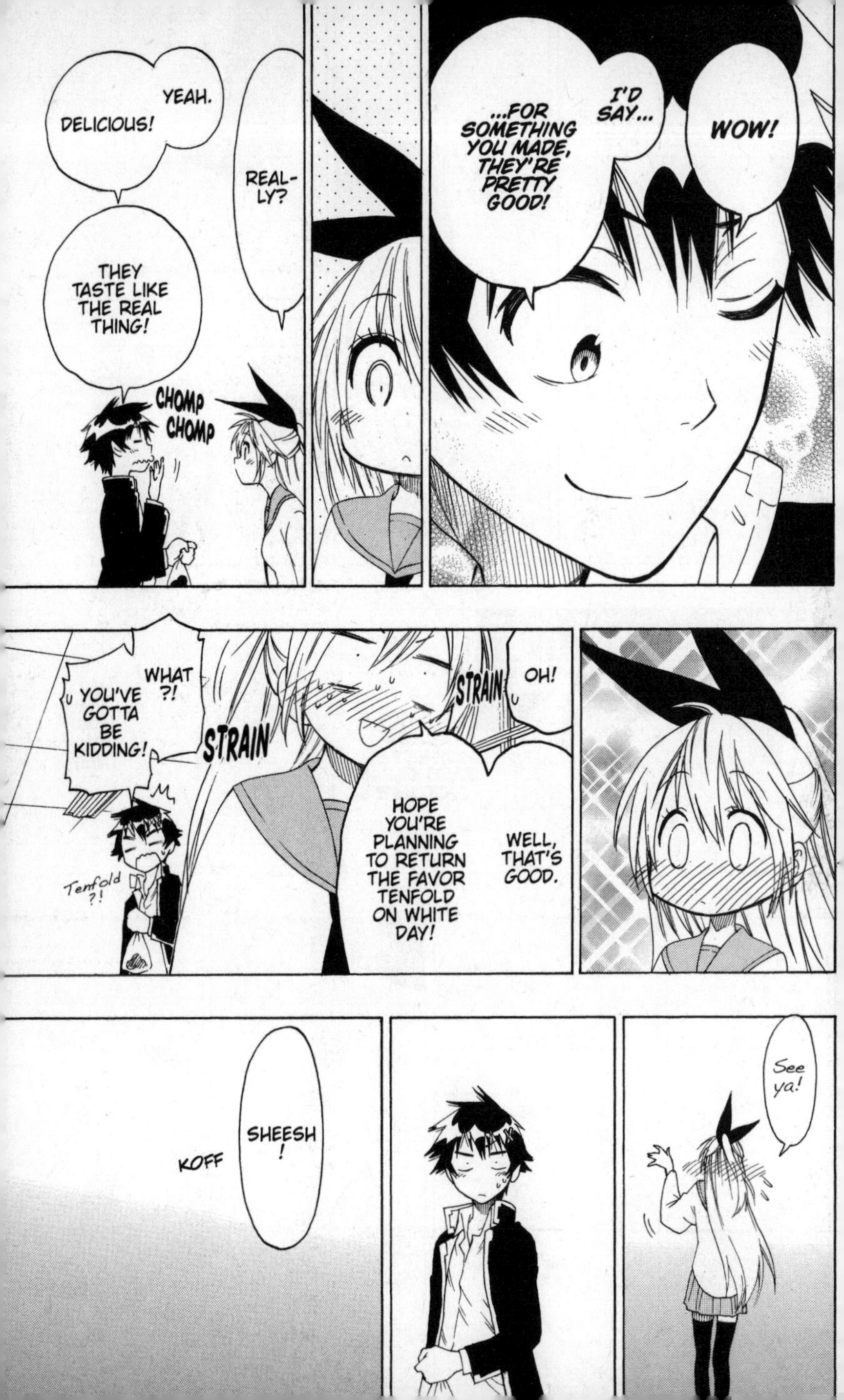
WOW!
I'D SAY...
...FOR SOMETHING YOU MADE, THEY'RE PRETTY GOOD!
REAL-LY?
YEAH. DELICIOUS!
THEY TASTE LIKE THE REAL THING!
CHOMP CHOMP
OH!
STRAIN
WELL, THAT'S GOOD.
HOPE YOU'RE PLANNING TO RETURN THE FAVOR TENFOLD ON WHITE DAY!
STRAIN
WHAT?!
YOU'VE GOTTA BE KIDDING!
Tenfold?!
See ya!
SHEESH!
KOFF

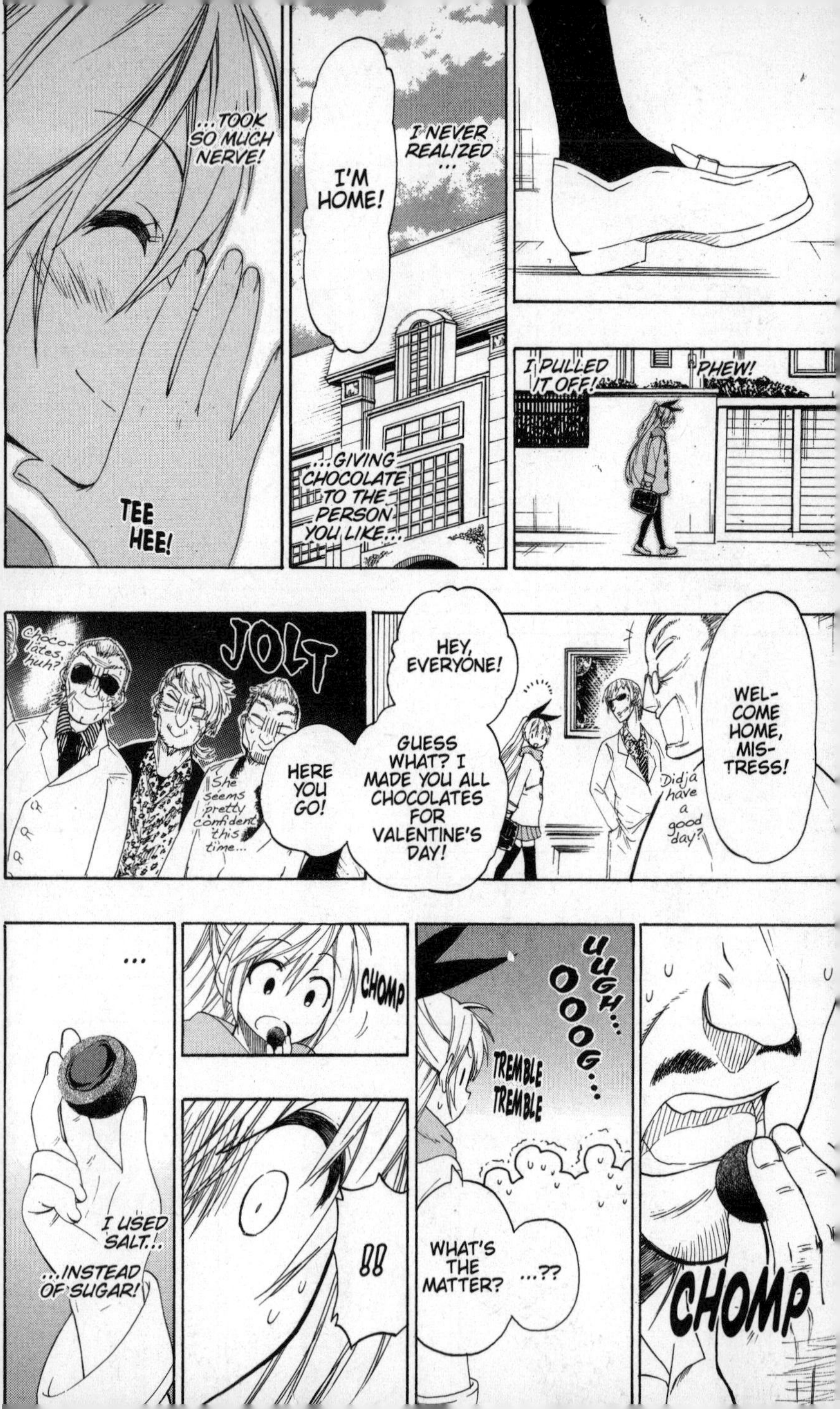
I PULLED IT OFF!
PHEW!
I NEVER REALIZED...
I'M HOME!
...GIVING CHOCOLATE TO THE PERSON YOU LIKE...
...TOOK SO MUCH NERVE!
TEE HEE!
WELCOME HOME, MISTRESS!
Didja have a good day?
HEY, EVERYONE!
GUESS WHAT? I MADE YOU ALL CHOCOLATES FOR VALENTINE'S DAY!
HERE YOU GO!
JOLT
Chocolates, huh?
She seems pretty confident this time...
CHOMP
UUGH... OOOG...
TREMBLE TREMBLE
...??
WHAT'S THE MATTER?
CHOMP
!!
...
I USED SALT...
...INSTEAD OF SUGAR!

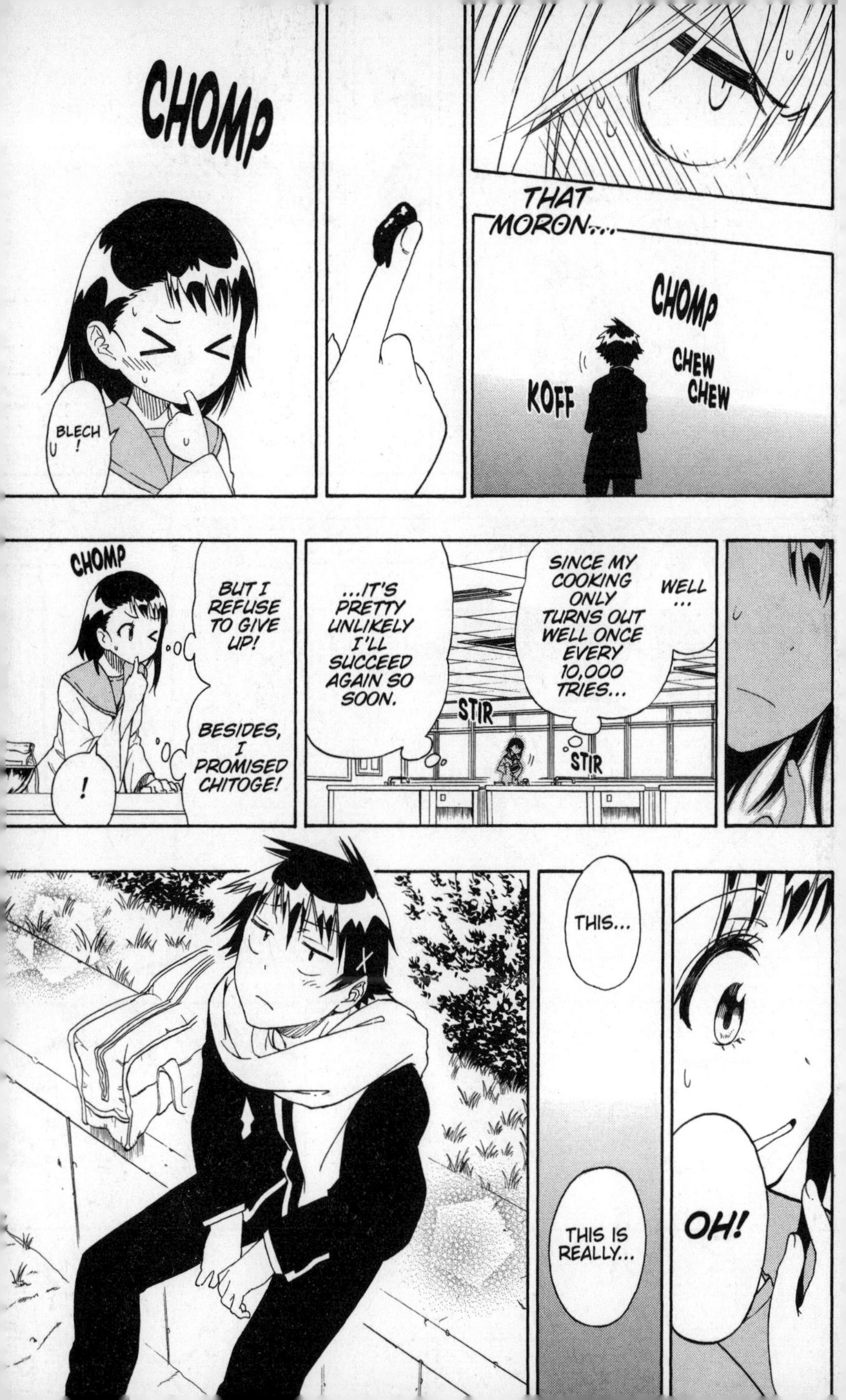
THAT MORON...
CHOMP
CHEW CHEW
KOFF
CHOMP
BLECH!
WELL...
SINCE MY COOKING ONLY TURNS OUT WELL ONCE EVERY 10,000 TRIES...
...IT'S PRETTY UNLIKELY I'LL SUCCEED AGAIN SO SOON.
STIR
STIR
CHOMP
BUT I REFUSE TO GIVE UP!
BESIDES, I PROMISED CHITOGE!
!
OH!
THIS...
THIS IS REALLY...

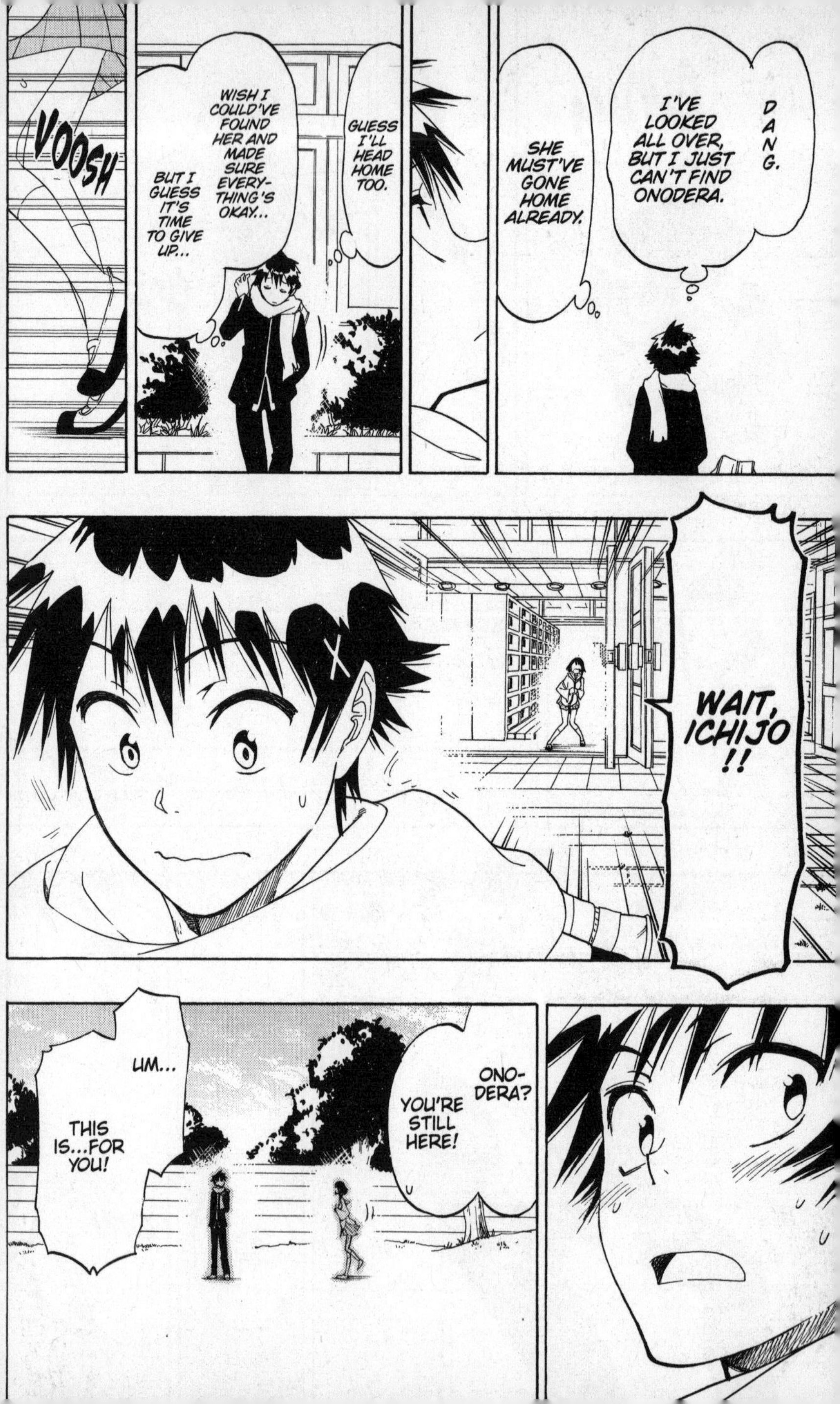
DANG.
I'VE LOOKED ALL OVER, BUT I JUST CAN'T FIND ONODERA.
SHE MUST'VE GONE HOME ALREADY.
GUESS I'LL HEAD HOME TOO.
WISH I COULD'VE FOUND HER AND MADE SURE EVERY-THING'S OKAY...
BUT I GUESS IT'S TIME TO GIVE UP...
VOOSH
WAIT, ICHIJO!!
ONO-DERA?
YOU'RE STILL HERE!
UM...
THIS IS...FOR YOU!

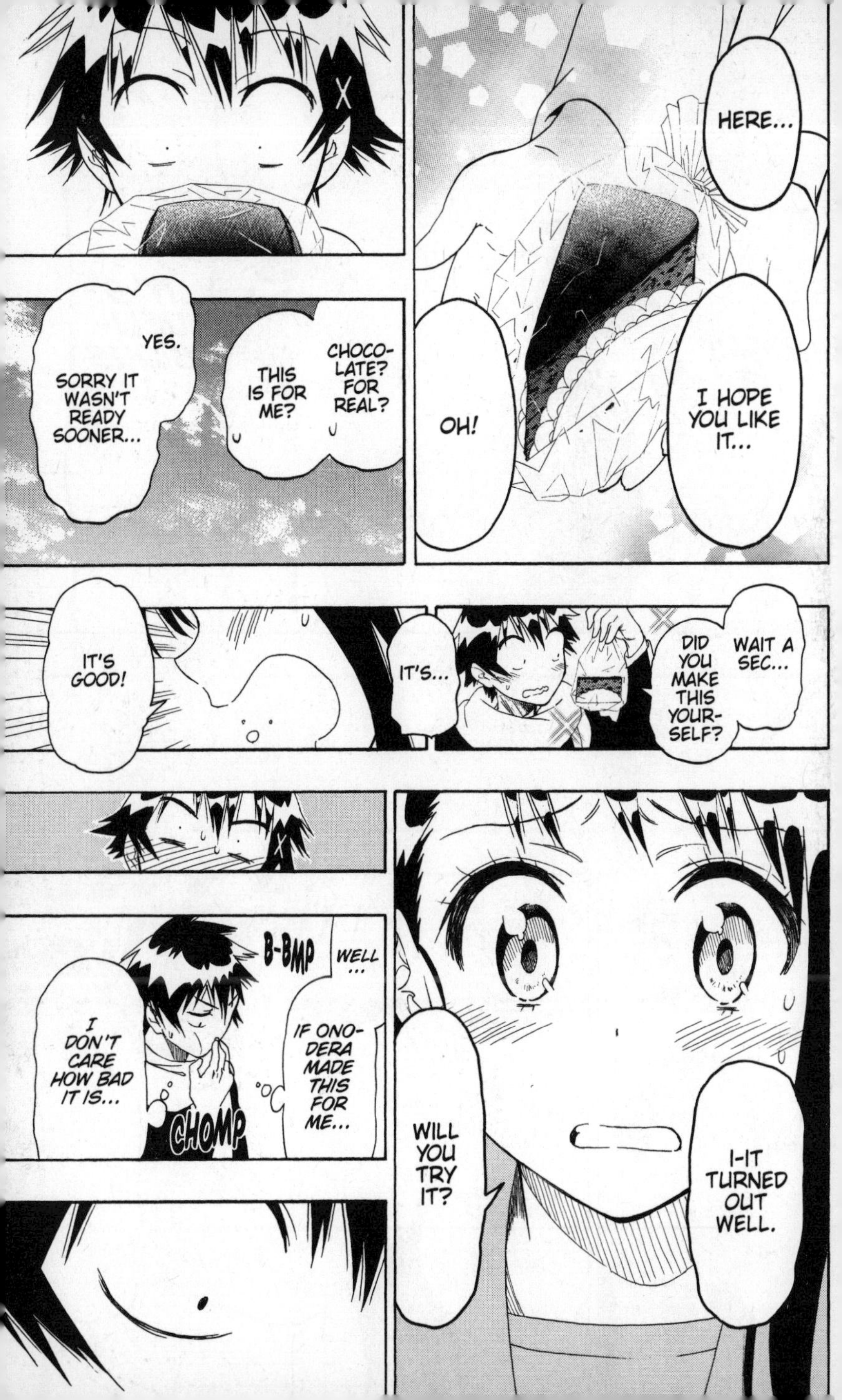
HERE...
I HOPE YOU LIKE IT...
OH!
CHOCO-LATE? FOR REAL?
THIS IS FOR ME?
YES.
SORRY IT WASN'T READY SOONER...
WAIT A SEC...
DID YOU MAKE THIS YOUR-SELF?
IT'S...
IT'S GOOD!
I-IT TURNED OUT WELL.
WILL YOU TRY IT?
WELL...
B-BMP
IF ONO-DERA MADE THIS FOR ME...
CHOMP
I DON'T CARE HOW BAD IT IS...

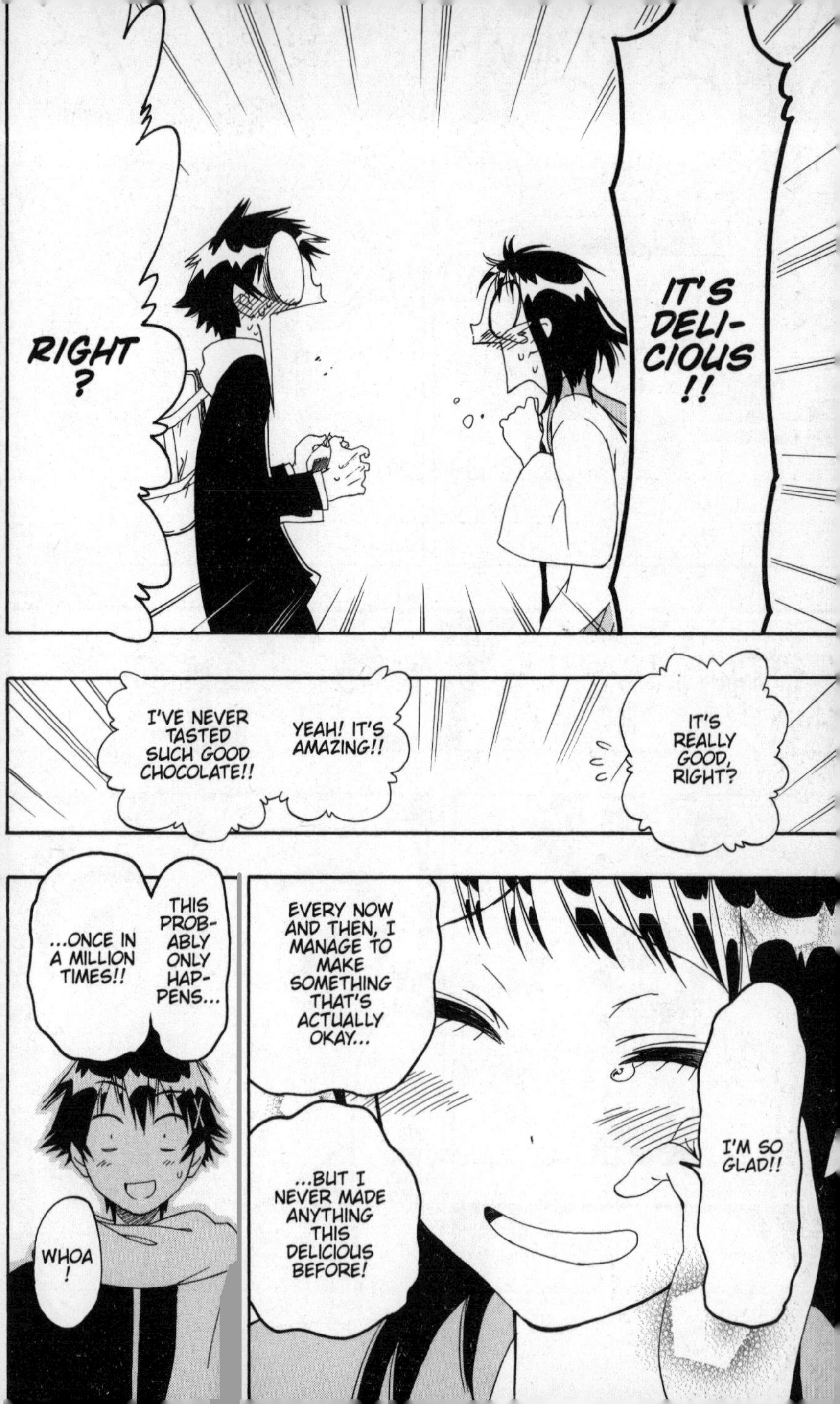
IT'S DELICIOUS!!
RIGHT?
IT'S REALLY GOOD, RIGHT?
YEAH! IT'S AMAZING!!
I'VE NEVER TASTED SUCH GOOD CHOCOLATE!!
I'M SO GLAD!!
EVERY NOW AND THEN, I MANAGE TO MAKE SOMETHING THAT'S ACTUALLY OKAY...
...BUT I NEVER MADE ANYTHING THIS DELICIOUS BEFORE!
THIS PROBABLY ONLY HAPPENS...
...ONCE IN A MILLION TIMES!!
WHOA!

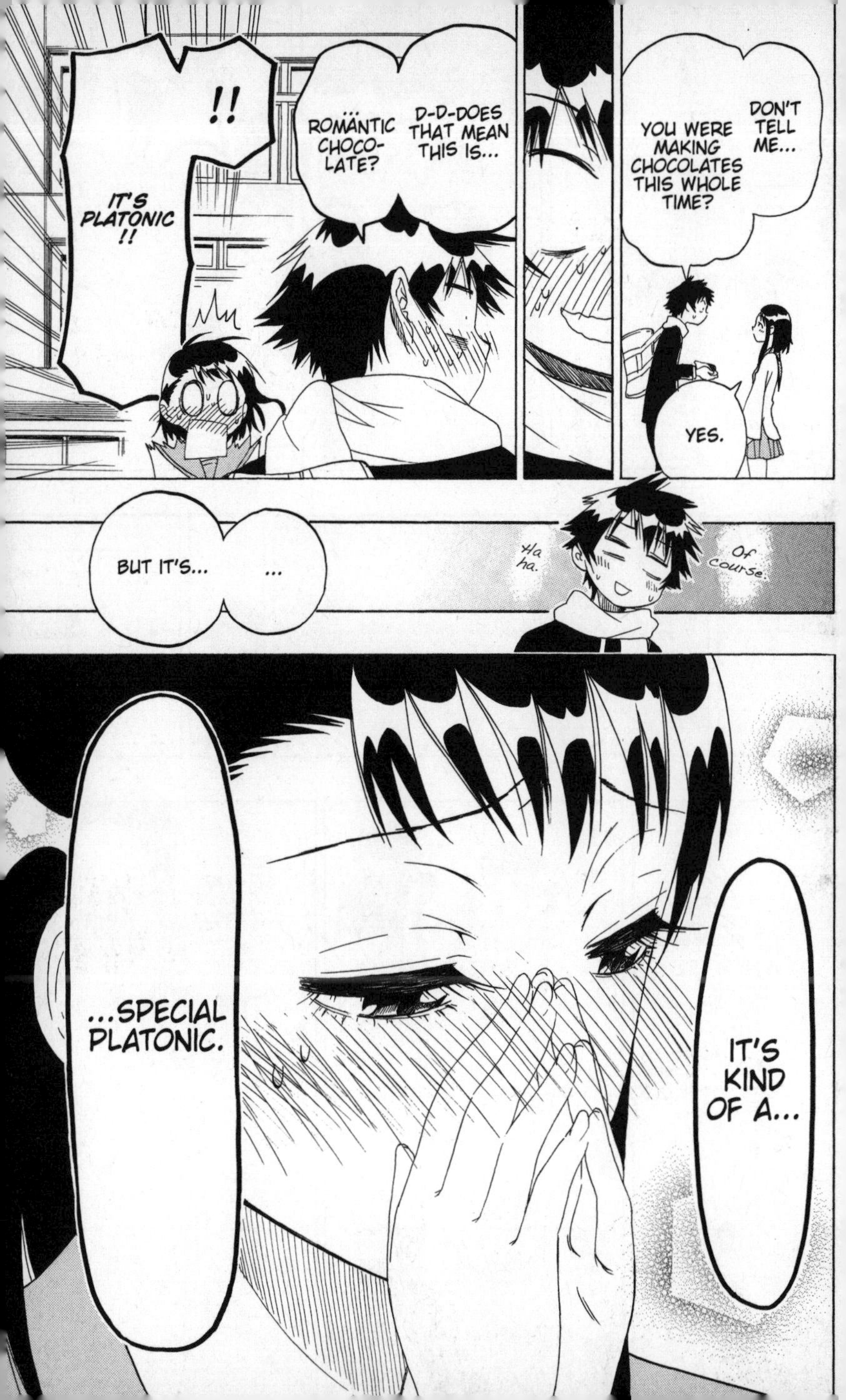
DON'T TELL ME...
YOU WERE MAKING CHOCOLATES THIS WHOLE TIME?
YES.
D-D-DOES THAT MEAN THIS IS...
...ROMANTIC CHOCOLATE?
!!
IT'S PLATONIC !!
Of course.
Ha ha.
BUT IT'S... ...
IT'S KIND OF A...
...SPECIAL PLATONIC.

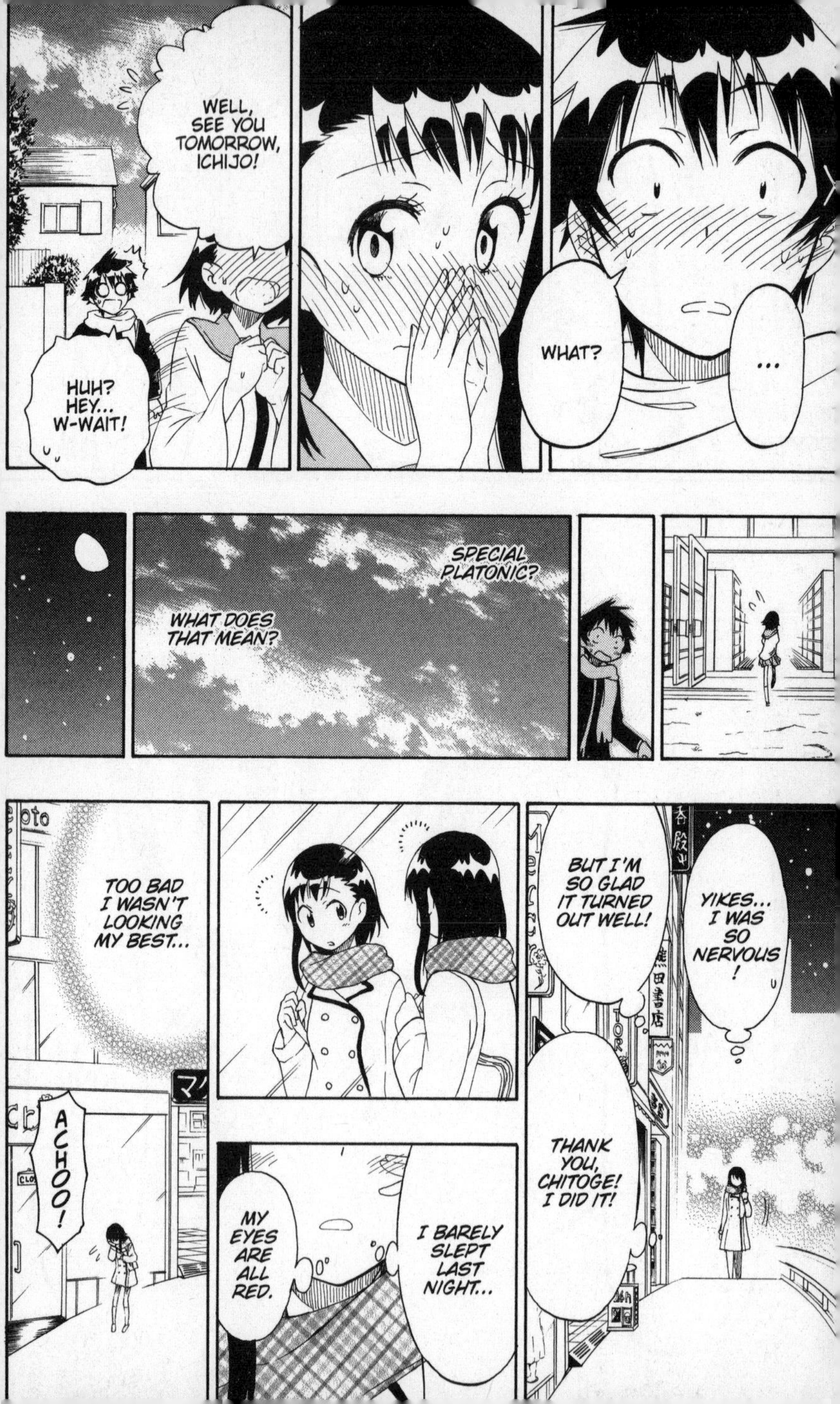
...
WHAT?
WELL, SEE YOU TOMORROW, ICHIJO!
HUH? HEY... W-WAIT!
SPECIAL PLATONIC?
WHAT DOES THAT MEAN?
YIKES... I WAS SO NERVOUS!
BUT I'M SO GLAD IT TURNED OUT WELL!
THANK YOU, CHITOGE! I DID IT!
I BARELY SLEPT LAST NIGHT...
MY EYES ARE ALL RED.
TOO BAD I WASN'T LOOKING MY BEST...
ACHOO!

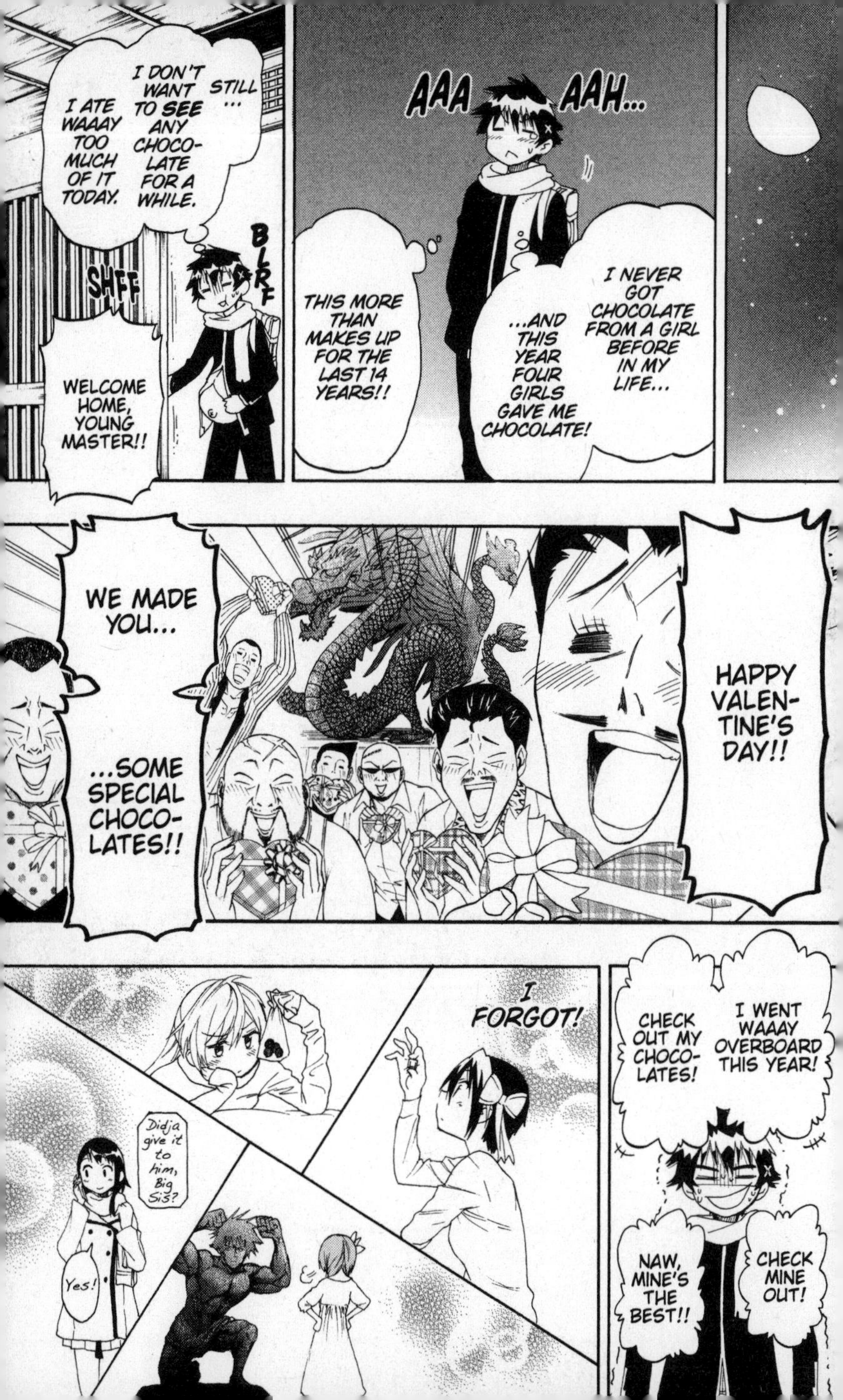
AAA AAH...
I NEVER GOT CHOCOLATE FROM A GIRL BEFORE IN MY LIFE...
...AND THIS YEAR FOUR GIRLS GAVE ME CHOCOLATE!
THIS MORE THAN MAKES UP FOR THE LAST 14 YEARS!!
STILL...
I DON'T WANT TO SEE ANY CHOCOLATE FOR A WHILE.
I ATE WAAAY TOO MUCH OF IT TODAY.
BLRF
SHFF
WELCOME HOME, YOUNG MASTER!!
HAPPY VALENTINE'S DAY!!
WE MADE YOU...
...SOME SPECIAL CHOCOLATES!!
I WENT WAAAY OVERBOARD THIS YEAR!
CHECK OUT MY CHOCOLATES!
CHECK MINE OUT!
NAW, MINE'S THE BEST!!
I FORGOT!
Didja give it to him, Big Sis?
Yes!

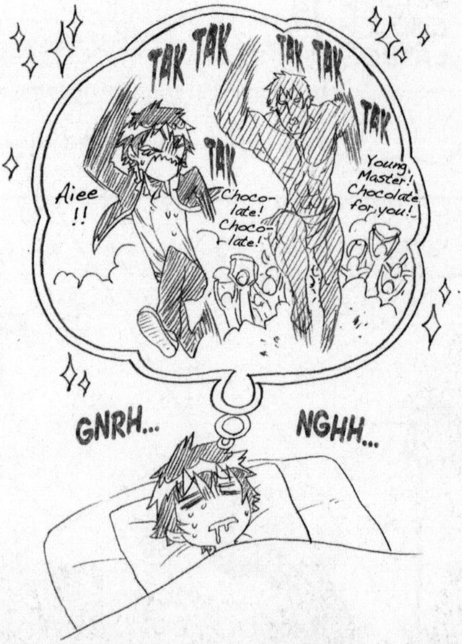
TAK TAK
TAK TAK
TAK
TAK
Young Master! Chocolate for you!
Chocolate! Chocolate!
Aiee !!
NGHH...
GNRH...

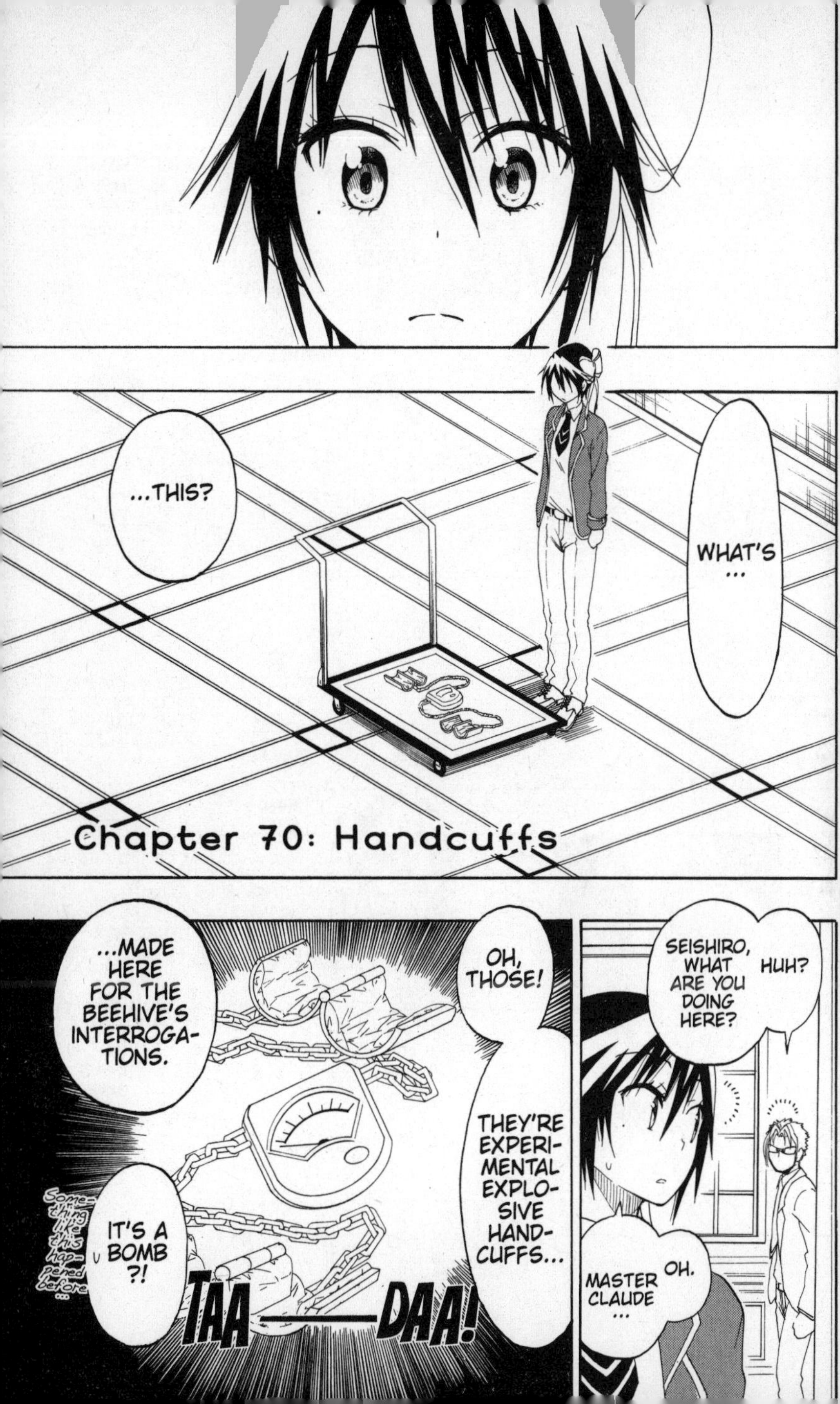
WHAT'S ...
...THIS?
Chapter 70: Handcuffs
HUH?
SEISHIRO, WHAT ARE YOU DOING HERE?
OH.
MASTER CLAUDE ...
OH, THOSE!
THEY'RE EXPERIMENTAL EXPLOSIVE HANDCUFFS...
...MADE HERE FOR THE BEEHIVE'S INTERROGATIONS.
TAA——DAA!
IT'S A BOMB ?!
Something like this happened before ...

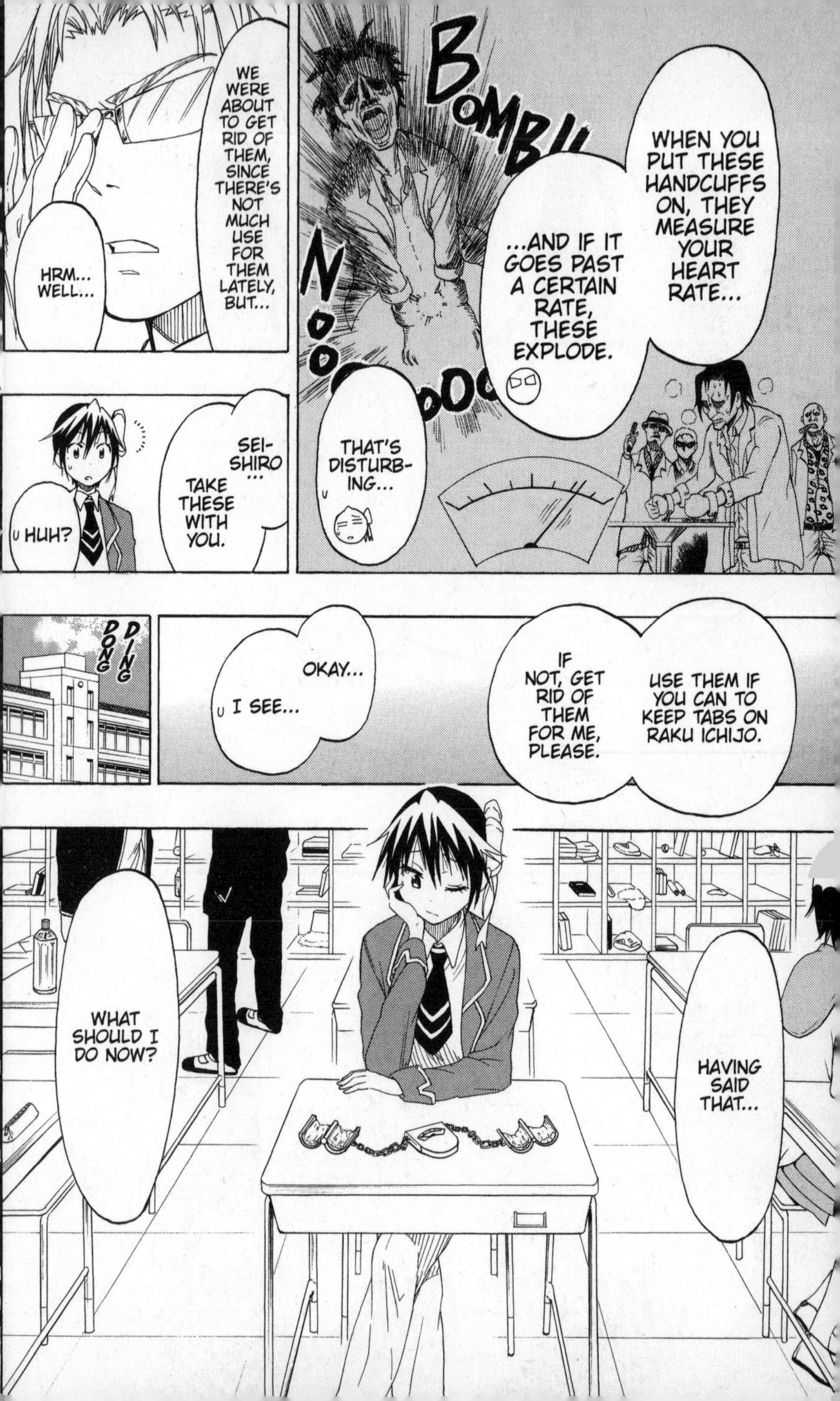
WHEN YOU PUT THESE HANDCUFFS ON, THEY MEASURE YOUR HEART RATE...
...AND IF IT GOES PAST A CERTAIN RATE, THESE EXPLODE.
BOMBU
THAT'S DISTURBING...
WE WERE ABOUT TO GET RID OF THEM, SINCE THERE'S NOT MUCH USE FOR THEM LATELY, BUT...
HRM... WELL...
SEI-SHIRO...
TAKE THESE WITH YOU.
HUH?
USE THEM IF YOU CAN TO KEEP TABS ON RAKU ICHIJO.
IF NOT, GET RID OF THEM FOR ME, PLEASE.
OKAY...
I SEE...
DING DONG
HAVING SAID THAT...
WHAT SHOULD I DO NOW?

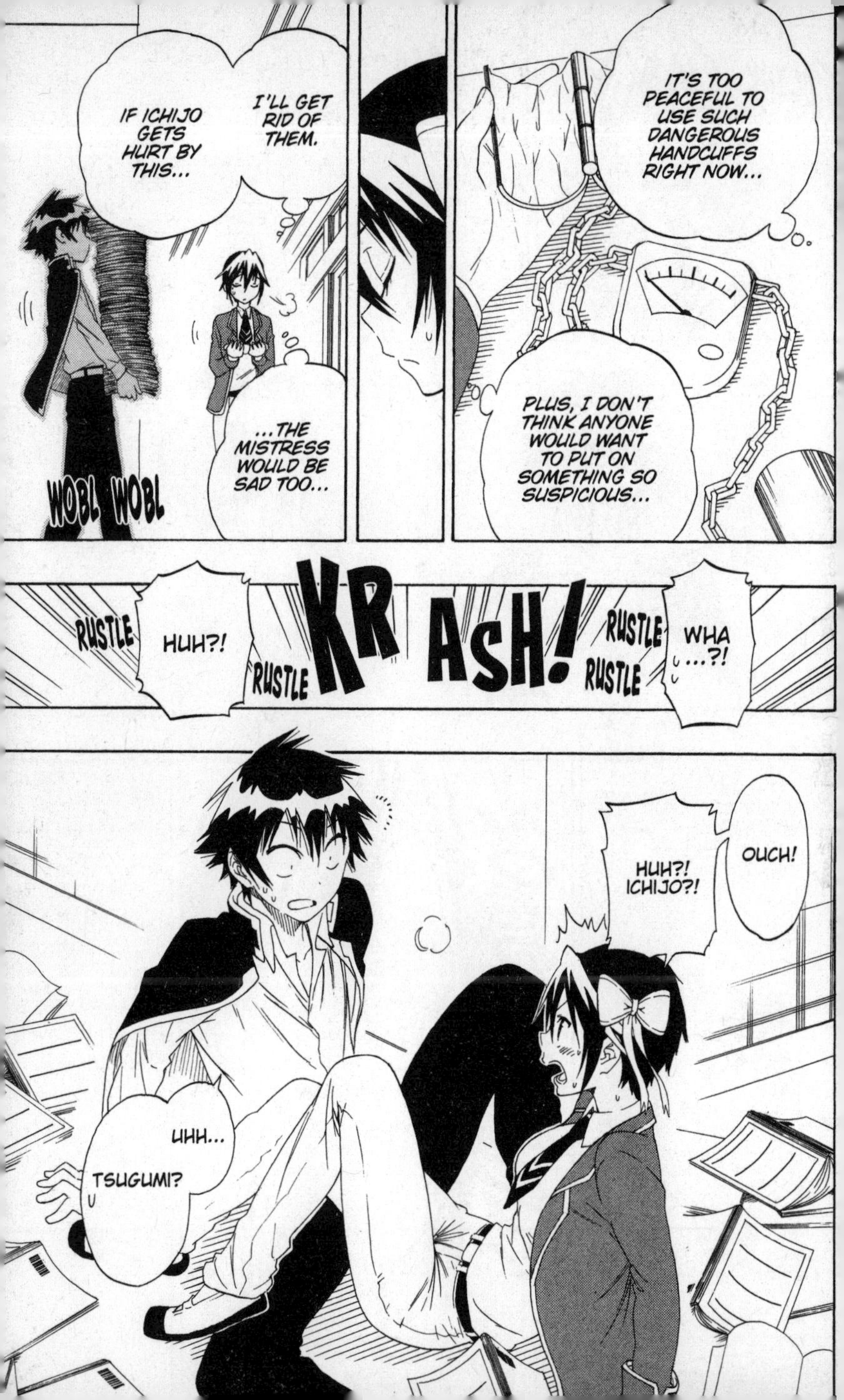
IT'S TOO PEACEFUL TO USE SUCH DANGEROUS HANDCUFFS RIGHT NOW...
PLUS, I DON'T THINK ANYONE WOULD WANT TO PUT ON SOMETHING SO SUSPICIOUS...
I'LL GET RID OF THEM.
IF ICHIJO GETS HURT BY THIS...
...THE MISTRESS WOULD BE SAD TOO...
WOBL WOBL
WHA ...?!
RUSTLE
RUSTLE
KRASH!
RUSTLE
HUH?!
RUSTLE
OUCH!
HUH?! ICHIJO?!
UHH...
TSUGUMI?

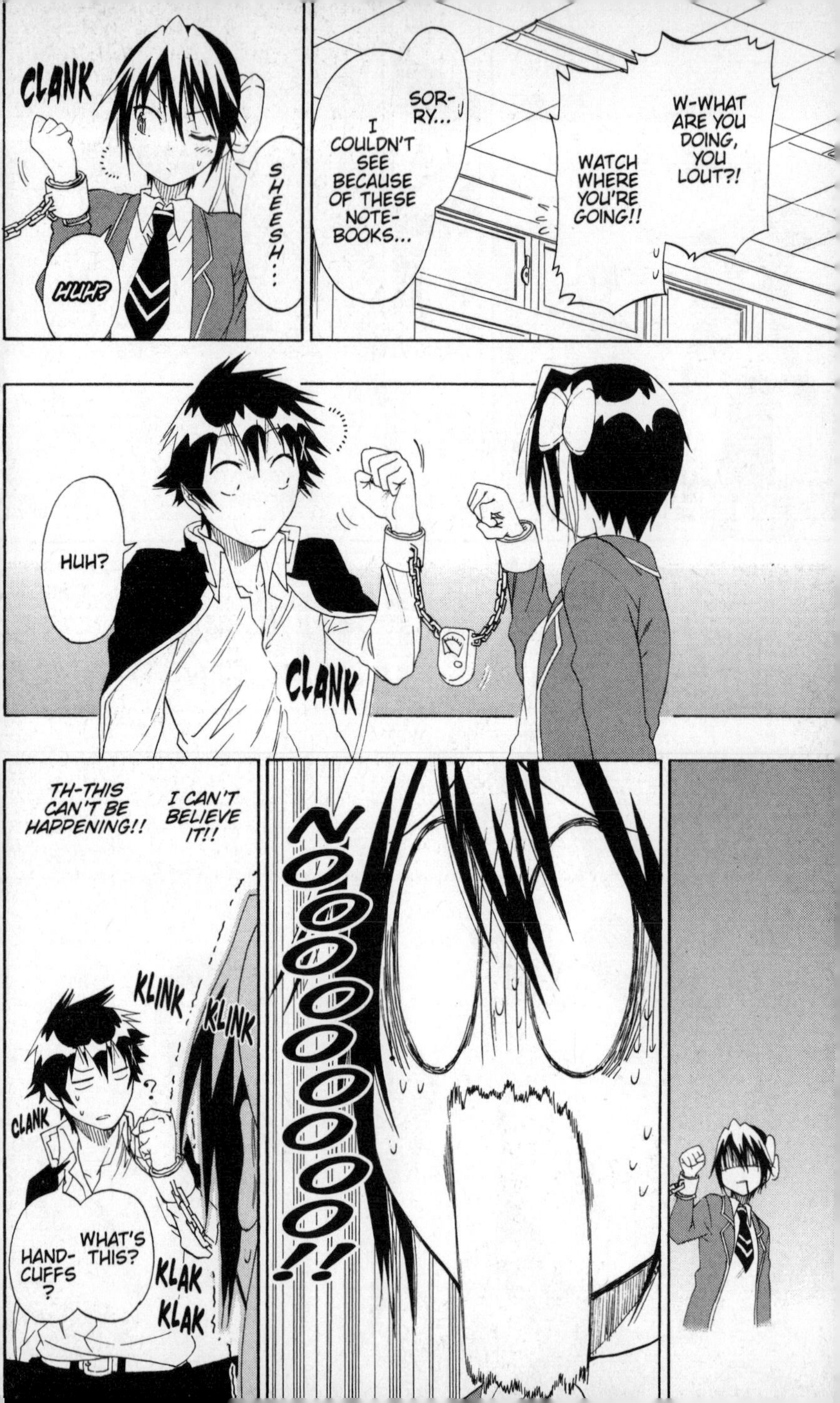

W-WHAT ARE YOU DOING, YOU LOUT?!
WATCH WHERE YOU'RE GOING!!
SORRY...
I COULDN'T SEE BECAUSE OF THESE NOTEBOOKS...
SHEESH...
CLANK
HUH?
HUH?
CLANK
NOOOOOOOOOOOO!!
I CAN'T BELIEVE IT!!
TH-THIS CAN'T BE HAPPENING!!
KLINK
KLINK
CLANK
WHAT'S THIS? HANDCUFFS?
KLAK
KLAK

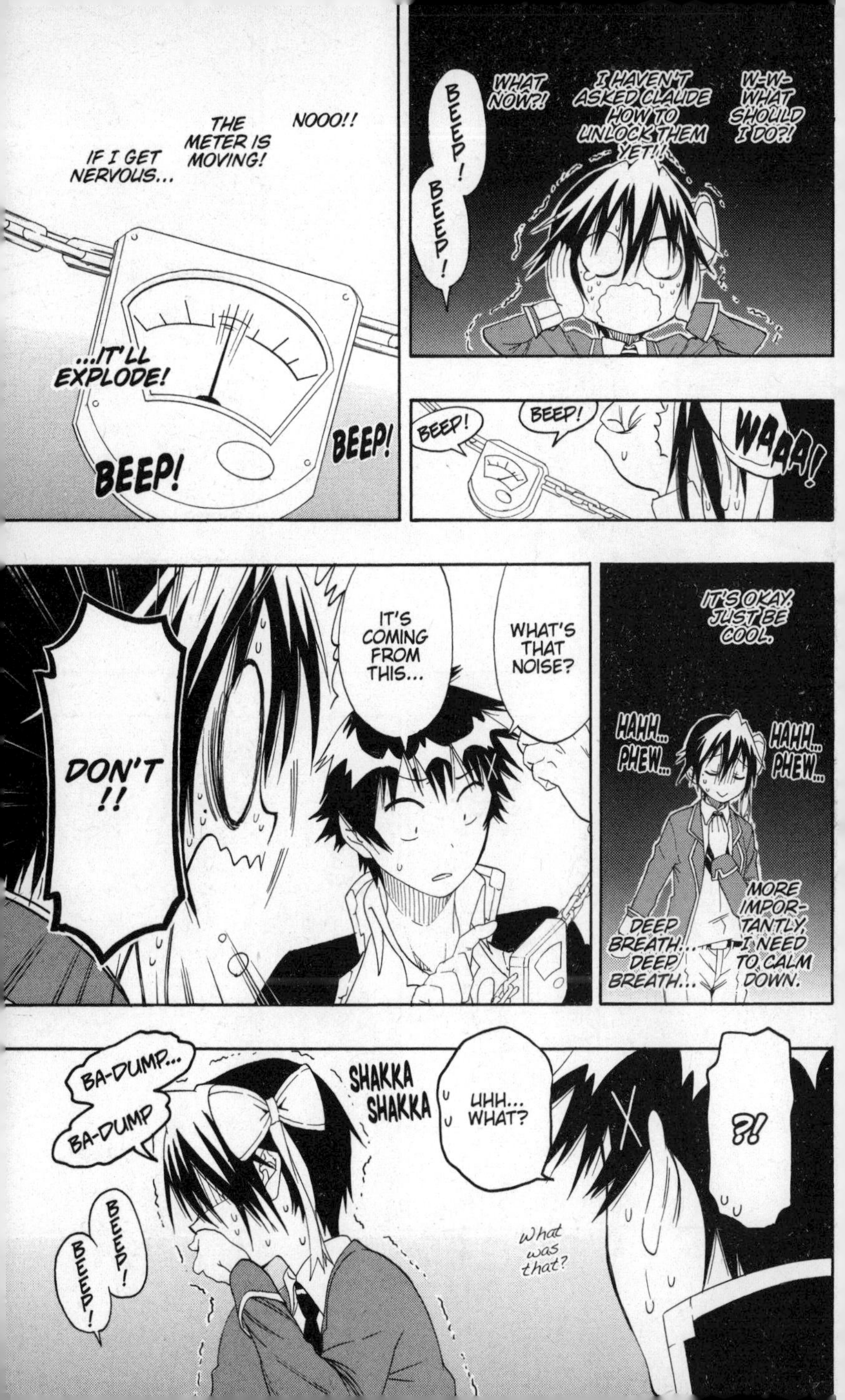

W-W-WHAT SHOULD I DO?!
I HAVEN'T ASKED CLAUDE HOW TO UNLOCK THEM YET!!
WHAT NOW?!
BEEP! BEEP!
WAAA!
BEEP!
BEEP!
NOOO!!
THE METER IS MOVING!
IF I GET NERVOUS...
...IT'LL EXPLODE!
BEEP!
BEEP!
IT'S OKAY. JUST BE COOL.
HAHH... PHEW...
HAHH... PHEW...
MORE IMPORTANTLY, I NEED TO CALM DOWN.
DEEP BREATH... DEEP BREATH...
WHAT'S THAT NOISE?
IT'S COMING FROM THIS...
DON'T!!
?!
UHH... WHAT?
What was that?
SHAKKA SHAKKA
BA-DUMP... BA-DUMP
BEEP! BEEP!

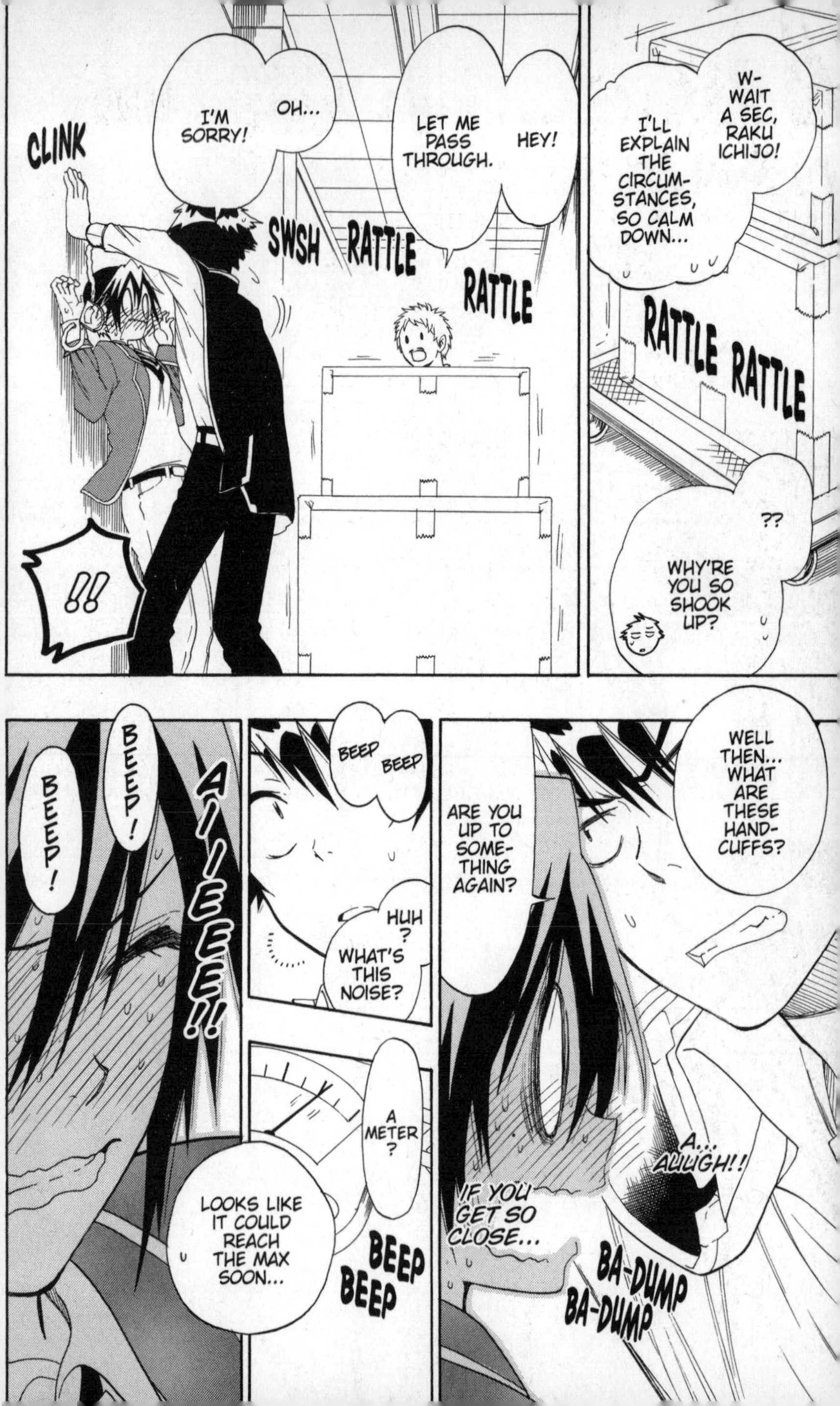
W-WAIT A SEC, RAKU ICHIJO!
I'LL EXPLAIN THE CIRCUM-STANCES, SO CALM DOWN...
RATTLE RATTLE
??
WHY'RE YOU SO SHOOK UP?
HEY!
LET ME PASS THROUGH.
RATTLE
OH...
I'M SORRY!
RATTLE
SWSH
CLINK
!!
WELL THEN... WHAT ARE THESE HAND-CUFFS?
ARE YOU UP TO SOME-THING AGAIN?
A... AUUGH!!
IF YOU GET SO CLOSE...
BA-DUMP BA-DUMP
BEEP BEEP
HUH? WHAT'S THIS NOISE?
A METER?
LOOKS LIKE IT COULD REACH THE MAX SOON...
BEEP BEEP
AIIIEEEE!!
BEEP! BEEP!

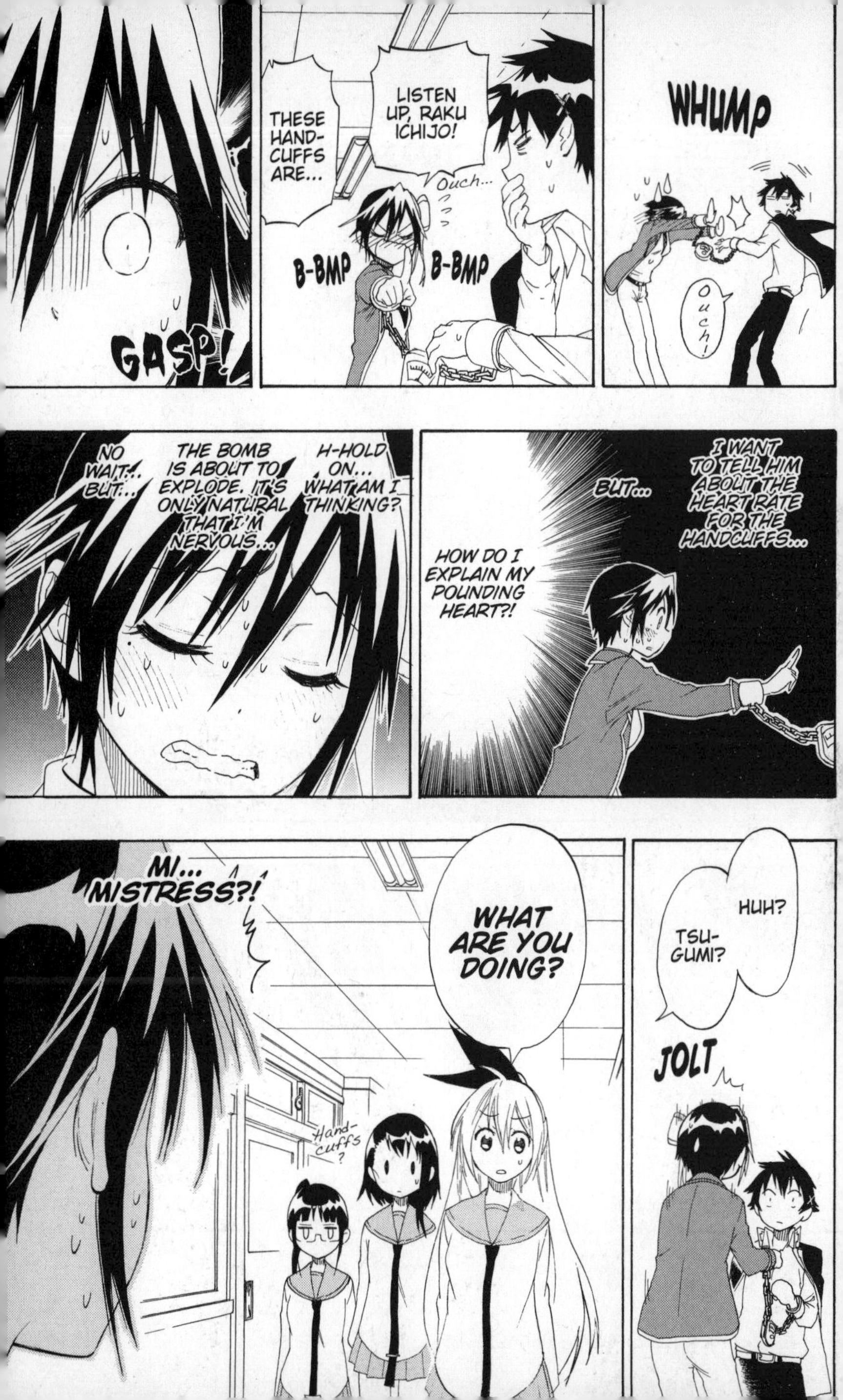
WHUMP
Ouch!
LISTEN UP, RAKU ICHIJO!
THESE HAND-CUFFS ARE...
Ouch...
B-BMP
B-BMP
GASP!
I WANT TO TELL HIM ABOUT THE HEART RATE FOR THE HANDCUFFS...
BUT...
HOW DO I EXPLAIN MY POUNDING HEART?!
H-HOLD ON... WHAT AM I THINKING?
THE BOMB IS ABOUT TO EXPLODE. IT'S ONLY NATURAL THAT I'M NERVOUS...
NO WAIT... BUT...
HUH?
TSU-GUMI?
JOLT
WHAT ARE YOU DOING?
Hand-cuffs?
MI... MISTRESS?!

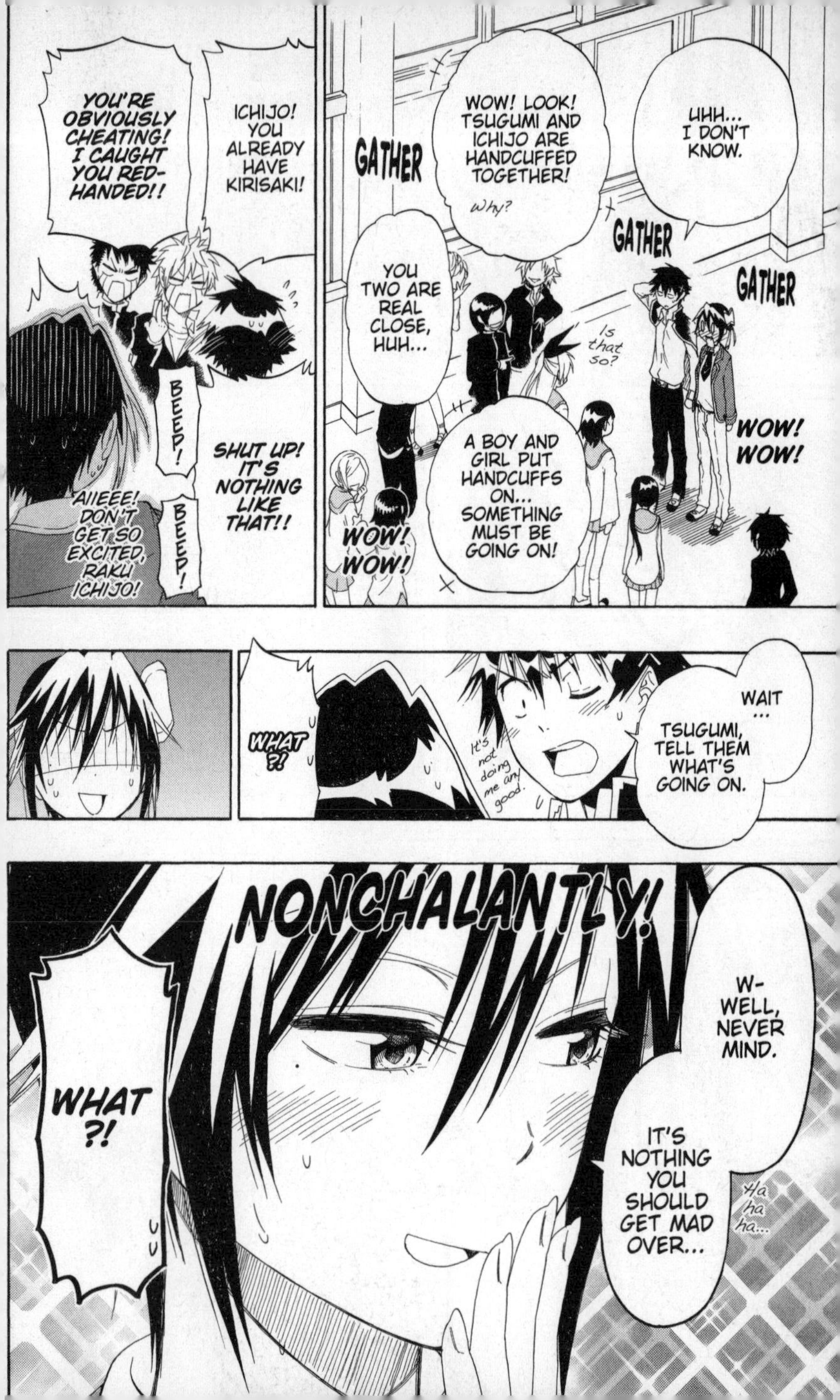

UHH... I DON'T KNOW.
WOW! LOOK! TSUGUMI AND ICHIJO ARE HANDCUFFED TOGETHER!
why?
GATHER
GATHER
GATHER
YOU TWO ARE REAL CLOSE, HUH...
Is that so?
WOW! WOW!
A BOY AND GIRL PUT HANDCUFFS ON... SOMETHING MUST BE GOING ON!
WOW! WOW!
ICHIJO! YOU ALREADY HAVE KIRISAKI!
YOU'RE OBVIOUSLY CHEATING! I CAUGHT YOU RED-HANDED!!
BEEP!
SHUT UP! IT'S NOTHING LIKE THAT!!
BEEP!
AIIEEE! DON'T GET SO EXCITED, RAKU ICHIJO!
WAIT... TSUGUMI, TELL THEM WHAT'S GOING ON.
It's not doing me any good.
WHAT?!
W-WELL, NEVER MIND.
IT'S NOTHING YOU SHOULD GET MAD OVER...
Ha ha ha...
NONCHALANTLY!
WHAT?!

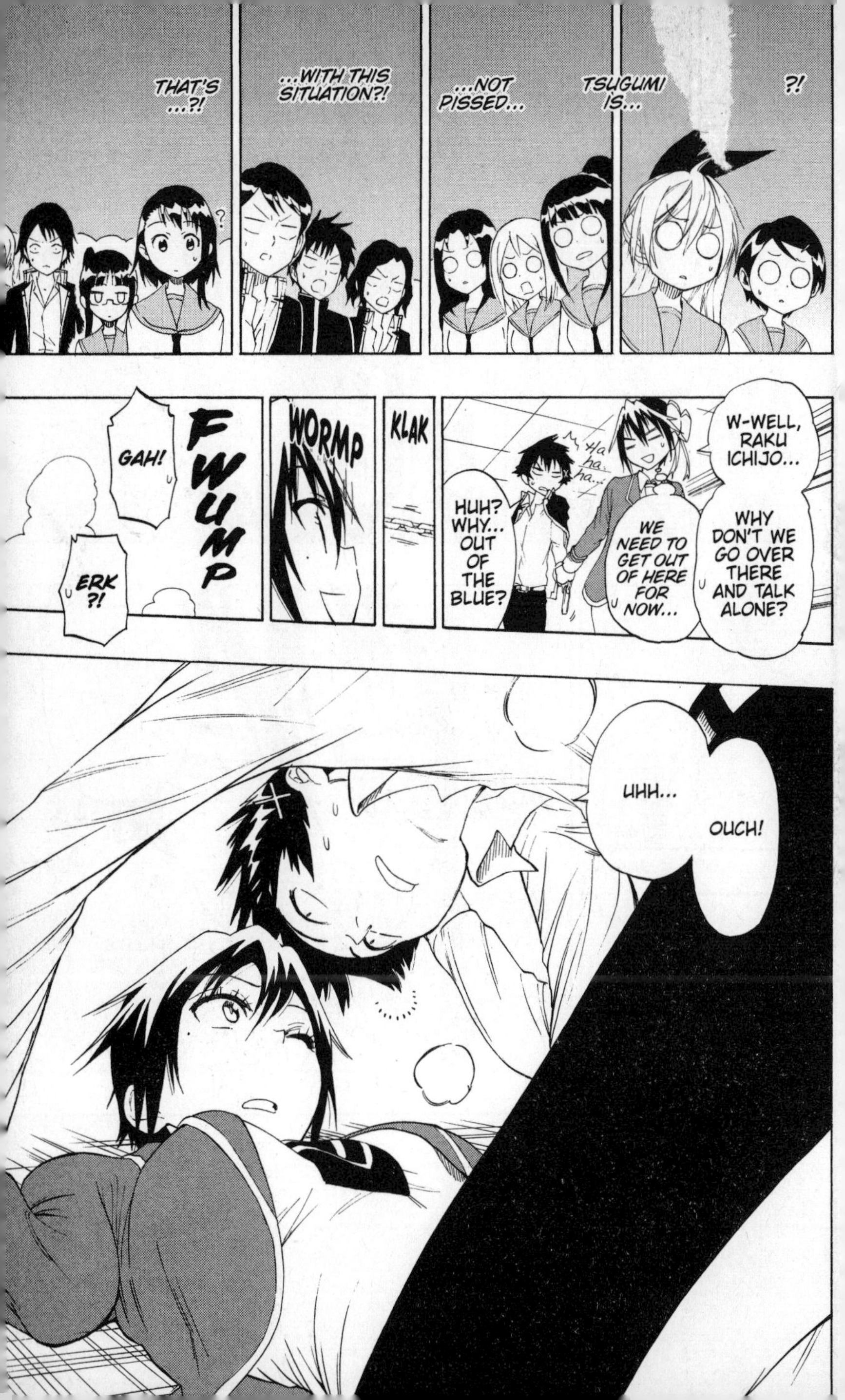

?!
TSUGUMI IS...
...NOT PISSED...
...WITH THIS SITUATION?!
THAT'S ...?!
W-WELL, RAKU ICHIJO...
WHY DON'T WE GO OVER THERE AND TALK ALONE?
WE NEED TO GET OUT OF HERE FOR NOW...
Ha ha ha...
HUH? WHY... OUT OF THE BLUE?
KLAK
WORMP
FWUMP
GAH!
ERK ?!
UHH...
OUCH!

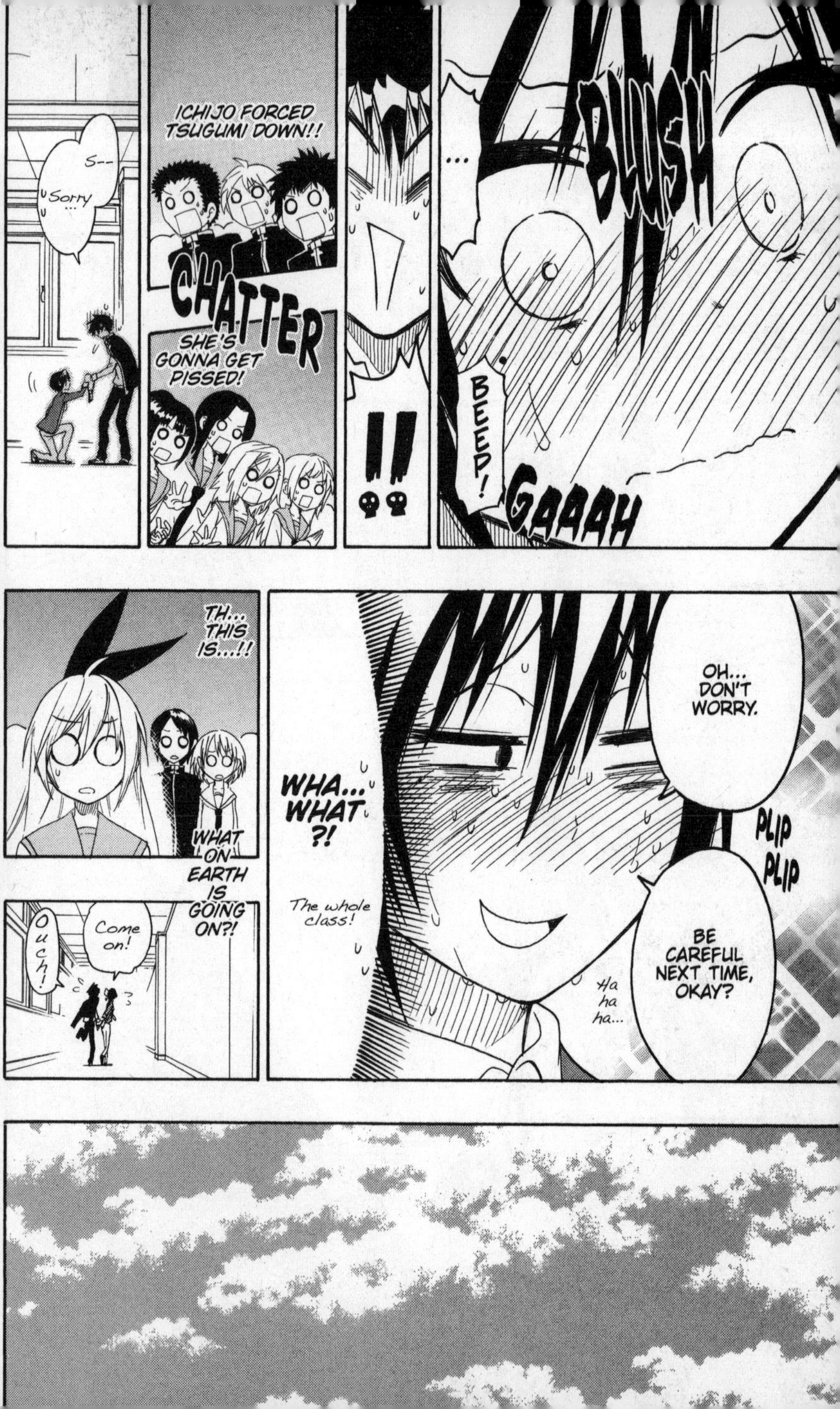
BLUSH
...
BEEP!
GAAAH
!!
ICHIJO FORCED TSUGUMI DOWN!!
CHATTER
SHE'S GONNA GET PISSED!
S--
Sorry...
OH... DON'T WORRY.
PLIP PLIP
BE CAREFUL NEXT TIME, OKAY?
Ha ha ha...
WHA... WHAT?!
The whole class!
TH... THIS IS...!!
WHAT ON EARTH IS GOING ON?!
Come on!
Ouch!

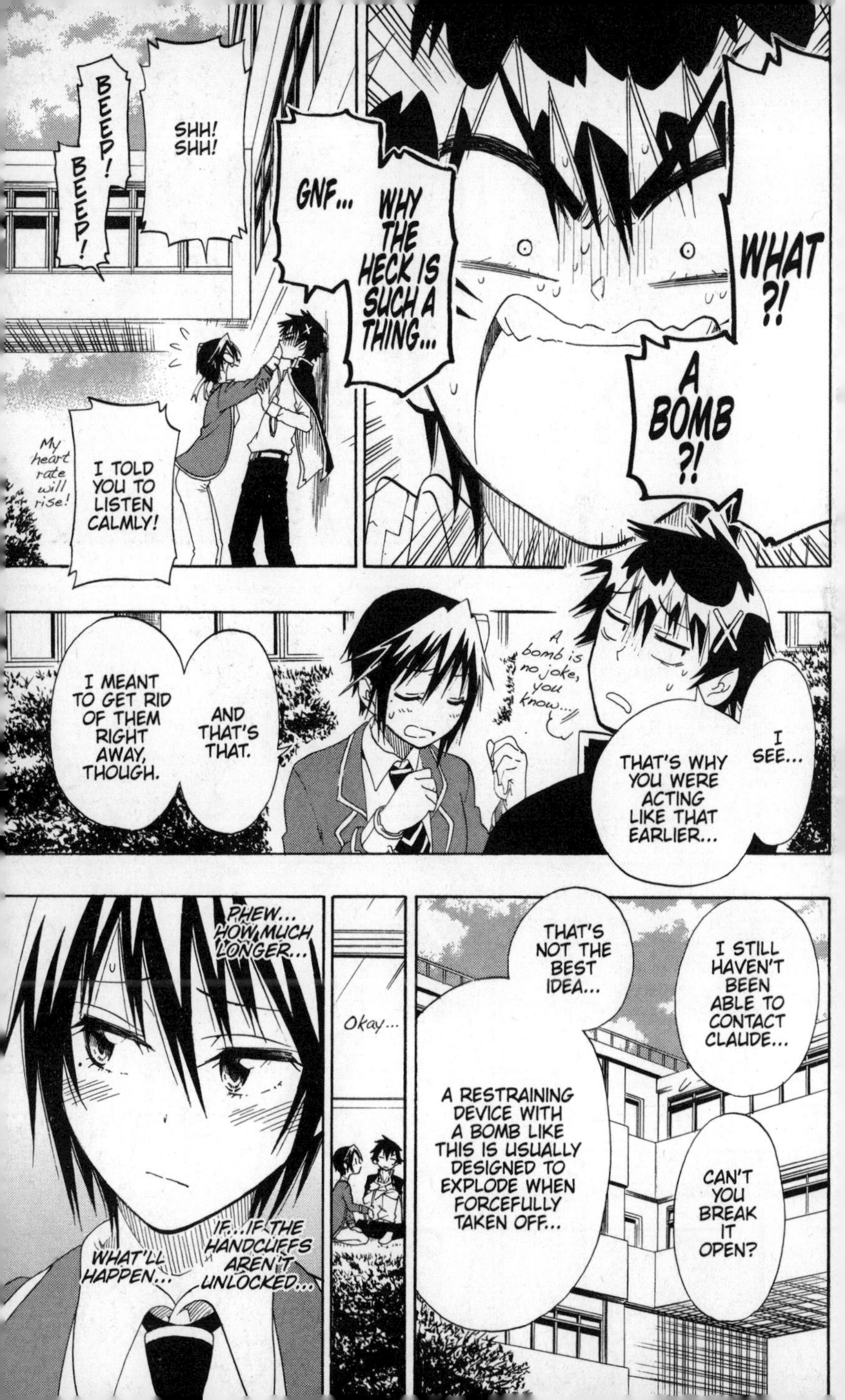
WHAT?!
A BOMB?!
GNF... WHY THE HECK IS SUCH A THING...
SHH! SHH!
BEEP! BEEP!
I TOLD YOU TO LISTEN CALMLY!
My heart rate will rise!
I SEE...
THAT'S WHY YOU WERE ACTING LIKE THAT EARLIER...
A bomb is no joke, you know...
AND THAT'S THAT.
I MEANT TO GET RID OF THEM RIGHT AWAY, THOUGH.
I STILL HAVEN'T BEEN ABLE TO CONTACT CLAUDE...
CAN'T YOU BREAK IT OPEN?
THAT'S NOT THE BEST IDEA...
A RESTRAINING DEVICE WITH A BOMB LIKE THIS IS USUALLY DESIGNED TO EXPLODE WHEN FORCEFULLY TAKEN OFF...
Okay...
PHEW... HOW MUCH LONGER...
IF...IF THE HANDCUFFS AREN'T UNLOCKED...
WHAT'LL HAPPEN...

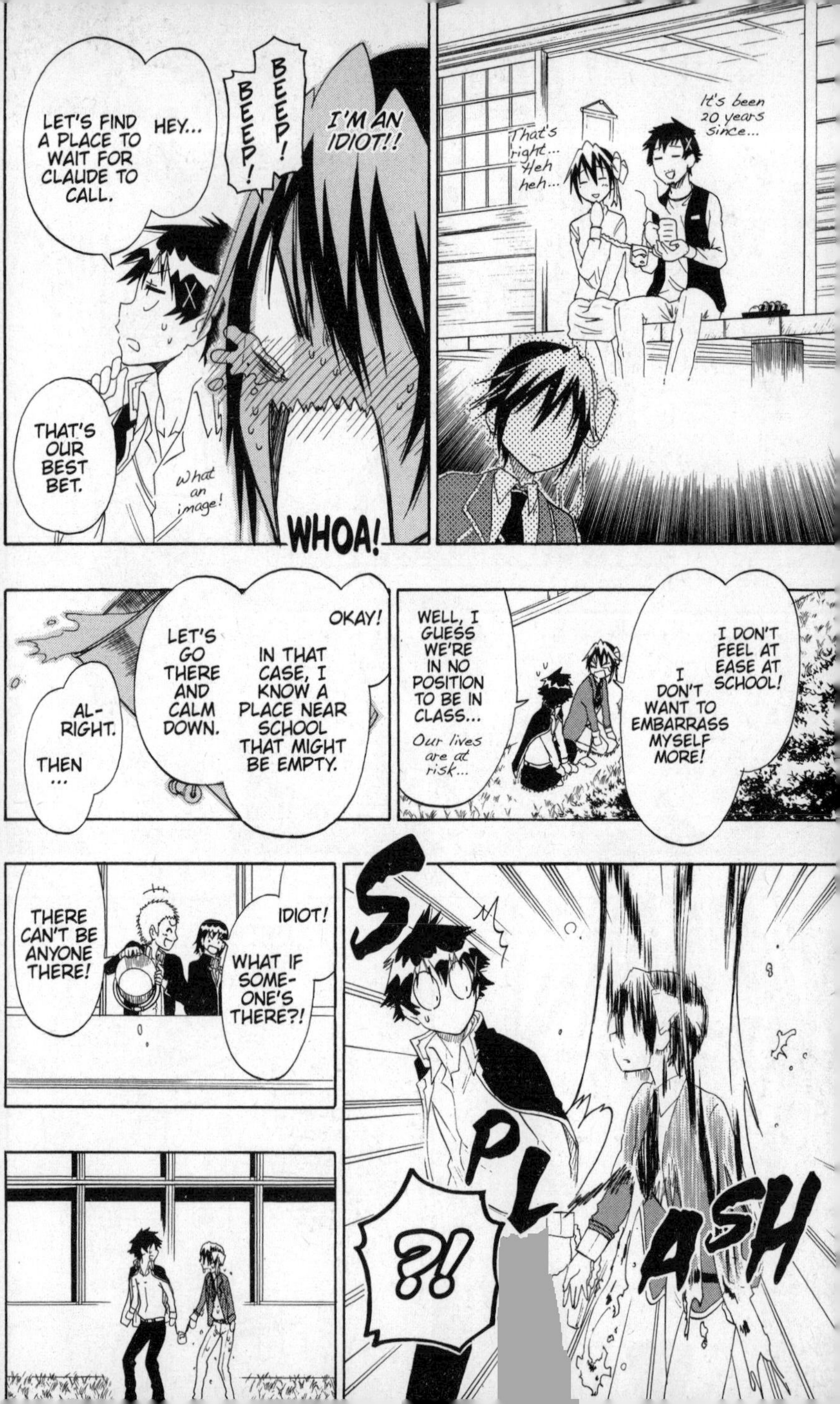
It's been 20 years since...
That's right... Heh heh...
I'M AN IDIOT!!
BEEP! BEEP! BEEP!
HEY...
LET'S FIND A PLACE TO WAIT FOR CLAUDE TO CALL.
What an image!
THAT'S OUR BEST BET.
WHOA!
I DON'T FEEL AT EASE AT SCHOOL!
I DON'T WANT TO EMBARRASS MYSELF MORE!
WELL, I GUESS WE'RE IN NO POSITION TO BE IN CLASS...
Our lives are at risk...
OKAY!
IN THAT CASE, I KNOW A PLACE NEAR SCHOOL THAT MIGHT BE EMPTY.
LET'S GO THERE AND CALM DOWN.
ALRIGHT.
THEN...
SPLASH
?!
IDIOT!
WHAT IF SOMEONE'S THERE?!
THERE CAN'T BE ANYONE THERE!

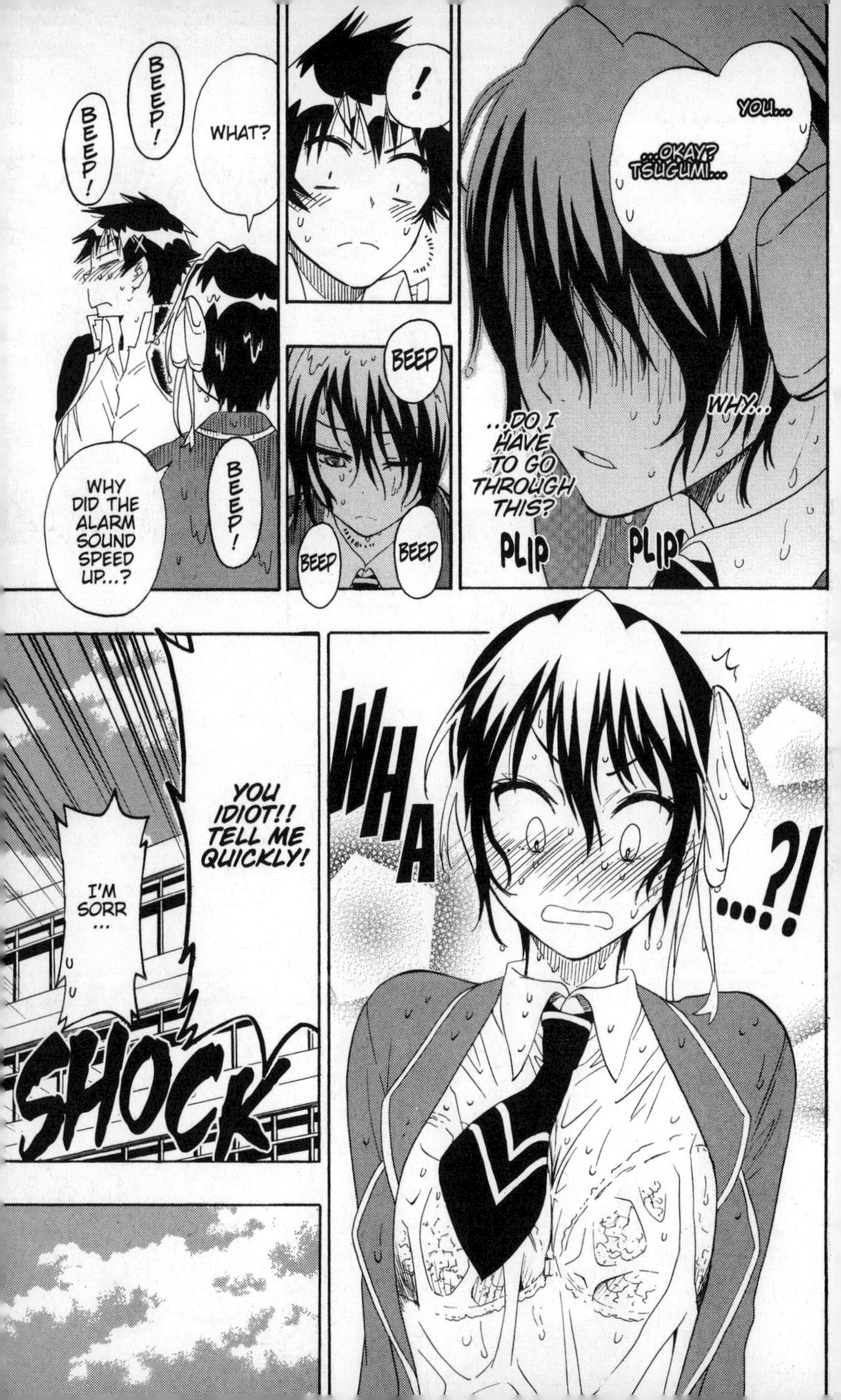
YOU...
...OKAY? TSUGUMI...
WHY...
...DO I HAVE TO GO THROUGH THIS?
PLIP
PLIP
!
BEEP
BEEP
BEEP
BEEP!
WHAT?
BEEP!
BEEP!
WHY DID THE ALARM SOUND SPEED UP...?
WHA
...?!
YOU IDIOT!! TELL ME QUICKLY!
I'M SORR...
SHOCK

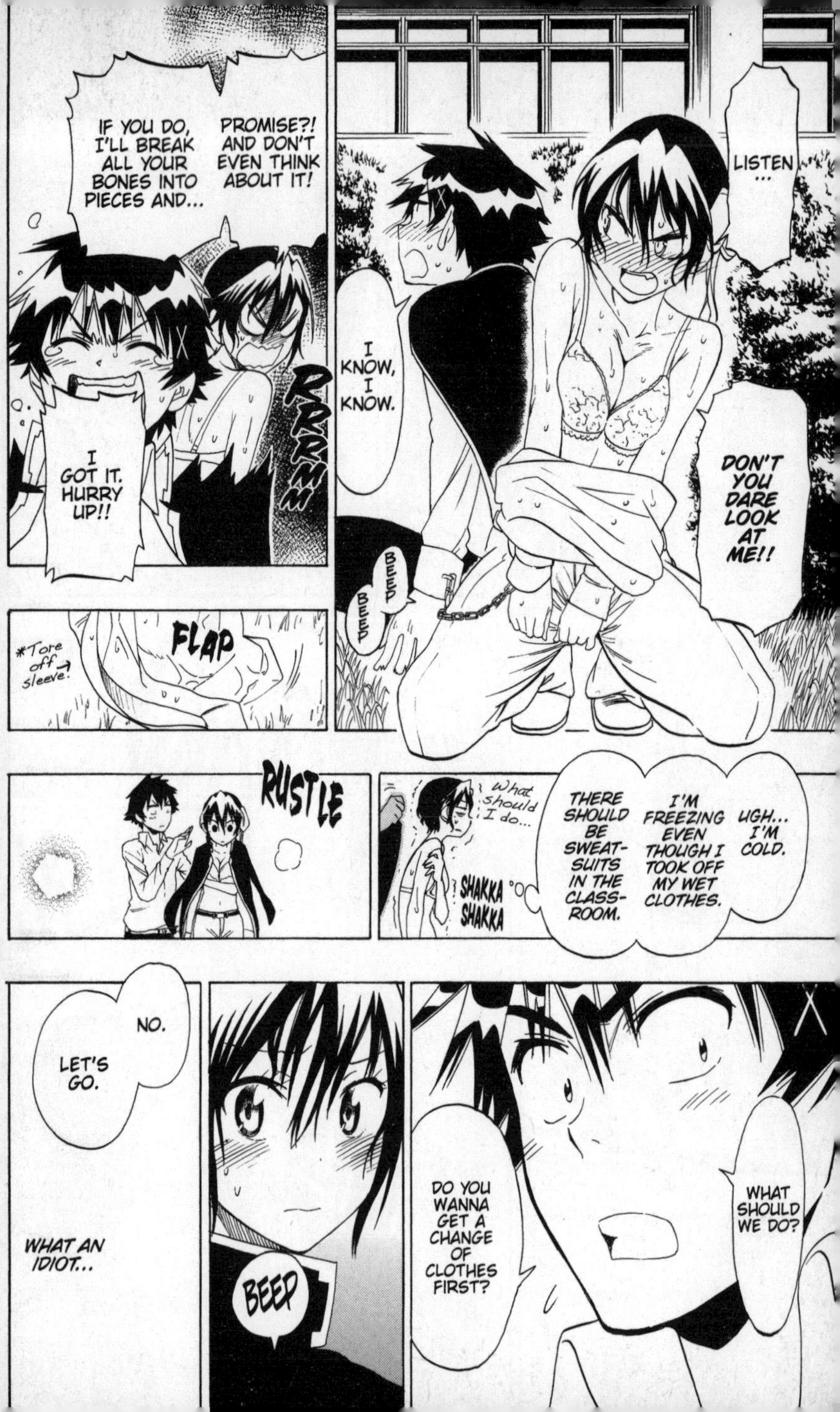
LISTEN...
DON'T YOU DARE LOOK AT ME!!
I KNOW, I KNOW.
BEEP BEEP
PROMISE?! AND DON'T EVEN THINK ABOUT IT!
IF YOU DO, I'LL BREAK ALL YOUR BONES INTO PIECES AND...
RRRMM
I GOT IT. HURRY UP!!
FLAP
*Tore off sleeve.
UGH... I'M COLD.
I'M FREEZING EVEN THOUGH I TOOK OFF MY WET CLOTHES.
THERE SHOULD BE SWEAT-SUITS IN THE CLASS-ROOM.
What should I do...
SHAKKA SHAKKA
RUSTLE
WHAT SHOULD WE DO?
DO YOU WANNA GET A CHANGE OF CLOTHES FIRST?
BEEP
NO.
LET'S GO.
WHAT AN IDIOT...

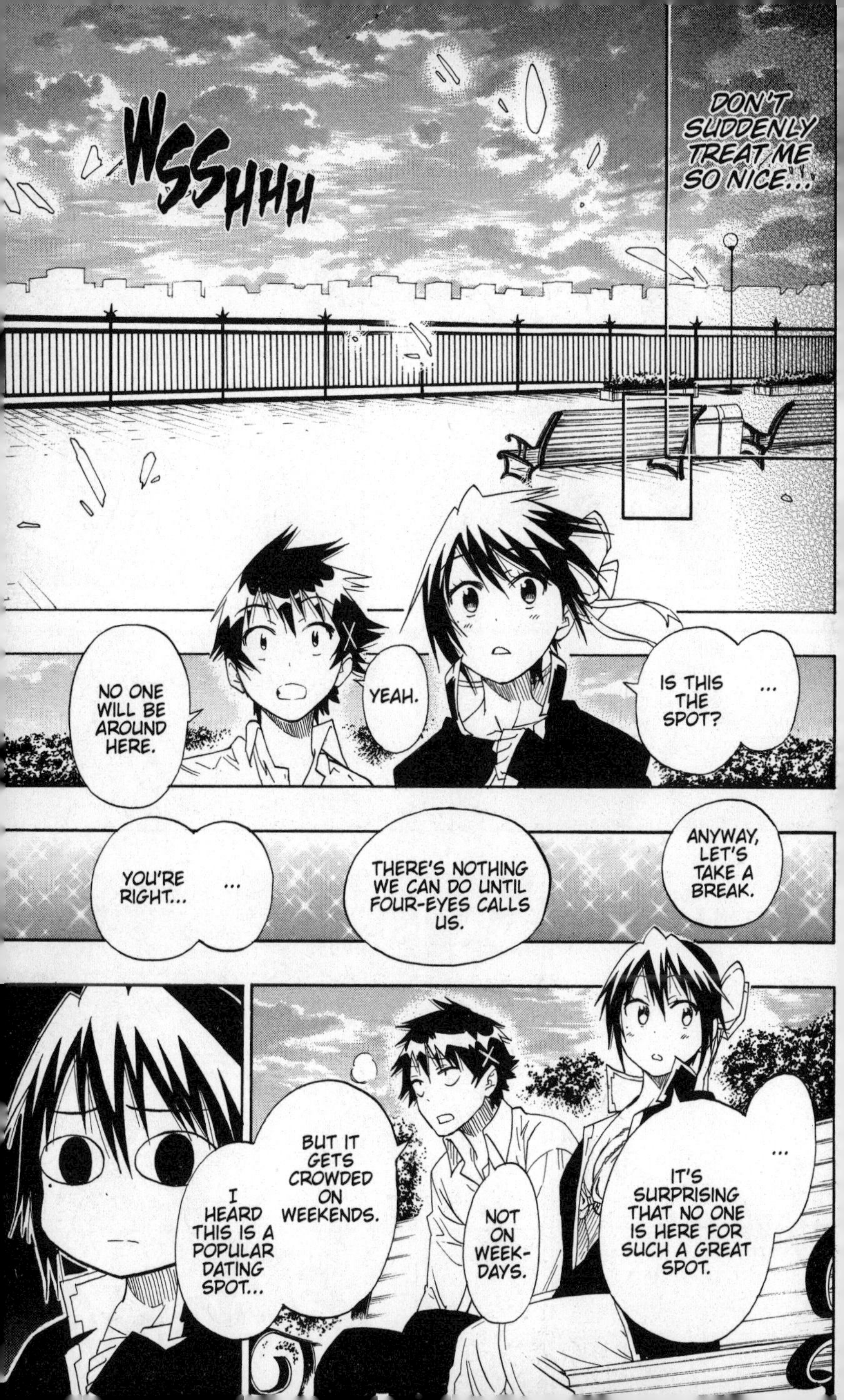
DON'T SUDDENLY TREAT ME SO NICE...!
WSSHHH
...
IS THIS THE SPOT?
YEAH.
NO ONE WILL BE AROUND HERE.
ANYWAY, LET'S TAKE A BREAK.
THERE'S NOTHING WE CAN DO UNTIL FOUR-EYES CALLS US.
...
YOU'RE RIGHT...
...
IT'S SURPRISING THAT NO ONE IS HERE FOR SUCH A GREAT SPOT.
NOT ON WEEK-DAYS.
BUT IT GETS CROWDED ON WEEKENDS.
I HEARD THIS IS A POPULAR DATING SPOT...

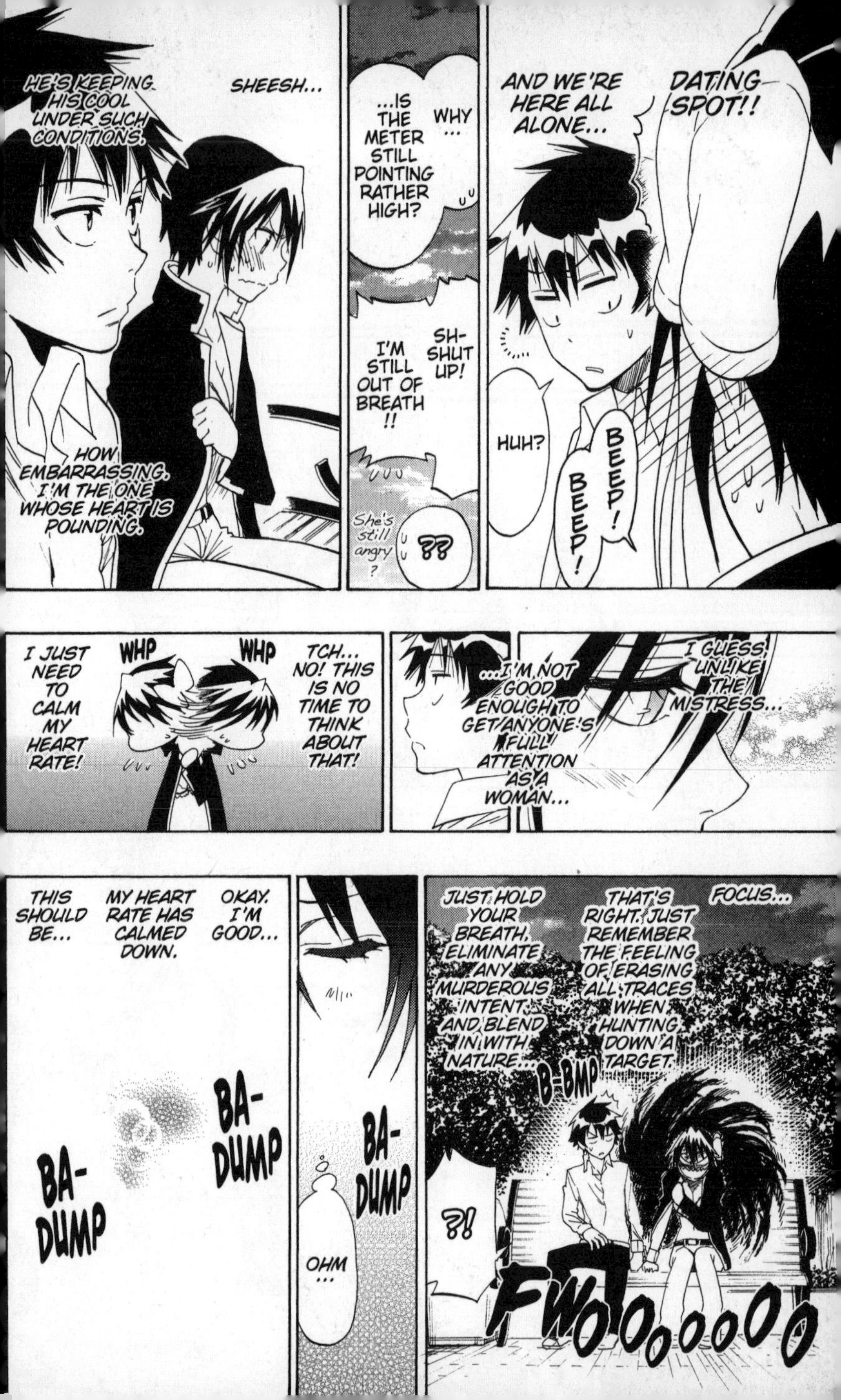
DATING SPOT!!
AND WE'RE HERE ALL ALONE...
BEEP! BEEP!
HUH?
WHY...
...IS THE METER STILL POINTING RATHER HIGH?
SH-SHUT UP!
I'M STILL OUT OF BREATH!!
She's still angry?
??
SHEESH...
HE'S KEEPING HIS COOL UNDER SUCH CONDITIONS.
HOW EMBARRASSING. I'M THE ONE WHOSE HEART IS POUNDING.
I GUESS UNLIKE THE MISTRESS...
...I'M NOT GOOD ENOUGH TO GET ANYONE'S FULL ATTENTION AS A WOMAN...
TCH... NO! THIS IS NO TIME TO THINK ABOUT THAT!
WHP
WHP
I JUST NEED TO CALM MY HEART RATE!
FOCUS...
THAT'S RIGHT. JUST REMEMBER THE FEELING OF ERASING ALL TRACES WHEN HUNTING DOWN A TARGET.
JUST HOLD YOUR BREATH. ELIMINATE ANY MURDEROUS INTENT, AND BLEND IN WITH NATURE...
B-BMP
?!
FWOOOOOOOO
BA-DUMP
OHM...
OKAY. I'M GOOD...
MY HEART RATE HAS CALMED DOWN.
THIS SHOULD BE...
BA-DUMP
BA-DUMP

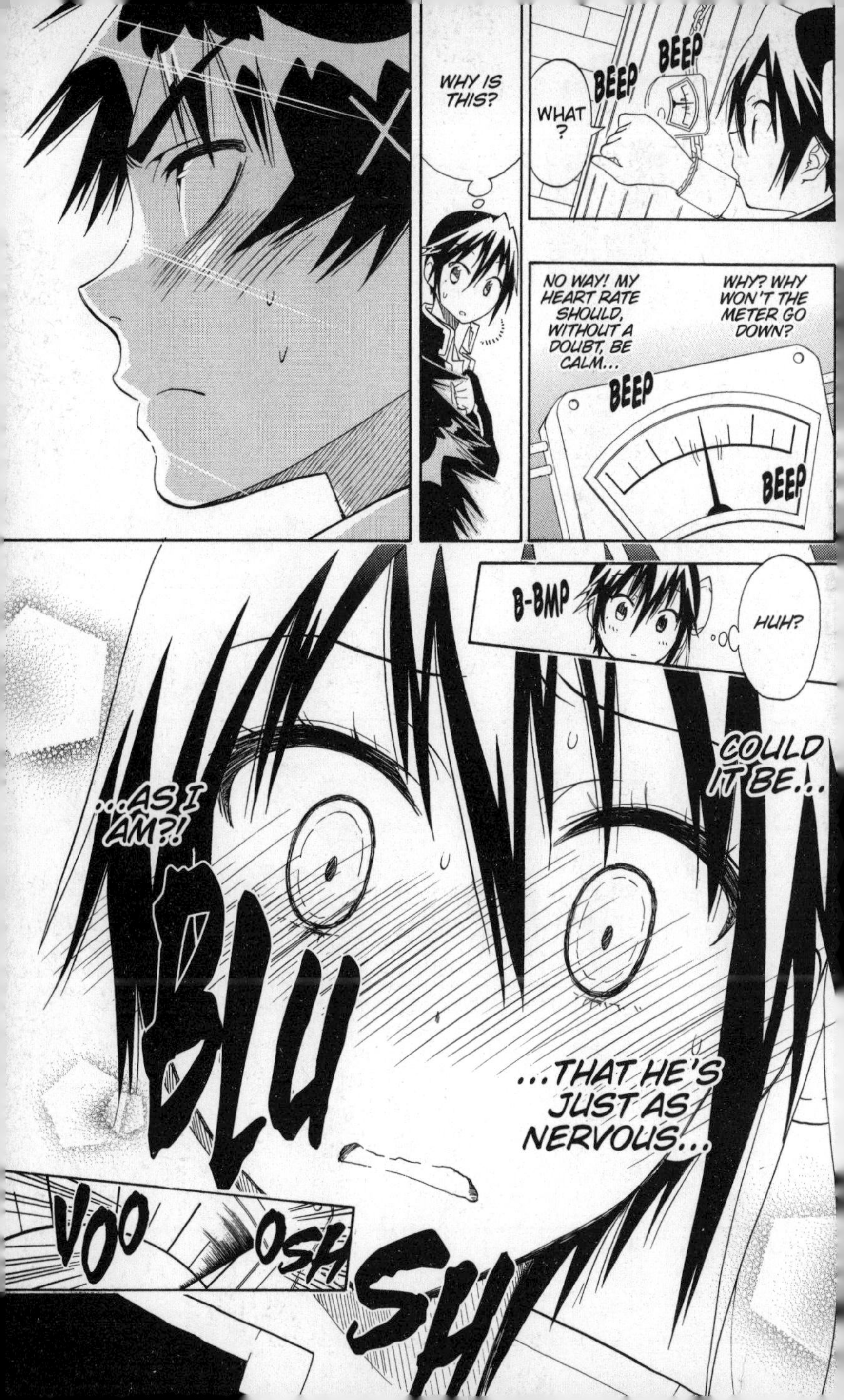
BEEP
BEEP
WHAT?
WHY? WHY WON'T THE METER GO DOWN?
NO WAY! MY HEART RATE SHOULD, WITHOUT A DOUBT, BE CALM...
BEEP
BEEP
WHY IS THIS?
HUH?
B-BMP
COULD IT BE...
...THAT HE'S JUST AS NERVOUS...
...AS I AM?!
BLUSH
VOOOSH

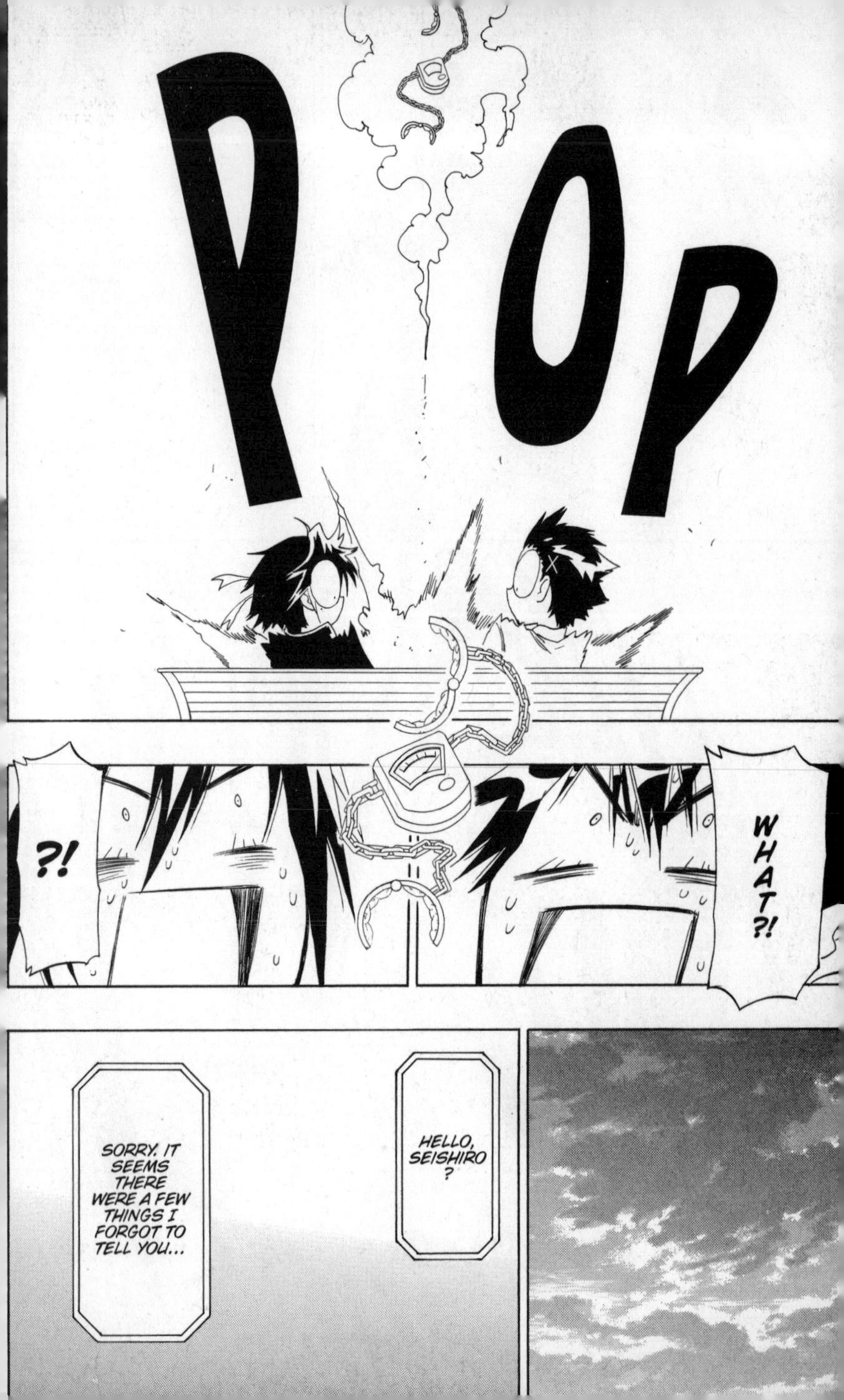
POP
WHAT?!
?!
HELLO, SEISHIRO?
SORRY. IT SEEMS THERE WERE A FEW THINGS I FORGOT TO TELL YOU...

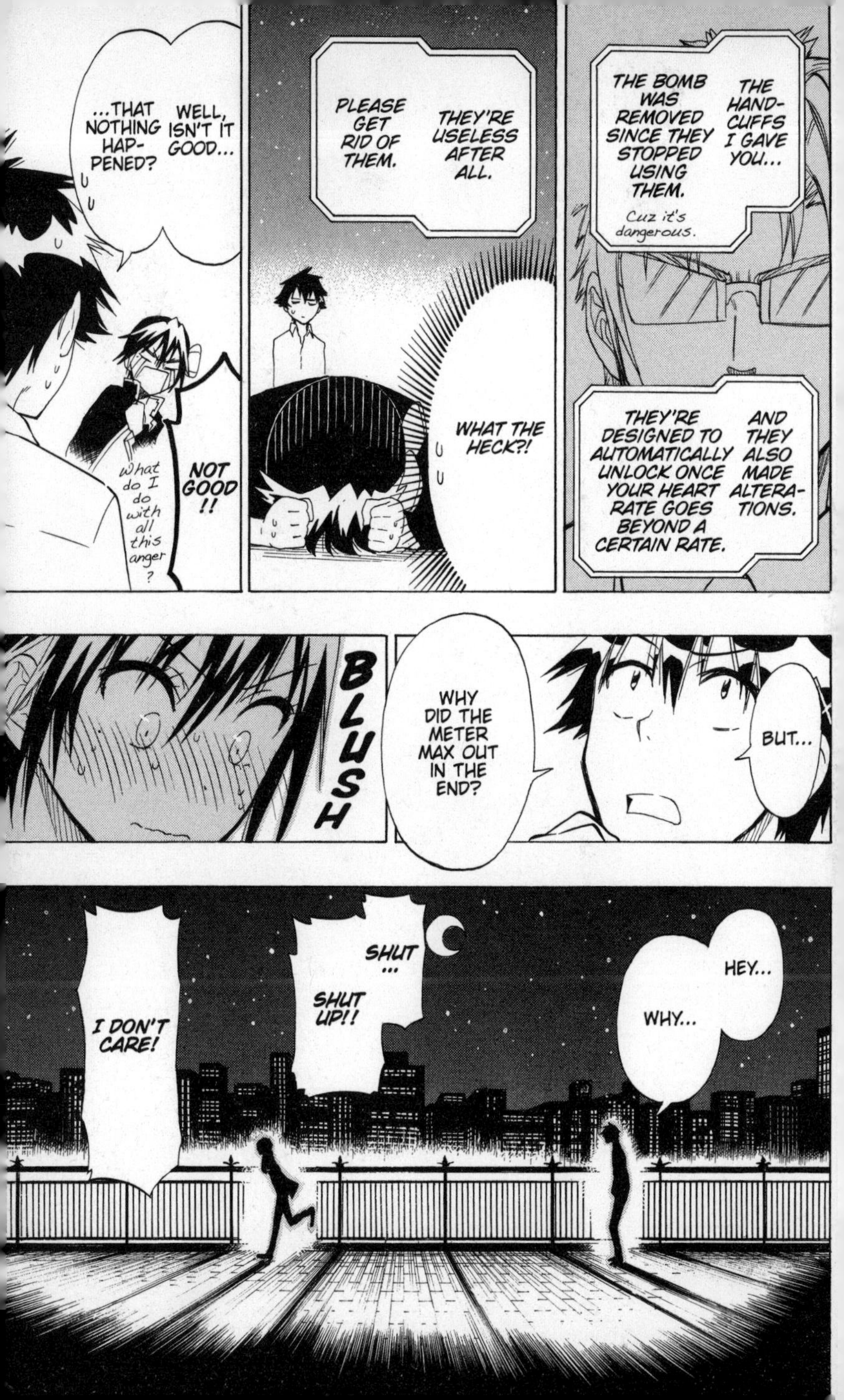
THE HANDCUFFS I GAVE YOU...
THE BOMB WAS REMOVED SINCE THEY STOPPED USING THEM.
Cuz it's dangerous.
AND THEY ALSO MADE ALTERATIONS.
THEY'RE DESIGNED TO AUTOMATICALLY UNLOCK ONCE YOUR HEART RATE GOES BEYOND A CERTAIN RATE.
THEY'RE USELESS AFTER ALL.
PLEASE GET RID OF THEM.
WHAT THE HECK?!
WELL, ISN'T IT GOOD...
...THAT NOTHING HAPPENED?
NOT GOOD!!
What do I do with all this anger?
BUT...
WHY DID THE METER MAX OUT IN THE END?
BLUSH
HEY...
WHY...
SHUT...
SHUT UP!!
I DON'T CARE!

So
warm...

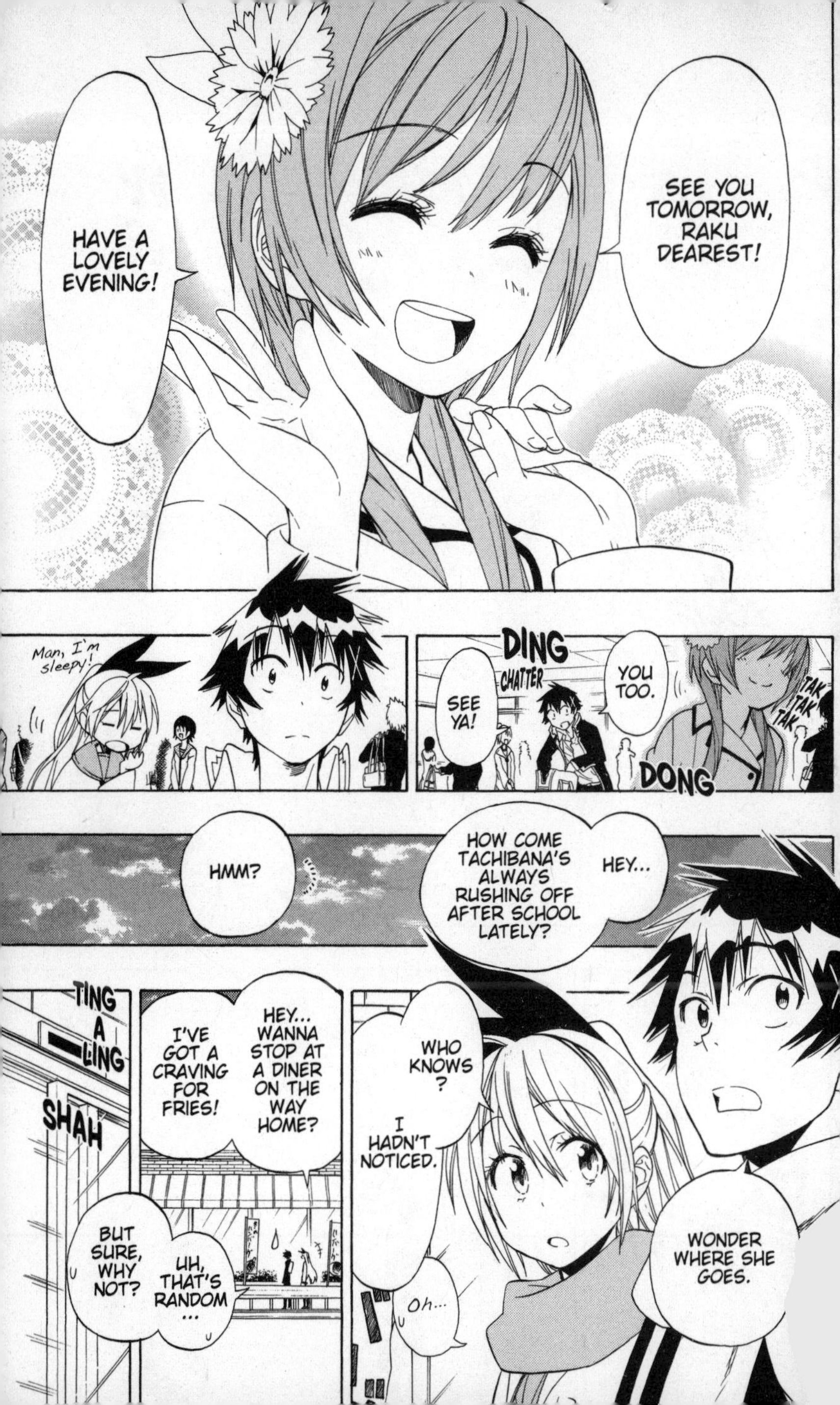
SEE YOU TOMORROW, RAKU DEAREST!
HAVE A LOVELY EVENING!
DING
CHATTER
YOU TOO.
SEE YA!
TAK TAK TAK
DONG
Man, I'm sleepy!
HEY...
HOW COME TACHIBANA'S ALWAYS RUSHING OFF AFTER SCHOOL LATELY?
HMM?
WHO KNOWS?
I HADN'T NOTICED.
WONDER WHERE SHE GOES.
Oh...
HEY... WANNA STOP AT A DINER ON THE WAY HOME?
I'VE GOT A CRAVING FOR FRIES!
UH, THAT'S RANDOM...
BUT SURE, WHY NOT?
TING A LING
SHAH

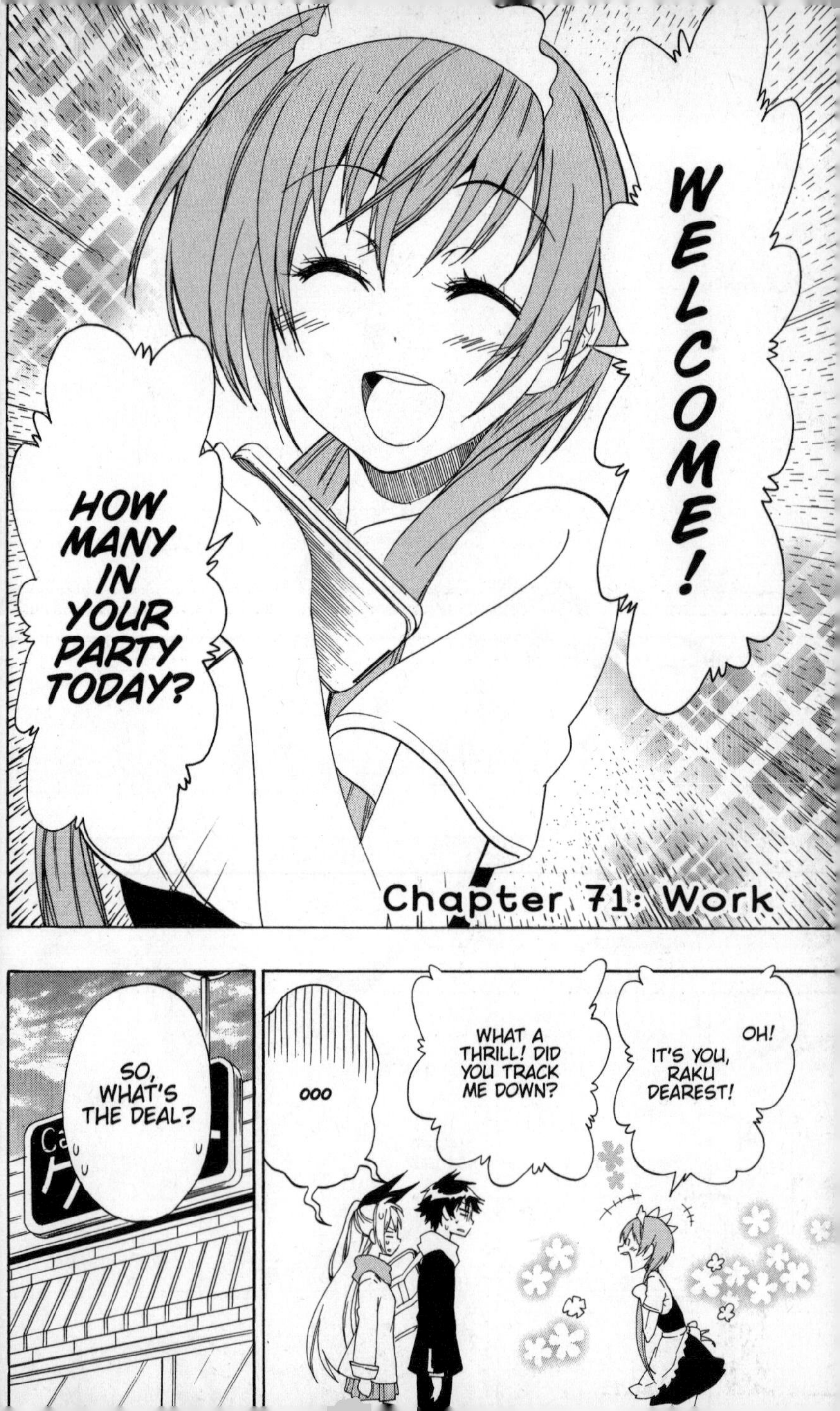
WELCOME!
HOW MANY IN YOUR PARTY TODAY?
Chapter 71: Work
OH! IT'S YOU, RAKU DEAREST!
WHAT A THRILL! DID YOU TRACK ME DOWN?
ooo
SO, WHAT'S THE DEAL?

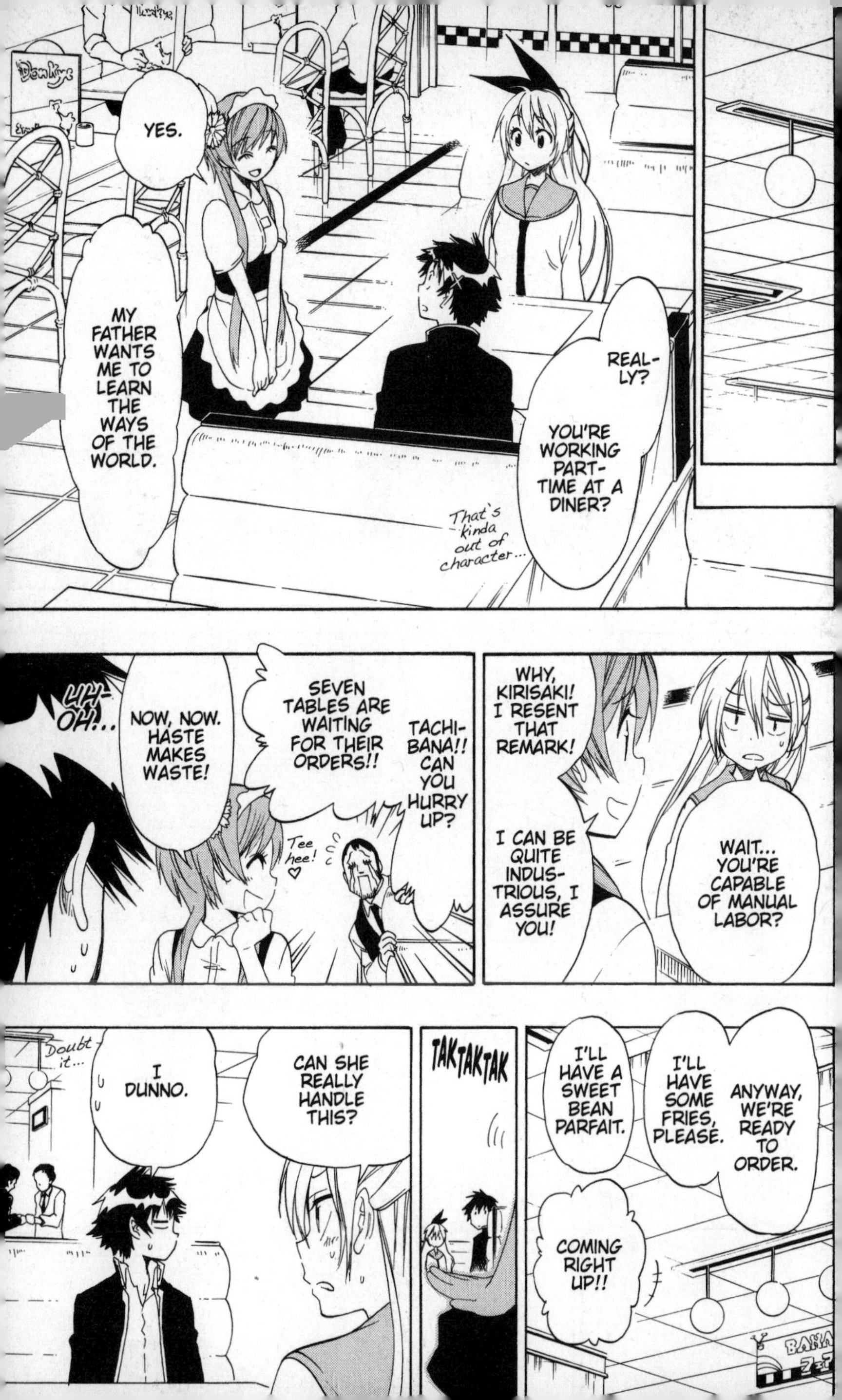
REAL-LY?
YOU'RE WORKING PART-TIME AT A DINER?
That's kinda out of character...
YES.
MY FATHER WANTS ME TO LEARN THE WAYS OF THE WORLD.
WAIT... YOU'RE CAPABLE OF MANUAL LABOR?
WHY, KIRISAKI! I RESENT THAT REMARK!
I CAN BE QUITE INDUSTRIOUS, I ASSURE YOU!
TACHI-BANA!! CAN YOU HURRY UP?
SEVEN TABLES ARE WAITING FOR THEIR ORDERS!!
Tee hee! ♥
NOW, NOW. HASTE MAKES WASTE!
UH-OH...
ANYWAY, WE'RE READY TO ORDER.
I'LL HAVE SOME FRIES, PLEASE.
I'LL HAVE A SWEET BEAN PARFAIT.
COMING RIGHT UP!!
TAKTAKTAK
CAN SHE REALLY HANDLE THIS?
I DUNNO.
Doubt it...

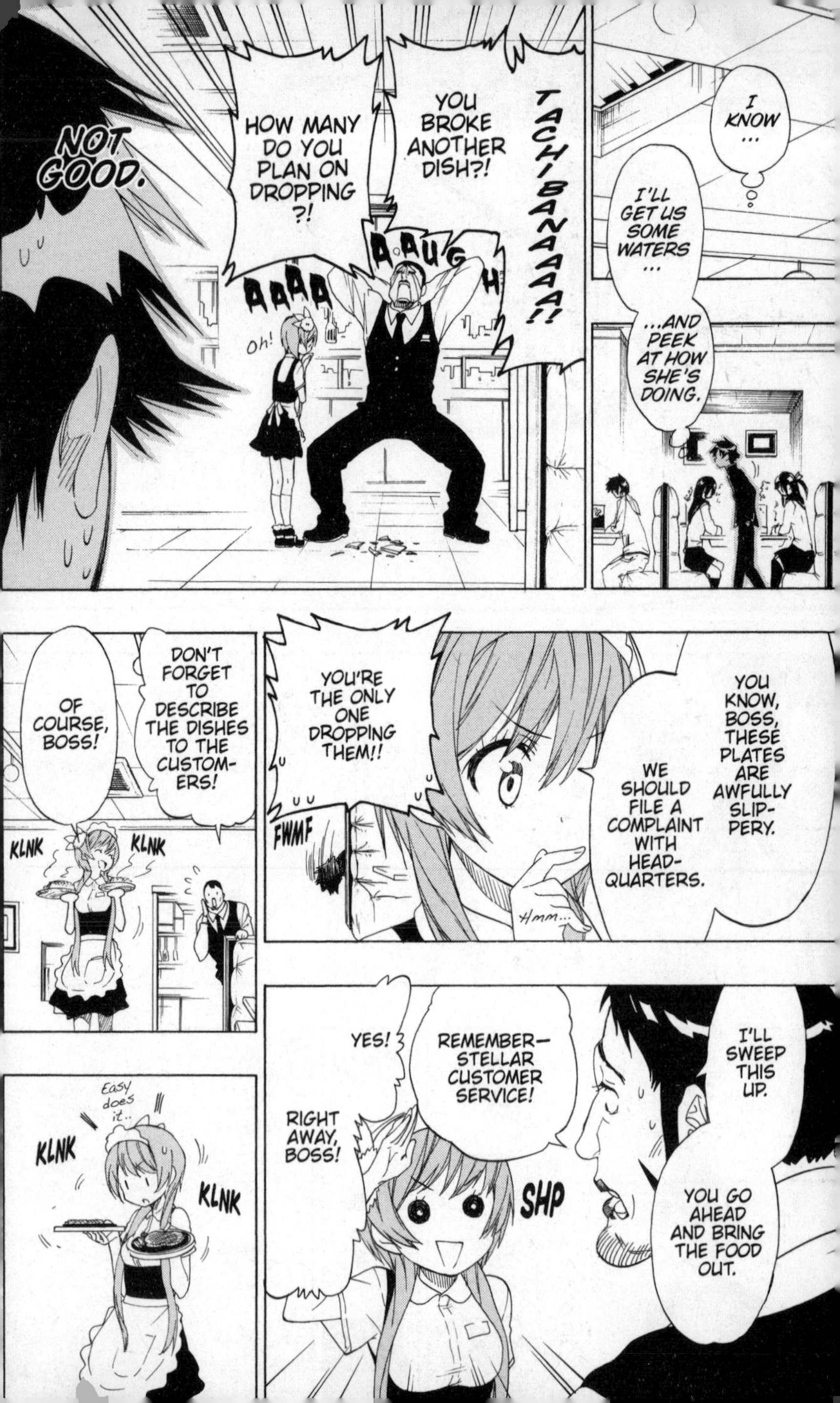
I KNOW...
I'LL GET US SOME WATERS...
...AND PEEK AT HOW SHE'S DOING.
TACHIBANAAAAA!!
YOU BROKE ANOTHER DISH?!
HOW MANY DO YOU PLAN ON DROPPING?!
AAUGH
AAAA
Oh!
NOT GOOD.
YOU KNOW, BOSS, THESE PLATES ARE AWFULLY SLIPPERY.
WE SHOULD FILE A COMPLAINT WITH HEADQUARTERS.
Hmm...
YOU'RE THE ONLY ONE DROPPING THEM!!
FWMF
DON'T FORGET TO DESCRIBE THE DISHES TO THE CUSTOMERS!
OF COURSE, BOSS!
KLNK
KLNK
I'LL SWEEP THIS UP.
YOU GO AHEAD AND BRING THE FOOD OUT.
REMEMBER—STELLAR CUSTOMER SERVICE!
YES!
RIGHT AWAY, BOSS!
SHP
Easy does it..
KLNK
KLNK

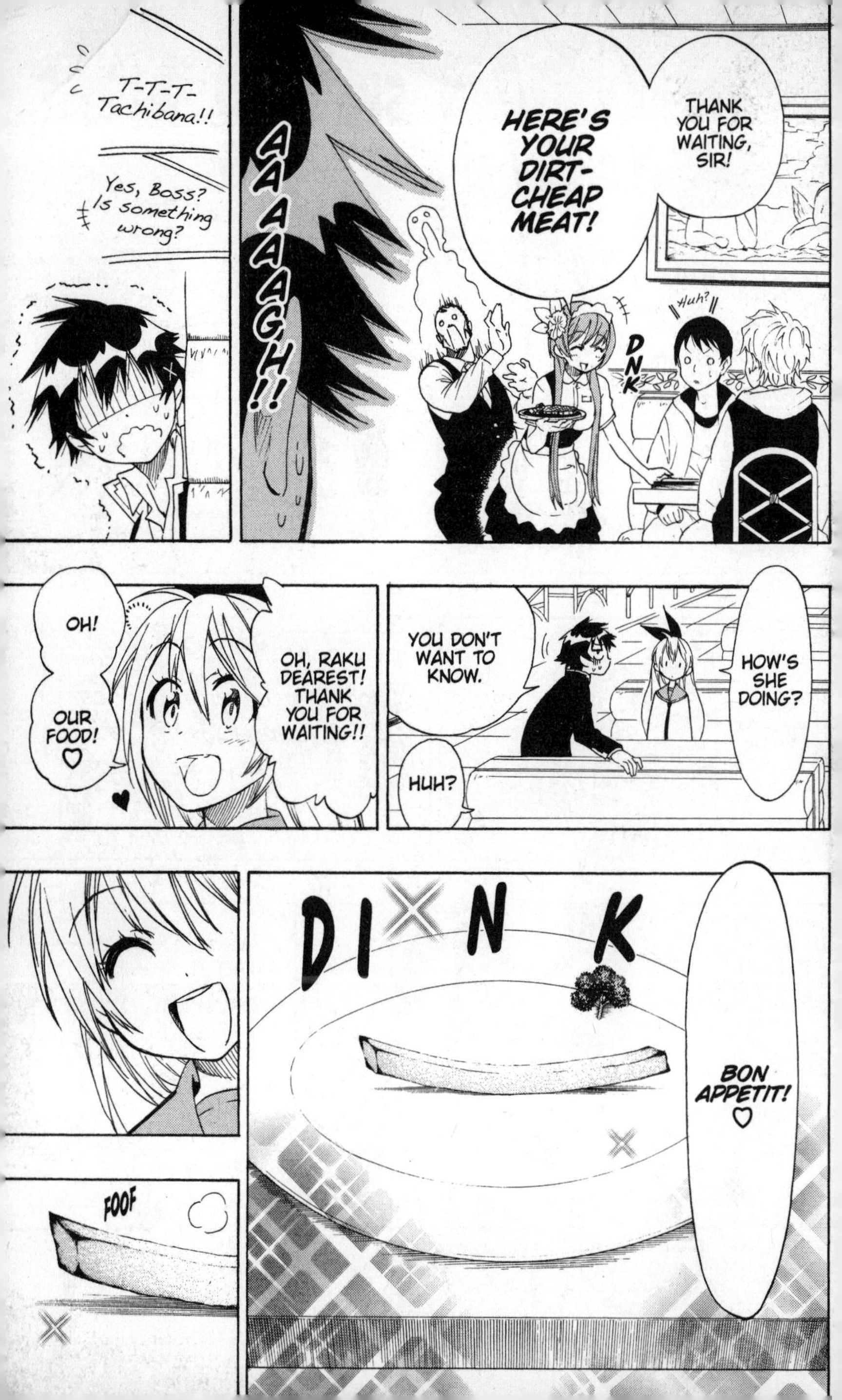
THANK YOU FOR WAITING, SIR!
HERE'S YOUR DIRT-CHEAP MEAT!
DNK
Huh?
AAAAAAGH!!
T-T-T-Tachibana!!
Yes, Boss? Is something wrong?
HOW'S SHE DOING?
YOU DON'T WANT TO KNOW.
HUH?
OH, RAKU DEAREST! THANK YOU FOR WAITING!!
OH! OUR FOOD! ♡
BON APPETIT! ♡
DINK
FOOF

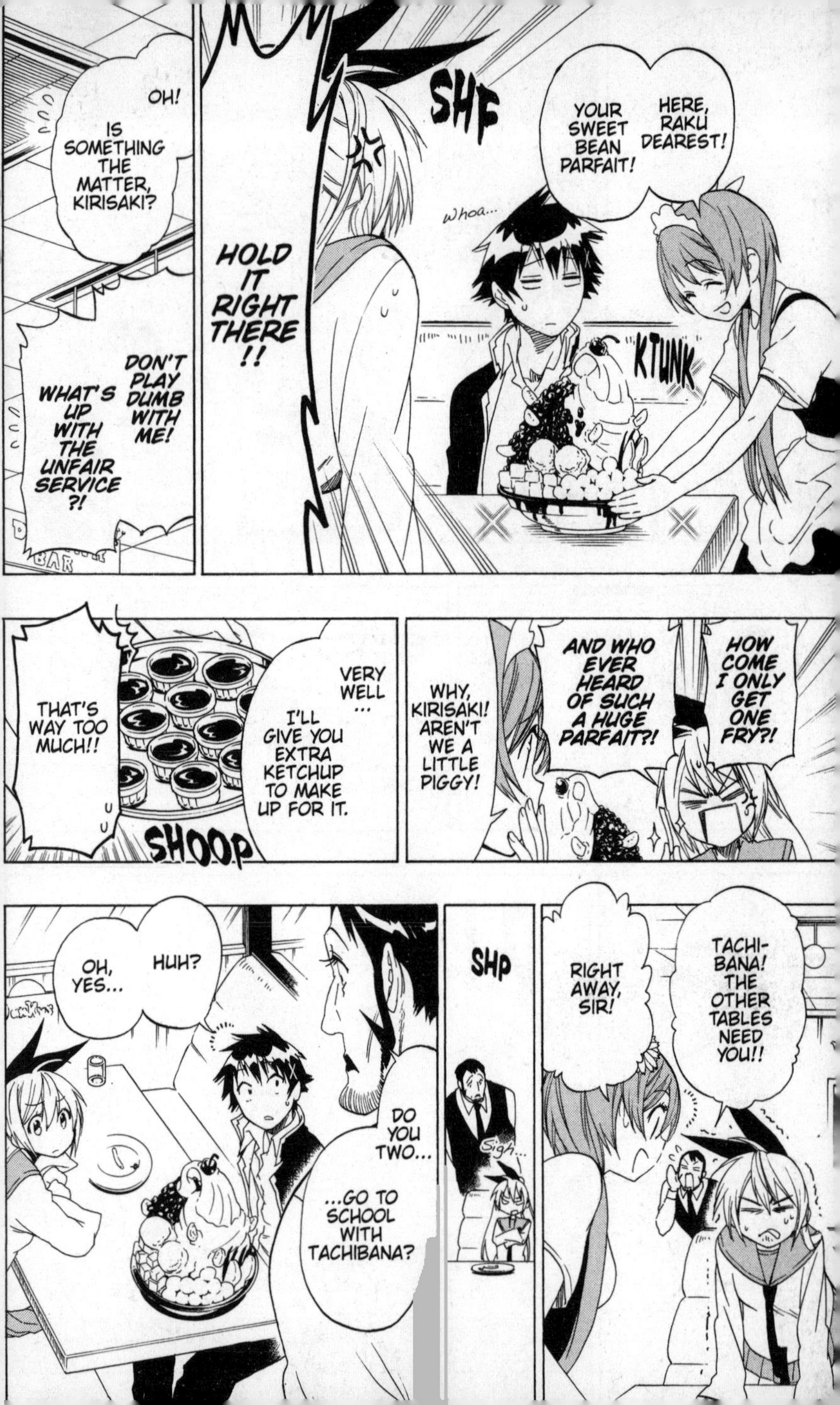
HERE, RAKU DEAREST!
YOUR SWEET BEAN PARFAIT!
Whoa...
KTUNK
SHF
HOLD IT RIGHT THERE!!
OH!
IS SOMETHING THE MATTER, KIRISAKI?
DON'T PLAY DUMB WITH ME!
WHAT'S UP WITH THE UNFAIR SERVICE?!
HOW COME I ONLY GET ONE FRY?!
AND WHO EVER HEARD OF SUCH A HUGE PARFAIT?!
WHY, KIRISAKI! AREN'T WE A LITTLE PIGGY!
VERY WELL...
I'LL GIVE YOU EXTRA KETCHUP TO MAKE UP FOR IT.
SHOOP
THAT'S WAY TOO MUCH!!
TACHIBANA! THE OTHER TABLES NEED YOU!!
RIGHT AWAY, SIR!
SHP
Sigh...
HUH?
OH, YES...
DO YOU TWO...
...GO TO SCHOOL WITH TACHIBANA?

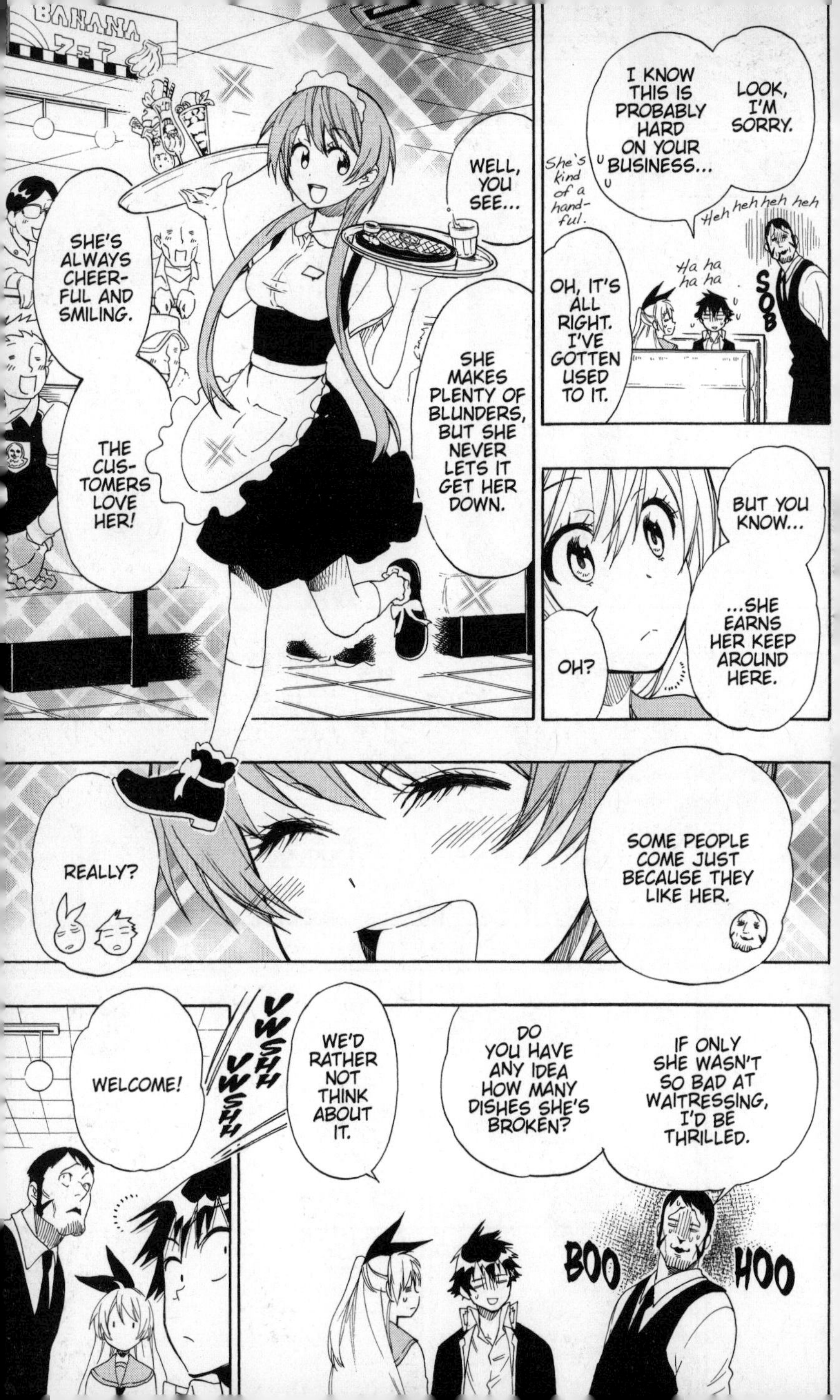
LOOK, I'M SORRY.
I KNOW THIS IS PROBABLY HARD ON YOUR BUSINESS...
Heh heh heh heh
SOB
She's kind of a handful.
Ha ha ha ha
OH, IT'S ALL RIGHT. I'VE GOTTEN USED TO IT.
BUT YOU KNOW...
...SHE EARNS HER KEEP AROUND HERE.
OH?
BANANA フェア
WELL, YOU SEE...
SHE MAKES PLENTY OF BLUNDERS, BUT SHE NEVER LETS IT GET HER DOWN.
SHE'S ALWAYS CHEERFUL AND SMILING.
THE CUSTOMERS LOVE HER!
SOME PEOPLE COME JUST BECAUSE THEY LIKE HER.
REALLY?
IF ONLY SHE WASN'T SO BAD AT WAITRESSING, I'D BE THRILLED.
BOO HOO
DO YOU HAVE ANY IDEA HOW MANY DISHES SHE'S BROKEN?
WE'D RATHER NOT THINK ABOUT IT.
VWSHH
VWSHH
WELCOME!

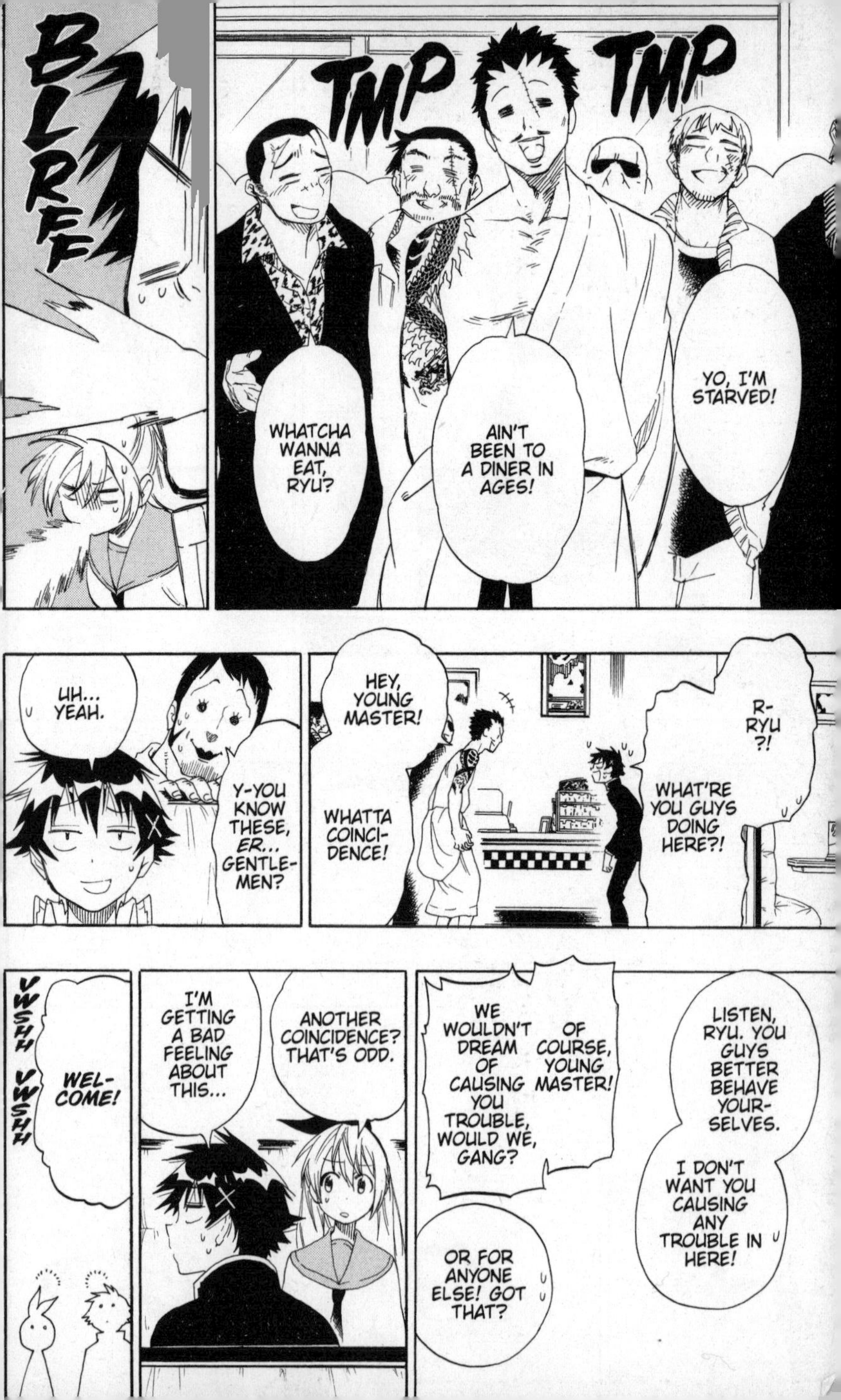
TMP TMP
YO, I'M STARVED!
AIN'T BEEN TO A DINER IN AGES!
WHATCHA WANNA EAT, RYU?
BLRFF
R-RYU?!
WHAT'RE YOU GUYS DOING HERE?!
HEY, YOUNG MASTER!
WHATTA COINCIDENCE!
Y-YOU KNOW THESE, ER... GENTLEMEN?
UH... YEAH.
LISTEN, RYU. YOU GUYS BETTER BEHAVE YOURSELVES.
I DON'T WANT YOU CAUSING ANY TROUBLE IN HERE!
OF COURSE, YOUNG MASTER!
WE WOULDN'T DREAM OF CAUSING YOU TROUBLE, WOULD WE, GANG?
OR FOR ANYONE ELSE! GOT THAT?
ANOTHER COINCIDENCE? THAT'S ODD.
I'M GETTING A BAD FEELING ABOUT THIS...
VWSHH VWSHH
WEL-COME!

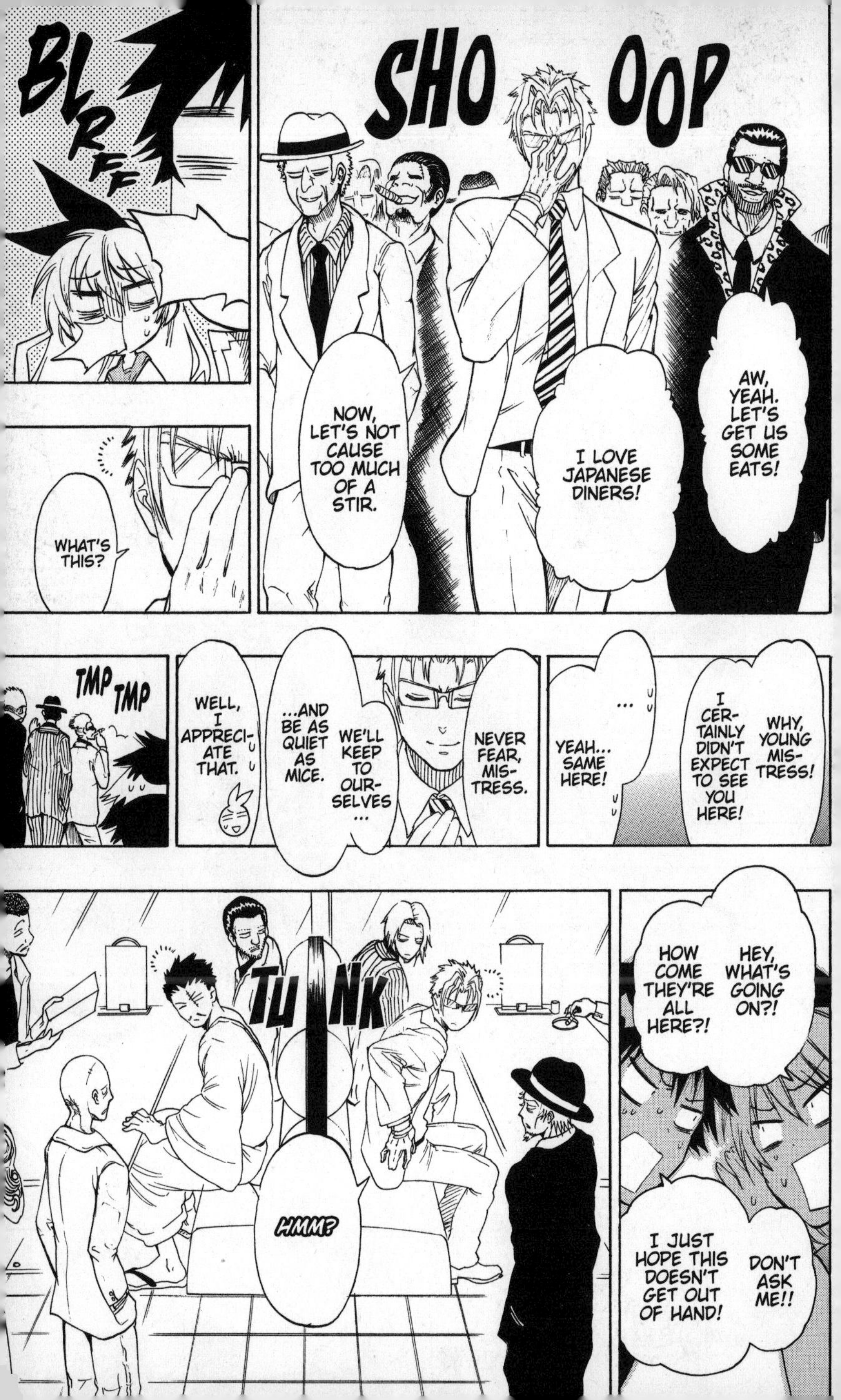
SHO OOP
AW, YEAH. LET'S GET US SOME EATS!
I LOVE JAPANESE DINERS!
NOW, LET'S NOT CAUSE TOO MUCH OF A STIR.
BLRFF
WHAT'S THIS?
WHY, YOUNG MIS-TRESS!
I CER-TAINLY DIDN'T EXPECT TO SEE YOU HERE!
...
YEAH... SAME HERE!
NEVER FEAR, MIS-TRESS.
WE'LL KEEP TO OUR-SELVES...
...AND BE AS QUIET AS MICE.
TMP TMP
WELL, I APPRECI-ATE THAT.
HEY, WHAT'S GOING ON?!
HOW COME THEY'RE ALL HERE?!
DON'T ASK ME!!
I JUST HOPE THIS DOESN'T GET OUT OF HAND!
TUNK
HMM?

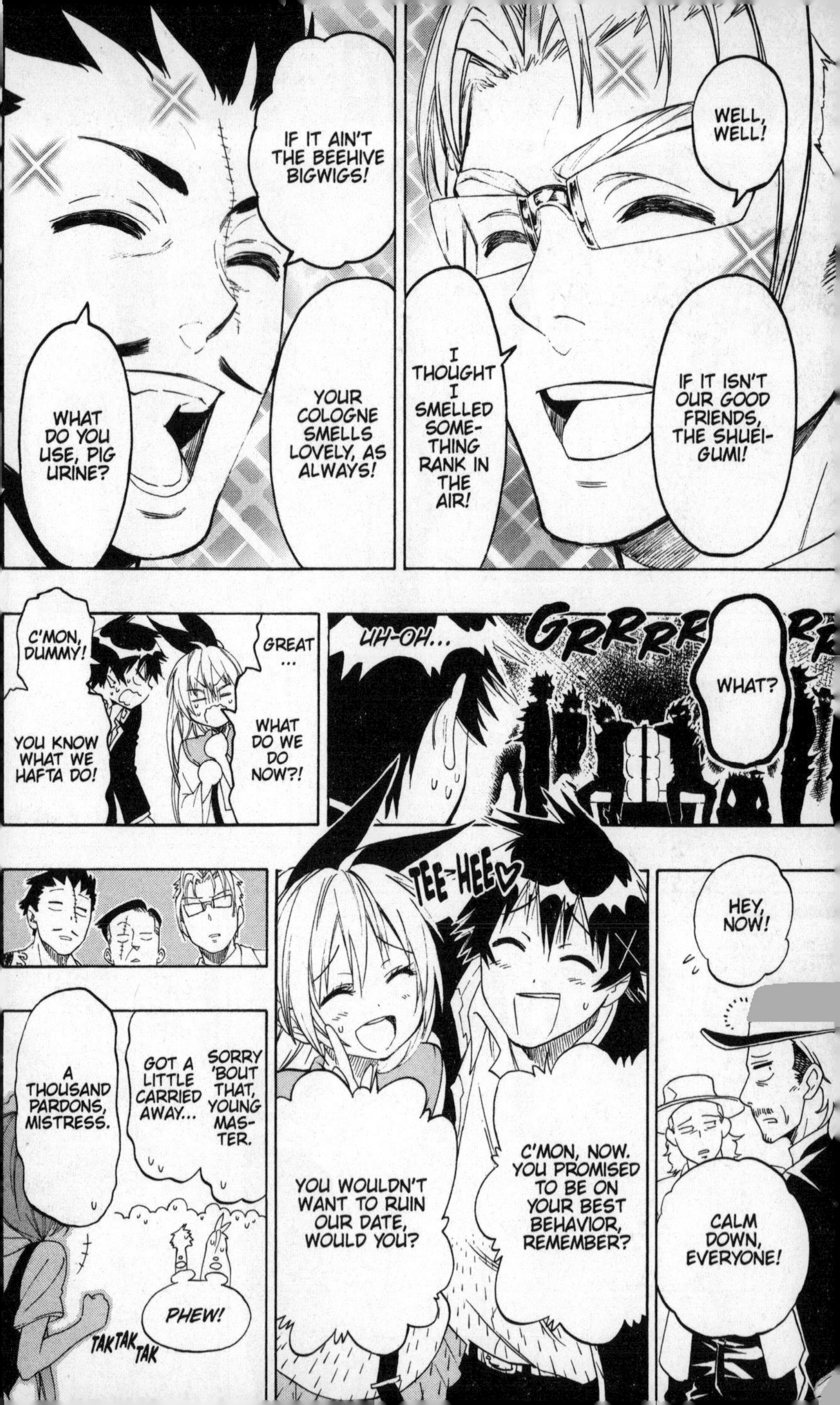
WELL, WELL!
IF IT ISN'T OUR GOOD FRIENDS, THE SHUEI-GUMI!
I THOUGHT I SMELLED SOME-THING RANK IN THE AIR!
IF IT AIN'T THE BEEHIVE BIGWIGS!
YOUR COLOGNE SMELLS LOVELY, AS ALWAYS!
WHAT DO YOU USE, PIG URINE?
GRRRR RR
WHAT?
UH-OH...
GREAT...
WHAT DO WE DO NOW?!
C'MON, DUMMY!
YOU KNOW WHAT WE HAFTA DO!
HEY, NOW!
CALM DOWN, EVERYONE!
TEE-HEE♥
C'MON, NOW. YOU PROMISED TO BE ON YOUR BEST BEHAVIOR, REMEMBER?
YOU WOULDN'T WANT TO RUIN OUR DATE, WOULD YOU?
SORRY 'BOUT THAT, YOUNG MAS-TER.
GOT A LITTLE CARRIED AWAY...
A THOUSAND PARDONS, MISTRESS.
PHEW!
TAKTAKTAK

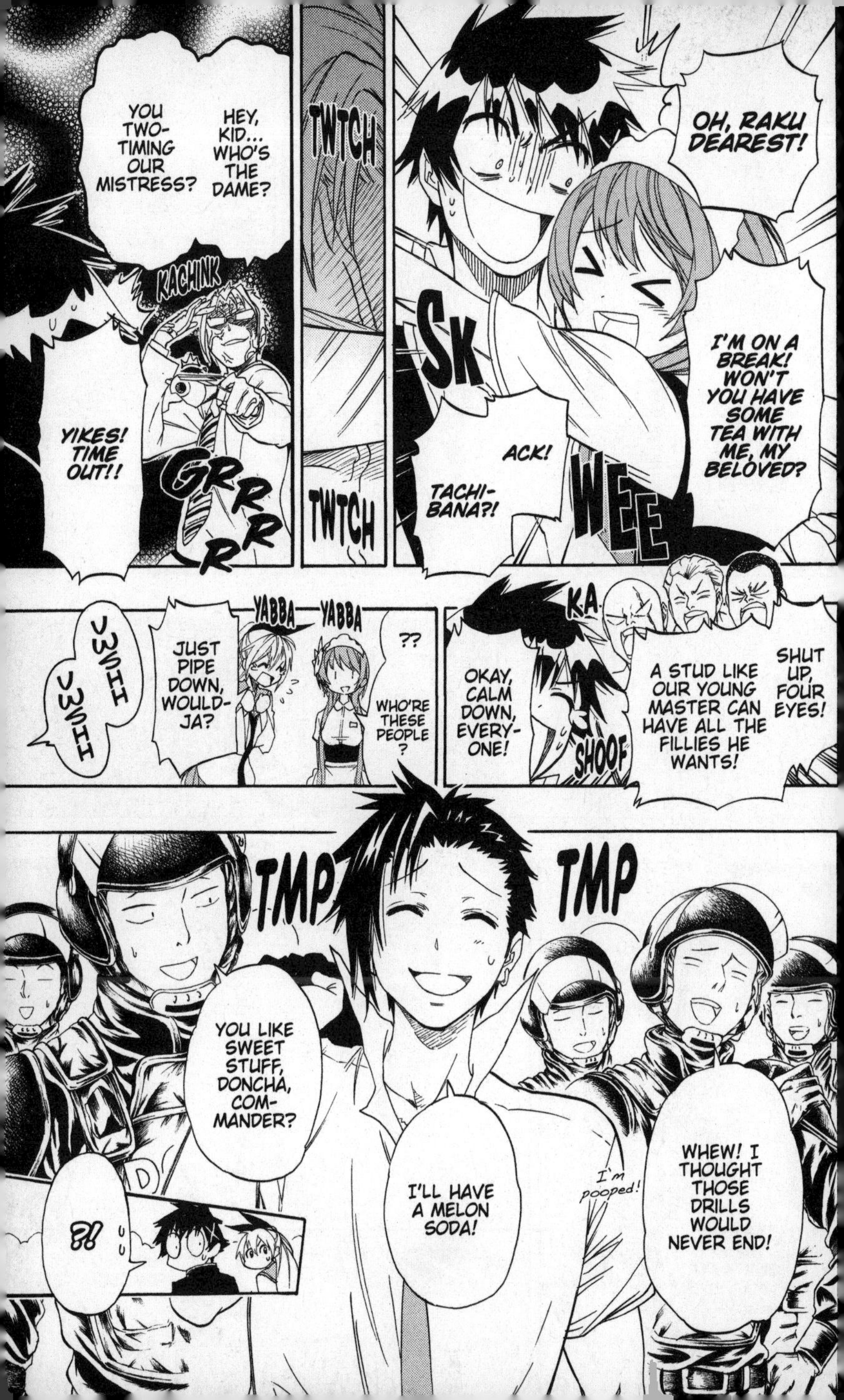
OH, RAKU DEAREST!
I'M ON A BREAK! WON'T YOU HAVE SOME TEA WITH ME, MY BELOVED?
SK
WEE
ACK!
TACHI-BANA?!
TWTCH
TWTCH
HEY, KID... WHO'S THE DAME?
YOU TWO-TIMING OUR MISTRESS?
KACHINK
YIKES! TIME OUT!!
GRRRR
KA
SHUT UP, FOUR EYES!
A STUD LIKE OUR YOUNG MASTER CAN HAVE ALL THE FILLIES HE WANTS!
OKAY, CALM DOWN, EVERY-ONE!
SHOOF
YABBA YABBA
??
WHO'RE THESE PEOPLE?
JUST PIPE DOWN, WOULD-JA?
VWSHH VWSHH
TMP TMP
WHEW! I THOUGHT THOSE DRILLS WOULD NEVER END!
I'm pooped!
I'LL HAVE A MELON SODA!
YOU LIKE SWEET STUFF, DONCHA, COM-MANDER?
?!

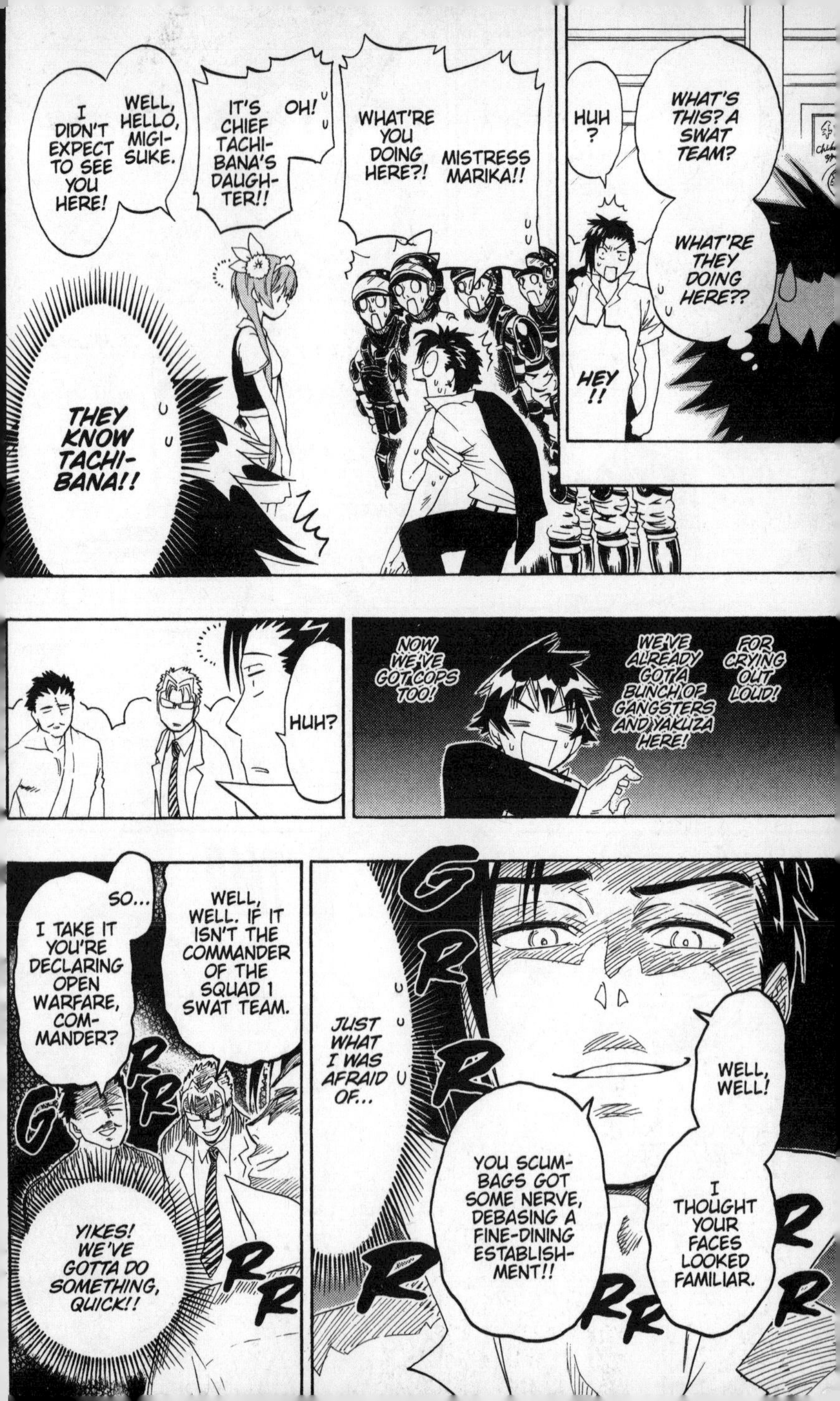
WHAT'S THIS? A SWAT TEAM?
WHAT'RE THEY DOING HERE??
HUH?
HEY!!
MISTRESS MARIKA!!
WHAT'RE YOU DOING HERE?!
OH!
IT'S CHIEF TACHIBANA'S DAUGHTER!!
WELL, HELLO, MIGISUKE.
I DIDN'T EXPECT TO SEE YOU HERE!
THEY KNOW TACHIBANA!!
FOR CRYING OUT LOUD!
WE'VE ALREADY GOT A BUNCH OF GANGSTERS AND YAKUZA HERE!
NOW WE'VE GOT COPS TOO!
HUH?
GRRRR
WELL, WELL!
I THOUGHT YOUR FACES LOOKED FAMILIAR.
YOU SCUMBAGS GOT SOME NERVE, DEBASING A FINE-DINING ESTABLISHMENT!!
JUST WHAT I WAS AFRAID OF...
WELL, WELL. IF IT ISN'T THE COMMANDER OF THE SQUAD 1 SWAT TEAM.
SO...
I TAKE IT YOU'RE DECLARING OPEN WARFARE, COMMANDER?
GRR
YIKES! WE'VE GOTTA DO SOMETHING, QUICK!!
RR

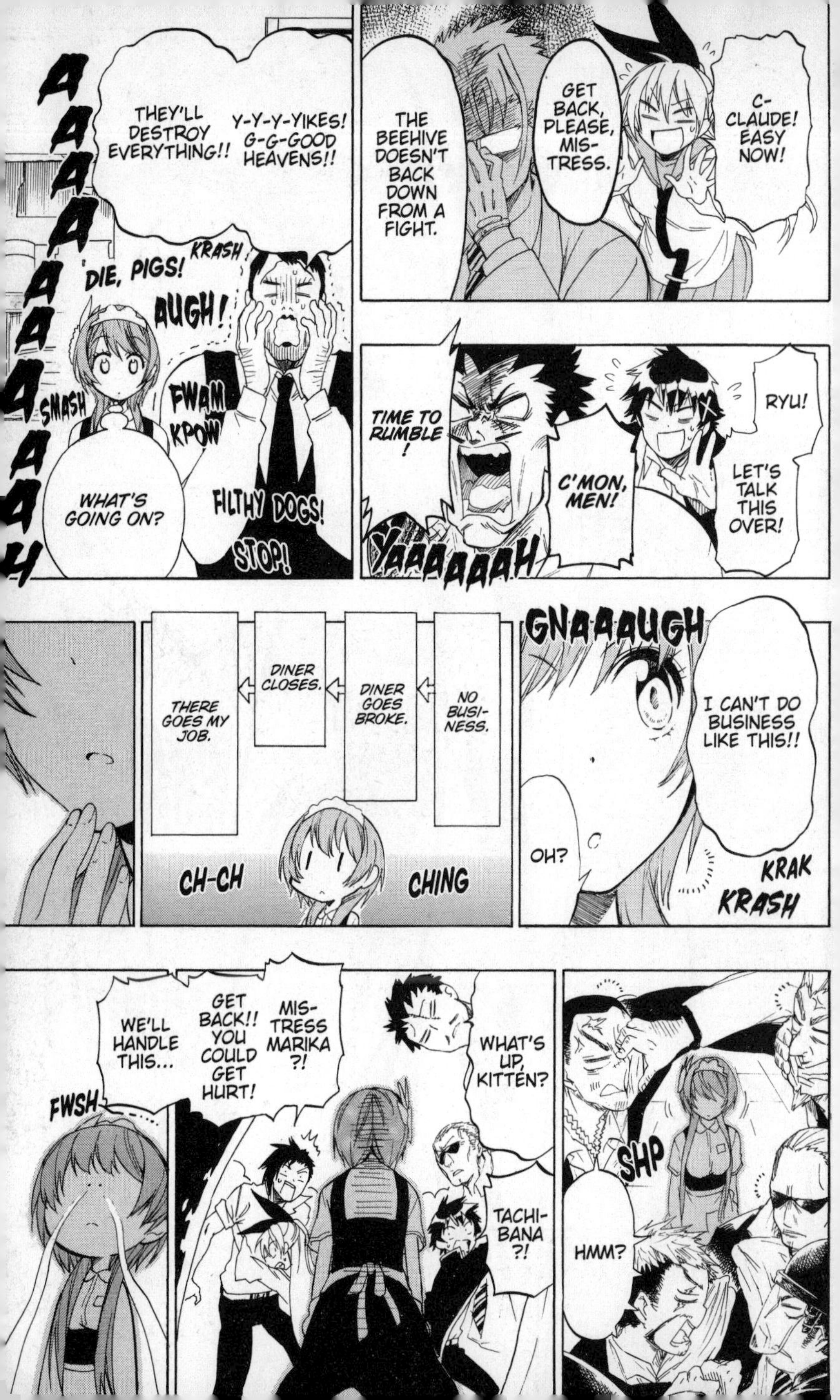
C-CLAUDE! EASY NOW!
GET BACK, PLEASE, MIS-TRESS.
THE BEEHIVE DOESN'T BACK DOWN FROM A FIGHT.
RYU!
LET'S TALK THIS OVER!
C'MON, MEN!
TIME TO RUMBLE!
YAAAAAAH
Y-Y-Y-YIKES! G-G-GOOD HEAVENS!!
THEY'LL DESTROY EVERYTHING!!
AAAAAAAAAAAH
KRASH
DIE, PIGS!
AUGH!
FWAM
KPOW
SMASH
FILTHY DOGS!
STOP!
WHAT'S GOING ON?
GNAAAUGH
I CAN'T DO BUSINESS LIKE THIS!!
OH?
KRAK
KRASH
NO BUSI-NESS.
DINER GOES BROKE.
DINER CLOSES.
THERE GOES MY JOB.
CH-CH
CHING
HMM?
SHP
WHAT'S UP, KITTEN?
TACHI-BANA ?!
MIS-TRESS MARIKA ?!
GET BACK!! YOU COULD GET HURT!
WE'LL HANDLE THIS...
FWSH

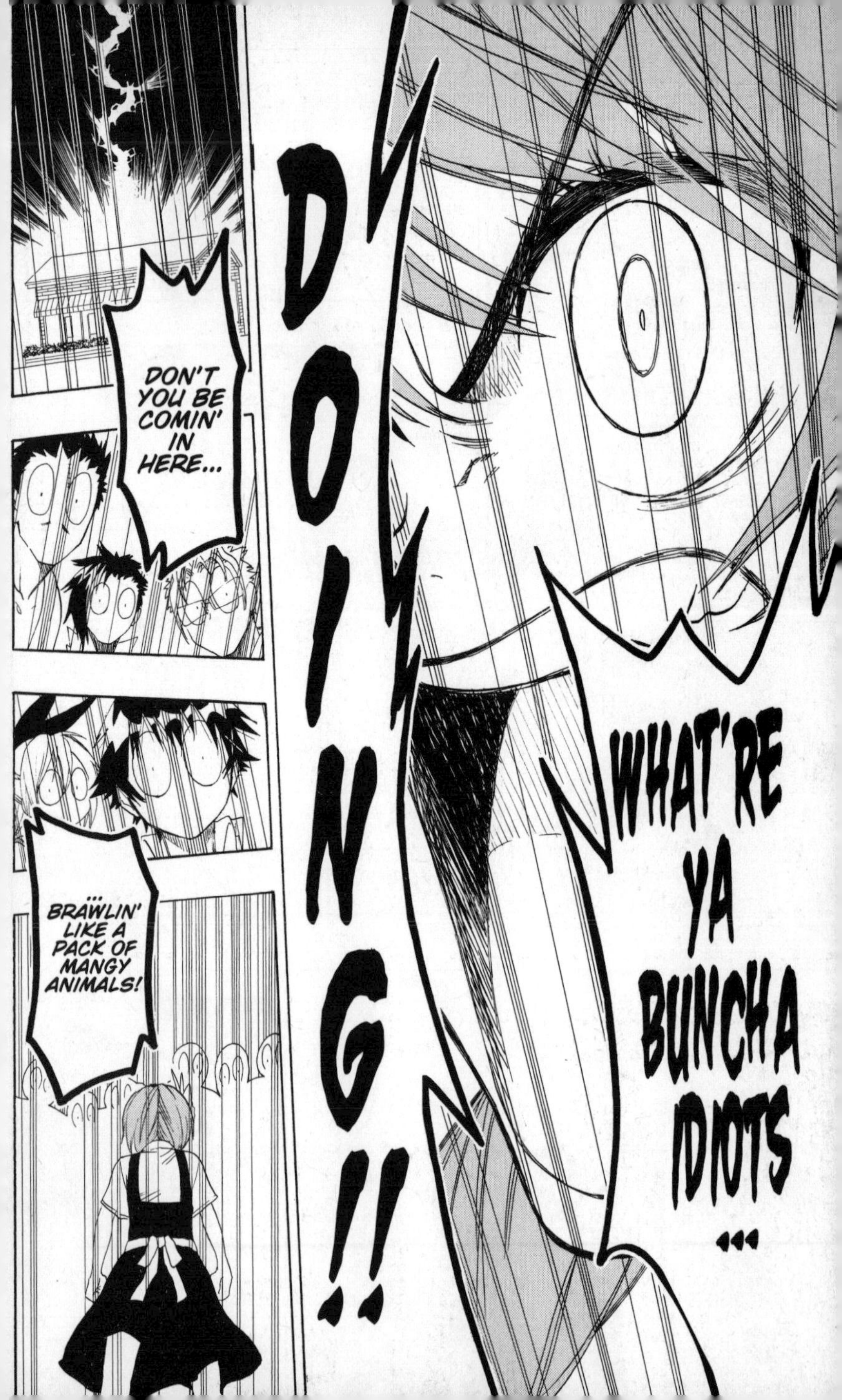

WHAT'RE YA BUNCHA IDIOTS ...
DOING!!
DON'T YOU BE COMIN' IN HERE...
...BRÄWLIN' LIKE A PACK OF MANGY ANIMALS!

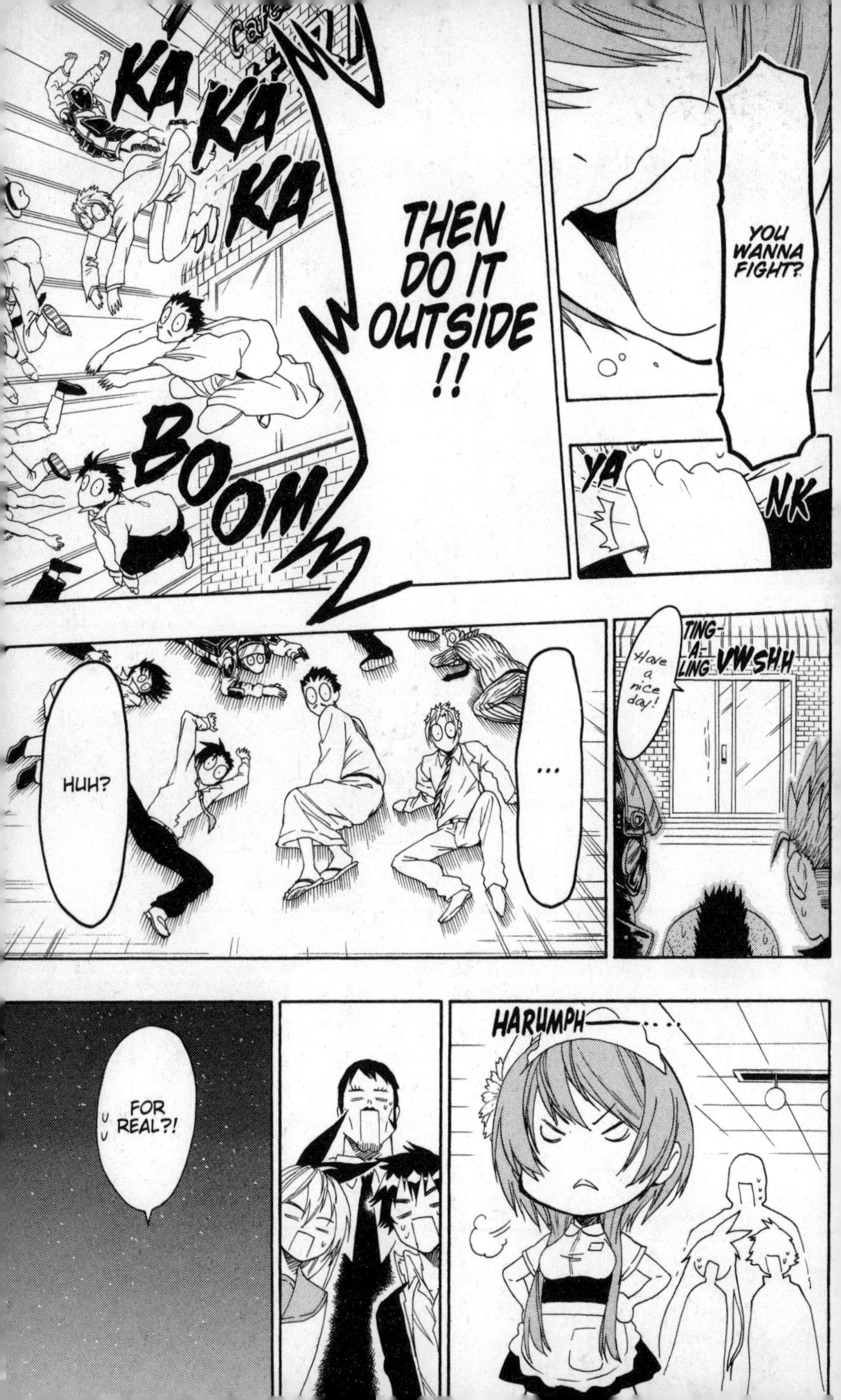
YOU WANNA FIGHT?
YA
NK
THEN DO IT OUTSIDE !!
KA KA KA KA KA
BOOM
TING-A-LING
VWSHH
Have a nice day!
...
HUH?
HARUMPH—...
FOR REAL?!

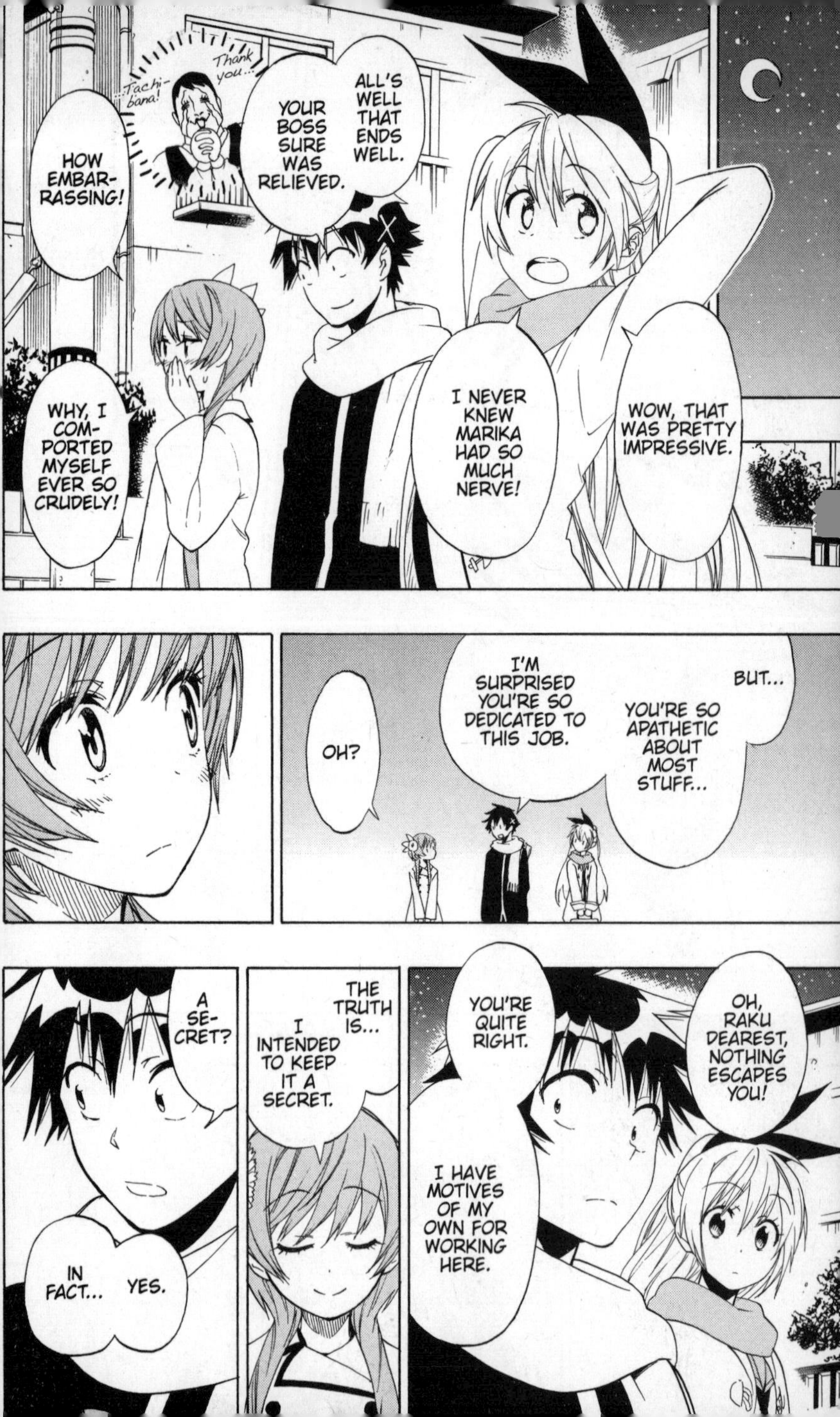
ALL'S WELL THAT ENDS WELL.
YOUR BOSS SURE WAS RELIEVED.
Thank you...
...Tachibana!
HOW EMBARRASSING!
WOW, THAT WAS PRETTY IMPRESSIVE.
I NEVER KNEW MARIKA HAD SO MUCH NERVE!
WHY, I COMPORTED MYSELF EVER SO CRUDELY!
BUT...
YOU'RE SO APATHETIC ABOUT MOST STUFF...
I'M SURPRISED YOU'RE SO DEDICATED TO THIS JOB.
OH?
OH, RAKU DEAREST, NOTHING ESCAPES YOU!
YOU'RE QUITE RIGHT.
I HAVE MOTIVES OF MY OWN FOR WORKING HERE.
THE TRUTH IS...
I INTENDED TO KEEP IT A SECRET.
A SECRET?
IN FACT... YES.

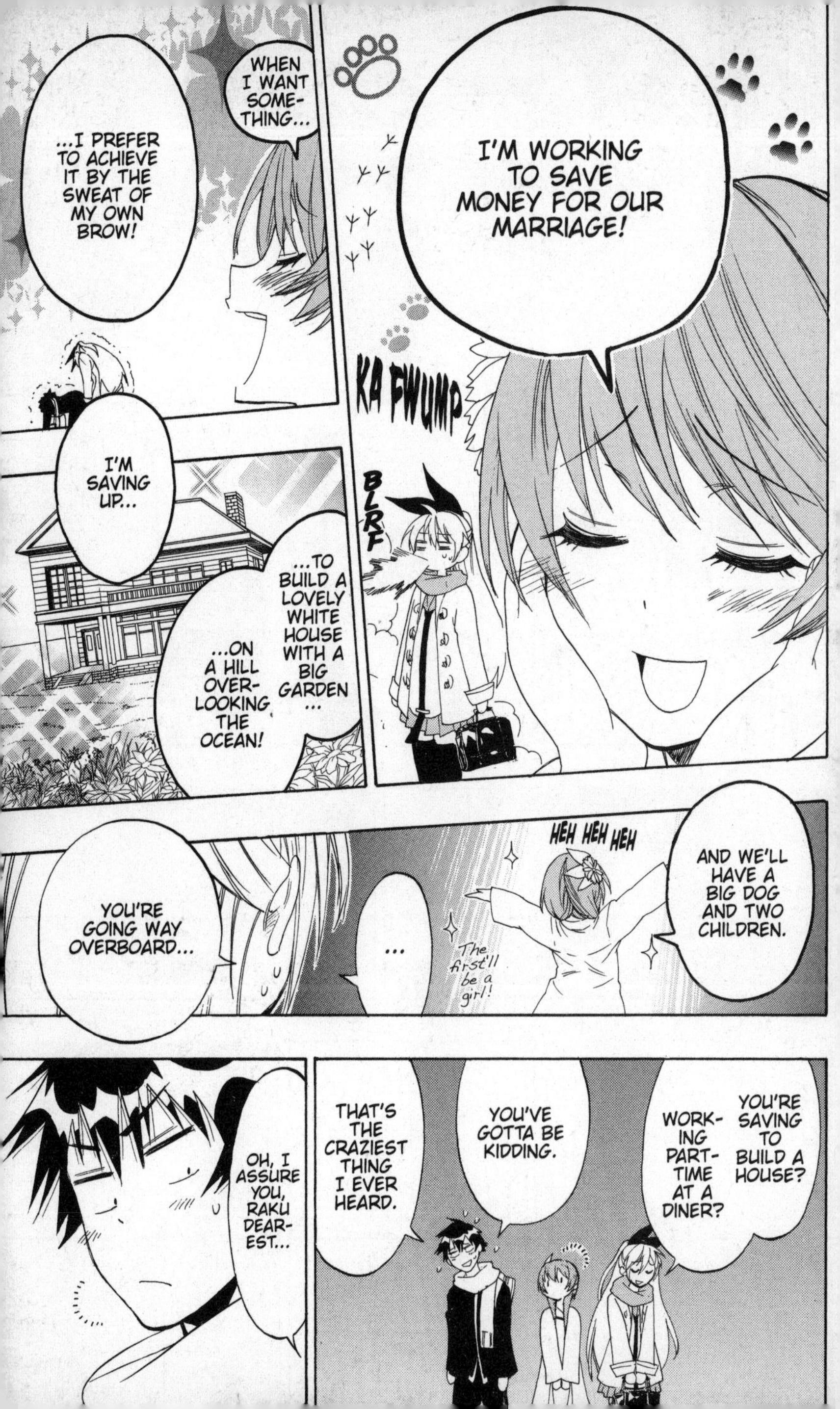
I'M WORKING TO SAVE MONEY FOR OUR MARRIAGE!
KA FWUMP
BLRF
WHEN I WANT SOMETHING...
...I PREFER TO ACHIEVE IT BY THE SWEAT OF MY OWN BROW!
I'M SAVING UP...
...TO BUILD A LOVELY WHITE HOUSE WITH A BIG GARDEN...
...ON A HILL OVERLOOKING THE OCEAN!
AND WE'LL HAVE A BIG DOG AND TWO CHILDREN.
HEH HEH HEH
The first'll be a girl!
...
YOU'RE GOING WAY OVERBOARD...
YOU'RE SAVING TO BUILD A HOUSE?
WORKING PART-TIME AT A DINER?
YOU'VE GOTTA BE KIDDING.
THAT'S THE CRAZIEST THING I EVER HEARD.
OH, I ASSURE YOU, RAKU DEAREST...

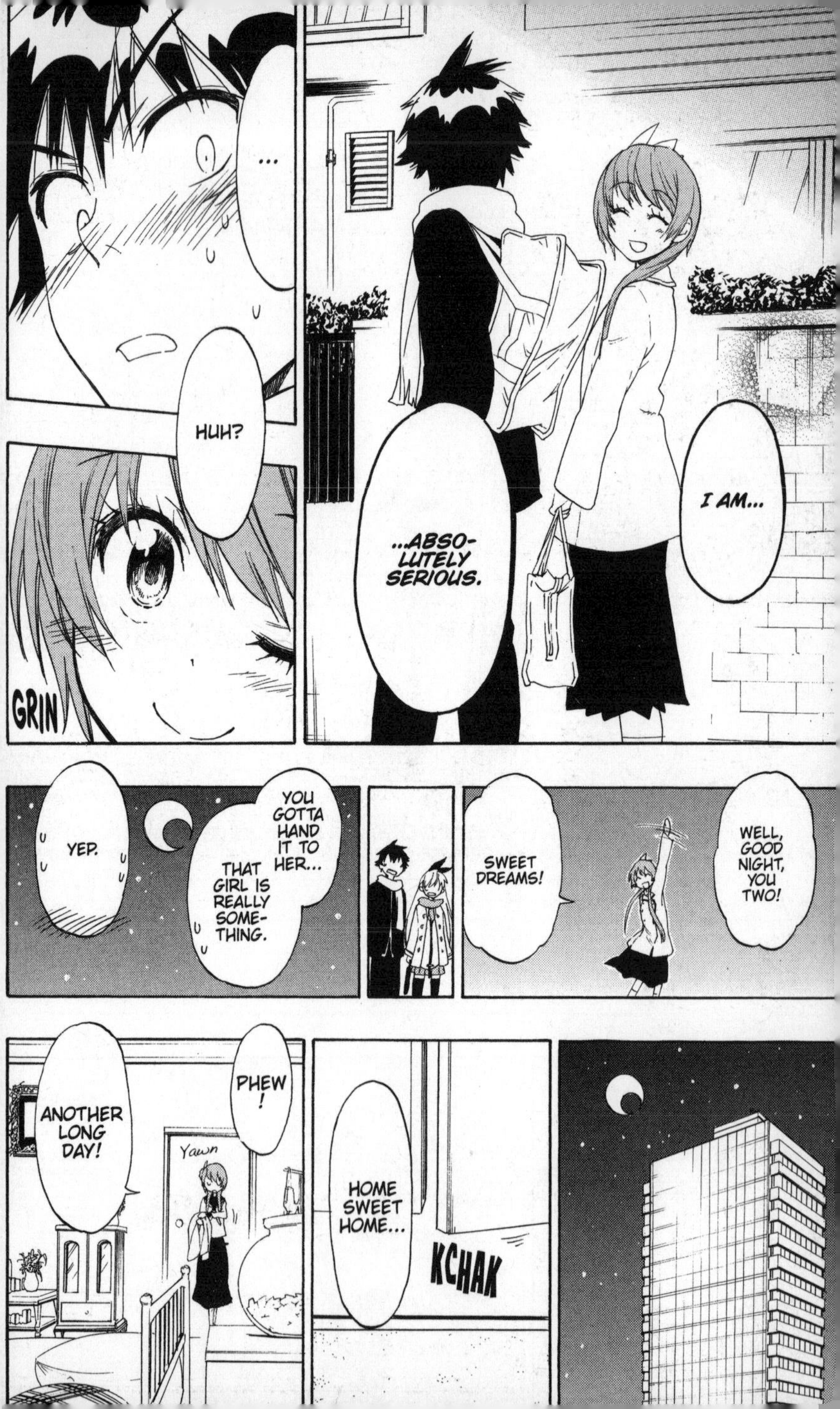
I AM...
...ABSOLUTELY SERIOUS.
...
HUH?
GRIN
WELL, GOOD NIGHT, YOU TWO!
SWEET DREAMS!
YOU GOTTA HAND IT TO HER...
THAT GIRL IS REALLY SOMETHING.
YEP.
KCHAK
HOME SWEET HOME...
PHEW!
ANOTHER LONG DAY!
Yawn

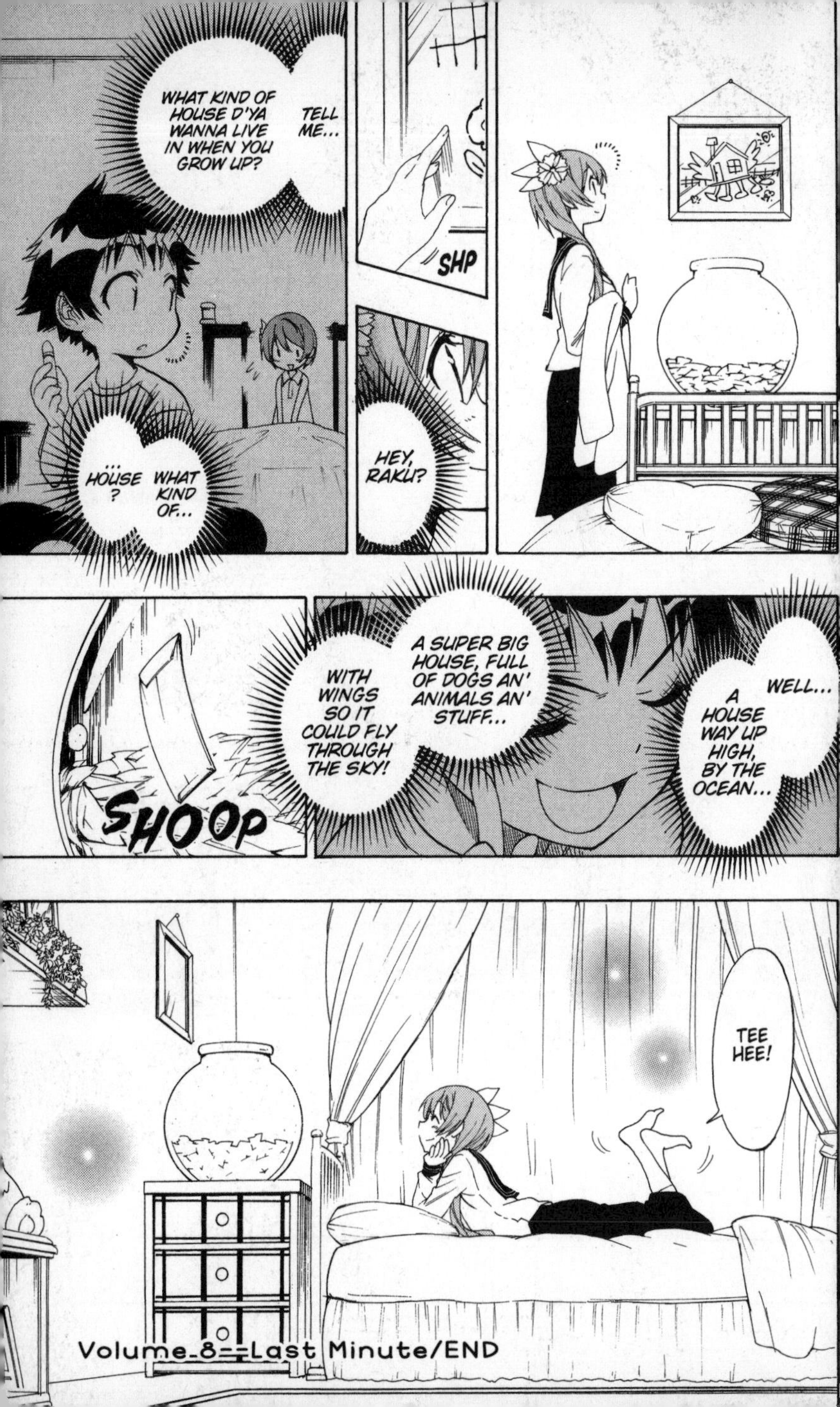
SHP
HEY, RAKU?
TELL ME...
WHAT KIND OF HOUSE D'YA WANNA LIVE IN WHEN YOU GROW UP?
WHAT KIND OF...
...HOUSE?
WELL...
A HOUSE WAY UP HIGH, BY THE OCEAN...
A SUPER BIG HOUSE, FULL OF DOGS AN' ANIMALS AN' STUFF...
WITH WINGS SO IT COULD FLY THROUGH THE SKY!
SHOOP
TEE HEE!
Volume 8 -- Last Minute/END

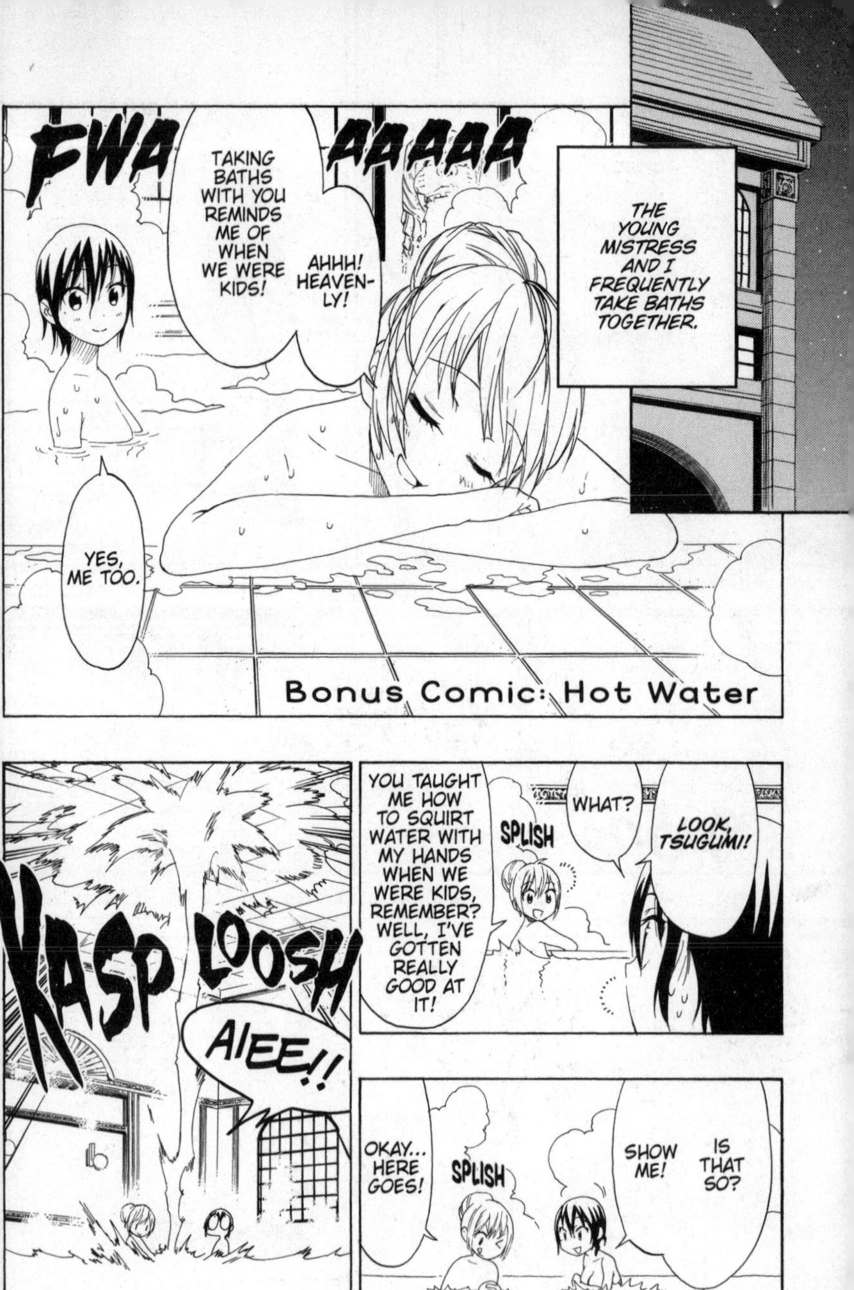
THE YOUNG MISTRESS AND I FREQUENTLY TAKE BATHS TOGETHER.
FWAAAAAA
AHHH! HEAVEN-LY!
TAKING BATHS WITH YOU REMINDS ME OF WHEN WE WERE KIDS!
YES, ME TOO.
Bonus Comic: Hot Water
LOOK, TSUGUMI!
WHAT?
SPLISH
YOU TAUGHT ME HOW TO SQUIRT WATER WITH MY HANDS WHEN WE WERE KIDS, REMEMBER? WELL, I'VE GOTTEN REALLY GOOD AT IT!
IS THAT SO?
SHOW ME!
SPLISH
OKAY... HERE GOES!
KASPLOOSH
AIEE!!

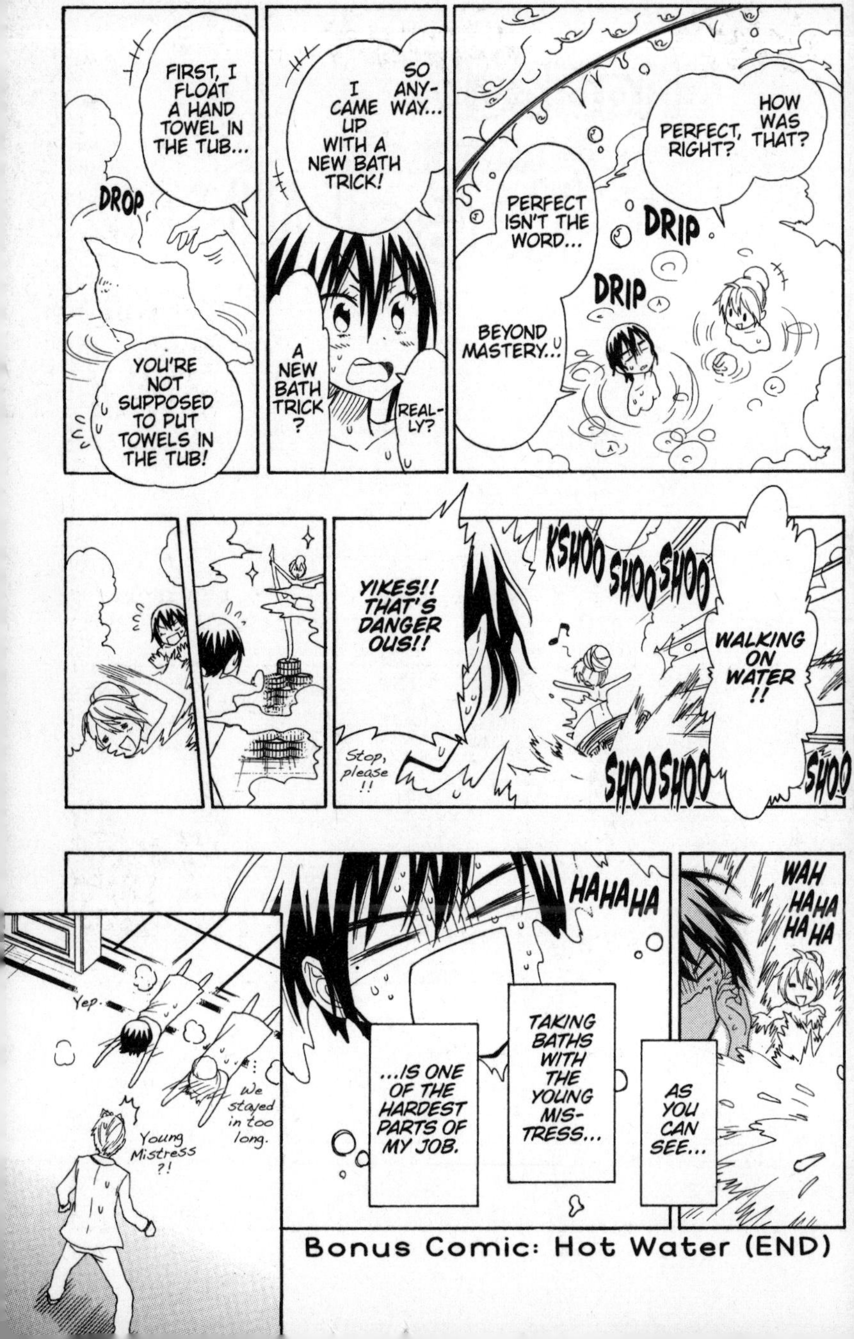
HOW WAS THAT?
PERFECT, RIGHT?
DRIP
PERFECT ISN'T THE WORD...
DRIP
BEYOND MASTERY...
SO ANYWAY...
I CAME UP WITH A NEW BATH TRICK!
REALLY?
A NEW BATH TRICK?
FIRST, I FLOAT A HAND TOWEL IN THE TUB...
DROP
YOU'RE NOT SUPPOSED TO PUT TOWELS IN THE TUB!
KSHOO SHOO SHOO
WALKING ON WATER!!
YIKES!! THAT'S DANGER OUS!!
SHOO SHOO
SHOO
Stop, please!!
WAH HAHA HAHA
AS YOU CAN SEE...
HAHAHA
TAKING BATHS WITH THE YOUNG MIS-TRESS...
...IS ONE OF THE HARDEST PARTS OF MY JOB.
Yep.
We stayed in too long.
Young Mistress?!

Bonus Comic: Hot Water (END)

# NISEKOI BONUS COMIC!!

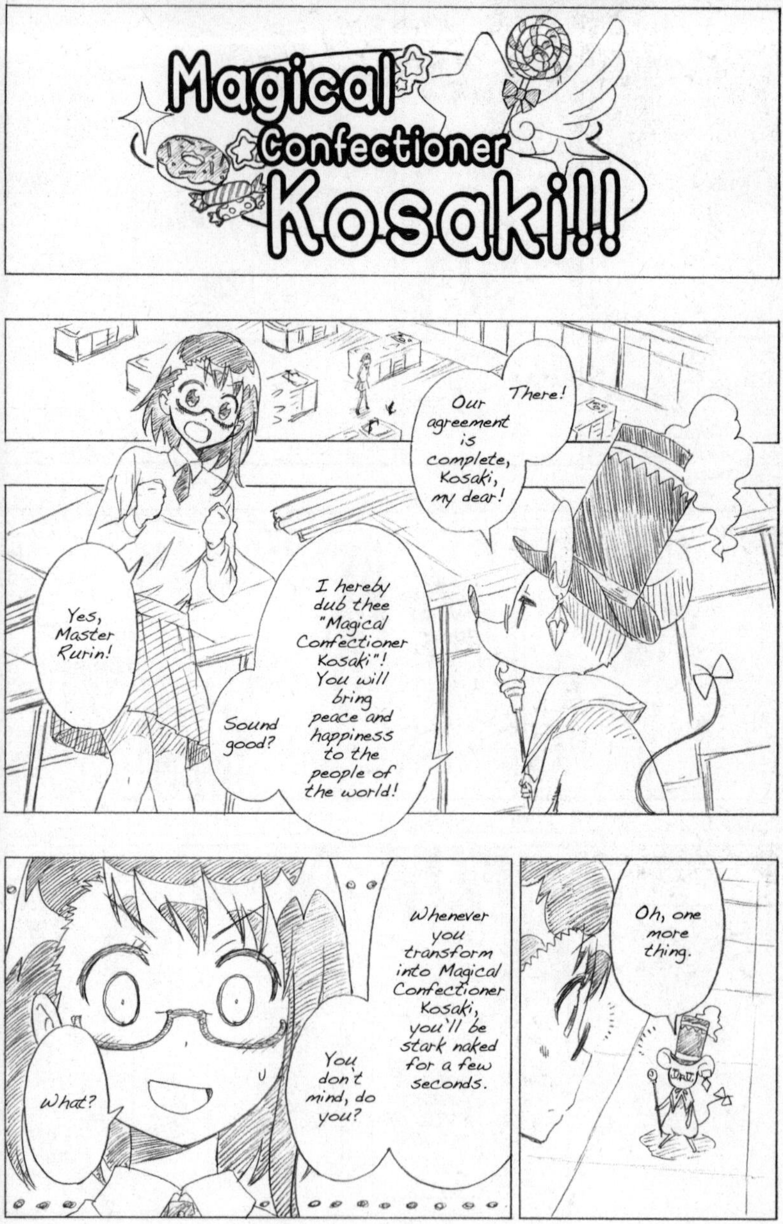
Magical Confectioner Kosaki!!
There! Our agreement is complete, Kosaki, my dear!
I hereby dub thee "Magical Confectioner Kosaki"! You will bring peace and happiness to the people of the world!
Sound good?
Yes, Master Rurin!
Oh, one more thing.
Whenever you transform into Magical Confectioner Kosaki, you'll be stark naked for a few seconds.
You don't mind, do you?
What?

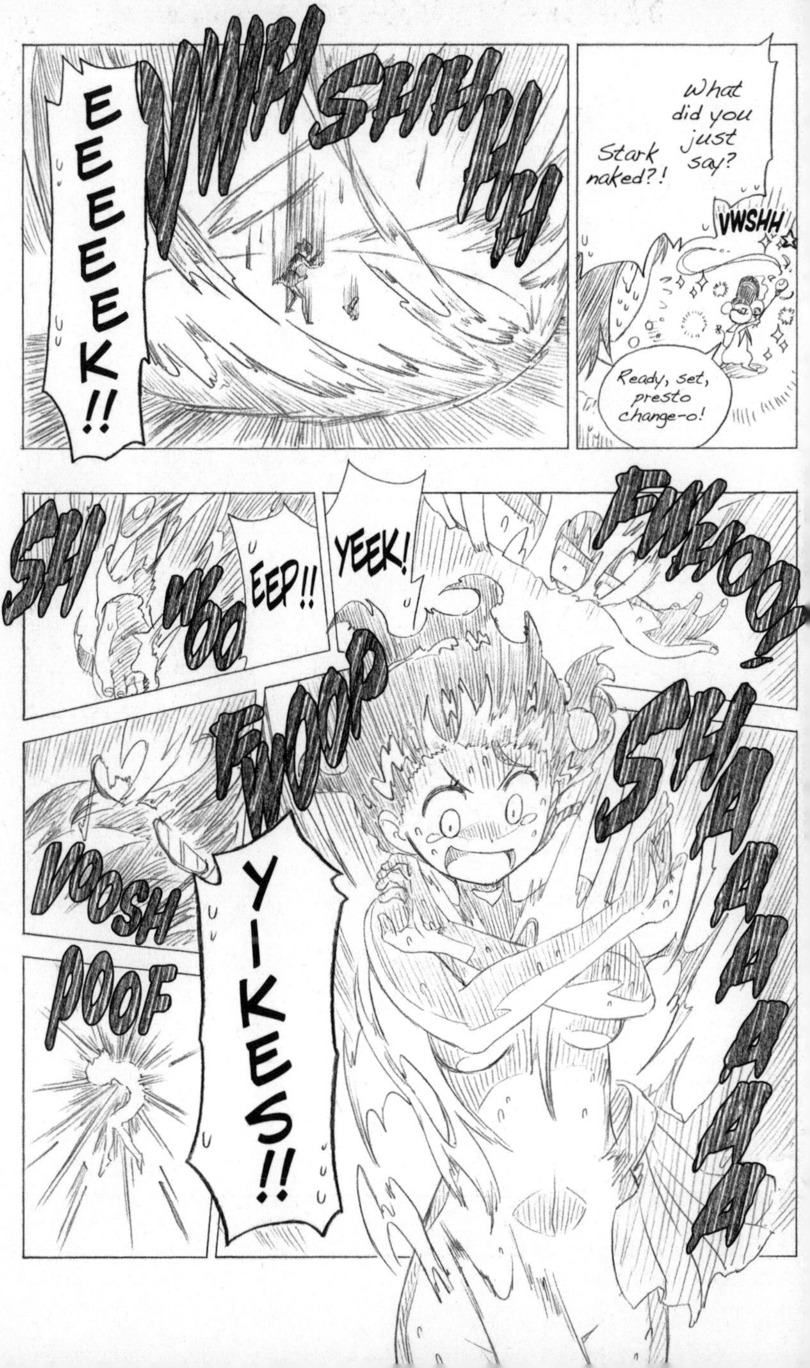
What did you just say?
Stark naked?!
VWSHH
Ready, set, presto change-o!
VWHSHHHH
EEEEEEK!!
FWHOOO!
YEEK!
SHAAAAAAA
FWOOP
YIKES!!
SHWOO
EEP!!
VOOSH
POOF

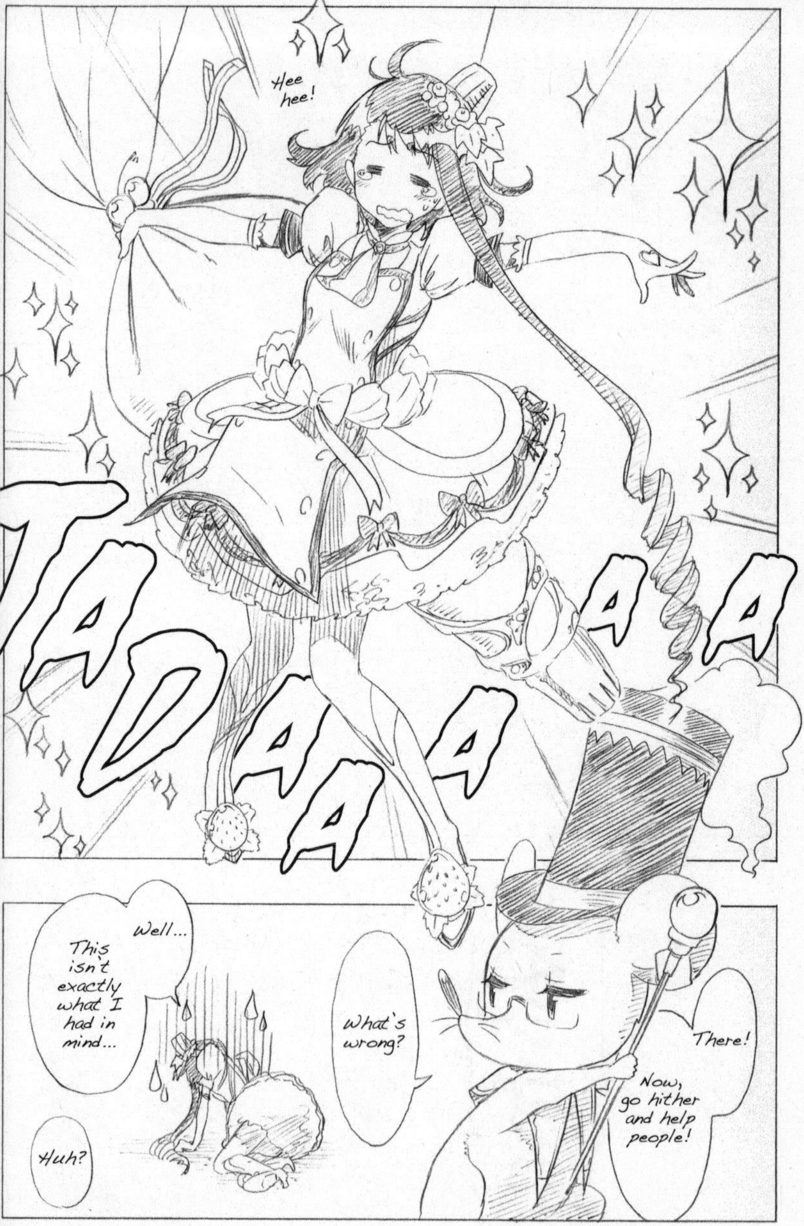
Hee hee!
TADAAAAAA
There!
Now, go hither and help people!
Huh?
What's wrong?
Well...
This isn't exactly what I had in mind...

To be continued?

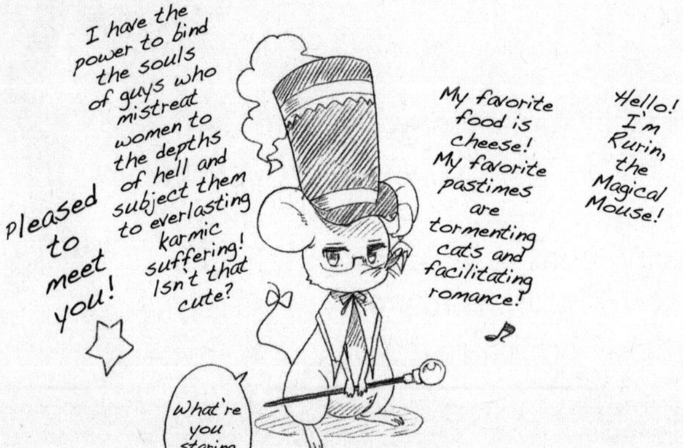
Hello! I'm Rurin, the Magical Mouse!
My favorite food is cheese! My favorite pastimes are tormenting cats and facilitating romance!
I have the power to bind the souls of guys who mistreat women to the depths of hell and subject them to everlasting karmic suffering! Isn't that cute?
Pleased to meet you!
What're you staring at?

# You're Reading the WRONG WAY!

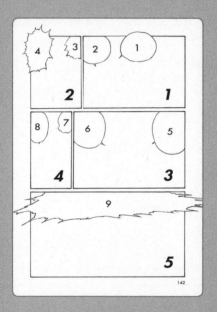

**NISEKOI** reads from right to left, starting in the upper-right corner. Japanese is read from right to left, meaning that action, sound effects, and word-balloon order are completely reversed from English order.